International Journal on Advances in Systems and Measurements

2016 vol. 9 nr. 3&4

Printed from e-media with permission by:

Curran Associates, Inc.
57 Morehouse Lane
Red Hook, NY 12571

Some format issues inherent in the e-media version may also appear in this print version.

Printed by Curran Associates, Inc. (2018)

International Academy, Research, and Industry Association (IARIA)
412 Derby Way
Wilmington, DE 19810

Phone: (408) 893-6407
Fax: (408) 527-6351

petre@iaria.org

Additional copies of this publication are available from:

Curran Associates, Inc.
57 Morehouse Lane
Red Hook, NY 12571 USA
Phone: 845-758-0400
Fax: 845-758-2633
Email: curran@proceedings.com
Web: www.proceedings.com

The *International Journal on Advances in Systems and Measurements* is published by IARIA.
ISSN: 1942-261x
journals site: http://www.iariajournals.org
contact: petre@iaria.org

Reference should mention:

> *International Journal on Advances in Systems and Measurements, issn 1942-261x*
> *vol. 9, no. 3 & 4, year 2016, http://www.iariajournals.org/systems_and_measurements/*

Reference to an article in the journal is as follows:

> *<Author list>, "<Article title>"*
> *International Journal on Advances in Systems and Measurements, issn 1942-261x*
> *vol. 9, no. 3 & 4, year 2016, http://www.iariajournals.org/systems_and_measurements/*

Sponsored by IARIA
www.iaria.org

International Journal on Advances in Systems and Measurements
Volume 9, Number 3 & 4, 2016

Dario Bottazzi, Laboratori Guglielmo Marconi, Italy
Diletta Romana Cacciagrano, University of Camerino, Italy
Javier Calpe, Analog Devices and University of Valencia, Spain
Jaime Calvo-Gallego, University of Salamanca, Spain
Maria-Dolores Cano Baños, Universidad Politécnica de Cartagena,Spain
Juan-Vicente Capella-Hernández, Universitat Politècnica de València, Spain
Vítor Carvalho, Minho University & IPCA, Portugal
Irinela Chilibon, National Institute of Research and Development for Optoelectronics, Romania
Soolyeon Cho, North Carolina State University, USA
Hugo Coll Ferri, Polytechnic University of Valencia, Spain
Denis Collange, Orange Labs, France
Noelia Correia, Universidade do Algarve, Portugal
Pierre-Jean Cottinet, INSA de Lyon - LGEF, France
Paulo Estevao Cruvinel, Embrapa Instrumentation Centre - São Carlos, Brazil
Marc Daumas, University of Perpignan, France
Jianguo Ding, University of Luxembourg, Luxembourg
António Dourado, University of Coimbra, Portugal
Daniela Dragomirescu, LAAS-CNRS / University of Toulouse, France
Matthew Dunlop, Virginia Tech, USA
Mohamed Eltoweissy, Pacific Northwest National Laboratory / Virginia Tech, USA
Paulo Felisberto, LARSyS, University of Algarve, Portugal
Javad Foroughi, University of Wollongong, Australia
Miguel Franklin de Castro, Federal University of Ceará, Brazil
Mounir Gaidi, Centre de Recherches et des Technologies de l'Energie (CRTEn), Tunisie
Eva Gescheidtova, Brno University of Technology, Czech Republic
Tejas R. Gandhi, Virtua Health-Marlton, USA
Teodor Ghetiu, University of York, UK
Franca Giannini, IMATI - Consiglio Nazionale delle Ricerche - Genova, Italy
Gonçalo Gomes, Nokia Siemens Networks, Portugal
Luis Gomes, Universidade Nova Lisboa, Portugal
Antonio Luis Gomes Valente, University of Trás-os-Montes and Alto Douro, Portugal
Diego Gonzalez Aguilera, University of Salamanca - Avila, Spain
Genady Grabarnik,CUNY - New York, USA
Craig Grimes, Nanjing University of Technology, PR China
Stefanos Gritzalis, University of the Aegean, Greece
Richard Gunstone, Bournemouth University, UK
Jianlin Guo, Mitsubishi Electric Research Laboratories, USA
Mohammad Hammoudeh, Manchester Metropolitan University, UK
Petr Hanáček, Brno University of Technology, Czech Republic
Go Hasegawa, Osaka University, Japan
Henning Heuer, Fraunhofer Institut Zerstörungsfreie Prüfverfahren (FhG-IZFP-D), Germany
Paloma R. Horche, Universidad Politécnica de Madrid, Spain
Vincent Huang, Ericsson Research, Sweden
Friedrich Hülsmann, Gottfried Wilhelm Leibniz Bibliothek - Hannover, Germany
Travis Humble, Oak Ridge National Laboratory, USA
Florentin Ipate, University of Pitesti, Romania

Patrick Meumeu Yomsi, INRIA Nancy-Grand Est, France
Alberto Yúfera, Centro Nacional de Microelectronica (CNM-CSIC) - Sevilla, Spain
Sergey Y. Yurish, IFSA, Spain
David Zammit-Mangion, University of Malta, Malta
Guigen Zhang, Clemson University, USA
Weiping Zhang, Shanghai Jiao Tong University, P. R. China

International Journal on Advances in Systems and Measurements
Volume 9, Numbers 3 & 4, 2016

CONTENTS

International Journal on Advances in Systems and Measurements, vol 9 no 3 & 4, year 2016, http://www.iariajournals.org/systems_and_measurements/

Butterfly-like Algorithms for GASPI Split Phase Allreduce

Vanessa End
and Ramin Yahyapour

Gesellschaft für wissenschaftliche
Datenverarbeitung mbH Göttingen
Göttingen, Germany
Email: <vanessa.end>,
<ramin.yahyapour>@gwdg.de

Christian Simmendinger
and Thomas Alrutz

T-Systems Solutions for Research GmbH
Stuttgart/Göttingen, Germany
Email: <christian.simmendinger>,
<thomas.alrutz>@t-systems-sfr.com

Abstract—**Collective communication routines pose a significant bottleneck of highly parallel programs. Research on different algorithms for disseminating information among all participating processes in a collective communication has brought forth many different algorithms, some of which have a butterfly-like communication scheme. While these algorithms have been abandoned from usage in collective communication routines with larger messages, due to the congestion that arises from their use, these algorithms have ideal properties for split-phase allreduce routines: all processes are involved in the computation of the result in each communication round and they have few communication rounds. This article will present several different algorithms with a butterfly-like communication scheme and examine their usability for a GASPI allreduce library routine. The library routines will be compared to state-of-the-art MPI implementations and also to a tree-based allreduce algorithm.**

Keywords–GASPI; Allreduce; Partitioned Global Address Space (PGAS); Collective Communication; Algorithms.

I. Introduction

In high performance computing (HPC), one of the main bottlenecks is always communication. As we are looking into the exascale age, this bottleneck becomes even more important than before: with more processes participating in the computation of a problem, also more communication between these processes is necessary. But already in the past, this bottleneck has been observed - especially when using collective communication routines, e.g., barrier or allreduce routines, where all processes (of a given group) are active in the communication. Therefore, many different algorithms have been developed in the course of time to reduce the runtime of collective routines and thus, the overall communication overhead. Key to this reduction of runtime is the underlying communication algorithm.

In this paper, we extend our work from [1], where we have introduced an adaption of the n-way dissemination algorithm, such that it is usable for split-phase allreduce operations, as they are defined in, e.g., the Global Address Space Programming Interface (GASPI) specification [2]. GASPI is based on one-sided communication semantics, distinguishing it from message-passing paradigms, libraries and application programming interfaces (API) like the Message-Passing Interface (MPI) standard [3]. In the spirit of hybrid programming (e.g., combined MPI and OpenMP communication) for improved performance, GASPI's communication routines are designed for inter-node communication and leaves it to the programmer to include another communication interface for intra-node, i.e., shared-memory communication. Thus, one GASPI process is started per node or cache coherent non-uniform memory access (ccNUMA) socket.

To enable the programmer to design a fault-tolerant application and to achieve perfect overlap of communication and computation, GASPI's non-local operations are equipped with a timeout mechanism. By either using one of the predefined constants `GASPI_BLOCK` or `GASPI_TEST` or by giving a user-defined timeout value, non-local routines can either be called in a blocking or a non-blocking manner. In the same way, GASPI also defines split-phase collective communication routines, namely `gaspi_barrier`, `gaspi_allreduce` and `gaspi_allreduce_user`, for which the user can define a personal reduce routine. The goal of our research is to find a fast algorithm for the allreduce operation, which has a small number of communication rounds and, whenever possible, uses all available resources for the computation of the partial results computed in each communication round.

Collective communication is an important issue in high performance computing and thus, research on algorithms for the different collective communication routines has been pursued in the last decades. In the area of the allreduce operation, influences from all other communication algorithms can be used, e.g., tree algorithms like the binomial spanning tree (BST) [4] or the tree algorithm of Mellor-Crummey and Scott [5]. These are then used to first reduce and then broadcast the data. Also, more barrier related algorithms like the butterfly barrier of Brooks [6] or the tournament algorithm described by Debra Hensgen et al. in the same paper as the dissemination algorithm [7] influence allreduce algorithms.

Yet, none of these algorithms seems fit for the challenges of split-phase remote direct memory access (RDMA) allreduce, with potentially computation-intense user-defined reduce operations over an InfiniBand network. The tree algorithms have a tree depth of $\lceil \log_2(P) \rceil$ and have to be run through twice, leading to a total of $2\lceil \log_2(P) \rceil$ communication rounds.

In each of these rounds, a large part of the participating ranks remain idling, while the n-way dissemination algorithm and Bruck's algorithm only need $\lceil \log_{n+1}(P) \rceil$ communication rounds and involve all ranks in every round. Also, the butterfly barrier has $k = \lceil \log_2(P) \rceil$ communication rounds to traverse, but it is also only fit for 2^k participants.

There are two key features which make (n-way) dissemination based allreduce operations very interesting for both split-phase implementations as well as user-defined reductions, like they are both defined in the GASPI specification [2].

1) Split-phase collectives either require an external active progress component or, alternatively, progress has to be achieved through suitable calls from the calling processes. Since the underlying algorithm for the split-phase collectives is unknown to the enduser, all participating processes have to repeatedly call the collective several times. Algorithms for split-phase collectives hence ideally both involve all processes in every communication step and moreover ideally require a minimum number of steps (and thus a minimum number of calls). The n-way dissemination algorithm exactly matches these requirements. It requires a very small number of communication rounds of order $\lceil \log_{n+1}(P) \rceil$ and additionally involves every process in all communication rounds.
2) User-defined collectives share some of the above requirements in the sense that CPU-expensive local reductions ideally should leverage every calling CPU in each round and ideally would require a minimum number of communication rounds (and hence a minimum number of expensive local reductions).

In the following section, we will describe related work. In Section III, we will shortly introduce the algorithms chosen for the experiments, elaborating on the adaption of the n-way dissemination algorithm. In addition to the adapted n-way dissemination algorithm, this paper will also present Bruck's algorithm [8] and the butterfly algorithm [6] with two adaptions for $P \neq 2^k$ in more detail. While we have only shown experimental results of the allreduce function with the sum operation in the former paper, we will now also show results using the minimum and the maximum operation in allreduce. The experimental setup and experimental results are presented in Section IV, where we also evaluate the results of the experiments. Section V will then give a conclusion of the work and an outlook on future work.

II. Related Work

Some related work, especially in terms of developed algorithms, has already been presented in the introduction. Still to mention is the group around Jehoshua Bruck, which has done much research on multi-port algorithms, hereby developing a k-port algorithm with a very similar communication scheme as that of the n-way dissemination algorithm [8], [9]. These works were found relatively late in the implementation phase of the adapted n-way dissemination algorithm, why an extensive comparison of the two has been postponed to this paper.

In the past years, more and more emphasis has been put on RDMA techniques and algorithms [10][11] due to hardware development, e.g., InfiniBand™[12] or RDMA over Converged Ethernet (RoCE) [13]. While Panda et al. [10] exploit the multicast feature of InfiniBand™, this is not an option for us because the multicast is a so called unreliable operation and in addition an optional feature of the InfiniBand™architecture [12]. Congestion in fat tree configured networks is still a topic in research, where for example Zahavi is an active researcher [14]. While a change of the routing tables or routing algorithm is often not an option for application programmers, the adaption of node orders within the API is a possible option.

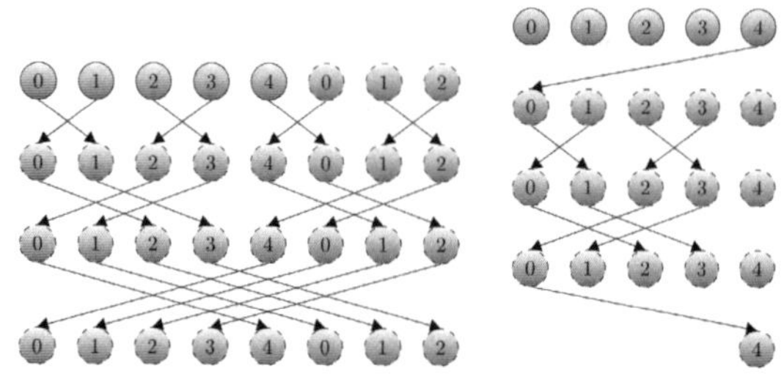

Figure 1. Comparison of the Butterfly Algorithm for $P = 5$ with virtual processes (left) to the Pairwise Exchange Algorithm for the same number of processes (right).

III. Algorithms

Since communication is one of the most important bottlenecks in parallel computing, many different algorithms have been developed for the numerous different collective communication routines. In this section, several algorithms, usable for collective communication routines, will be presented. Our focus lies on algorithms with butterfly-like communication schemes, as these are at the moment not used for communication with large messages, but our initial research shows that in modern architecture, the congestion does not arise in the way expected. In addition to this, the algorithms are not used for allreduce operations at all, because they potentially deliver wrong results for some numbers of participating processes, if implemented in their original design. With some adaptions, this is no longer true for these algorithms. We start the presentation of algorithms with the name-giving algorithm, the butterfly algorithm.

A. *Butterfly Algorithm and Pairwise Exchange Algorithm*

Eugene D. Brooks introduced the butterfly algorithm in the *Butterfly Barrier* in 1986 [6]. It has been designed for operations with $P = 2^k$ participants. It then has $k = \lceil \log_2 P \rceil$ communication rounds, where in each round l, rank p communicates with $p \pm 2^{l-1}$. Since this algorithm was not intended for the use with $P = 2^{k-1} + q < 2^k$ processes, a first adaption was made: *virtual processes* were introduced to virtually have $P' = 2^k$ processes to use the algorithm on. Existing processes adopted the role of these virtual processes as depicted in Figure 1. Processes 0 to 2 act as if they were additional processes 5, 6 and 7 to comply to the communication scheme for $P = 8$. This introduces unnecessary additional communication and overhead. While this is not too dramatic in the case of a barrier, this becomes very interesting when the message sizes increase. Even when $P = 2^k$, the symmetric communication scheme of the butterfly algorithm quickly leads to congestion in network topologies where there is exactly one link from one processor to another, as this link will be used in both directions

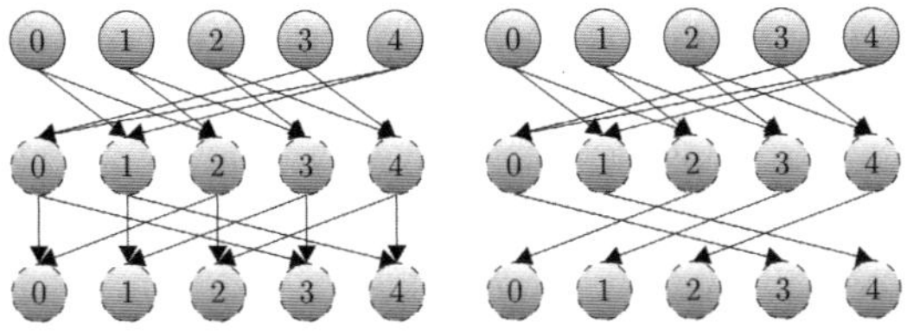

Figure 2. Comparison of the 2-way dissemination algorithm (left) to the adapted 2-way dissemination algorithm (right) for 5 ranks.

at the same time. In addition, the adaption makes the algorithm unusable for non-idempotent allreduce operations, as data is transferred and processed more than once.

A different adaption to the original algorithm leads to the *Pairwise Exchange Algorithm* (PE). This algorithm is identical to the previous algorithm if $P = 2^k$ and is for example described in [15]. If the number of processes is not a power of two, but rather $2^k + q$, then the q "leftover" processes first communicate with the first q processes and then wait until the 2^k remaining processes have finished the algorithm, as shown in Figure 1.

The first adaption of the butterfly algorithm would make it possible to use this algorithm for $P \neq 2^k$, but it would lead to a repeated inclusion of initial data from the virtual processes, if used for an allreduce. The pairwise exchange algorithm also solves this problem, why this will be the only adaption used in the experiments shown below.

B. (n-way) Dissemination Algorithm

The basis of the n-way dissemination algorithm is the dissemination algorithm developed by Hensgen et al. in 1988 [7]. To be exact, this algorithm is equivalent to a 1-way dissemination algorithm as it is defined by Hoefler et al. in 2006 [16]. In Hoefler's n-way dissemination algorithm, each participating process sends and receives n messages per communication round - instead of just one as presented by Hensgen et al.

Similar to the butterfly algorithm for $P \neq 2^k$, the n-way dissemination algorithm transfers certain data elements more than once to the participating ranks if $P \neq (n+1)^k$. This is exemplarily shown for a 2-way dissemination algorithm with 5 ranks in Figure 2 on the left. Nevertheless, the algorithm shows excellent performance in barrier operations, where it does not matter, whether a flag is communicated once or twice. It does not seriously impact the runtime and especially it does not alter the result of the routine. Using this algorithm for allreduce is not practicable in these cases though - the result will be wrong and different on all participating nodes. To still use this algorithm for allreduce operations, we have presented an adaption to the n-way dissemination algorithm, which overcomes these problems in [1]. The below described adaption of the communication scheme is depicted in Figure 2 in direct comparison to the original communication scheme.

The n-way dissemination algorithm, as presented in [16] has been developed for spreading data among the participants, where n is the number of messages transferred in each communication round. As the algorithm is not exclusive to nodes, cores, processes or threads, the term *ranks* will be used

TABLE I. ROUND-WISE COMPUTATION OF PARTIAL RESULTS IN A 2-WAY DISSEMINATION ALGORITHM (FROM [1])

rank	round 0	round 1	round 2
0	x_0	$S_1^0 = x_0 \circ x_8 \circ x_7$	$S_2^0 = S_1^0 \circ S_1^6 \circ S_1^3$
1	x_1	$S_1^1 = x_1 \circ x_0 \circ x_8$	$S_2^1 = S_1^1 \circ S_1^7 \circ S_1^4$
2	x_2	$S_1^2 = x_2 \circ x_1 \circ x_0$	$S_2^2 = S_1^2 \circ S_1^8 \circ S_1^5$
3	x_3	$S_1^3 = x_3 \circ x_2 \circ x_1$	$S_2^3 = S_1^3 \circ S_1^0 \circ S_1^6$
4	x_4	$S_1^4 = x_4 \circ x_3 \circ x_2$	$S_2^4 = S_1^4 \circ S_1^1 \circ S_1^7$
5	x_5	$S_1^5 = x_5 \circ x_4 \circ x_3$	$S_2^5 = S_1^5 \circ S_1^2 \circ S_1^8$
6	x_6	$S_1^6 = x_6 \circ x_5 \circ x_4$	$S_2^6 = S_1^6 \circ S_1^3 \circ S_1^0$
7	x_7	$S_1^7 = x_7 \circ x_6 \circ x_5$	$S_2^7 = S_1^7 \circ S_1^4 \circ S_1^1$
8	x_8	$S_1^8 = x_8 \circ x_7 \circ x_6$	$S_2^8 = S_1^8 \circ S_1^5 \circ S_1^2$

rank	round 0	round 1	round 2
0	x_0	$S_1^0 = x_0 \circ x_7 \circ x_6$	$S_2^0 = S_1^0 \circ S_1^5 \circ S_1^2$
1	x_1	$S_1^1 = x_1 \circ x_0 \circ x_7$	$S_2^1 = S_1^1 \circ S_1^6 \circ S_1^3$
2	x_2	$S_1^2 = x_2 \circ x_1 \circ x_0$	$S_2^2 = S_1^2 \circ S_1^7 \circ S_1^4$
3	x_3	$S_1^3 = x_3 \circ x_2 \circ x_1$	$S_2^3 = S_1^3 \circ S_1^0 \circ S_1^5$
4	x_4	$S_1^4 = x_4 \circ x_3 \circ x_2$	$S_2^4 = S_1^4 \circ S_1^1 \circ S_1^6$
5	x_5	$S_1^5 = x_5 \circ x_4 \circ x_3$	$S_2^5 = S_1^5 \circ S_1^2 \circ S_1^7$
6	x_6	$S_1^6 = x_6 \circ x_5 \circ x_4$	$S_2^6 = S_1^6 \circ S_1^3 \circ S_1^0$
7	x_7	$S_1^7 = x_7 \circ x_6 \circ x_5$	$S_2^7 = S_1^7 \circ S_1^4 \circ S_1^1$

in the following. The P participants in the collective operation are numbered consecutively from $0, \ldots, P-1$ and this number is their rank. With respect to rank p, the ranks $p+1$ and $p-1$ are called p's *neighbors*, where $p-1$ will be the *left-hand neighbor*.

Let P be the number of ranks involved in the collective communication. Then $k = \lceil \log_{n+1}(P) \rceil$ is the number of communication rounds the n-way dissemination algorithm needs to traverse, before all ranks have all information. In every communication round $l \in \{1, \ldots, k\}$, every process p has n peers $s_{l,i}$, to which it transfers data and also n peers $r_{l,j}$, from which it receives data:

$$\begin{aligned} s_{l,i} &= p + i \cdot (n+1)^{l-1} \mod P \\ r_{l,j} &= p - j \cdot (n+1)^{l-1} \mod P, \end{aligned} \tag{1}$$

with $i, j \in \{1, \ldots, n\}$. Thus, in every round p gets (additional) information from $n(n+1)^{l-1}$ participating ranks - either directly or through the information obtained by the sending ranks in the preceding rounds.

When using the dissemination algorithm for an allreduce, the information received in every round is the partial result the sending rank has computed in the round before. The receiving rank then computes a new local partial result from the received data and the local partial result already at hand.

Let S_l^p be the partial result of rank p in round l, $\circ$ be the reduction operation used and x_p be the rank's initial data. Then rank p receives n partial results $S_{l-1}^{r_{l,i}}$ in round l and computes

$$S_l^p = S_{l-1}^p \circ S_{l-1}^{r_{l,1}} \circ S_{l-1}^{r_{l,2}} \circ \cdots \circ S_{l-1}^{r_{l,n}}, \tag{2}$$

which it transfers to its peers $s_{l+1,i}$ in the next round. This data movement is shown in Table I for an allreduce based on a 2-way dissemination algorithm. First for 9 ranks, then for 8 participating ranks. By expanding the result of rank 0 in round

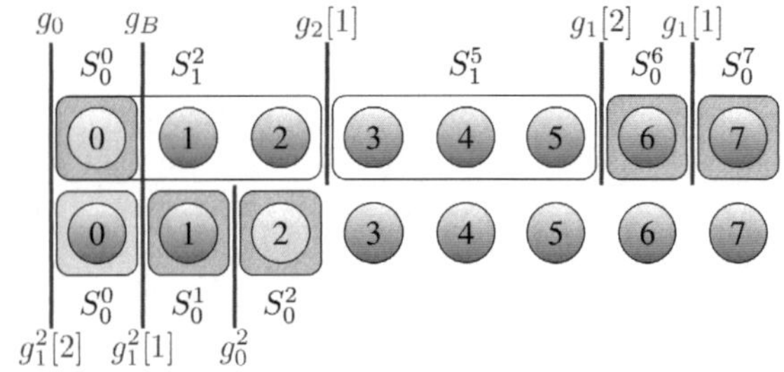

Figure 3. The data boundaries g and received partial results $S_i^{r_{l,j}}$ of ranks 0 and 2 (from [1]).

2 from the second table, it becomes visible, that the reduction operation has been applied twice to x_0:

$$S_2^0 = (x_0 \circ x_7 \circ x_6) \circ (x_5 \circ x_4 \circ x_3) \circ (x_2 \circ x_1 \circ x_0). \quad (3)$$

In general, if $P \neq (n+1)^k$, the final result will include data of at least one rank twice: In every communication round l, each rank receives n partial results each of which is the reduction of the initial data of its $(n+1)^{l-1}$ left-hand neighbors. Thus, the number of included initial data elements is described through

$$\sum_{i=1}^{l} n(n+1)^{i-1} + 1 = (n+1)^l \quad (4)$$

for every round l.

In the cases of the maximum or minimum operation to be performed in the allreduce, this does not matter. In the case of a summation though, this dilemma will result into different final sums on the participating ranks. In general, the adaption is needed for all operations, where the repeated application of the function to the same element changes the final result, so called *non-idempotent* functions.

The adaption of the n-way dissemination algorithm is mainly based on these two properties: (1) in every round l, p receives n new partial results. (2) These partial results are the result of the combination of the data of the next $\sum_{i=0}^{l-1} n(n+1)^{i-1} + 1$ left-hand neighbors of the sender. This is depicted in Figure 3 through boxes. Highlighted in green are those ranks, whose data view is represented, that is rank 0's in the first row and rank 2's in the second row. Each box encloses those ranks, whose initial data is included in the partial result the right most rank in the box has transferred in a given round. This means for rank 0, it has its own data, received S_0^6 and S_0^7 in the first round (gray boxes) and will receive S_1^5 and S_1^2 from ranks 2 and 5 in round 2 (white boxes).

As each of the boxes describes one of the partial results received, the included initial data items can not be retrieved by the destination rank. The change from one box to the next is thus defined as a *data boundary*. The main idea of the adaption is to find data boundaries in the data of the source ranks in the last round, which coincide with data boundaries in the destination rank's data. When such a correspondence is found, the data sent in the last round is reduced accordingly. To be able to do so, it is necessary to describe these boundaries in a mathematical manner. Considering the data elements included in each partial result received, the data boundaries of the receiver p can be described as:

$$g_{l_{\text{rcv}}}[j_{\text{rcv}}] = p - n \sum_{i=0}^{l_{\text{rcv}}-2} (n+1)^i - j_{\text{rcv}}(n+1)^{l_{\text{rcv}}-1} \bmod P, \quad (5)$$

where $j_{\text{rcv}}(n+1)^{l_{\text{rcv}}-1}$ describes the boundary created through the data transferred by rank $r_{l_{\text{rcv}},j_{\text{rcv}}}$ in round l_{rcv}.

Also, the sending ranks have received partial results in the preceding rounds, which are marked through corresponding boundaries. From the view of rank p in the last round k, these boundaries are then described through

$$g^s_{l_{\text{snd}}}[j_{\text{snd}}] = p - s(n+1)^{k-1} - n \sum_{i=0}^{l_{\text{snd}}-2} (n+1)^i - j_{\text{snd}}(n+1)^{l_{\text{snd}}-1} \bmod P, \quad (6)$$

with $s \in \{1, \ldots, n\}$ distinguishing the n senders and j_{snd}, l_{snd} corresponding to the above j_{rcv}, l_{rcv} for the sending rank. To also consider those cases, where only the initial data of the sending or the receiving rank is included more than once in the final result, we let $l_{\text{snd}}, l_{\text{rcv}} \in \{0, \ldots, k-1\}$ and introduce an additional *base border* g_B in the destination rank's data.

These boundaries are also depicted in Figure 3 for the previously given example of a 2-way dissemination algorithm with 8 ranks. The figure depicts the data present on ranks 0 and 2 after the first communication round in the gray boxes with according boundaries g_B, g_0, $g_1[1]$ and $g_1[2]$ on rank 0 and g_0^2, $g_1^2[1]$ and $g_1^2[2]$ on rank 2. Since the boundaries g_B and $g_1^2[1]$ coincide, the first sender in the last round, that is rank 5, transfers its partial result but rank 2 only transfers a reduction $S' = x_2 \circ x_1$ instead of $x_2 \circ x_1 \circ x_0$.

More generally speaking, the algorithm is adaptable, if there are boundaries on the source rank that coincide with boundaries on the destination rank, i.e.,

$$g^s_{l_{\text{snd}}}[j_{\text{snd}}] = g_{l_{\text{rcv}}}[j_{\text{rcv}}] \quad (7)$$

or $g^s_{l_{\text{snd}}}[j_{\text{snd}}] = g_B$. Then the last source rank, defined through s, transfers only the data up to the given boundary and the receiving rank takes the partial result up to its given boundary out of the final result. Taking out the partial result in this context means: if the given operation has an inverse $\circ^{-1}$, apply this to the final result and the partial result defined through $g_{l_{\text{rcv}}}[j_{\text{rcv}}]$. If the operation does not have an inverse, recalculate the final result, hereby omitting the partial result defined through $g_{l_{\text{rcv}}}[j_{\text{rcv}}]$. Since this boundary is known from the very beginning, it is possible to store this partial result in the round it is created, thus saving additional computation time at the end.

From this, one can directly deduce the number of participating ranks P, for which the n-way dissemination algorithm is adaptable in this manner:

$$\begin{aligned} P &= g^s_{l_{\text{snd}}}[j_{\text{snd}}] - g_{l_{\text{rcv}}}[j_{\text{rcv}}] \\ &= s(n+1)^{k-1} + n\sum_{i=0}^{l_{\text{snd}}-2}(n+1)^i + j_{\text{snd}}(n+1)^{l_{\text{snd}}-1} \\ &\quad - n\sum_{i=0}^{l_{\text{rcv}}-2}(n+1)^i - j_{\text{rcv}}(n+1)^{l_{\text{rcv}}-1} . \end{aligned} \tag{8}$$

For given P, a 5-tuple $(s, l_{\text{snd}}, l_{\text{rcv}}, j_{\text{snd}}, j_{\text{rcv}})$ can be precalculated for different n. Then this 5-tuple also describes the adaption of the algorithm:

Theorem 1: Given the 5-tuple $(s, l_{\text{snd}}, l_{\text{rcv}}, j_{\text{snd}}, j_{\text{rcv}})$, the last round of the n-way dissemination algorithm is adapted through one of the following cases:

1) $l_{\text{rcv}}, l_{\text{snd}} > 0$
The sender $p - s(n+1)^{k-1}$ sends its partial result up to $g^s_{l_{\text{snd}}}[j_{\text{snd}}]$ and the receiver takes out its partial result up to the boundary $g_{l_{\text{rcv}}}[j_{\text{rcv}}]$.
2) $l_{\text{rcv}} > 0, l_{\text{snd}} = 0$
The sender $p - s(n+1)^{k-1}$ sends its own data and the receiver takes out its partial result up to the boundary $g_{l_{\text{rcv}}}[j_{\text{rcv}}]$.
3) $l_{\text{rcv}} = 0, l_{\text{snd}} = 0$
The sender $p - (s-1)(n+1)^{k-1}$ sends its last calculated partial result. If $s = 1$ the algorithm ends after $k-1$ rounds.
4) $l_{\text{rcv}} = 0, l_{\text{snd}} = 1$
The sender $p - s(n+1)^{k-1}$ sends its partial result up to $g^s_{l_{\text{snd}}}[j_{\text{snd}} - 1]$. If $j_{\text{snd}} = 1$, the sender only sends its initial data.
5) $l_{\text{rcv}} = 0, l_{\text{snd}} > 1$
The sender $p - s(n+1)^{k-1}$ sends its partial result up to $g^s_{l_{\text{snd}}}[j_{\text{snd}}]$ and the receiver takes out its initial data from the final result.

Proof: We show the correctness of the above theorem by using that at the end each process will have to calculate the final result from P different data elements. We therefore look at (8) and how the given 5-tuple changes the terms of relevance. We will again need the fact, that the received partial results are always a composition of the initial data of neighboring elements.

1) $l_{\text{rcv}}, l_{\text{snd}} > 0$:

$$\begin{aligned} P &= s(n+1)^{k-1} + n\sum_{i=0}^{l_{\text{snd}}-2}(n+1)^i + j_{\text{snd}}(n+1)^{l_{\text{snd}}-1} \\ &\quad - n\sum_{i=0}^{l_{\text{rcv}}-2}(n+1)^i - j_{\text{rcv}}(n+1)^{l_{\text{rcv}}-1} \\ &= g^s_{l_{\text{snd}}}[j_{\text{snd}}] - g_{l_{\text{rcv}}}[j_{\text{rcv}}] . \end{aligned} \tag{9}$$

In order to have the result of P elements, the sender must thus transfer the partial result including the data up to $g^s_{l_{\text{snd}}}[j_{\text{snd}}]$ and the receiver takes out the elements up to $g_{l_{\text{rcv}}}[j_{\text{rcv}}]$.

2) $l_{\text{rcv}} > 0, l_{\text{snd}} = 0$:

$$\begin{aligned} P &= s(n+1)^{k-1} - n\sum_{i=0}^{l_{\text{rcv}}-2}(n+1)^i - j_{\text{rcv}}(n+1)^{l_{\text{rcv}}-1} \\ &= s(n+1)^{k-1} - g_{l_{\text{rcv}}}[j_{\text{rcv}}] \end{aligned} \tag{10}$$

and thus we see that the sender must send only its own data, while the receiver takes out data up to $g_{l_{\text{rcv}}}[j_{\text{rcv}}]$.

3) $l_{\text{rcv}} = 0, l_{\text{snd}} = 0$:

$$P = s(n+1)^{k-1} . \tag{11}$$

In the first $k-1$ rounds, the receiving rank will already have the partial result of $n\sum_{i=1}^{k-1}(n+1)^i = (n+1)^{k-1} - 1$ elements. In the last round it then receives the partial sums of $(s-1)(n+1)^{k-1}$ further elements by the first $s-1$ senders and can thus compute the partial result from a total of $(s-1)(n+1)^{k-1} + (n+1)^{k-1} = s(n+1)^{k-1} - 1$ elements. Including its own data makes the final result of $s(n+1)^{k-1} = P$ elements. If $s = 1$ the algorithm is done after $k-1$ rounds.

4) $l_{\text{rcv}} = 0, l_{\text{snd}} = 1$:

$$P = s(n+1)^{k-1} + j_{\text{snd}} \tag{12}$$

Following the same argumentation as above, the receiving rank will have the partial result of $s(n+1)^{k-1} - 1$ elements. It thus still needs

$$\begin{aligned} & P - \left(s(n+1)^{k-1} - 1\right) \\ = \ & s(n+1)^{k-1} + j_{\text{snd}} - s(n+1)^{k-1} + 1 \\ = \ & j_{\text{snd}} + 1 \end{aligned} \tag{13}$$

elements. Now, taking into account its own data it still needs j_{snd} data elements. The data boundary $g_1[j_{\text{snd}}]$ of the sender includes j_{snd} elements plus its own data, i.e., $j_{\text{snd}}+1$ elements. The $j^{\text{th}}_{\text{snd}}$ element will then be the receiving rank's data, thus it suffices to send up to $g_1[j_{\text{snd}} - 1]$.

5) $l_{\text{rcv}} = 0, l_{\text{snd}} > 1$:

$$\begin{aligned} P &= s(n+1)^{k-1} \\ &\quad + n\sum_{i=0}^{l_{\text{snd}}-2}(n+1)^i + j_{\text{snd}}(n+1)^{l_{\text{snd}}-1} \end{aligned} \tag{14}$$

In this case, the sender sends a partial result which necessarily includes the initial data of the receiving rank. This means that the receiving rank has to take out its own initial data from the final result. Due to $l_{\text{snd}} > 1$ the sender will not be able to take a single initial data element out of the partial result to be transferred. ■

Note that the case where a data boundary on the sending side corresponds to the base border on the receiving side, i.e., $g^s_{l_{snd}}[j_{snd}] = g_B$, has not been covered above. In this case, there is no 5-tuple like above, but rather $P - 1 = g^s_{l_{snd}}[j_{snd}]$ and the adaption and reasoning complies to case 4 in the above theorem.

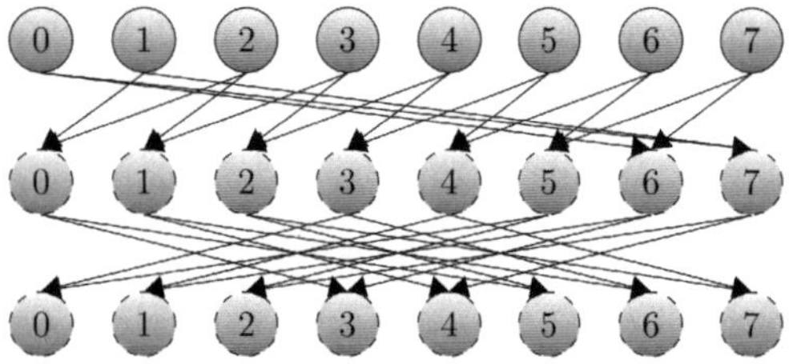

Figure 4. Communication scheme of Bruck's global combine algorithm for $P = 8$.

C. Bruck's Algorithm

In [8], Jehoshua Bruck and Ching-Tien Ho present two algorithms for global combine operations in n-port message-passing systems[1] The first of the two shows many similarities to the n-way dissemination algorithm presented above. While the dissemination algorithm and the n-way dissemination algorithm were both designed for barrier operations, Bruck's algorithm is explicitly designed for global combine operations, i.e., allreduces.

In $\lceil \log_{n+1}(P) \rceil$ communication rounds, every participating process transfers and receives n partial reduction results from other processes. Let $\circ$ be the reduction operation used and x_p be the initial data of process p. The partial results transferred by rank p in round l are computed in two versions: $S_l^p[0]$ is the reduction of all previously received results without the initial data of the computing process and $S_l^p[1] = x_p \circ S_l^p[0]$. In each round, the group of destination ranks is split up into two groups, one of which will receive S_p^0, and the other will receive S_p^1. For determining these groups, two things are necessary: the base $(n+1)$ representation of $P-1$ and the counter c, which counts the number of elements on which the reduction has already been performed.

For ease of readability, the algorithm will here be described with the help of an example for $P = 8$ and $n = 2$ from the view of rank 0. The complete communication scheme for this example is depicted in Figure 4. The general description and the proof can be found in [8]. The algorithm will need $k = \lceil \log_3(8) \rceil = 2$ communication rounds. For each of these rounds l, an α_{l-1} is needed to split the destination ranks in two groups: one receiving $S_l^p[0]$ and the other $S_l^p[1]$. These α_i are computed through the representation of $P-1 = 7$ in a base 3 notation:

$$7 = (21)_3 = (\alpha_1 \alpha_0)_3. \tag{15}$$

In the first round, only the partial result $S_1^0[1] = x_0$ is transferred to $\alpha_{k-1} = \alpha_1 = 2$ process. The destination processes are

$$s_{1,1} \equiv p-1 \mod (P) \equiv -1 \mod 8 \equiv 7 \tag{16}$$
$$s_{1,2} \equiv p-2 \mod (P) \equiv -2 \mod 8 \equiv 6. \tag{17}$$

At the same time, rank 0 will receive partial results from its peers $r_{1,1} \equiv p+1 \mod (P) \equiv 1$ and $r_{1,2} = 2$, namely $S_1^1[1] = x_1$ and $S_1^2[1] = x_2$. Rank 0 can then calculate new partial results to be transferred in the following round:

$$S_2^0[0] = S_1^0[0] \circ S_1^1[1] \circ S_1^2[1] = x_1 \circ x_2 \tag{18}$$
$$S_2^0[1] = S_1^0[1] \circ S_1^1[1] \circ S_1^2[1] = x_0 \circ x_1 \circ x_2. \tag{19}$$

At the same time, c is increased to $c = \alpha_1 = 2$, which will be needed for the computation of the communication peers in the next round. Rank 0 will now transfer $S_2^0[1]$ to $\alpha_0 = 1$ rank:

$$s_{2,1} \equiv p - \alpha_0 \cdot (c+1) \mod (P) \equiv -3 \mod 8 \equiv 5, \tag{20}$$

and $S_2^0[0]$ to the remaining $n - \alpha_0 = 2 - 1 = 1$ rank:

$$s_{2,2} \equiv p - c - \alpha_0 \cdot (c+1) \mod (P) \equiv -5 \mod 8 \equiv 3. \tag{21}$$

At the same time, rank 0 will receive partial results from ranks

$$\begin{aligned} r_{2,1} &\equiv p + (c+1) \mod (P) \\ &\equiv 3 \mod 8 \equiv 3 \end{aligned} \tag{22}$$
$$\begin{aligned} r_{2,2} &\equiv p + c + \alpha_0(c+1) \mod (P) \\ &\equiv 5 \mod 8 \equiv 5. \end{aligned} \tag{23}$$

Then, rank 0 can compute the final result

$$\begin{aligned} S_3^0[1] &= S_2^0[1] \circ S_2^3[1] \circ S_2^5[0] \\ &= x_0 \circ x_1 \circ x_2 \circ (x_3 \circ x_4 \circ x_5) \circ (x_6 \circ x_7). \end{aligned} \tag{24}$$

Bruck's algorithm was the last to be presented in this paper, and a comparison of the different algorithms will be given in the next subsection.

D. Comparison

The algorithms with a butterfly-like communication scheme presented in this paper have some significant differences, starting with the number of communication rounds needed to complete the algorithm. The pairwise exchange algorithm needs $\lfloor \log_2(P) \rfloor + 2$ communication rounds, while the adapted n-way dissemination algorithm and Bruck's algorithm only need $\lceil \log_{n++1}(P) \rceil$ communication rounds. In a split-phase allreduce, this will lead to a significant difference in the number of repeated calls to the allreduce routine. In addition to that, q ranks will be idling in the PE algorithm, while the other $P - q$ ranks need to do some computation between the communication steps. To still exploit the full potential of a split-phase allreduce, an application will have to distribute the workload accordingly.

Even though Bruck's algorithm and the adapted n-way dissemination algorithm need the same number of communication rounds to complete an allreduce, an important difference is the applicability to different group sizes P. While Bruck's algorithm works for all pairs (n, P), the n-way dissemination algorithm can not be adapted for all pairs. In those cases, where the algorithm is not adaptable, alternative solutions need to be found for the n-way dissemination algorithm. One possibility could be, to transfer larger messages in the communication rounds, carrying not only a given partial result but maybe some additional initial data items to complete the allreduce properly. Nevertheless, the adaption to the n-way dissemination algorithm can be an important addition to the repertoire of allreduce algorithms in a communication library, because it makes sense to have different algorithms for different combinations of message sizes, number of participating ranks and reduction routines, as described, e.g., in [17].

[1]The notation has been heavily changed from the original paper to fit the notation throughout the rest of the paper.

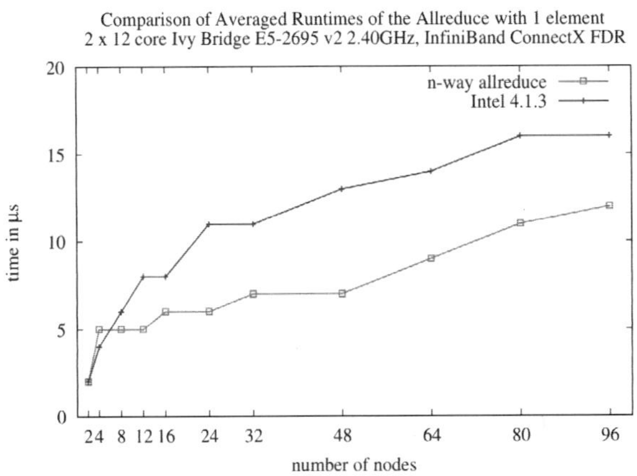

Figure 5. GASPI allreduce with 1 integer and SUM implemented on top of ibverbs in comparison to MPI allreduce (from [1]).

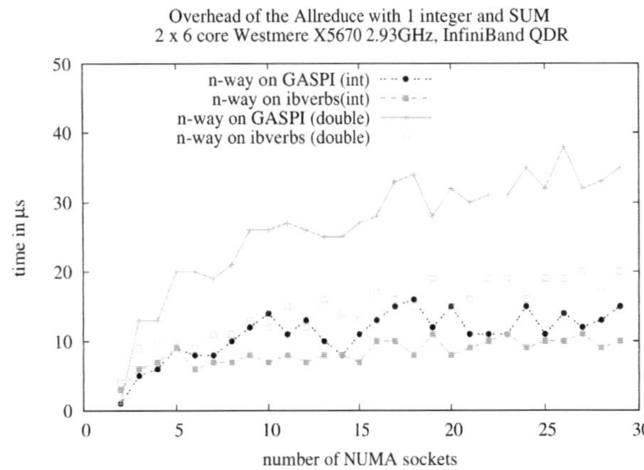

Figure 6. Comparison of allreduce with sum, implemented with ibverbs and implemented as GASPI library routine Cluster 1. One GASPI process per socket.

A possibly very important advantage of Bruck's algorithm and the n-way dissemination algorithm in comparison to the PE is the choice of communication peers. While the PE algorithm has a true butterfly communication scheme, the other two algorithms do not. Depending on the underlying network and routing, two messages will be transferred in opposite directions on the same path in a true butterfly scheme. This will not happen in the butterfly-like schemes of Bruck's algorithm and the n-way dissemination algorithm.

In this paper, we cannot show experiments and results for all different use-case scenarios, but will show a comparison of the three algorithms, implemented as allreduce library routines on top of GASPI.

IV. Experiments and Results

We have implemented the described algorithms as allreduce library functions, using only GASPI routines, in the scope of a GASPI collective library and tested the routines on two different systems:

Cluster 1: A system with 14 nodes, each having two sockets with 6-core Westmere X5670 @2.93GHz processors and an InfiniBand QDR network in fat tree configuration. On this system, the algorithm was compared to the allreduce routines of MVAPICH 2.2.0 and OpenMPI 1.6.5, because no Intel MPI implementation is available on this system. In the following plots, only the OpenMPI runtime is shown, because the MVAPICH implementation is much slower. Thus, a user would not use this implementation for allreduce-heavy jobs and for a better readability, we do not plot these runtimes.

Cluster 2: A system with two sockets nodes of with 8-core Sandy Bridge E5-2670/1600 @2.6GHz processors and an InfiniBand FDR10 network in fat tree configuration. On this system, the algorithm was compared to the allreduce routines of Intel MPI 4.1.3.049 and OpenMPI 1.8.1. In the following plots, only the Intel MPI runtime is shown, because it was always the faster implementation.

The cluster that was used for the tests in the previous paper was no longer available for experiments. In the previous paper [1], we had implemented only the n-way dissemination algorithm directly on top of ibverbs, which showed a significant performance improvement when compared to an Intel MPI, as seen in Figure 5. To enable portability to different GASPI implementations, the option of implementing library routines was now chosen. The GASPI implementation used, is the GPI2-1.1.1 by the Fraunhofer ITWM [18].

We will show runtime comparisons for the smallest possible message size (one integer) and the largest possible message size (255 doubles) in GASPI allreduce routines. In the second case, the reduction operation is applied element-wise to an array of 255 doubles. The runtimes shown are average times from 10^4 runs to balance single higher runtimes which may be caused through different deterministically irreproducible aspects like jitter, contention in the network and similar. Timings were taken right before the call and then again immediately after the call returned. Between two calls of an allreduce, a barrier was called to eliminate caching effects.

We have started one GASPI process per NUMA socket, which is the maximum number of GASPI processes that can be started per node. In addition to a comparison with the fastest MPI implementation on each cluster, we have also implemented a binomial spanning tree as a GASPI allreduce library routine, to show the difference between a good performing tree implementation and an implementation with butterfly-like algorithms. For better readability of the plots, we have omitted the graphical representation of the runtimes of the GPI2 allreduce, because it was, as to be expected, faster than the library routines in most cases.

To convey an idea of the overhead induced through the implementation of the allreduce as a GASPI library routine instead of implementing the allreduce directly with ibverbs, this overhead is depicted in Figure 6. The runtime for the allreduce with one integer increases by a factor of up to 1.84 and with 255 doubles, it even increases by a factor of up to 2.18. This will have to be kept in mind, when regarding the following results.

While the BST and the PE transfer a fixed number of messages per communication round, the n-way dissemination

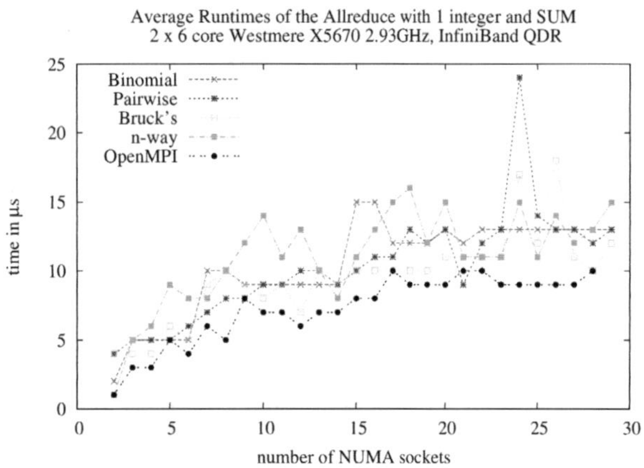

Figure 7. Comparison of Allreduce implementations with 1 integer and sum as reduction operation on Cluster 1. One GASPI process per socket.

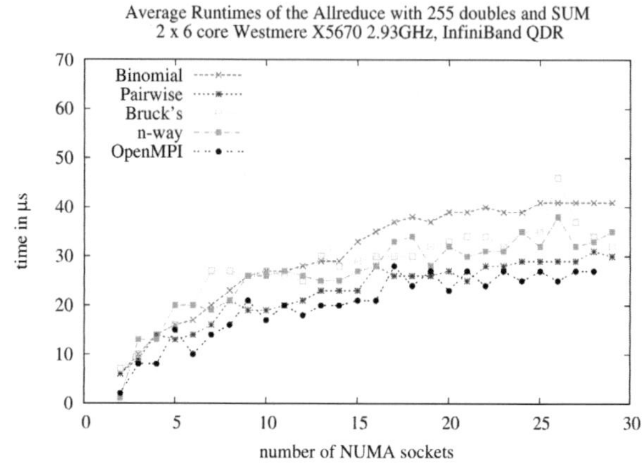

Figure 9. Comparison of Allreduce implementations with 255 doubles and sum as reduction operation on Cluster 1. One GASPI process per socket.

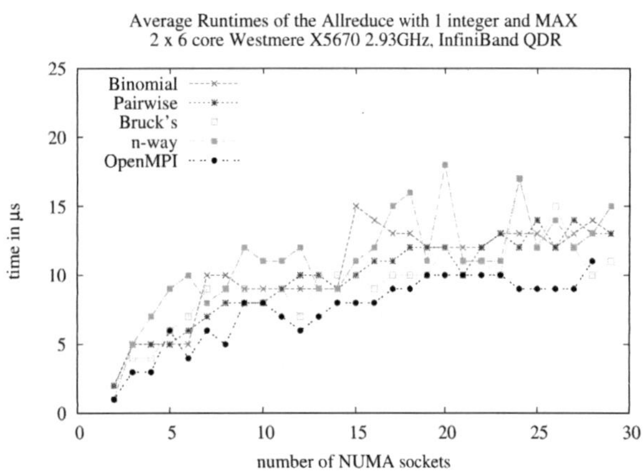

Figure 8. Comparison of Allreduce implementations with 1 integer and maximum as reduction operation on Cluster 1. One GASPI process per socket.

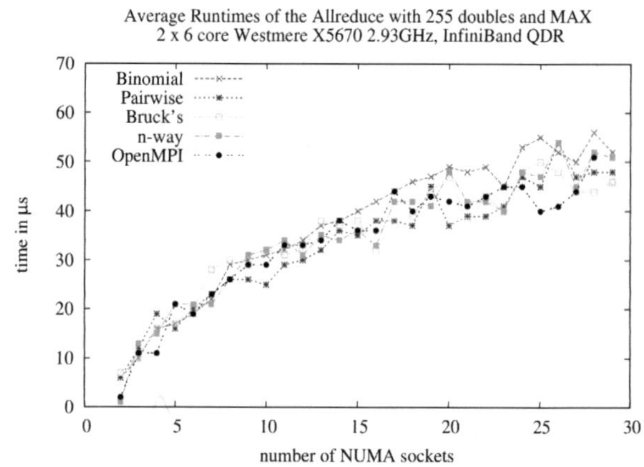

Figure 10. Comparison of Allreduce implementations with 255 doubles and maximum as reduction operation on Cluster 1. One GASPI process per socket.

algorithm and Bruck's algorithm may transfer different numbers of messages per communication round. Since Bruck's algorithm works for all combinations of (n, P), we have fixed $n = 5$ for these experiments. For the n-way dissemination algorithm the n is chosen in the first call of the allreduce routine and the smallest n possible is chosen. This procedure differs from the procedure in the former paper, where a number of allreduces was started in the first call and the fastest n was chosen. Further research has shown, that the overhead induced by calling a sufficiently high number of allreduces to chose a n in this first call is not necessarily compensated through the potentially faster following allreduces. In the future, static but network dependent lookup tables need to be developed or further research on the choice of n depending on the bandwidth, latency and message rate of the underlying network needs to be done.

In Figures 7 to 10 the runtime results on Cluster 1 are shown with one GASPI process started per NUMA socket. Figures 7 and 8 show the runtime results for the allreduce with one integer and sum, respectively maximum reduction operation. Figures 9 and 10 show the same for 255 doubles. In all cases except the maximum operation with 255 doubles, none of the library routines are faster than the OpenMPI implementation. This comes as no surprise, as the allreduce library routines are implemented on top of GASPI routines, while the OpenMPI allreduce may make direct use of ibverbs routines. The runtimes of the GASPI library allreduce are steadier when using the allreduce on 255 doubles than on one integer. When increasing the message size, the butterfly-like algorithms have faster runtimes than the BST. Even though it has been suggested, that the symmetric communication scheme of the PE algorithm will lead to a high congestion in the network, this is not confirmed by the results of the experiments: The pairwise exchange algorithm has a runtime close to the OpenMPI implementation. When using the maximum as reduction operation, all butterfly-like algorithms have similar runtimes and are even faster than the OpenMPI allreduce

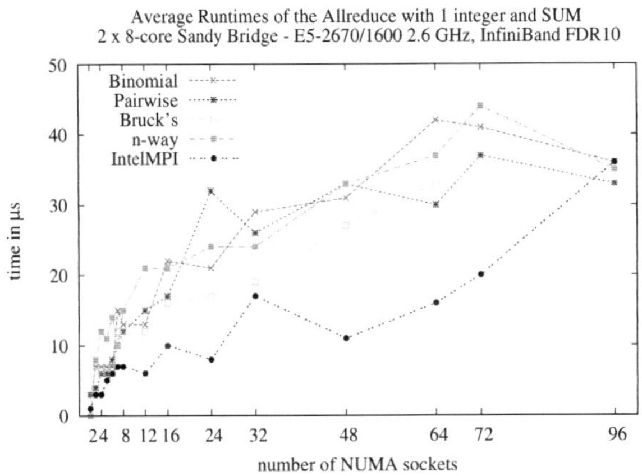

Figure 11. Comparison of Allreduce implementations with one integer and sum as reduction operation on Cluster 2. One GASPI process per socket.

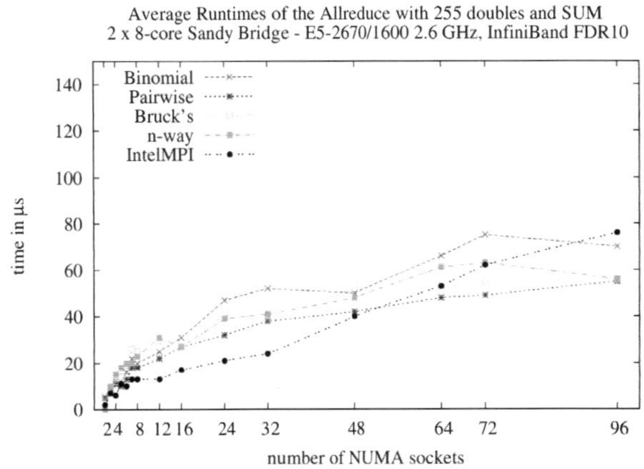

Figure 13. Comparison of Allreduce implementations with 255 doubles and sum as reduction operation on Cluster 2. One GASPI process per socket.

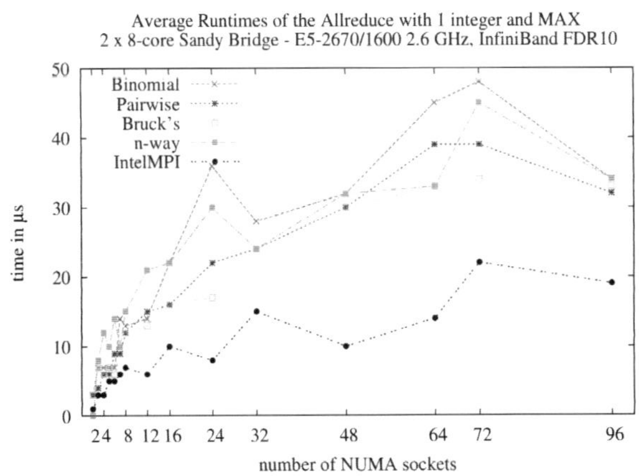

Figure 12. Comparison of Allreduce implementations with one integer and max as reduction operation on Cluster 2. One GASPI process per socket.

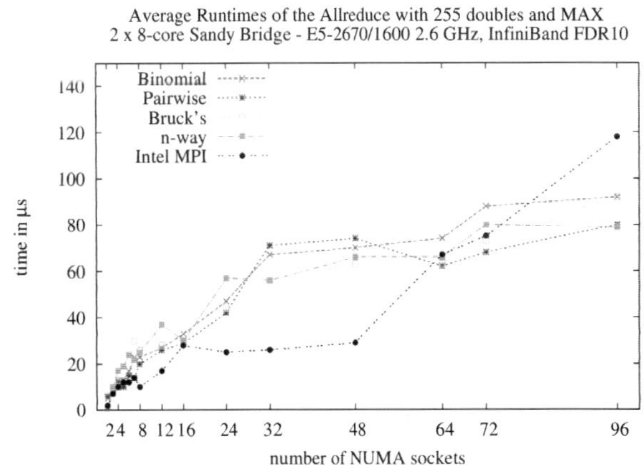

Figure 14. Comparison of Allreduce implementations with 255 doubles and max as reduction operation on Cluster 2. One GASPI process per socket.

implementation for several process numbers. Overall, Bruck's algorithm shows best results for small messages, i.e., one integer, and the PE algorithm shows the best results for large messages, i.e., allreduces on 255 doubles. The adapted n-way dissemination algorithm runtime plot is very volatile, especially for small messages. At least for larger messages, it shows consistently faster runtimes than the BST. For all algorithms, the allreduce with large messages and the maximum operation is significantly slower than the equivalent allreduce with summation as reduction routine.

Figures 11 to 14 show the averaged runtime results on Cluster 2. Here, the difference in runtime between the Intel MPI allreduce and the GASPI allreduce routines is significant for small messages, as can be seen in Figures 11 and 12. Only for larger numbers of involved processes the runtimes of the GASPI routines and those of the Intel MPI implementation converge (Figure 11). While the plots are not as erratic as on Cluster 1, this might be due to the fact, that on this system we could not test every process count. Especially Bruck's algorithm outperforms the other butterfly-like algorithms and the BST for allreduces with small messages. For large messages, i.e., 255 doubles, the GASPI library implementations of the allreduce and the Intel MPI implementation have similar runtimes. Even though the Intel MPI implementation is still faster for a process count up to 48, the gap to the runtimes of the GASPI library has closed to a great extent. With higher number of processes, the GASPI library routines are even faster than the Intel MPI allreduce. Again, the PE shows surprisingly good results, especially for large messages and the sum operation, while the BST's runtimes are at the upper limit of the library runtimes.

V. CONCLUSION AND FUTURE WORK

We have examined different algorithms with a butterfly-like communication scheme for the suitability in a GASPI allreduce library function. In [1] we had presented an adaption to the n-way dissemination algorithm, which was here compared to other algorithms with a similar communication structure. Two important properties of these algorithms are their low number of communication rounds while at the same time involving all processes in each computation step of the algorithm. This makes them ideal candidates for a split-phase allreduce routine as defined in the GASPI specification.

We have seen in the experiments, that algorithms with a butterfly-like communication scheme are often significantly faster than, e.g., the BST and sometimes even reach the performance of existing MPI implementations. This is especially important to note, because the results presented in this article are results obtained from library implementations, i.e., not directly implemented on ibverbs but rather with GASPI routines. As shown in Figure 6, the overhead induced through this additional layer of indirection can slow a routine down by a factor of 2. Considering this, an implementation of the allreduce routine with ibverbs should accelerate the routine to approximately the level of the MPI implementations shown for small messages and even faster in the case of large messages. This is a relevant starting point for future research.

Another important comparison to make is the influence of the different network interconnects on the algorithm. While in the former paper, the FDR network had an immense influence on the runtime of the n-way dissemination algorithm. In this case, we are comparing a QDR network to a FDR-10 network and do not see the same performance increase. Instead, we partially even see a decrease in speed. While Bruck's algorithm does not need more than 10 μs for small messages Cluster 1, it needs 16 μs on Cluster 2. For large messages we see a speedup from 32 μs to 30 μs for the global maximum and from 30 μs to 27 μs for the global sum. This again highlights the importance of adjusting the used algorithms to the underlying network and will be investigated further in the scope of a library with collective routines for GASPI implementations.

All in all, algorithms with a butterfly-like communication scheme should not be ignored for new communication routines and libraries. The increasing message rates and network topology developments might make the use of these algorithms very feasible again.

REFERENCES

[1] V. End, R. Yahyapour, C. Simmendinger, and T. Alrutz, "Adapting the n-way Dissemination Algorithm for GASPI Split-Phase Allreduce," in INFOCOMP 2015, The Fifth International Conference on Advanced Communications and Computation, June 2015, pp. 13 – 19.

[2] GASPI Consortium, "GASPI: Global Address Space Programming Interface, Specification of a PGAS API for communication Version 16.1," https://raw.githubusercontent.com/GASPI-Forum/GASPI-Forum.github.io/master/standards/GASPI-16.1.pdf, February 2016, retrieved 2016.11.29 at 13:07.

[3] Message-Passing Interface Forum, MPI: A Message Passing Interface Standard, Version 3.0. High-Performance Computing Center Stuttgart, 09 2012.

[4] N.-F. Tzeng and H.-L. Chen, "Fast compaction in hypercubes," IEEE Transactions on Parallel and Distributed Systems, vol. 9, 1998, pp. 50–55.

[5] J. M. Mellor-Crummey and M. L. Scott, "Algorithms for scalable synchronization on shared-memory multiprocessors," ACM Transactions on Computer Systems, vol. 9, no. 1, Feb. 1991, pp. 21–65.

[6] E. D. Brooks, "The Butterfly Barrier," International Journal of Parallel Programming, vol. 15, no. 4, 1986, pp. 295–307.

[7] D. Hensgen, R. Finkel, and U. Manber, "Two algorithms for barrier synchronization," International Journal of Parallel Programming, vol. 17, no. 1, Feb. 1988, pp. 1–17.

[8] J. Bruck and C.-T. Ho, "Efficient global combine operations in multi-port message-passing systems," Parallel Processing Letters, vol. 3, no. 04, 1993, pp. 335–346.

[9] J. Bruck, C.-T. Ho, S. Kipnis, E. Upfal, and D. Weathersby, "Efficient algorithms for all-to-all communications in multi-port message-passing systems," in IEEE Transactions on Parallel and Distributed Systems, 1997, pp. 298–309.

[10] S. P. Kini, J. Liu, J. Wu, P. Wyckoff, and D. K. Panda, "Fast and Scalable Barrier using RDMA and Multicast Mechanisms for InfiniBand-based Clusters," in Recent Advances in Parallel Virtual Machine and Message Passing Interface. Springer, 2003, pp. 369–378.

[11] V. Tipparaju, J. Nieplocha, and D. Panda, "Fast collective operations using shared and remote memory access protocols on clusters," in Proceedings of the 17th International Symposium on Parallel and Distributed Processing, ser. IPDPS '03. Washington, DC, USA: IEEE Computer Society, 2003, pp. 84.1–.

[12] InfiniBand Trade Association, "Infiniband architecture specification volume 1, release 1.3," https://cw.infinibandta.org/document/dl/7859, March 2015, retrieved 2016.11.29 at 13:09.

[13] ——, "Infiniband architecture specification volume 1, release 1.2.1, annex a16," https://cw.infinibandta.org/document/dl/7148, 2010, retrieved 2016.11.29 at 13:08.

[14] E. Zahavi, "Fat-tree Routing and Node Ordering Providing Contention Free Traffic for MPI Global Collectives," J. Parallel Distrib. Comput., vol. 72, no. 11, Nov. 2012, pp. 1423–1432.

[15] R. Gupta, V. Tipparaju, J. Nieplocha, and D. Panda, "Efficient Barrier using Remote Memory Operations on VIA-Based Clusters," in IEEE Cluster Computing. IEEE Computer Society, 2002, p. 83ff.

[16] T. Hoefler, T. Mehlan, F. Mietke, and W. Rehm, "Fast Barrier Synchronization for InfiniBand," in Proceedings of the 20th International Conference on Parallel and Distributed Processing, ser. IPDPS'06. Washington, DC, USA: IEEE Computer Society, 2006, pp. 272–272.

[17] R. Thakur, R. Rabenseifner, and W. Gropp, "Optimization of Collective Communication Operations in MPICH," International Journal of High Performance Computing Applications, vol. 19, 2005, pp. 49–66.

[18] Fraunhofer ITWM, "GPI2 homepage," www.gpi-site.com/gpi2, retrieved 2016.11.29 at 13:11.

Influences of Meshing and High-Performance Computing towards Advancing the Numerical Analysis of High-Velocity Impacts

Arash Ramezani and Hendrik Rothe
University of the Federal Armed Forces
Hamburg, Germany
Email: ramezani@hsu-hh.de, rothe@hsu-hh.de

Abstract—**By now, computers and software have spread into all fields of industry. The use of finite-difference and finite-element computer codes to solve problems involving fast, transient loading is commonplace. A large number of commercial codes exist and are applied to problems ranging from fairly low to extremely high damage levels. Therefore, extensive efforts are currently made in order to improve the safety by applying certain numerical solutions. For many engineering problems involving shock and impact, there is no single ideal numerical method that can reproduce the various aspects of a problem. An approach which combines different techniques in a single numerical analysis can provide the "best" solution in terms of accuracy and efficiency. But, what happens if code predictions do not correspond with reality? This paper discusses various factors related to the computational mesh that can lead to disagreement between computations and experience. Furthermore, the influence of high-performance computing is a main subject of this work. The goal is to find an appropriate technique for simulating composite materials and thereby improve modern armor to meet current challenges. Given the complexity of penetration processes, it is not surprising that the bulk of work in this area is experimental in nature. Terminal ballistic test techniques, aside from routine proof tests, vary mainly in the degree of instrumentation provided and hence the amount of data retrieved. Here, both the ballistic trials as well as the analytical methods will be discussed.**

Keywords-solver methologies; simulation models; meshing; high-performance computing; high-velocity impact; armor systems.

I. INTRODUCTION

In the security sector, failing industrial components are ongoing problems that cause great concern as they can endanger people and equipment. Therefore, extensive efforts are currently made in order to improve the safety of industrial components by applying certain computer-based solutions. To deal with problems involving the release of a large amount of energy over a very short period of time, e.g., explosions and impacts, there are three approaches, which are discussed in detail in [1].

As the problems are highly non-linear and require information regarding material behavior at ultra-high loading rates, which are generally not available, most of the work is experimental and may cause tremendous expenses. Analytical approaches are possible if the geometries involved are relatively simple and if the loading can be described through boundary conditions, initial conditions, or a combination of the two. Numerical solutions are far more general in scope and remove any difficulties associated with geometry [2].

For structures under shock and impact loading, numerical simulations have proven to be extremely useful. They provide a rapid and less expensive way to evaluate new design ideas. Numerical simulations can supply quantitative and accurate details of stress, strain, and deformation fields that would be very costly or difficult to reproduce experimentally. In these numerical simulations, the partial differential equations governing the basic physics principles of conservation of mass, momentum, and energy are employed. The equations to be solved are time-dependent and nonlinear in nature. These equations, together with constitutive models describing material behavior and a set of initial and boundary conditions, define the complete system for shock and impact simulations.

The governing partial differential equations need to be solved in both time and space domains (see Figure 1). The solution for the time domain can be achieved by an explicit method. In the explicit method, the solution at a given point in time is expressed as a function of the system variables and parameters, with no requirements for stiffness and mass matrices. Thus, the computing time at each time step is low but may require numerous time steps for a complete solution.

The solution for the space domain can be obtained utilizing different spatial discretization techniques, such as Lagrange [3], Euler [4], Arbitrary Lagrange Euler (ALE) [5], or "mesh free" methods [6]. Each of these techniques has its unique capabilities, but also limitations. Usually, there is not a single technique that can cope with all the regimes of a problem [7].

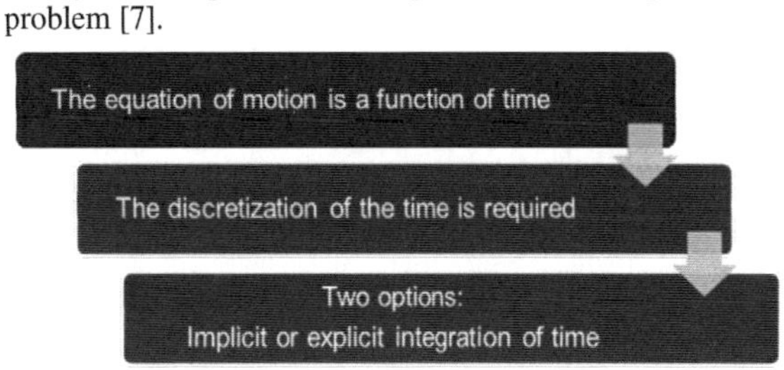

Figure 1. Discretization of time and space is required.

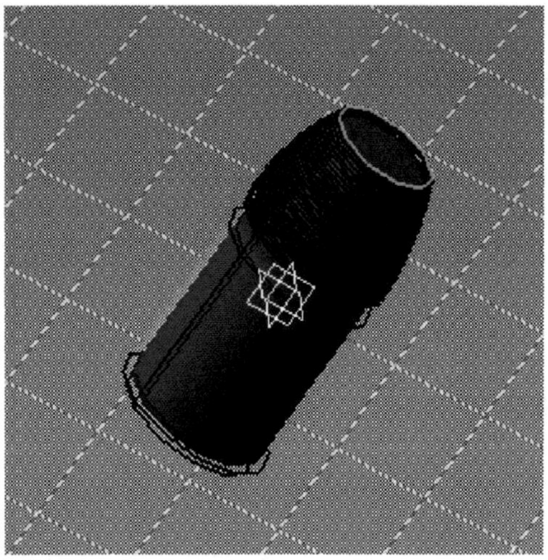

Figure 2. Native CAD geometry of an exemplary projectile.

This work will focus on high-speed dynamics, esp. impact simulations. By using a computer-aided design (CAD) neutral environment that supports direct, bidirectional, and associative interfaces with CAD systems, the geometry can be optimized successively. Native CAD geometry can be used directly without a translation to IGES or other intermediate geometry formats [8]. An example is given in Figure 2.

The work will also provide a brief overview of ballistic tests to offer some basic knowledge of the subject, serving as a basis for the comparison and verification of the simulation results.

The objective of this work is to compare current simulation methodologies to find the most suitable model for high-speed dynamics and impact studies. Lagrange, Euler, ALE, and "mesh free" methods, as well as combinations of these methods, are described and applied to a modern amor structure impacted by a projectile. It aims to clarify the following issues: What is the most suitable simulation model? How does the mesh density affect the results? What are the benefits of high-performance computing?

The results shall be used to improve the safety of ballistic structures, esp. for armored vehicles. Instead of running expensive trials, numerical simulations should be applied to identify vulnerabilities of structures. Contrary to the experimental results, numerical methods allow an easy and comprehensive study of all mechanical parameters.

Modeling will also help to understand how the armor schemes behave during impact and how the failure processes can be controlled to our advantage.

After a brief introduction and description of the different methods of space discretization in Section III, there is a short section on ballistic trials where the experimental set-up is depicted, followed by Section V describing the analysis with numerical simulations. In Section VI, the possible deployment of high-performance computing is discussed. The paper ends with a concluding paragraph.

II. State-of-the-Art

Simulating penetration and perforation events requires a numerical technique that allows one body (penetrator) to pass through another (target). Traditionally, these simulations have been performed using either an Eulerian approach, i.e., a non-deformable (fixed) mesh with material advecting among the cells, or using a Lagrangian approach, i.e., a deformable mesh with large deformations. The main point of criticism of the Eulerian approach has been that the shape of the penetrating body, usually an idealized rigid projectile, becomes "fuzzy" as the penetration simulation proceeds, due to the mixing of advected materials in the fixed Eulerian cells. Lagrangian methods require some form of augmentation to minimize or eliminate large mesh distortions. The so-called "pilot hole" technique and the material erosion are the two most often used augmentations for Lagrangian penetration simulations. In the pilot hole technique, elements are removed a priori from the target mesh along the penetrator trajectory, which works well for normal impacts where the trajectory is known a priori. The latter technique removes distorted elements from the simulation based upon a user supplied criterion. They are also removed along the penetrator trajectory, but with no general guidance for selecting certain criteria, i.e., they are ad hoc.

The focus of the present work is to assess a relatively new class of numerical methods, so-called mesh free methods, which offer analysts an alternate analytical technique for simulating this class of ballistic problems without a priori trajectory knowledge or the need to resort to ad hoc criteria. The assessment is made by comparing projectile residual speeds provided by the various techniques, when used to simulate a ballistic impact experiment. The techniques compared are the mesh free method known as Smooth Particle Hydrodynamics (SPH), a multi-material ALE technique, and Lagrangian with material erosion. Given that comparing these inherently different methods is hardly possible, large efforts have been made to minimize the numerous ancillary aspects of the different simulations and focus on the unique capabilities of the techniques.

III. Methods of Space Discretization

The spatial discretization is performed by representing the fields and structures of the problem using computational points in space, usually connected with each other through computational grids. Generally, the following applies: the finer the grid, the more accurate the solution. For problems of dynamic fluid-structure interaction and impact, there typically is no single best numerical method which is applicable to all parts of a problem. Techniques to couple types of numerical solvers in a single simulation can allow the use of the most appropriate solver for each domain of the problem [9].

The most commonly used spatial discretization methods are Lagrange, Euler, ALE (a mixture of Lagrange and Euler), and mesh-free methods, such as Smooth Particles Hydrodynamics (SPH) [10].

A. *Lagrange*

The Lagrange method of space discretization uses a mesh that moves and distorts with the material it models as a result of forces from neighboring elements (meshes are imbedded in material). There is no grid required for the external space, as the conservation of mass is automatically satisfied and material boundaries are clearly defined. This is the most efficient solution methodology with an accurate pressure history definition.

The Lagrange method is most appropriate for representing solids, such as structures and projectiles. If however, there is too much deformation of any element, it results in a very slowly advancing solution and is usually terminated because the smallest dimension of an element results in a time step that is below the threshold level.

B. *Euler*

The Euler (multi-material) solver utilizes a fixed mesh, allowing materials to flow (advect) from one element to the next (meshes are fixed in space). Therefore, an external space needs to be modeled. Due to the fixed grid, the Euler method avoids problems of mesh distortion and tangling that are prevalent in Lagrange simulations with large flows. The Euler solver is very well-suited for problems involving extreme material movement, such as fluids and gases. To describe solid behavior, additional calculations are required to transport the solid stress tensor and the history of the material through the grid. Euler is generally more computationally intensive than Lagrange and requires a higher resolution (smaller elements) to accurately capture sharp pressure peaks that often occur with shock waves.

C. *ALE*

The ALE method of space discretization is a hybrid of the Lagrange and Euler methods. It allows redefining the grid continuously in arbitrary and predefined ways as the calculation proceeds, which effectively provides a continuous rezoning facility. Various predefined grid motions can be specified, such as free (Lagrange), fixed (Euler), equipotential, equal spacing, and others. The ALE method can model solids as well as liquids. The advantage of ALE is the ability to reduce and sometimes eliminate difficulties caused by severe mesh distortions encountered by the Lagrange method, thus allowing a calculation to continue efficiently. However, compared to Lagrange, an additional computational step of rezoning is employed to move the grid and remap the solution onto a new grid [7].

D. *SPH*

The mesh-free Lagrangian method of space discretization (or SPH method) is a particle-based solver and was initially used in astrophysics. The particles are imbedded in material and they are not only interacting mass points but also interpolation points used to calculate the value of physical variables based on the data from neighboring SPH particles, scaled by a weighting function. Because there is no grid defined, distortion and tangling problems are avoided as well. Compared to the Euler method, material boundaries and interfaces in the SPH are rather well defined and material separation is naturally handled. Therefore, the SPH solver is ideally suited for certain types of problems with extensive material damage and separation, such as cracking. This type of response often occurs with brittle materials and hypervelocity impacts. However, mesh-free methods, such as SPH, can be less efficient than mesh-based Lagrangian methods with comparable resolution.

Figure 3 gives a short overview of the solver technologies mentioned above. The crucial factor is the grid that causes different outcomes.

The behavior (deflection) of the simple elements is well-known and may be calculated and analyzed using simple equations called shape functions. By applying coupling conditions between the elements at their nodes, the overall stiffness of the structure may be built up and the deflection/distortion of any node – and subsequently of the whole structure – can be calculated approximately [12].

Due to the fact that all engineering simulations are based on geometry to represent the design, the target and all its components are simulated as CAD models [13]. Therefore, several runs are necessary: from modeling to calculation to the evaluation and subsequent improvement of the model (see Figure 4).

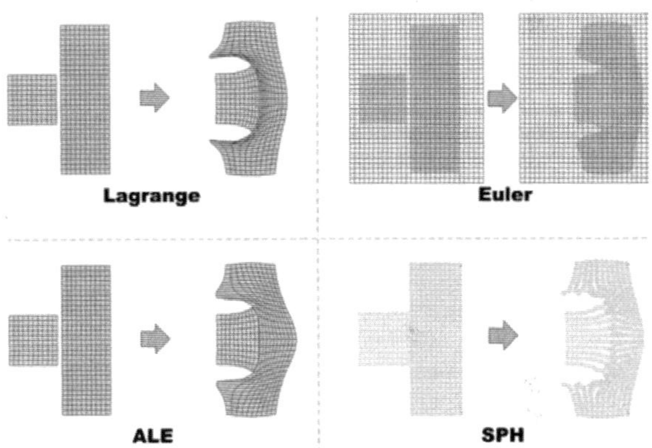

Figure 3. Examples of Lagrange, Euler, ALE, and SPH simulations on an impact problem [11].

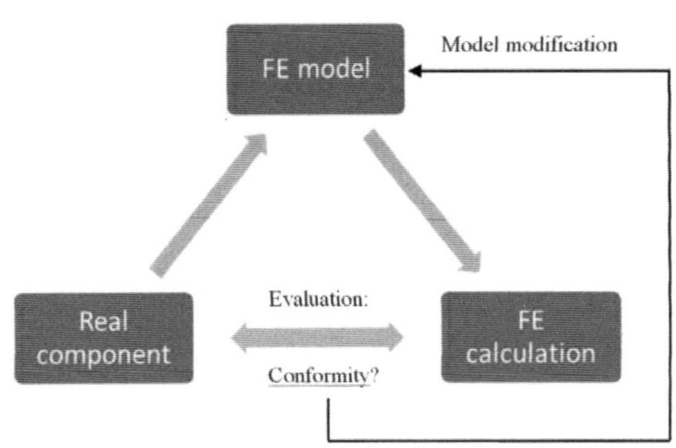

Figure 4. Iterative procedure of a typical FE analysis [12].

The most important steps during an FE analysis are the evaluation and interpretation of the outcomes followed by suitable modifications of the model. For that reason, ballistic trials are necessary to validate the simulation results. They can be used as the basis of an iterative optimization process.

IV. Effects of Meshing

Engineers and scientists use finite element analysis (FEA) software to build predictive computational models of real-world scenarios. The use of FEA software begins with a CAD model that represents the physical parts being simulated as well as knowledge of the material properties and the applied loads and constraints. This information enables the prediction of real-world behavior, often with very high levels of accuracy.

The numerical model becomes complete once the mesh is created. Different phenomena and analyses require varied mesh settings. For example, in wave propagation problems, such as modeling elastic waves in structural mechanics or electromagnetic waves in radio frequency analysis, the size of the largest element has to be substantially smaller than the wavelength in order to resolve the problem. In fluid flow, boundary layer meshes may be required in order to resolve boundary layers, while the cell Reynolds number may determine the element size in the bulk of the fluid.

In many cases, different parts of a CAD geometry have to be meshed separately. The model variables have to be matched by the FEA software at the interfaces between the different parts. The matching can be done through continuity constraints (i.e., boundary conditions that relate the finite element discretizations of the different parts to each other). Due to the possible non-local character of these conditions, they are often called multi-point constraints.

The accuracy that can be obtained from any FEA model is directly related to the finite element mesh that is used. The finite element mesh is used to subdivide the CAD model into smaller domains called elements, over which a set of equations are solved. These equations approximately represent the governing equation of interest via a set of polynomial functions defined over each element. As these elements are made smaller and smaller, as the mesh is refined, the computed solution will approach the true solution.

This process of mesh refinement is a key step in validating any finite element model and gaining confidence in the software, the model, and the results.

A good finite element analyst starts with both an understanding of the physics of the system that is to be analyzed and a complete description of the geometry of the system. This geometry is represented via a CAD model. A typical CAD model will accurately describe the shape and structure, but often also contain cosmetic features or manufacturing details that can prove to be extraneous for the purposes of finite element modeling. The analyst should put some engineering judgment into examining the CAD model and deciding if these features and details can be removed or simplified prior to meshing. Starting with a simple model and adding complexity is almost always easier than starting with a complex model and simplifying it.

The analyst should also know all of the physics that are relevant to the problem, the materials properties, the loads, the constraints, and any elements that can affect the results of interest. These inputs may have uncertainties in them. For instance, the material properties and loads may not always be precisely known. It is important to keep this in mind during the modeling process, as there is no benefit in trying to resolve a model to greater accuracy than the input data admits.

Once all of this information is assembled into an FEA model, the analyst can begin with a preliminary mesh. Early in the analysis process, it makes sense to start with a mesh that is as coarse as possible – a mesh with very large elements. A coarse mesh will require less computational resources to solve and, while it may give a very inaccurate solution, it can still be used as a rough verification and as a check on the applied loads and constraints.

After computing the solution on the coarse mesh, the process of mesh refinement begins. In its simplest form, mesh refinement is the process of resolving the model with successively finer and finer meshes, comparing the results between these different meshes. This comparison can be done by analyzing the fields at one or more points in the model or by evaluating the integral of a field over some domains or boundaries.

By comparing these scalar quantities, it is possible to judge the convergence of the solution with respect to mesh refinement. After comparing a minimum of three successive solutions, an asymptotic behavior of the solution starts to emerge, and the changes in the solution between meshes become smaller. Eventually, these changes will be small enough that the analyst can consider the model to be converged. This is always a judgment call on the part of the analyst, who knows the uncertainties in the model inputs and the acceptable uncertainty in the results.

When it comes to mesh refinement, there is a suite of techniques that are commonly used. An experienced user of FEA software should be familiar with each of these techniques and the trade-offs between them.

Reducing the element size is the easiest mesh refinement strategy, with element sizes reduced throughout the modeling domains. This approach is attractive due to its simplicity, but the drawback is that there is no preferential mesh refinement in regions where a locally finer mesh may be needed (see Figure 5).

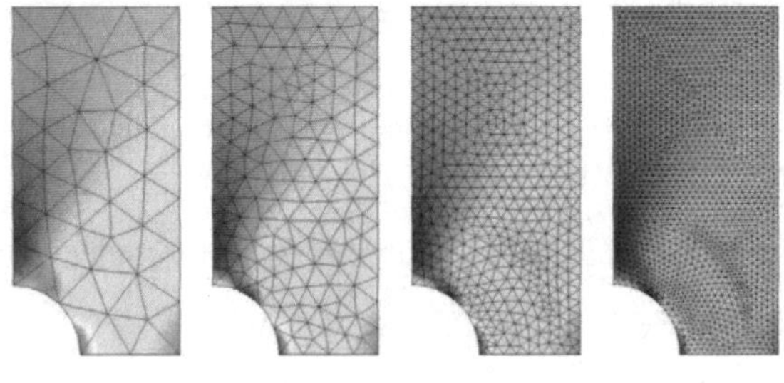

Figure 5. The stresses in a plate with a hole, solved with different element sizes.

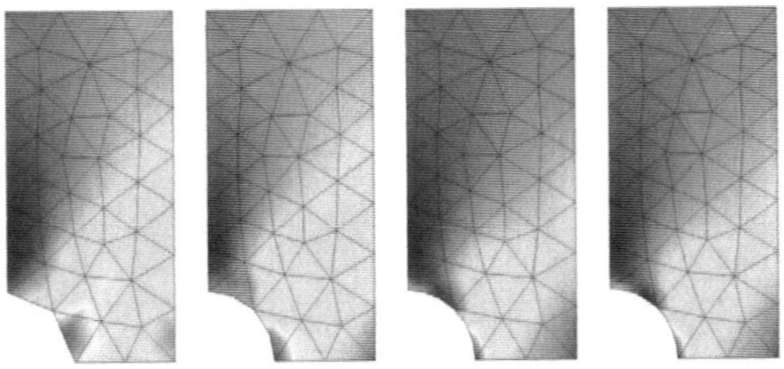

Figure 6. The same finite element mesh, but solved with different element orders.

Increasing the element order is advantageous in the sense that no remeshing is needed; the same mesh can be used, but with different element orders. Remeshing can be time consuming for complex 3D geometries or the mesh may come from an external source and cannot be altered. The disadvantage to this technique is that the computational requirements increase faster than with other mesh refinement techniques (see Figure 6).

V. BALLISTIC TRIALS

Ballistics is an essential component for the evaluation of our results. Here, terminal ballistics is the most important sub-field. It describes the interaction of a projectile with its target. Terminal ballistics is relevant for both small and large caliber projectiles. The task is to analyze and evaluate the impact and its various modes of action. This will provide information on the effect of the projectile and the extinction risk.

Given that a projectile strikes a target, compressive waves propagate into both the projectile and the target. Relief waves propagate inward from the lateral free surfaces of the penetrator, cross at the centerline, and generate a high tensile stress. If the impacts were normal, we would have a two-dimensional stress state. If the impacts were oblique, bending stresses would be generated in the penetrator. When the compressive wave was to reach the free surface of the target, it would rebound as a tensile wave. The target could fracture at this point. The projectile could change direction in case of perforation (usually towards the normal of the target surface). A typical impact response is illustrated in Figure 7.

Because of the differences in target behavior due to the proximity of the distal surface, we must categorize targets into four broad groups. In a semi-infinite target, there is no influence of distal boundary on penetration. A thick target is one in which the boundary influences penetration after the projectile has already travelled some distance into the target. An intermediate thickness target is a target where the boundaries exert influence throughout the impact. Finally, a thin target is one in which stress or deformation gradients are negligible throughout the thickness.

There are several methods which may cause a target to fail when subjected to an impact. The major variables are the target and penetrator material properties, the impact velocity, the projectile shape (especially the ogive), the geometry of the target supporting structure, and the dimensions of the projectile and target.

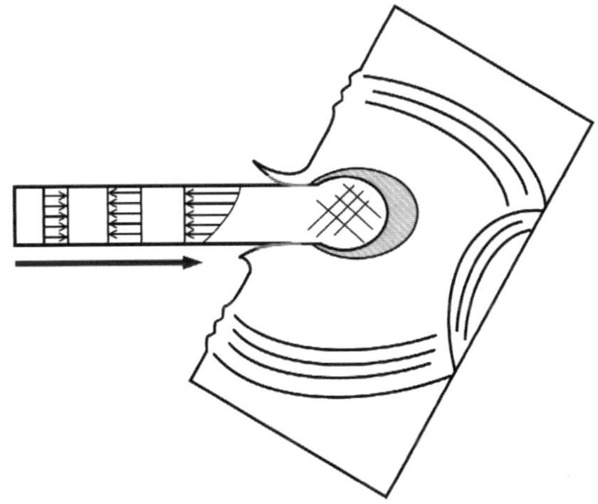

Figure 7. Wave propagation after impact.

The results of the ballistic tests were provided prior to the simulation work to aid calibration. A series of metal plate impact experiments, using several projectile types, have been performed. For the present comparative study, the only target considered is 0.5 inch (12.7 mm) thick 6061-T6 aluminum plate. The plate has a free span area of 8 by 8 inches (203 by 203 mm) and was fixed in place.

The plate was nominally center impacted by a blunt projectile, also made from 6061-T6 aluminum, with an impact speed of 3181 feet/second (970 meters/second). The orientation of the projectile impact was intended to be normal to the target. The projectile is basically a right circular cylinder of length 0.974 inches (24.7 mm) and diameter 0.66 inch (16.7 mm), with a short length of reduced diameter (shoulder) at the rear of the projectile.

The projectile's observed exit speed was 1830 feet/second. The deformed target and projectile are shown in Figures 8 and 9, respectively. As can be seen the target is essentially "drilled out" by the projectile, i.e., a clean hole remains in the target plate. Also, the lack of "petals" on the exit surface of the target indicates the hole was formed by concentrated shear around the perimeter of the hole.

The deformed projectiles, shown in Figure 9, indicate the increasing amount of projectile deformation as it perforates increasingly thicker targets: 0.125 to 0.5 inch. The deformed projectile on the right is the case of present interest. It is worth noting that the simulation of deformable projectiles perforating deformable targets is a challenging class of ballistic simulations. The vast majority of perforation simulations involve nearly rigid projectiles impacting deformable targets. Although deformable projectile calculations form a special, and limited, class in ballistics, establishing confidence in the simulation of this challenging class of problems will lend further confidence to the comparatively easier simulation of near rigid projectile perforating deformable targets [14].

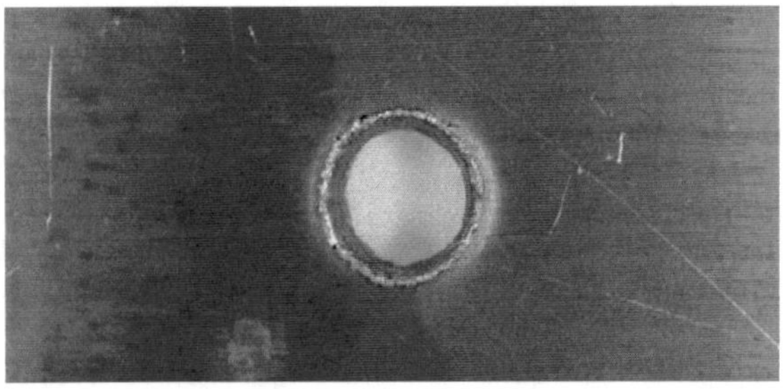

Figure 8. Front view of a perforated aluminum 0.5 inch thick target.

Figure 9. Deformed 6061-T6 aluminum projectiles after perforation 0.125, 0.25, and 0.5 inch thick (left-to- right) aluminum targets.

VI. NUMERICAL SIMULATION

The ballistic tests are followed by computational modeling of the experimental set-up.

Three mesh refinement models were constructed using the two-dimension axisymmetric solver in ANSYS. While the three-dimensional solver could also be used, using the two-dimension axisymmetric solver allows more efficient solutions, especially with a large number of elements. The particulars of the three meshes are summarized in Table I.

Figure 10 shows two of the three axisymmetric mesh configurations. The mesh discretizations are similar in that each mesh uses one number as the basis for determining the number and size of all the elements in the mesh. The target plate elements immediately below the projectile have the same mesh refinement as the projectile. The configuration is based on [14].

A suite of impact simulations was performed using the above-described 6061-T6 aluminum projectile and 6061-T6 aluminum target. The projectile was given an initial velocity of 3181 feet/second (970 meters/second) and the projectile's speed was recorded at a point near the rear of the projectile. The resulting residual speed was thought to best correspond to the experimental measurement technique for residual speed.

TABLE I. SUMMARY OF MESH CONFIGURATIONS

	Smallest Element (mm)	Number of Elements
Coarse	0.4445	3,174
Medium	0.22225	12,913
Fine	0.14816	28,922

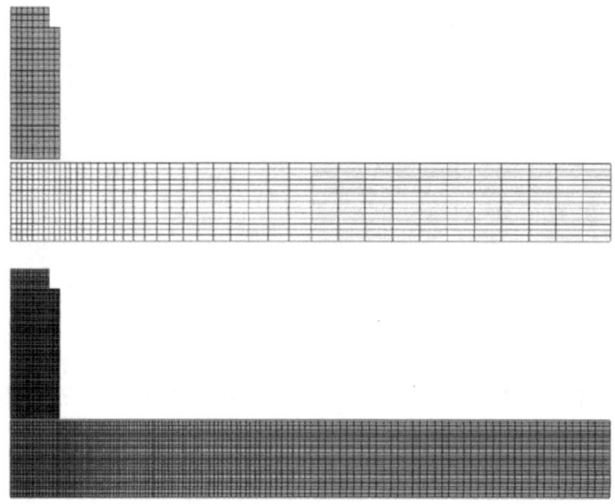

Figure 10. Two of the three axisymmetric mesh discretizations.

The overall projectile and target plate dimensions were previously given in the description of the ballistic experiment. The axisymmetric model is fully constrained around the outer diameter of the target plate, i.e., fully fixed (clamped). Different solver methodologies have been applied. The comparison is presented in the following section.

A. Solver Evaluation

Using the Johnson-Cook failure criterion eliminates the need to select an erosion criterion and a value for the criterion at which to erode elements. These are two significant difficulties most often overlooked when using an erosion-based simulation technique. Many users select an ad hoc erosion criterion and assign ad hoc values for erosion. In so doing, they seem to ignore the fact that the results are then also ad hoc, which is not desirable when making predictive calculations.

As mentioned above, the Johnson-Cook failure model is not regularized via element characteristic lengths. Thus, we expect the results to be mesh-dependent. It is the purpose of this section to assess this mesh dependency using four successively refined meshes. Subsequently, theses Lagrange erosion results will be compared with the corresponding ALE and SPH results.

1) Lagrange method: Figure 11 shows the initial and deformed (t = 0.053 ms) mesh configurations for the medium discretized mesh. Also shown is an illustration of the eroded element distribution at the end of the simulation. The eroded elements are indicated relative to their initial position using a different color to differentiate them from the non-eroded elements of the same part. Table II summarizes the residual speed of the projectile for the three mesh configurations considered. With the exception of the medium mesh speed, which indicates a somewhat larger projectile speed reduction, the projectile speeds are decreasing nearly uniformly with increasing mesh refinement.

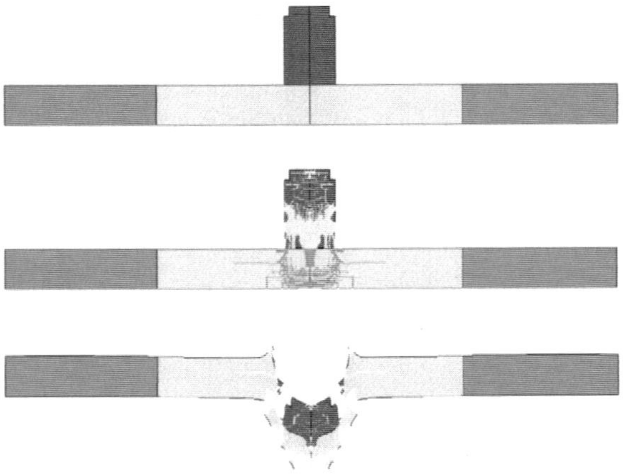

Figure 11. Initial, eroded, and deformed Lagrange elements with a medium mesh configuration.

Figure 12 shows a plot of the residual speed versus the mesh refinement parameter. This plot indicates that the results do not follow the developing trend. Based on this plot, no claim can be made that the results are in the asymptotic regime, much less converged. This is disappointing since the mesh densities for these two cases are likely to be much greater than it would have been attempted in typical three dimensional simulations.

2) ALE method: As mentioned above, failure criteria such as the Johnson-Cook failure criterion, cannot be used with Eulerian formulations as cell (element) deletion is not allowed. If a user attempts to use a failure model, the deletion of failed cells will eventually cause the calculation to terminate inaccurately. Thus, all the ALE simulations in this section omit the Johnson-Cook failure model.

In the absence of a failure criterion, it will be demonstrated that the residual speed of the projectile is quite low. It is the purpose of this section to assess the mesh dependency of the ALE solution using successively refined meshes. Subsequently, these results will be compared with the corresponding Lagrange and SPH results.

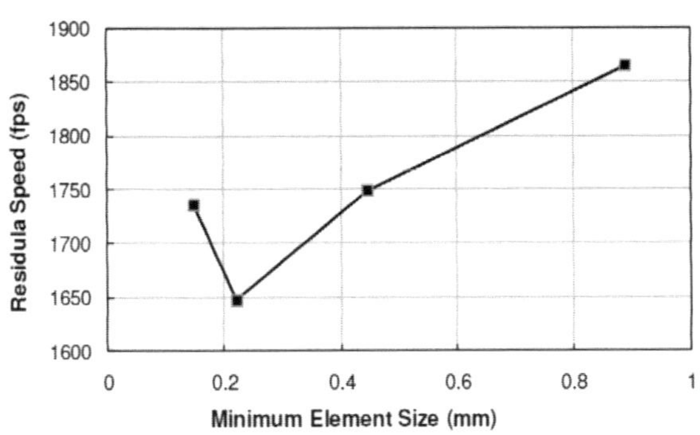

Figure 12. Plot of residual speed versus mesh refinement parameter.

TABLE II. COMPARISON OF LAGRANGE WITH EROSION AND ALE PROJECTILE RESIDUAL SPEEDS

	Residual Speed (fps)	
Mesh	**Lagrange**	**ALE**
Coarse	1748	1693
Medium	1647	1788
Fine	1737	1834
Experiment	1830	

Note: although the same mesh densities are used in both the Lagrange and ALE simulations in this demonstration, ALE mesh densities generally need to be greater than corresponding Lagrange with erosion mesh densities. The advection of materials from cell-to-cell, and especially the assumption of uniform strain-rate increments for all materials occupying a cell, introduces numerical errors to the ALE solution that can only be minimized by increasing the mesh densities. For the present demonstration, it is posited that the Lagrange mesh densities are greater than they would typically be for such a perforation simulation, making the ALE mesh densities probably appear typical in terms of expectations.

Table II compares the previous Lagrange with erosion results with the corresponding ALE projectile residual speeds. The vast majority of perforation simulations involve nearly rigid projectiles impacting deformable targets. Figure 13 shows the ALE simulation at t = 0.1 ms with a medium number of elements. It is interesting to note that the ALE deformed projectile is quite similar in shape to the deformed projectile after the test.

3) SPH method: Failure criteria like the Johnson-Cook failure criterion, are not typically used with the Smooth Particle Hydrodynamic (SPH) formulations, as particle methods are designed to avoid mesh distortions, which is the primary motivation for using failure/erosion criteria. It is the purpose of this section to assess the mesh dependency of the SPH solution using three successively refined particle meshes. These results will be compared with the corresponding Lagrange with erosion and ALE results.

Figure 13. ALE simulation with a medium discretized mesh (t = 0.1 ms).

Much like the mesh refinements used in the Lagrange and ALE calculations, refinements of the SPH particle spacing requires changing the spacing in both the impacted region of the target plate and the projectile, which is also modeled using SPH particles. Figure 14 shows the coarsest SPH model with the projectile and center of the target plate. It was modeled using SPH particles, while the outer portion of the plate was modeled with Lagrange solid elements. Table III summarizes the three SPH meshes.

Figure 15 shows the initial and final (t = 0.1 ms) deformed projectile and target plate configuration for the finest SPH mesh. In addition to the target plate 'plug' being removed from the plate by the projectile (darker brown particles on the right side of target plate), there is considerable front surface ejecta of both the projectile (light brown particles) and the target plate (darker brown particles). For this mesh refinement, the deformed projectile remains relatively intact, with the exception of the front surface ejecta and portions of the projectile that remain attached to the target plate.

B. *Simulation Results*

In the previous sections, the results from a laboratory experiment were used as a basis to assess the accuracy of the numerical simulations with respect to mesh refinement.

Examining the Lagrange results first without considering the experimental observation, it would seem like the Lagrange method provides the "best" results. All three sets of the Lagrange-with-erosion results have an observed order of convergence which is less than two and thus considered a favorable indication, since few numerical methods have orders of accuracy greater than two.

A general trend seems to be that, as the mesh is refined, the resulting deformed projectile more closely resembles the observed deformed projectile. The exception to this trend is the "point" that protrudes from the front of the projectile. Due to target elements, this "point" appears to be eroded erroneously along the axis of symmetry.

Also, it can be deduced that, for ALE simulations, meshes need to be more dense than it is required for the corresponding Lagrange mesh density. The current status is as follows: the ALE meshes were refined enough, and the Lagrange meshes were more refined than necessary. It is more likely that the advection of material, e.g., from target plate into the surrounding vacuum, over-predicts the motion of the target plate, thus effectively reducing its stiffness and allowing for a "soft catch" of the projectile and an associated reduced projectile residual speed.

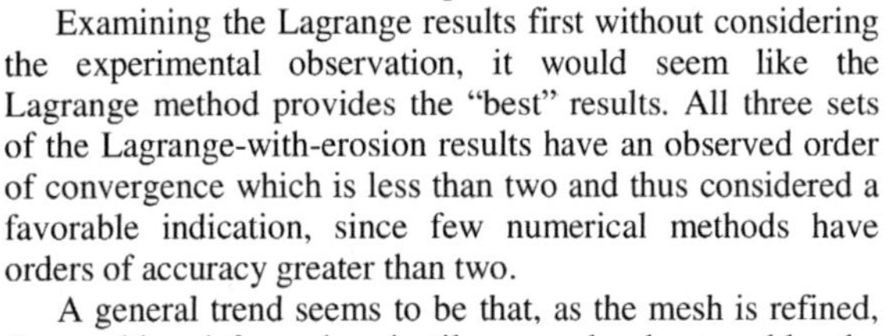

Figure 14. Coarsest SPH model (0.96 mm particle spacing).

TABLE III. SUMMARY OF SPH RESIDUAL SPEEDS FOR THREE PARTICLE MESH REFINEMENTS

		Number of Particles		
Mesh	**Particle Spacing (mm)**	**Projectile**	**Target**	**Residual Speed (fps)**
Coarse	0.96	1,536	28,665	1094
Medium	0.64	4,860	98,080	1312
Fine	0.43	17,064	333,840	1424
Experiment				1830

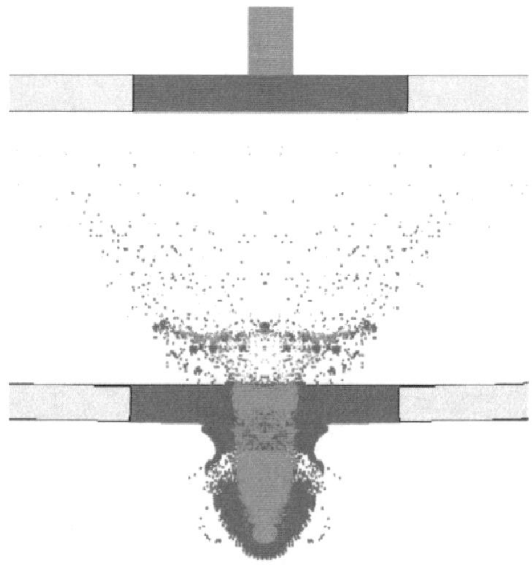

Figure 15. Initial and final (t = 0.1 ms) configurations for finest SPH mesh (0.43 mm spacing).

Here, it needs to be recalled that the Johnson-Cook failure model cannot be included in the Eulerian simulations as the notion of removal of a cell in the Eulerian context is not permitted. However, these results do indicate that they converge in or at least near the asymptotic range.

Just like the ALE results, the SPH residual speeds increase with increasing mesh density, thus being opposite to the general trend for the Lagrange results. An increasing speed with mesh refinement leads to predictions for a converged result that is greater than the calculated values. Finally, the SPH deformed projectile, previously shown in Figure 15, bears little or no resemblance to the deformed projectile recovered after the perforation test (see Figure 9). Thus, the SPH residual speed results should perhaps be considered reasonable, at least compared to the ALE results. However, the lack of uniformity of the deformed projectile shape between the SPH simulations and the actual experiment might be an indication that the "right" answer might be obtained for the "wrong" reason. Future perforation experiments should include additional diagnostics, e.g., strain measurements on the target plates, so that assessments of agreement can be more extensive than solely considering residual speed.

The SPH deformed projectile looked the least like the observed deformed projectile of any of the three simulation techniques reported. Rather than forming a rounded impact end on the projectile, the SPH deformed projectile seems to form more of a "jet" with a narrow diameter at the fore and a tapered diameter toward the rear. Also, only the refined mesh appears to maintain the integrity of the projectile, i.e., the other two mesh configurations indicate the projectile separating into two parts. Finally, it appears as if some of the projectile material remains on the inner diameter of the hole formed in the target plate. However, it is uncertain if this was observed in the test.

VII. High-Performance Computing

The objective is to develop and improve the modern armor used in the security sector. To develop better, smarter constructions requires an analysis of a wider range of parameters. However, there is a simple rule of thumb: the more design iterations that can be simulated, the more optimized is the final product. As a result, a high-performance computing (HPC) solution has to dramatically reduce overall engineering simulation time [15].

High-performance computing, otherwise known as HPC, refers to the use of aggregated computing power for handling compute- and data-intensive tasks – including simulation, modeling, and rendering – that standard workstations are unable to address. Typically, the problems under consideration cannot be solved on a commodity computer within a reasonable amount of time (too many operations are required) or the execution is impossible, due to limited available resources (too much data is required). HPC is the approach to overcome these limitations by using specialized or high-end hardware or by accumulating computational power from several units. The corresponding distribution of data and operations across several units requires the concept of parallelization [16]. When it comes to hardware setups, there are two types that are commonly used:

- Shared memory machines.
- Distributed memory clusters.

In shared memory machines, random-access memory (RAM) can be accessed by all of the processing units [17]. Meanwhile, in distributed memory clusters, the memory is inaccessible between different processing units, or nodes [18]. When using a distributed memory setup, there must be a network interconnect to send messages between the processing units (or to use other communication mechanisms), since they do not have access to the same memory space. Modern HPC systems are often a hybrid implementation of both concepts, as some units share a common memory space and some do not.

HPC is primarily used for two reasons. First, thanks to the increased number of central processing units (CPUs) and nodes, more computational power is available. Greater computational power enables specific models to be computed faster, since more operations can be performed per time unit. This is known as the speedup [19].

The speedup is defined as the ratio between the execution time on the parallel system and the execution time on the serial system. The upper limit of the speedup depends on how well the model can be parallelized. Consider, for example, a fixed-size computation where 50% of the code is able to be parallelized. In this case, there is a theoretical maximum speedup of 2. If the code can be parallelized to 95%, it is possible to reach a theoretical maximum speedup of 20. For a fully parallelized code, there is no theoretical maximum limit when adding more computational units to a system. Amdahl's law explains such a phenomenon (see Figure 16) [20].

Second, in the case of a cluster, the amount of memory available normally increases in a linear fashion with the inclusion of additional nodes. As such, larger and larger models can be computed as the number of units grows. This is referred to as the scaled speedup. Applying such an approach makes it possible to, in some sense, "cheat" the limitations posed by Amdahl's law, which considers a fixed-size problem. Doubling the amount of computational power and memory allows for a task that is twice as large as the base task to be computed within the same stretch of time. Gustafson-Barsis' law explains this phenomenon (see Figure 17) [21].

HPC adds tremendous value to engineering simulation by enabling the creation of large, high-fidelity models that yield accurate and detailed insights into the performance of a proposed design. HPC also adds value by enabling greater simulation throughput. Using HPC resources, many design variations can be analyzed.

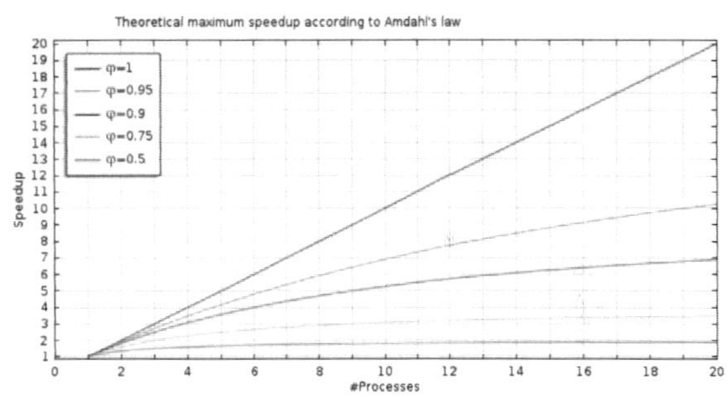

Figure 16. The theoretical maximum speedup, as noted by Amdahl's law.

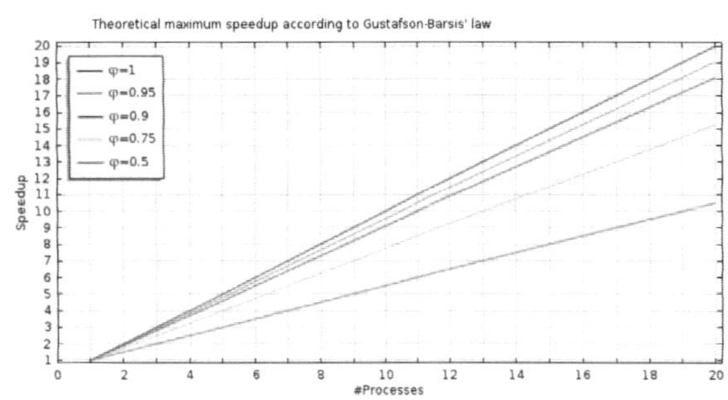

Figure 17. The theoretical maximum speedup, as noted by Gustafson-Barsis' law.

In 1965, Gordon Moore made a prediction that would set the pace for our modern digital revolution. From careful observation of an emerging trend, Moore extrapolated that computing would dramatically increase in power, and decrease in relative cost, at an exponential pace [22]. Moore's Law predicts that the number of transistors that can be economically placed on an integrated circuit will double about every two years. The insight, known as Moore's Law, became the golden rule for the electronics industry, and a springboard for innovation.

Moore's observation transformed computing from a rare and expensive venture into a pervasive and affordable necessity. All of the modern computing technology we know and enjoy sprang from the foundation laid by Moore's Law. From the Internet itself, to social media and modern data analytics, all these innovations stem directly from Moore and his findings.

Performance and cost are two key drivers of technological development. As more transistors fit into smaller spaces, processing power increased and energy efficiency improved, all at a lower cost for the end user. This development not only enhanced existing industries and increased productivity, but it has spawned whole new industries empowered by cheap and powerful computing.

This research will evaluate the performance of the following server generations: HP ProLiant SL390s G7, HP ProLiant DL580 G7, and HP ProLiant DL380p G8.

Taking the influence of the software into account, different versions of ANSYS will be applied here. Regarding the Lagrange solver in a complex 3D multi-material simulation model (modern composite armor structure instead of 6061-T6 aluminum target), the following benchmark is obtained for the different simulations (see Table IV below).

The results indicate the importance of high-performance computing in combination with competitive simulation software to solve current problems of the computer-aided engineering sector.

VIII. Conclusion

This work focuses on the comparison of current simulation methodologies to find the most suitable model for high-speed dynamics and impact studies. The influence of meshing on the simulation results is pointed out based on an example. The benefits of high-performance computing are discussed in detail.

The reader is reminded that the ballistic simulation attempted in this work is among the most difficult as both the projectile and target experience significant deformation. The deformation of the projectile as it interacts with the target affects the deformation of the target, and vice versa.

TABLE IV. Benchmark to illustrate the influence of different server and software generations

	ANSYS 14.5	ANSYS 15.0
SL390s G7	27m31s	24m47s
DL580 G7	21m44s	19m51s
DL380p G8	19m16s	14m32s

The introduction of a failure criterion, such as the Johnson-Cook failure criterion, is clearly necessary for Lagrange models, and appears to also be necessary for SPH models. A better overall approach than on-off failure models, like the Johnson-Cook failure model, would be the use of continuum damage models. These models allow for the gradual reduction in strength of highly deformed materials and can be used in all three solution techniques.

Many modern computer-aided modeling, analysis, and manufacturing systems provide both interactive and automatic finite element mesh generation of surface and solid entities that describe the parts or products being virtually engineered as new designs. Unfortunately, for complex products, the interactive approach is too time consuming to factor into the design process and the quality of automatically created meshes often does not meet engineers' criteria for element shape and density. Though commercial finite element analysis packages have some ability to control and direct the automatic mesh generation process, determining a correlation between these user controlled mesh parameters and acceptable quality of the generated mesh is difficult if not impossible. Since the validity of analysis results is heavily dependent upon mesh quality, obtaining better meshes in the shortest amount of time is essential for the integration of FEA into the automated design process.

The importance of mesh refinement has been emphasized in this work. This relatively simple to perform assessment of how the key results change with mesh density is all too often overlooked in computational solid mechanics. Further, establishing that the results are in the asymptotic regime provides some confidence that the mesh density is adequate.

When predictions are required, analysts want as many checks and assurances as possible that their results are credible. Mesh refinement studies provide the analyst some confidence the results are at a minimum not being affected by ad hoc choices of discretization.

A technique that is frequently employed in industry is that of modifying existing nodes and elements. Mesh smoothing routines have likewise long been an effective method of improving mesh quality in a pre-existing mesh. Many techniques are available for performing mesh smoothing. Some of the more advanced ones use gradient-based optimization techniques to quickly determine the optimal distribution of existing nodes. Others iterate using brute-force methods, such as Laplacian smoothing, to improve mesh distribution and corresponding element quality. Beyond this geometrical optimization of element shape, some schemes have been developed to modify and optimize the topology of the mesh by editing the node-adjacency structure of the mesh. Routines and optimizers include methods and operators such as edge swapping, vertex removing, edge collapsing, etc. to edit and improve the mesh topology. Special operators are required for maintaining a valid mesh in the case of quadrilateral and hexahedral meshes. Still other mesh improvement methods involve generating a new mesh based on information learned from previous attempts. Several algorithms use a posteriori techniques to improve the mesh once regions of inaccuracy are located.

Although the above techniques have undoubtedly improved the quality of meshes available to the mesh researcher, the accessibility to such techniques within commercial FEA is still limited. It is a well-accepted fact that it takes software companies years to adopt and dispense new methods and techniques. Often the effectiveness of their implementation is called into question: smoothing algorithms, for example, are restricted by the node/element configuration of the starting mesh and may not be able to improve a mesh to meet the desired criteria. This paper proposes a strategy for generating an optimal mesh within the framework of existing FEA software. Rather than optimizing initial node placement or operations to be performed on existing elements, the mesh control parameters available in a commercial FEA package can be optimized to yield a high-quality mesh [23].

Meshing is considered to be one of the most difficult tasks of preprocessing in traditional FEA. In modern FEA packages, an initial mesh may be automatically altered, during the solution process in order to minimize or reduce the error in the numerical solution. This is referred to as adaptive meshing.

If creating the mesh is considered a difficult task, then selecting and setting the solvers and obtaining a solution to the equations (which constitute the numerical model) in a reasonable computational time is an even more difficult task. The difficulty is associated with a variety of challenges.

This work demonstrates how a small number of well-defined experiments can be used to develop, calibrate, and validate solver technologies used for simulating the impact of projectiles on armor systems.

New concepts and models can be developed and easily tested with the help of modern hydrocodes. The initial design approach of the units and systems has to be as safe and optimal as possible. Therefore, most design concepts are analyzed on the computer.

The gained experience is of prime importance for the development of modern armor. By applying the numerical model, a large number of potential armor schemes can be evaluated and the understanding of the interaction between different materials under ballistic impact can be improved.

The most important steps during an FE analysis are the evaluation and interpretation of the outcomes followed by suitable modifications of the model. For that reason, ballistic trials are necessary to validate the simulation results.

They are designed to obtain information about

- the velocity and trajectory of the projectile prior to the impact,
- changes in configuration of the projectile and target due to the impact,
- masses, velocities, and trajectories of fragments generated by the impact process.

The combined use of computations, experiments and high-strain-rate material characterization has, in many cases, supplemented the data achievable by experiments alone at considerable savings in both cost and engineering manhours.

References

[1] A. Ramezani and H. Rothe, "Simulation Methodologies for the Numerical Analysis of High-Speed Dynamics," The Seventh International Conference on Advances in System Simulation (SIMUL 2015) IARIA, Nov. 2015, pp. 59-66, ISBN 978-1-61208-442-8

[2] J. Zukas, "Introduction to Hydrocodes," Elsevier Science, February 2004.

[3] A. M. S. Hamouda and M. S. J. Hashmi, "Modelling the impact and penetration events of modern engineering materials: Characteristics of computer codes and material models," Journal of Materials Processing Technology, vol. 56, Jan. 1996, pp. 847–862.

[4] D. J. Benson, "Computational methods in Lagrangian and Eulerian hydrocodes," Computer Methods in Applied Mechanics and Engineering, vol. 99, Sep. 1992, pp. 235–394, doi: 10.1016/0045-7825(92)90042-I.

[5] M. Oevermann, S. Gerber, and F. Behrendt, "Euler-Lagrange/DEM simulation of wood gasification in a bubbling fluidized bed reactor," Particuology, vol. 7, Aug. 2009, pp. 307-316, doi: 10.1016/j.partic.2009.04.004.

[6] D. L. Hicks and L. M. Liebrock, "SPH hydrocodes can be stabilized with shape-shifting," Computers & Mathematics with Applications, vol. 38, Sep. 1999, pp. 1-16, doi: 10.1016/S0898-1221(99)00210-2.

[7] X. Quan, N. K. Birnbaum, M. S. Cowler, and B. I. Gerber, "Numerical Simulations of Structural Deformation under Shock and Impact Loads using a Coupled Multi-Solver Approach," 5th Asia-Pacific Conference on Shock and Impact Loads on Structures, Hunan, China, Nov. 2003, pp. 152-161.

[8] N. V. Bermeo, M. G. Mendoza, and A. G. Castro, "Semantic Representation of CAD Models Based on the IGES Standard," Computer Science, vol. 8265, Dec. 2001, pp. 157-168, doi: 10.1007/ 978-3-642-45114-0_13.

[9] G. S. Collins, "An Introduction to Hydrocode Modeling," Applied Modelling and Computation Group, Imperial College London, August 2002, unpublished.

[10] R. F. Stellingwerf and C. A. Wingate, "Impact Modeling with Smooth Particle Hydrodynamics," International Journal of Impact Engineering, vol. 14, Sep. 1993, pp. 707–718.

[11] ANSYS Inc. Available Solution Methods. [Online]. Available from: http://www.ansys.com/Products/Simulation+Technology/Structural+Analysis/Explicit+Dynamics/Features/Available+Solution+Methods [retrieved: August, 2015]

[12] P. Fröhlich, "FEM Application Basics," Vieweg Verlag, September 2005.

[13] H. B. Woyand, "FEM with CATIA V5," J. Schlembach Fachverlag, April 2007.

[14] L. E. Schwer, "Aluminum Plate Perforation: A Comparative Case Study using Lagrange with Erosion, Multi-Material ALE, and Smooth Particle Hydrodynamics," 7th European LS-DYNA Conference, Salzburg, Austria, May. 2009.

[15] ANSYS Inc. "The Value of High-Performance Computing for Simulation," [Online]. Available from: http://investors.ansys.com/~/media/Files/A/Ansys-IR/annual-reports/whitepapers/the-value-of-high-performance-computing-for-simulation.pdf [retrieved: November, 2016]

[16] G. S. Almasi, and G. Allan. "Highly parallel computing," Benjamin-Cummings Publishing Co., Inc., 1988.

[17] H. El-Rewini, and A. Mostafa, "Advanced computer architecture and parallel processing," Vol. 42, John Wiley & Sons, 2005.

[18] J. E. Savage, "Models of computation," Exploring the Power of Computing, 1998.

[19] J. L. Hennessy, and D. A. Patterson, "Computer architecture: a quantitative approach," Elsevier, 2011.

[20] G. M. Amdahl, "Validity of the single processor approach to achieving large scale computing capabilities," Proceedings of the April 18-20, 1967, spring joint computer conference. ACM, 1967.

[21] J. L. Gustafson, "Reevaluating Amdahl's law," Communications of the ACM 31.5: 532-533, 1988.

[22] G. E. Moore, "Cramming more components onto integrated circuits, Reprinted from Electronics, volume 38, number 8, April 19, 1965, pp. 114 ff." IEEE Solid-State Circuits Newsletter 3.20:33-35, 2006.

[23] J. P. Dittmer, C. G. Jensen, M. Gottschalk, and T. Almy, "Mesh Optimization Using a Genetic Algorithm to Control Mesh Creation Parameters," Computer-Aided Design & Applications, vol. 3, May 2006, pp. 731–740.

A Complete Automatic Test Set Generator for Embedded Reactive Systems: From AUTSEG V1 to AUTSEG V2

Mariem Abdelmoula, Daniel Gaffé, and Michel Auguin

LEAT, University of Nice-Sophia Antipolis, CNRS
Email: Mariem.Abdelmoula@unice.fr
Email: Daniel.Gaffe@unice.fr
Email: Michel.Auguin@unice.fr

***Abstract*—One of the biggest challenges in hardware and software design is to ensure that a system is error-free. Small defects in reactive embedded systems can have disastrous and costly consequences for a project. Preventing such errors by identifying the most probable cases of erratic system behavior is quite challenging. Indeed, tests performed in industry are non-exhaustive, while state space analysis using formal verification in scientific research is inappropriate for large complex systems. We present in this context a new approach for generating exhaustive test sets that combines the underlying principles of the industrial testing technique with the academic-based formal verification. Our method consists in building a generic model of the system under test according to the synchronous approach. The goal is to identify the optimal preconditions for restricting the state space of the model such that test generation can take place on significant subspaces only. So, all the possible test sets are generated from the extracted subspace preconditions. Our approach exhibits a simpler and efficient quasi-flattening algorithm compared with existing techniques, and a useful compiled internal description to check security properties while minimizing the state space combinatorial explosion problem. It also provides a symbolic processing technique for numeric data that provides an expressive and concrete test of the system, while improving system verification (Determinism, Death sequences) and identifying all possible test cases. We have implemented our approach on a tool called AUTSEG V2. This testing tool is an extension of the first version AUTSEG V1 to integrate data manipulations. We present in this paper a complete description of our automatic testing approach including all features presented in AUTSEG V1 and AUTSEG V2.**

Keywords–AUTSEG; Quasi-flattening; SupLDD; Backtrack; Test Sets Generation.

I. INTRODUCTION

System verification generates great interest today, especially for embedded reactive systems which have complex behaviors over time and which require long test sequences. This kind of system is increasingly dominating safety-critical domains, such as the nuclear industry, health insurance, banking, the chemical industry, mining, avionics and online payment, where failure could be disastrous. Preventing such failure by identifying the most probable cases of erratic system behavior is quite challenging. A practical solution in industry uses intensive test patterns in order to discover bugs, and increase confidence in the system, while researchers concentrate their efforts instead on formal verification. However, testing is obviously non-exhaustive and formal verification is impracticable on real systems because of the combinatorial explosion nature of the state space.

AUTSEG V1 [2] combines these two approaches to provide an automatic test set generator, where formal verification ensures automation in all phases of design, execution and test evaluation and fosters confidence in the consistency and relevance of the tests. In a first version of AUTSEG, only Boolean inputs and outputs were supported, while most of actual systems handle numerical data. Numerical data manipulation represents a big challenge for most of existing test generation tools due to the difficulty to express formal properties on those data using a concise representation. In our approach, we consider symbolic test sets which are thereby more expressive, safer and less complex than the concrete ones.

Therefore, we have developed a second version AUTSEG V2 [1] to take into account numerical data manipulation in addition to Boolean data manipulation. This was achieved by developing a new library for data manipulation called SupLDD. Prior automatic test set generation methods have been consequently extended and adapted to this new numerical context. Symbolic data manipulations in AUTSEG V2 allow not only symbolic data calculations, but also system verification (Determinism, Death sequences), and identification of all possible test cases without requiring coverage of all system states and transitions. Hence, our approach bypasses in numerous cases the state space explosion problem.

We present in this paper a complete description of our automatic testing approach that includes all operations introduced in AUTSEG V1 and AUTSEG V2. In the remainder of this paper, we give an overview of related work in Section II. We present in Section III our global approach to test generation. A case study is presented in Section IV. We show in Section V experimental results. Finally, we conclude the paper in Section VI with some directions for future works.

II. RELATED WORK

Lutess V2 [3] is a test environment, written in Lustre, for synchronous reactive systems. It automatically generates tests that dynamically feed the program under test from the formal description of the program environment and properties. This version of Lutess deals with numeric inputs and outputs unlike the first version [4]. Lutess V2 is based on Constraint Logic Programming (CLP) and allows the introduction of hypotheses to the program under test. Due to CLP solvers' capabilities, it is possible to associate occurrence probabilities to any Boolean expression. However, this tool requires the conversion of tested models to the Lustre format, which may cause a few issues in our tests.

B. Blanc presents in [5] a structural testing tool called GATeL, also based on CLP. GATeL aims to find a sequence that satisfies both the invariant and the test purpose by solving the constraints problem on program variables. Contrary to Lutess, GATeL interprets the Lustre code and starts from the final state and ends with the first one. This technique relies on human intervention, which is stringently averted in our paper.

C. Jard and T. Jeron present TGV (Test Generation with Verification technology) in [6], a powerful tool for test generation from various specifications of reactive systems. It takes as inputs a specification and a test purpose in IOLTS (Input Output Labeled Transition System) format and generates test cases in IOLTS format as well. TGV allows three basic types of operations: First, it identifies sequences of the specification accepted by a test purpose, based on the synchronous product. It then computes visible actions from abstraction and determination. Finally, it selects test cases by computation of reachable states from initial states and co-reachable states from accepting states. A limitation lies in the non-symbolic (enumerative) dealing with data. The resulting test cases can be big and therefore relatively difficult to understand.

D. Clarke extends this work in [7], presenting a symbolic test generation tool called STG. It adds the symbolic treatment of data by using OMEGA tool capabilities. Test cases are therefore smaller and more readable than those done with enumerative approaches in TGV. STG produces the test cases from an IOSTS specification (Input Output Symbolic Transition System) and a test purpose. Despite its effectiveness, this tool is no longer maintained.

STS (Symbolic Transition Systems) [8] is quite often used in systems testing. It enhances readability and abstraction of behavioral descriptions compared to formalisms with limited data types. STS also addresses the states explosion problem through the use of guards and typed parameters related to the transitions. At the moment, STS hierarchy does not appear very enlightening outside the world of timed/hybrid systems or well-structured systems. Such systems are outside of the scope of this paper.

ISTA (Integration and System Test Automation) [9] is an interesting tool for automated test code generation from High-Level Petri Nets. ISTA generates executable test code from MID (Model Implementation Description) specifications. Petri net elements are then mapped to implementation constructs. ISTA can be efficient for security testing when Petri nets generate threat sequences. However, it focuses solely on liveness properties checking, while we focus on security properties checking.

J. Burnim presents in [10] a testing tool for C called CREST. It inserts instrumentation code using CIL (C Intermediate Language) into a target program. Symbolic execution is therefore performed concurrently with the concrete execution. Path constraints are then solved using the YICES solver. CREST currently reasons symbolically only about linear, integer arithmetic. Closely related to CREST, KLOVER [11] is a symbolic execution and automatic test generation tool for C++ programs. It basically presents an efficient and usable tool to handle industrial applications. Both KLOVER and CREST cannot be adopted in our approach, as they accommodate tests on real systems, whereas we target tests on systems still being designed.

III. Architectural Test Overview

We introduce in this section the principles of our automatic testing approach including data manipulation. Fig. 1 shows five main operations including: i) the design of a global model of the system under test, ii) a quasi-flattening operation, iii) a compilation process, iv) a generation process of symbolic sequences mainly related to the symbolic data manipulation entity, v) and finally the backtrack operation to generate all possible test cases.

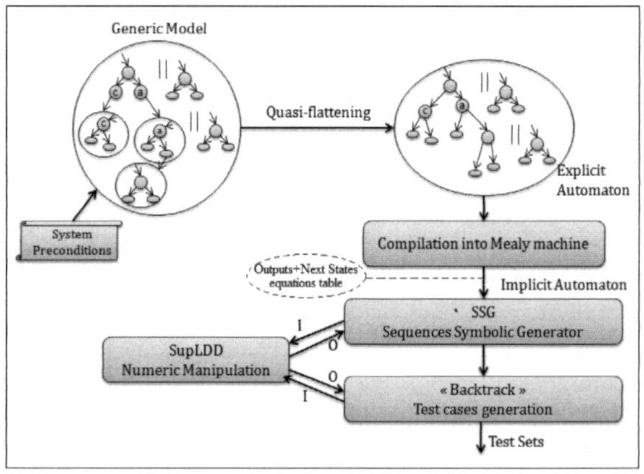

Figure 1. Global Test Process.

1. Global model: it presents the main input of our test. The global architecture is composed of hierarchical and parallel concurrent FSM based on the synchronous approach. It should conform to the specification of the system under test.

2. Quasi-flattening process: it flattens only hierarchical automata while maintaining parallelism. This offers a simple model, faster compilation, and brings more flexibility to identify all possible system evolutions.

3. Compilation process: it generates an implicit automaton represented by a Mealy machine from an explicit automaton. This process compiles the model, checks the determinism of all automata and ensures the persistence of the system behavior.

4. Symbolic data manipulation (SupLDD): it offers a symbolic means to characterize system preconditions by numerical constraints. It is solely based on the potency of the LDD library [4]. The symbolic representation of these preconditions shows an important role in the subsequent operations for generating symbolic sequences and performing test cases "Backtrack". It evenly enhances system security by analyzing the constraints computations.

5. Sequences Symbolic Generation (SSG): it works locally on significant subspaces. It automatically extracts necessary preconditions which lead to specific, significant states of the system from generated sequences. It relies on the effective representation of the global model and the robustness of numerical data processing to generate the exhaustive list of

possible sequences, avoiding therefore the manual and explicit presentation of all possible combinations of system commands.

6. Backtrack operation: it allows the verification of the whole system behavior through the manipulation of extracted preconditions from each significant subspace. It verifies the execution context of each significant subspace. Specifically, it identifies all paths satisfying each final critical state preconditions to reach the root state.

A. Global model

In this paper, we particularly focus on verification of embedded software controlling reactive systems behavior. The design of such systems is generally based on the synchronous approach [12] that presents clear semantics to exceptions, delays and actions suspension. This notably reduces the programming complexity and favors the application of verification methods. In this context, we present the global model by hierarchical and parallel concurrent Finite States Machines (FSMs) based on the synchronous approach. The hierarchical machine describes the global system behavior, while parallel automata act as observers for control data of the hierarchical automaton. Our approach allows for testing many types of systems at once. In fact, we present a single generic model for all types of systems, the specification of tests can be done later using particular Boolean variables called system preconditions (type of system, system mode, etc.). Hence, a specific test generation could be done at the end of test process through analysis of the system preconditions. This prevents generating as many models as system types, which can highly limit the legibility and increase the risk of specification bugs.

B. Quasi-flattening process

A straightforward way to analyze a hierarchical machine is to flatten it first (by recursively substituting in a hierarchical FSM, each super state with its associated FSM and calculating the Cartesian product of parallel sub-graphs), then apply on the resulting FSM a verification tool such as a model-checking or a test tool. We will show in our approach that we do not need to apply the Cartesian product, we can flatten only hierarchical automata: This is why we call it "Quasi-flattening".

Let us consider the model shown in Fig. 2, which shows automata interacting and communicating between each other. Most of them are sequential, hierarchical automata (e.g., automata 1 and 2), while others are parallel automata (e.g., automata 6 and 8). We note in this architecture 13122 ($3 \times 6 \times 3 \times 3 \times 3 \times 3 \times 3 \times 3$) possible states derived from parallel executions (graphs product) while there are many fewer reachable states at once. This model is designed by the graphic form of Light Esterel language [13]. This language is inspired by SyncCharts [14] in its graphic form, Esterel [15] in its textual form and Lustre [16] in its equational form. It integrates high-level concepts of synchronous languages in an expressive graphical formalism (taking into account the concept of multiple events, guaranteeing the determinism, providing a clear interpretation, rationally integrating the preemption concept, etc.).

A classical analysis is to transform this hierarchical structure in Light Esterel to the synchronous language Esterel. Such a transformation is not quite optimized. In fact, Esterel is not able to realize that there is only one active state at once. In practice, compiling such a structure using Esterel generates 83

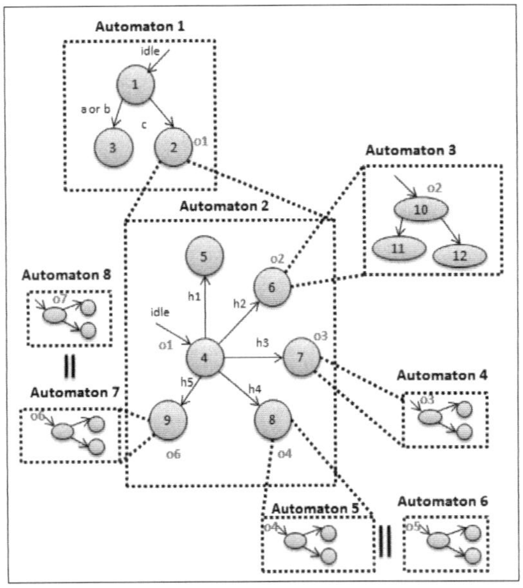

Figure 2. Model Design.

registers making roughly 9.6×10^{24} states. Hence, the behoof of our process. Opting for a quasi-flattening, we have flattened only hierarchical automata, while the global structure remained parallel. Thus, state 2 of automaton 1 in Fig. 2 is substituted by the set of states $\{4, 5, 6, 7, 8, 9\}$ of automaton 2 and so on. Required transitions are rewritten thereafter. Parallel automata are acting as observers that manage the model's control flags. Flattening parallel FSMs explode usually in terms of number of states. Thus, there is no need to flatten them, as we can compile them separately thanks to the synchronous approach, then concatenate them with the flat model retrieved at the end of the compilation process. This quasi-flattening operation allows for flattening the hierarchical automata and maintaining the parallelism. This offers a simpler model, faster compilation, and brings more flexibility to identify all possible evolutions of the system as detailed in the following steps.

Algorithm 1 details our quasi-flattening operation. We denote downstream the initial state of a transition and upstream the final one. This algorithm implements three main operations. Overall, it replaces each macro state with its associated FSM. It first interconnects the internal initial states. It then replaces normal terminations (Refers to SyncCharts "normal termination" transition [14]) with internal transitions in a recursive manner. Finally, it interconnects all states of the internal FSM.

We show in Fig. 3 the operation of linking internal initial states described in lines 3 to 9 of algorithm 1. This latter starts by marking the super state *St* to load it in a list and to be deleted later. Then, it considers all associated sub-states *sub-St* (states 3, 4, 5). For each transition in the global automaton, if the upstream state of this transition is the super state *St*, then this transition will be interconnected to the transition of the initial state of *St* (state 3). This corresponds to relinking *t0, t1, t2*.

Algorithm 1 Flattening operation

```
1: St ← State; SL ← State List of FSM; t ← transition in FSM
2: while (SL ≠ empty) do
3:   Consider each St from SL
4:   if (St is associated to a sub-FSM) then
5:     mark the deletion of St
6:     load all sub-St from sub-FSM (particularly init-sub-St)
7:     for (all t of FSM) do
8:       if (upstream(t) == St) then
9:         upstream(t) ← init-sub-St
10:        // illustration in Fig. 3 (t0, t1, t2 relinking)
11:    for (all t of FSM) do
12:      if (downstream(t) == St) then
13:        if (t is a normal-term transition) then
14:          // illustration in Fig. 4
15:          for (all sub-St of sub-FSM) do
16:            if (sub-St is associated to a sub-sub-FSM) then
17:              create t' (sub-St, upstream(t)) // Keep recursion
18:            if (sub-St is final) then
19:              for (all t'' of sub-FSM) do
20:                if (upstream(t'') == sub-St) then
21:                  upstream(t'') ← upstream(t); merge effect(t) to effect(t'')
22:        else
23:          // weak/strong transition: illustration in Fig. 3
24:          // For example t3 is less prior than t6 and replaced by ¬t6.t3 and t6
25:          for (all sub-St of sub-FSM) do
26:            if (t is a weak transition) then
27:              create t'(sub-St,upstream(t),trigger(t), weak-effect(t))
28:            else
29:              create t'(sub-St,upstream(t),trigger(t))
30:          for (all sub-t of sub-FSM) do
31:            turn-down the sub-t priority (or turn up t' priority)
32:        delete t
```

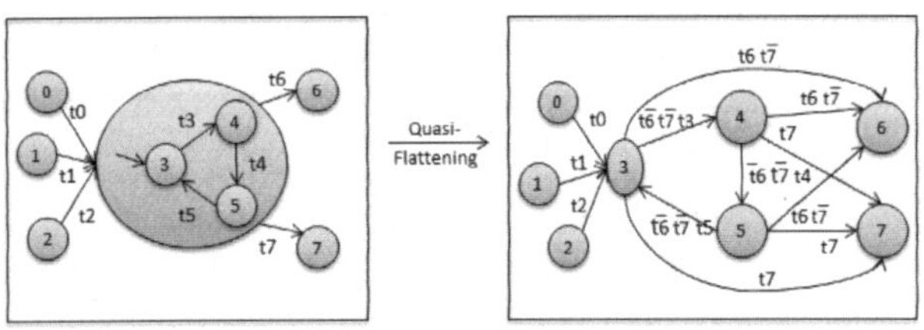

Figure 3. Interconnection of Internal States.

Fig. 4 illustrates the connection of a normal termination transition (lines 10 to 20 of algorithm 1). If the downstream state of a normal termination transition (t5) is a super state *St*, then the associated sub-states (1,2,3,4) are considered. If these sub-states are super states too, then a connection is created between these states and the upstream state of the normal termination transition.

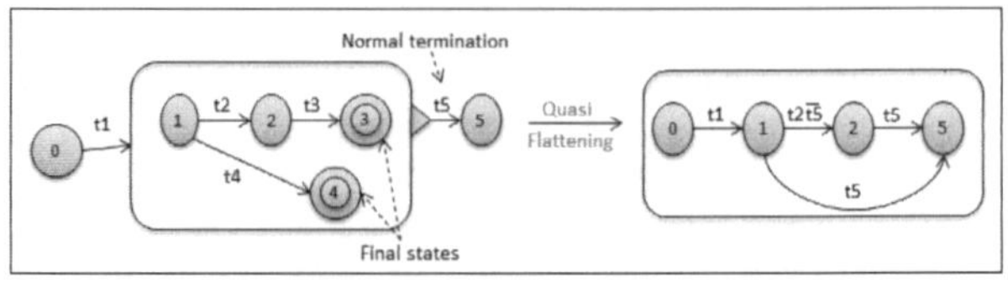

Figure 4. Normal Transition Connection.

Otherwise, if these sub-states are final states (3,4), then they will be merged with the upstream state of the normal termination transition (state 5). Finally, the outputs of the merged states are redirected to the resulted state. *St* is marked in a list to be deleted at the end of the algorithm.

Besides, in case of a weak or a strong preemption transition (According to SyncCharts and Esterel: in case of weak preemption, preempted outputs are emitted a last time, contrary to the strong preemption), we create transitions between all sub-states of the super state *St* and their upstream states, as described in lines 21 to 31 of algorithm 1. Fig. 3 illustrates this step, where *t6* and *t7* are considered to be preemption transitions: all the internal states (3,4,5) of the super state *St* are connected to their upstream states (6,7). Then, the priority of transitions is managed: the upper level transitions are prior to those of lower levels. In this context, *t3* is replaced by $\overline{t7}.\overline{t6}.t3$ to show that *t6* and *t7* are prior than *t3* and so on. At the end of this algorithm, all marked statements are deleted. In case of weak preemption transition, the associated outputs are transferred to the new transitions.

Flattening the hierarchical model of Fig. 2 results in a flat structure shown in Fig. 5. As the activation of state 2 is a trigger for state 4, these two states will be merged, just as state 6 will be merged to state 10, etc. Automata 6 and 8 (observers) remain parallel in the expanded automaton; they are small and do not increase the computational complexity. The model in Fig. 5 contains now only 144 ($16 \times 3 \times 3$) state combinations. In practice, compiling this model according to our process generates merely 8 registers, equivalent to 256 states.

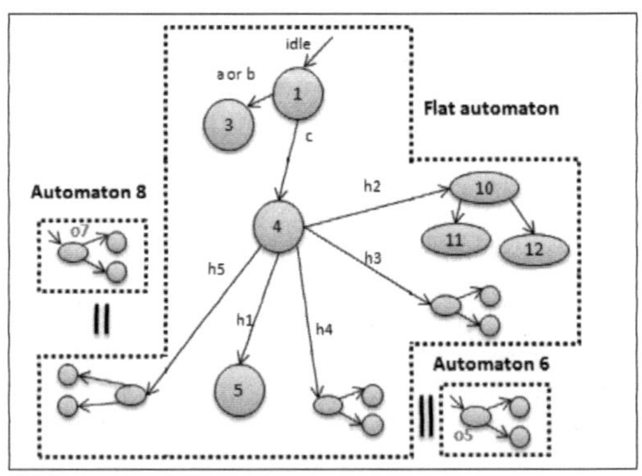

Figure 5. Flat Model.

Our flattening differs substantially from those of [17] and [18]. We assume that a transition, unlike the case of the states diagram in Statecharts, cannot exit from different hierarchical levels. Several operations are thus executed locally, not on

the global system. This yields a simpler algorithm and faster compilation. To this end, we have integrated the following assumptions in our algorithm:
-Normal termination. Fig. 4 shows an example of normal termination carried when a final internal state is reached. It allows a unique possible interpretation and facilitates code generation.
-Strong preemption. Unlike the weak preemption, internal outputs of the preempted state are lost during the transition.

C. Compilation process

We proceed in our approach to a symbolic compilation of the global model into Mealy machines, implicitly represented by a set of Boolean equations (circuit of logic gates and registers presenting the state of the system). In fact, the flat automata and concurrent automata are compiled separately. Compilation results of these automata are concatenated at the end of this process. They are represented by a union of sorted equations rather than a Cartesian product of graphs to support the synchronous parallel operation and instantaneous diffusion of signals as required by the synchronous approach. Accordingly, the system model is substantially reduced. Our compilation requires only $log_2(nbstates)$ registers, while classical works uses one register per state [19]. It also allows checking the determinism of all automata, which ensures the persistence of the system behavior.

Algorithm 2 describes the compilation process in details. First, it counts the number of states in the automaton and deduces the size of the states vector. Then, it develops the function of the next state for a given state variable. Finally, the generated vector is characterized by a set of Boolean expressions. It is represented by a set of BDDs.

Let us consider an automaton with 16 states as an example. The vector characterizing the next state is created by 4 ($log_2(16)$) expressions derived from inputs data and the current state. For each transition from state "k" to state "l", two types of vectors encoded by n (n = 4 bits in this example) bits are created: V_k vector specifying the characteristic function of transition BDD_{cond}, and V_l vector characterizing the function of the future state $BDD - NextState$. If $V_k(i)$ is valued to 1, then the state variable y_i is considered positively. Otherwise, y_i is reversed (lines 18-22). In this context, the BDD characterizing the transition condition is deduced by the combination of "y_i" and the condition "$cond$" on transition. For instance, $BDD_{cond} = y_0 \times \bar{y_1} \times \bar{y_2} \times y_3 \times cond$ for $V_k = (1, 0, 0, 1)$.

We show in lines (23-27) the construction of the Next State function $BDD - NextState(i) = BDD_{y(i)^+} \times notBDD_{y(i)'^+}$. $BDD_{y(i)^+}$ characterizes all transitions that turns y_i^+ to 1 (Set registers to 1). Conversely, $BDD_{y(i)'^+}$ characterizes all transitions that turns y_i^+ to 0 (Reset registers to 0). So, each function satisfying y^+ and not $(y^{'+})$ is a possible solution. In this case, parsing all states of the system is not necessary. Fig. 6 shows an example restricted to only 2 states variables where it is possible to find an appropriate function "$BDD^+_{y1\ respect} = y0.x + \overline{y0}.\overline{x}$" for y_1^+ and "$BDD^+_{y0\ respect} = y0.\overline{x} + \overline{y1}.\overline{y0}.x$" for y_0^+ even if the system state is not specified for "$y_1 y_0 = 11$".Thus, $BDD - NextState$ $(BDD_{y(i)^+})$ is specified by the two $BDD_{respect}$ looking for the simplest expressions to check on one hand y_0^+ and not($y_0^{'+}$) and on the other hand y_1^+ and not($y_1^{'+}$).

Algorithm 2 Compilation process

1: R ← Vector of states
2: R-I ← Initial vector of states (initial value of registers)
3: Next-State ← Vector of transitions
4: N ← Size of R and Next-State
5: f,f' ← Vectors of Boolean functions
6: N ← $\log_2(Statesnumber - 1) + 1$
7: Define N registers encapsulated in R.
8: **for** (i=0 to $N - 1$) **do**
9:     $BDD_{f(i)}$ ← BDD-0 // BDD initialisation
10:     $BDD_{f'(i)}$ ← BDD-0
11: **for** (j=0 to $Noutputs - 1$) **do**
12:     $Output_{O(j)}$ ← BDD-0
13: R-I ← binary coding of initial state
14: **for** (transition t_{kl}=k to l) **do**
15:     V_k ← Binary coding of k
16:     V_l ← Binary coding of l
17:     BDD_{cond} ← cond (t_{kl});
18:     **for** (i=0 to $N - 1$) **do**
19:         **if** V_k(i)==1 **then**
20:             BDD_{cond} ← BDD_{and}(R(i), BDD_{cond}) // BDD_{cond}: t_{kl} BDD characteristics
21:         **else**
22:             BDD_{cond} ← $BDD_{and}(BDD_{not}$ (R(i)), $BDD_{cond})$
23:         **if** (Vl(i)==1) **then**
24:             $BDD_{f(i)}$ ← $BDD_{or}(BDD_{f(i)}, BDD_{cond}$)// $BDD_{f(i)}$: set of register
25:         **else**
26:             $BDD_{f'(i)}$ ← $BDD_{or}(BDD_{f'(i)}, BDD_{cond})$)// $BDD_{f'(i)}$: reset of register
27:         $output_O$(output(t_{kl}))← BDD_{or} ($output_O$(output(t_{kl})), $BDDcond$)
28: **for** (i=0 to $N - 1$) **do**
29:     BDD-NextState(i)← $BDD_{respect}$ (BDD_f, BDD'_f)
30:     // respect: every BDD_h such us $BDD_f \rightarrow BDD_h$ AND $BDD_h \rightarrow not(BDD'_f)$

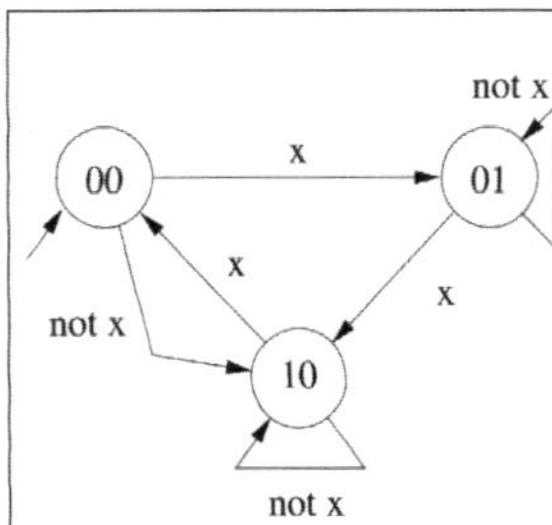

y1	y0	x	$y1^+$	$y1'^+$	$y1^+_{respect}$	$y0^+$	$y0'^+$	$y0^+_{respect}$
0	0	0	1	X	1	X	0	0
0	0	1	X	0	0	1	X	1
0	1	0	X	0	0	1	X	1
0	1	1	1	X	1	X	0	0
1	0	0	1	X	1	X	0	0
1	0	1	X	0	0	X	0	0
1	1	0	X	X	0	X	X	1
1	1	1	X	X	1	X	X	0

Figure 6. Next State Function.

As we handle automata with numerical and Boolean variables, each data inequation was first replaced by a Boolean variable (abstraction). Then at the end of the compilation process, data were re-injected to be processed by SupLDD later.

D. Symbolic data manipulation

In addition to Boolean functions, our approach allows numerical data manipulation. This provides more expressive and concrete system tests.

1) Related work: Since 1986, Binary Decision Diagrams (BDDs) have successfully emerged to represent Boolean functions for formal verification of systems with large state space. BDDs, however, cannot represent quantitative information such as integers and real numbers. Variations of BDDs have been proposed thereafter to support symbolic data manipulations that are required for verification and performance analysis of systems with numeric variables. For example, Multi-Terminal Binary Decision Diagrams (MTBDDs) [20] are a generalization of BDDs in which there can be multiple terminal nodes, each labelled by an arbitrary value. However, the size of nodes in an MTBDD can be exponential (2^n) for systems with large ranges of values. To support a larger number of values, Yung-Te Lai has developed Edge-Valued Binary Decision Diagrams (EVBDDs) [21] as an alternative to MTBDDs to offer a more compact form. EVBDDs associate multiplicative weights with the true edges of an EVBDD function graph to allow an optimal sharing of subgraphs. This suggests a linear evolution of non-terminal node sizes rather than an exponential one for MTBDDs. However, EVBDDs are limited to relatively simple calculation units, such as adders and comparators, implying a high cost per node for complex calculations such as $(X \times Y)$ or (2^X).

To overcome this exponential growth, Binary Moment Diagrams (BMDs) [22], another variation of BDDs, have been specifically developed for arithmetic functions considered to be linear functions, with Boolean inputs and integer outputs, to perform a compact representation of integer encodings and operations. They integrate a moment decomposition principle giving way to two sub-functions representing the two moments (constant and linear) of the function, instead of a decision. This representation was later extended to Multiplicative Binary Moment Diagrams (*BMDs) [23] to include weights on edges, allowing to share common sub-expressions. These edges' weights are multiplicatively combined in a *BMD, in contrast to the principle of addition in an EVBDD. Thus, the following arithmetic functions $X + Y$, $X - Y$, $X \times Y$, 2^X show representations of linear size. Despite their significant success in several cases, handling edges' weights in BMDs and *BMDs is a costly task. Moreover, BMDs are unable to verify the satisfiability property, and function outputs are non-divisible integers in order to separate bits, causing a problem for applications with output bit analysis. BMDs and MTBDDs were combined by Clarke and Zhao in Hybrid Decision Diagrams (HDDs) [24]. However, all of these diagrams are restricted to hardware arithmetic circuit checking and are not suitable for the verification of software system specifications.

Within the same context of arithmetic circuit checking, Taylor Expansion Diagrams (TEDs) [25] have been introduced to supply a new formalism for multi-value polynomial functions, providing a more abstract, standard and compact design representation, with integer or discrete input and output values. For an optimal fixed order of variables, the resulting graph is canonical and reduced. Unlike the above data structures, TED is defined on a non-binary tree. In other words, the number of child nodes depends on the degree of the relevant variable. This makes TED a complex data structure for particular functions such as (a^x). In addition, the representation of the function $(x < y)$ is an important issue in TED. This is particularly challenging for the verification of most software system specifications. In this context, Decision Diagrams for Difference logic (DDDs) [26] have been proposed to present functions of first order logic by inequalities of the form $\{x - y \leq c\}$ or $\{x - y < c\}$ with integer or real variables. The key idea is to present these logical formulas as BDD nodes labelled with atomic predicates. For a fixed variables order, a DDD representing a formula f is no larger than a BDD of a propositional abstraction of f. It supports as well dynamic programming by integrating an algorithm called QELIM, based on Fourier-Motzkin elimination [27]. Despite their proved efficiency in verifying timed systems [28], the difference logic in DDDs is too restrictive in many program analysis tasks. Even more, dynamic variable ordering (DVO) is not supported in DDDs. To address those limitations, LDDs [29] extend DDDs to full Linear Arithmetic by supporting an efficient scheduling algorithm and a QELIM quantification. They are BDDs with non-terminal nodes labelled by linear atomic predicates, satisfying a scheduling theory and local constraints reduction. Data structures in LDDs are optimally ordered and reduced by considering the many implications of all atomic predicates. LDDs have the possibility of computing arguments that are not fully reduced or canonical for most LDD operations. This suggests the use of various reduction heuristics that trade off reduction potency for calculation cost.

2) SupLDD: We summarize from the above data structures that LDD is the most relevant work for data manipulation in our context. Accordingly, we have developed a new library called Superior Linear Decision Diagrams (SupLDD) built on top of Linear Decision Diagrams (LDD) library. Fig. 7 shows an example of representation in SupLDD of the arithmetic formula $F1 = \{(x \geq 5) \wedge (y \geq 10) \wedge (x + y \geq 25)\} \vee \{(x < 5) \wedge (z > 3)\}$. Nodes of this structure are labelled by the linear predicates $\{(x < 5); (y < 10); (x + y < 25); (-z < -3)\}$ of formula F1, where the right branch evaluates its predicates to 1 and the left branch evaluates its predicates to 0. In fact, the choice of a particular comparison operator within the 4 possible operators $\{<, \leq, >, \geq\}$ is not important since the 3 other operators can always be expressed from the chosen operator: $\{x < y\} \Leftrightarrow \{NEG(x \geq y)\}; \{x < y\} \Leftrightarrow \{-x > -y\}$ and $\{x < y\} \Leftrightarrow \{NEG(-x \leq -y)\}$.

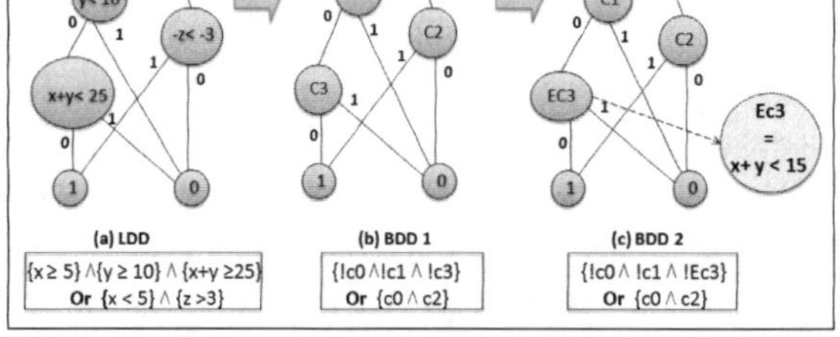

Figure 7. Representation in SupLDD of F1.

We show in Fig. 7.b that the representation of F1 in SupLDD has the same structure as a representation in BDD that labels its nodes by the corresponding Boolean variables

$\{C0; C1; C2; C3\}$ to each SupLDD predicate. But, a representation in SupLDD is more advantageous. In particular, it ensures the numerical data evaluation and manipulation of all predicates along the decision diagram. This furnishes a more accurate and expressive representation in Fig. 7.c than the original BDD representation. Namely, the Boolean variable C3 is replaced by EC3 which evaluates the corresponding node to $\{x+y < 15\}$ instead of $\{x+y < 25\}$ taking into account prior predicates $\{x < 5\}$ and $\{y < 10\}$. Besides, SupLDD relies on an efficient T-atomic scheduling algorithm [29] that makes compact and non-redundant diagrams for SupLDD where a node labelled for example by $\{x \leq 15\}$ never appears as a right child of a node labelled by $\{x \leq 10\}$. As well, nodes are ordered by a set of atoms $\{x, y, etc.\}$ where a node labelled by $\{y < 2\}$ never appears between two nodes labelled by $\{x < 0\}$ and $\{x < 13\}$. Further, SupLDD diagrams are optimally reduced, including the LDD reduction rules. First, the QELIM quantification introduced in LDDs allows the elimination of multiples variables: For example, the QELIM quantification of the expression $\{(x-y \leq 3) \wedge (x-t \geq 8) \wedge (y-z \leq 6) \wedge (t-k \geq 2)\}$ eliminates the intermediate variables *y* and *t* and generates the simplified expression $\{(x - z \leq 9) \wedge (x - k \geq 10)\}$. Second, the LDD high implication [29] rule enables getting the smallest geometric space: For example, simplifying the expression $\{(x \leq 3) \wedge (x \leq 8)\}$ in high implication yields the single term $\{x \leq 3\}$. Finally, the LDD low implication [29] rule generates the largest geometric space where the expression $\{(x \leq 3) \wedge (x \leq 8)\}$ becomes $\{x \leq 8\}$.

SupLDD operations- SupLDD operations are primarily generated from basic LDD operations [29]. They are simpler and more adapted to our needs. We present functions to manipulate inequalities of the form $\{\sum a_i x_i \leq c\}$; $\{\sum a_i x_i < c\}$; $\{\sum a_i x_i \geq c\}$; $\{\sum a_i x_i > c\}$; where $\{a_i, x_i, c \in Z\}$. Given two inequalities I_1 and I_2, the main operations in SupLDD include:

-SupLDD conjunction (*I1*, *I2*): This absolutely corresponds to the intersection on *Z* of subspaces representing *I1* and *I2*.

-SupLDD disjunction (*I1*, *I2*): As well, this operation absolutely corresponds to the union on *Z* of subspaces representing *I1* and *I2*.

Accordingly, all the space *Z* can be represented by a union of two inequalities $\{x \leq a\} \cup \{x > a\}$. As well, the empty set can be inferred from the intersection of inequalities $\{x \leq a\} \cap \{x > a\}$.

-Equality operator $\{\sum a_i x_i = c\}$: It is defined by the intersection of two inequalities $\{\sum a_i x_i \leq c\}$ and $\{\sum a_i x_i \geq c\}$.

-Resolution operator: It simplifies arithmetic expressions using QELIM quantification, and both low and high implication rules introduced in LDD. For example, the QELIM resolution of $\{(x-y \leq 3) \wedge (x-t \geq 8) \wedge (y-z \leq 6) \wedge (x-t \geq 2)\}$ gives the simplified expression $\{(x - z \leq 9) \wedge (x - t \geq 8) \wedge (x - t \geq 2)\}$. This expression can be further simplified to $\{(x - z \leq 9) \wedge (x - t \geq 8)\}$ in case of high implication and to $\{(x - z \leq 9) \wedge (x - t \geq 2)\}$ in case of low implication.

-Reduction operator: It solves an expression *A* with respect to an expression *B*. In other words, if *A* implies *B*, then the reduction of *A* with respect to *B* is the projection of *A* when *B* is true. For example, the projection of *A* $\{(x - y \leq 5) \wedge (z \geq 2) \wedge (z - t \leq 2)\}$ with respect to *B* $\{x - y \leq 7\}$ gives the reduced set $\{(z \geq 2) \wedge (z - t \leq 2)\}$.

We report in this paper on the performance of these functions to enhance our tests. More specifically, by means of the SupLDD library, we present next the Sequences Symbolic Generation operation that integrates data manipulation and generates more significant and expressive sequences. Moreover, we track and analyze test execution to spot the situations where the program violates its properties (Determinism, Death sequences). On the other hand, our library ensures the analysis of the generated sequences context to carry the backtrack operation and generate all possible test cases.

E. Sequences Symbolic Generation (SSG)

Contrary to the classical sequences generator that follows only one of the possible paths, we proceed to a symbolic execution [30] to automatically explore all possible paths of the studied system. The idea is to manipulate logical formulas matching interrelated variables instead of updating directly the variables in memory, in the case of concrete classical execution. Fig. 8 presents a set of possible sequences describing the behavior of a given system. It is a classical representation of the dynamic system evolutions. It shows a very large tree or even an infinite tree. Accordingly, exploring all possible program executions is not at all feasible. This requires imagining all possible combinations of the system commands, which is almost impossible. We will show in the next session the weakness of this classical approach when testing large systems.

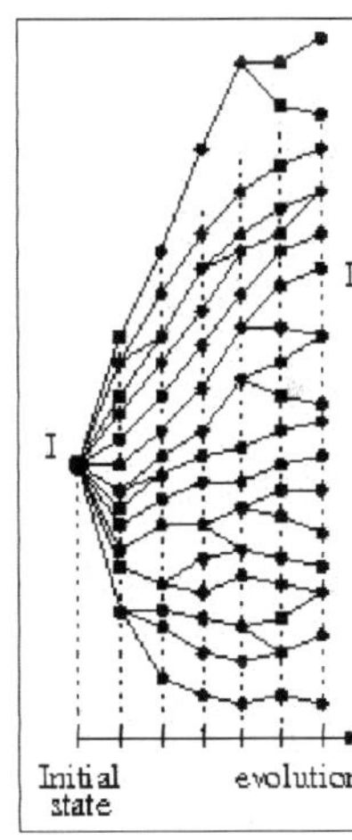

Figure 8. Classical Sequences Generation.

If we consider the representation of the system by a sequence of commands executed iteratively, the previous sequences tree becomes a repetition of the same subspace pattern as shown in Fig. 9. Instead of considering all the state space, we seek in our approach to restrict the state space and confine only on significant subspaces. This represents a specific system command, which can be repeated through possible generated sequences. Each state in the subspace is specified by 3 main variables: symbolic values of the program variables, path condition and command parameters (next byte-code to be executed). The path condition represents preconditions that should be satisfied by the symbolic values to successfully advance the current path execution.

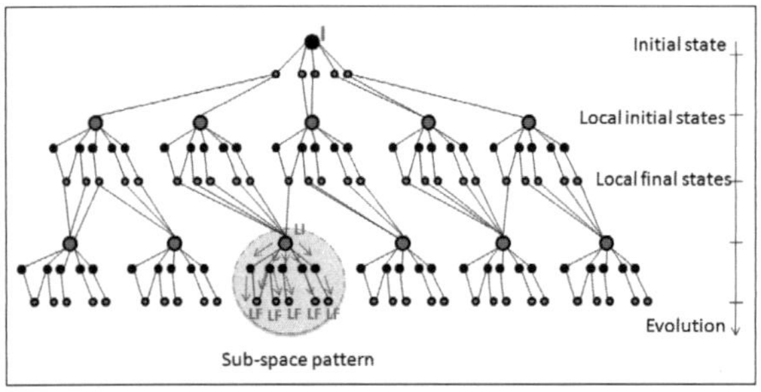

Figure 9. AUTSEG Model Representation.

In other words, it defines the preconditions to successfully follow that path. We particularly define two types of preconditions:

- Boolean global preconditions that define the execution context of a given command. They appear as input constraints of the tested command. They state the list of commands that should be executed beforehand. They arise as well as command output if the latter is properly executed.
- Numerical local preconditions that define numerical constraints on commands parameters. They are presented and manipulated by SupLDD functions mentioned in Section III-D2. Thus, they are presented in the form of $\{\sum a_i x_i \leq c\}$; $\{\sum a_i x_i < c\}$; $\{\sum a_i x_i \geq c\}$; $\{\sum a_i x_i > c\}$; where x_i presents the several commands parameters.

Our approach is primarily designed to test systems running iterative commands. In this context, the SSG operation occurs in the significant subspace representing a system command instead of considering all the state space. It generates the exhaustive list of possible sequences in each significant subspace and extracts the optimal preconditions defining its execution context. In fact, we test all system commands, but a single command is tested at once. The restriction was done by characterizing all preconditions defining the execution context in each subspace. Hence, the major complex calculation is intended to be locally performed in each significant subspace avoiding the state space combinatorial explosion problem.

Indeed, the safety of the tested system is checked by means of SupLDD analysis on numerical local preconditions and BDD analysis on Boolean global preconditions. First, we check if there are erroneous sequences. To this end, we apply the SupLDD conjunction function on all extracted numerical preconditions within the analyzed path. If the result of this conjunction is null, the analyzed sequence is then impossible and should be rectified! Second, we check the determinism of the system behavior. To this end, we verify if the SupLDD conjunction of all outgoing transitions from each state is empty. In other words, we verify if the SupLDD disjunction of all outgoing transitions from each state is equal to all of the space covering all possible system behaviors. Finally, we check the execution context of each command. This is to identify and verify that all extracted global preconditions are met. If the context is verified, then the generated sequence is considered safe. This verification operation is performed by the "Backtrack" operation detailed below.

Algorithm 3 shows in detail the symbolic sequences generation operation executed in each subspace. This allows automatically generating all possible sequences in a command and extract its global pre-conditions. This operation is quite simple because it relies on the flexibility of the designed model, compiled through the synchronous approach. We have applied symbolic analysis (Boolean via BDD-analysis and numeric via SupLDDs) from the local initial state (initial state of the command) to local final states of the specified subspace. For each combination of registers, BDD and SupLDD manipulations are applied to determine and characterize the next state and update the state variables. Required preconditions for this transition are identified as well. If these preconditions are global, then they are inserted into the GPLIST of global preconditions to be displayed later in the context of the generated sequence. Otherwise, if these preconditions are local, then they are pushed into a stack LPLIST, in conjunction with the previous ones. If the result of this conjunction is null, then the generated sequence is marked impossible and should be rectified. Outputs are calculated as well and pushed into a stack OLIST. Finally, the sequence is completed by the new established state. Once the necessary global preconditions are extracted, a next step is to backtrack the tree until the initial sequence fulfilling these preconditions is found.

Algorithm 3 SSG operation

```
Seq ← sequence
BDS ← BDD State
BDA ← BDD awaited
BDAC ← BDD awaited context
OLIST ← Outputs list
GPLIST ← Global Precondition list
LPLIST ← Local Precondition list
BDS ← Initial state
BDAC ← 0
OLIST ← empty
GPLIST ← empty
LPLIST ← All the space
Push (BDS, OLIST, BDAC)
while (stack is not empty) do
   Pull (BDS, OLIST, BDAC)
   list(BDA)← Compute the BDD awaited expressions list(BDS)
   for (i=0 to |list(BDA)|) do
      Input ← extract(BDA)
      if (Input is a global precondition) then
         GPLIST ← Push(GPLIST, Input)
      else
         if (Input is a local precondition) then
            LPLIST ← SupLDD-AND(LPLIST, Input)
            if (GPLIST is null) then
               Display ( Impossible Sequence !)
               Break
      NextBDS ← Compute future(BDS, BDA)
      OLIST ← Compute output (BDS, BDA)
      New-seq ← seq BDA | BDA
      if (New New-seq size < maximum diameter) then
         Push (NextBDS, OLIST, BDAC)
      else
         Display (GPLIST)
         Display (New-seq)
```

F. Backtrack operation

Once the necessary preconditions are extracted, the next step consists in backtracking paths from each final critical state toward the initial state, finding the sequence fulfilling these preconditions. This operation is carried by robust calculations on SupLDD and the compilation process, which kept enough knowledge to find later the previous states (Predecessors) that lead to the initial state. Algorithm 4 details this operation in two main phases: The first one (lines 11-20) labels the state space nodes, which are not yet analyzed. From the initial state ($e \leftarrow 0$), all successors are labelled by ($e \leftarrow e+1$). If a state is already labelled, its index is not incremented. This operation is repeated for all states until the whole state space is covered. The second phase (lines 21-30) identifies the best previous states. For each state *St*, the predecessor with the lowest label is introduced into the shortest path to reach the initial state: This is an important result of graph theory [31]. In other words, previous states always converge to the same global initial state. This approach easily favors the backtracking execution.

Algorithm 4 Search for Predecessors

```
1: St ← State
2: LSt ← List of States
3: LS ← List of Successors
4: LabS ← State Label
5: IS ← Initial State
6: S ← State
7: LabS(IS) ← 1
8: LSt ← IS
9: LP ← List of Predecessors
10: SMin ← Minimum Lab State
11: // Expansion
12: while (LSt != 0) do
13:   for (all St of LSt) do
14:     LS ← Get-Successors(St)
15:     if (LS != 0) then
16:       for (all S of LS) do
17:         if (!LabS(S)) then
18:           LabS(S) ← LabS(St)+1
19:       NLSt ← Push(LS)
20:   LSt ← NLSt
21: // Search for Predecessors
22: for (all St) do
23:   LP ← Get-Predecessor(St)
24:   SMin ← LabS(first(LP))
25:   StMin ← first(LP)
26:   for (all St' in LP) do
27:     if (LabS(St') < SMin) then
28:       SMin ← LabS(St')
29:       StMin ← St'
30:     Memorise-Backtrack(St,StMin)
```

Let us consider the example in Fig. 9. From the initial local state "IL" (initial state of a command), the symbolic sequences generator applies BDDs and SupLDDs analysis to generate all possible paths that lead to final local states of the tested subspace. Taking into account "LF" as a critical final state "FS" of the tested system, the backtrack operation is executed from "LF" state until the sequence that satisfies the extracted global preconditions. Assuming state "I" as the final result of this backtrack, the sequence from "I" to "LF" is an example of a good test set. However, considering the representation of Fig. 8, a test set from "I" to "LF" will be performed by generating all paths of the tree. Such a test becomes unfeasible if the number of steps to reach "LF" is greatly increased. The Backtrack operation includes two main actions:

- Global backtrack: It verifies the execution context of the tested subspace. It is based on Boolean global preconditions to identify the list of commands that should be executed before the tested command.

- Local backtrack: Once the list of commands is established, a next step is to execute a local backtrack. It determines the final path connecting all commands to be executed to reach the specified final state. It uses numeric local preconditions of each command from the list.

Fig. 10 details the global backtrack operation: Given the global extracted preconditions (GP1, GP2, etc.) from the SSG operation at this level (Final state FS of command C1), we search in the global actions table for actions (Commands C2 and C3) that emit each parsed global precondition. Next, we put on a list SL the states that trigger each identified action (SL= $\{C2, C3\}$). This operation is iteratively executed on all found states (C2,C3) until the root state I with zero preconditions (C4 with zero preconditions) is reached.

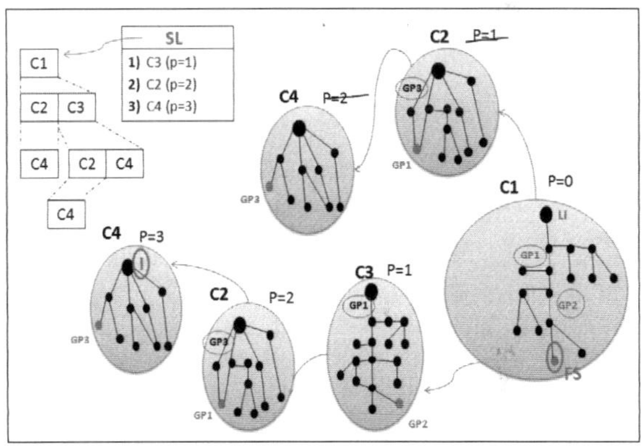

Figure 10. Global Backtrack.

The identified states can be repeated on *SL* (*C2* and *C4* are repeated on *SL*) as many times as there are commands that share the same global preconditions (*C1* and *C3* share the same precondition *GP1*). To manage this redundancy, we allocate a priority *P* to each found state, where each state of priority *P* should precede the state of priority *P+1*. More specifically, if an identified state already exists in *SL*, then its priority is incremented by 1 (Priority of commands *C2* and *C4* are incremented by 1). By the end of this operation, we obtain the list *SL* (*SL*= $\{$ *C3,C2,C4* $\}$) of final states referring to subspaces that should be traced to reach *I*.

A next step is to execute a local backtrack on each identified subspace (*C1,C3,C2,C4*), starting from the state with the lowest priority and so on to trace the final path from *FS* to *I*. The sequence from *I* to *FS* is an example of a good test set. Fig. 11 presents an example of local backtracking in command *C3*. In fact, during the SSG operation each state *S* was labelled by (1) a Local numeric Precondition (*LP*)

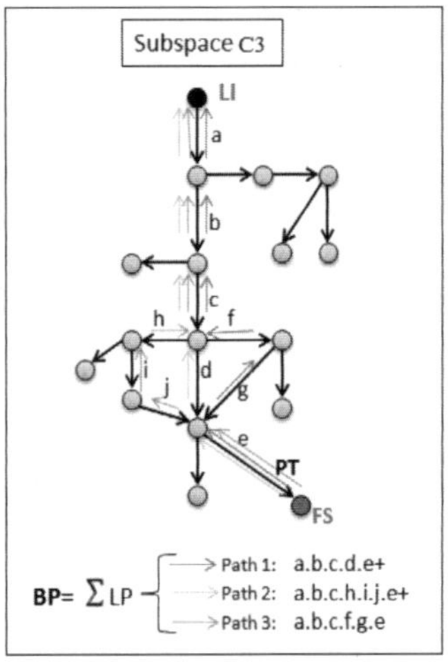

Figure 11. Local Backtrack.

presenting numerical constraints that should be satisfied on its ongoing transition and (2) a Total Local numeric precondition (*TL*) that presents the conjunction of all *LP* along the executed path from *I* to *S*. To execute the local backtrack, we start from the ongoing transition *PT* to *FS* to find a path that satisfies the backtrack precondition *BP* initially defined by *TL*. If the backtrack precondition is satisfied by the total precondition $\{TL \geq BP\}$, then if the local precondition *LP* of the tested transition is not null, we remove this verified precondition *LP* from *BP* by applying the SupLDD projection function. Next, we move to the amount state of *PT* and test its ongoing transitions, etc. However, if $\{TL < BP\}$, we move to the test of other ongoing transitions to find the transition from which *BP* can be satisfied. This operation is iteratively executed until reaching the initial state on which the backtrack precondition is null (fully satisfied). In short, if the context is verified, the generated sequence is considered correct. At the end of this process, we join all identified paths from each traced subspace according to the given priority order from the global backtrack operation.

IV. USE CASE

To illustrate our approach, we studied the case of a contactless smart card for the transportation sector manufactured by the company ASK [32], a world leader in this technology. We specifically targeted the verification of the card's functionality and security features. Security of such systems is critical: it can concern cards for access security, banking, ID, etc. Card complexity makes it difficult for a human to identify all possible delicate situations, or to validate them by classical methods. We need approximately 500,000 years to test the first 8 bytes if we consider a classical Intel processor able to generate 1000 test sets per second. As well, combinatorial explosion of possible modes of operation makes it nearly impossible to attempt a comprehensive simulation. The problem is exacerbated when the system integrates numerical data processing. We will show in the next session the results of applying our tool to this transportation card, taking into account the complexity of data manipulation. We compared our testing approach to that of ASK. We also compared our results to those obtained with a classical approach.

The smart card operation is defined by a transport standard called Calypso that presents 33 commands. The succession of these commands (e.g., Open Session, SV Debit, Get Data, Change Pin) gives the possible scenarios of card operation. We used Light Esterel [13] to interpret the card specification (Calypso) into hierarchical automata while taking advantages of this synchronous language. We designed the generic model of the studied card by 52 interconnected automata including 765 states. Forty-three of them form a hierarchical structure. The remaining automata operate in parallel and act as observers to control the global context of hierarchical automaton (Closed Session, Verified PIN, etc.). We show in Fig. 12 a small part of our model representing the command Open Session. Each command in Calypso is presented by an APDU (Application Protocol Data Unit) that presents the next byte-code to be executed (CLA,INS,P1,P2, etc.). We expressed these parameters by SupLDD local preconditions on various transitions. For instance, AUTSEGINT($h10 < P1 < h1E$) means that the corresponding transition can only be executed if $(10 < P1 < 30)$. Back-Autseg-Open-Session and Back-Autseg-Verify-PIN are examples of global preconditions that appear as outputs of respectively Open Session and Verify PIN commands when they are correctly executed. They appear also as inputs for other commands as SV Debit command to denote that the card can be debited only if the PIN code is correct and a session is already open.

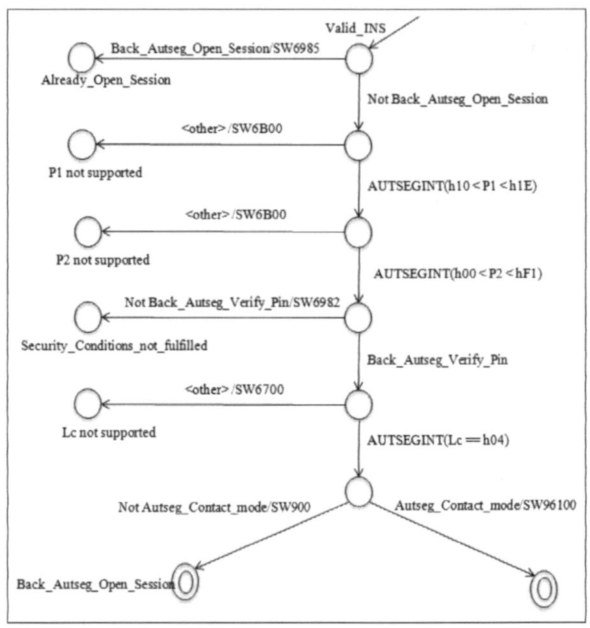

Figure 12. Open Session Command.

According to the Calypso standard, several card types and configurations are defined (contact/contactless, with/without Stored-Value, etc.). Typically, these characteristics must be initially configured to specify each test. However, changing card parameters requires recompiling each new specification separately and re-running the tests. This approach is unrealistic, because this can take many hours or even days to compile in industry. In addition, this would generate as many models as system types, which can highly limit the legibility and increase the risk of specification bugs. Contrary to this complex testing process, our approach yields a single appropriate generic model for all card types and applications. The model's explicit test sets are to be filtered at the end of the test process through analysis of system preconditions. For instance, Autseg-Contact-mode is an example of a system precondition specifying that Open Session command should be executed in a Contactless Mode. In this context, checking a contactless card involves evaluating Autseg-Contact-mode to 0 and then verifying the corresponding execution context. Accordingly, sequences with the precondition Autseg-Contact-mode are false and should be rectified!

V. Experimental Results

In this section, we show experimental results of applying our tool to the contactless transportation card. We intend to test the security of all possible combinations of 33 commands of the Calypso standard. This validation process is extremely important to determine whether the card performs to specification. Each command in the Calypso standard is encoded on a minimum of 8 bytes. We conducted our experiments on a PC with an Intel Dual Core GHz Processor, 8 GB RAM.

We have achieved a vast reduction of the state space due to the quasi-flattening process on the smart card hierarchical model. Compared to classical flattening works, we have moved from 9.6 10^{24} states in the designed model to only 256 per branch of parallel. Then, due to the compilation process, we have moved from 477 registers to only 22. More impressive results are obtained on sequences generation and test coverage with data processing. A classical test of this card can be achieved by browsing all paths of the tree in Fig. 13 without any restriction. This tree represents all possible combinations of 33 commands of the Calypso standard.

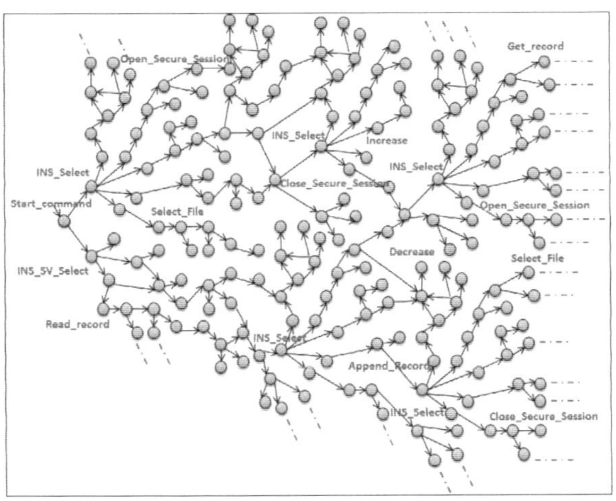

Figure 13. Classical Test of Calypso Card.

Such a test shows in plot C1 of Fig. 14 an exponential evolution of the number of sequences versus the number of tested bytes. We are not even able to test just a simple sequence of two commands. Our model explodes by 13 bytes generating 3,993,854,132 possible sequences. That is why AUTSEG tests only one command at once, but it introduces a notion of preconditions and behavior backtracking to abstract the effects of the previous commands in the sequence under test.

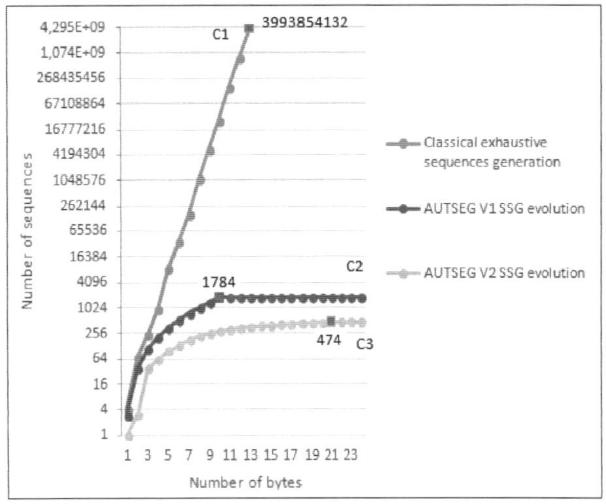

Figure 14. SSG Evolutions.

Hence, a second test applies AUTSEG V1 (without data processing) on the card model represented in the same manner as Fig. 9. It generates all possible paths in each significant subspace (command) separately. Results show in plot C2 a lower evolution that stabilizes at 10 steps and 1784 paths, allowing for coverage of all states of the tested model. More interesting results are shown in plot C3 by AUTSEG V2 tests taking into account numerical data manipulation. Our approach enables coverage of the global model in a substantially short time (a few seconds). It allows separately testing 33 commands (all of the system commands) in only 21 steps, generating a total of solely 474 paths. Covering all states in only 21 steps, our results demonstrate that we test separately one command (8 bytes) at once in our approach thanks to the backtrack operation. The additional steps (13 bytes) correspond to the test of system preconditions (e.g., AUTSEG-Contact-mode, etc.), global preconditions (e.g., Back-Autseg-Open-Session, etc.) and other local preconditions (e.g.,AUTSEGINT($h00 \leq buffer-size \leq hFF$)). Whereas, only fewer additional steps (2 bytes) are required within the first version of AUTSEG that stabilizes at 10 steps. This difference proves a complete handling of system constraints using the new version of AUTSEG, performing therefore more expressive and real tests: we integrate a better knowledge of the system.

Plot C4 in Fig. 15 exhibits results of AUTSEG V2 tests simulated with 3 anomalies on the smart card model. We note fewer generated sequences by the 5 steps. We obtain a total of 460 sequences instead of 474 at the end of the tests. Fourteen sequences are removed since they are unfeasible (dead sequences) according to SupLDD calculations. Indeed, the SupLDD conjunction of parsed local preconditions AUTSEGINT($01h \leq RecordNumber \leq 31h$) and AUTSEGINT($RecordNumber \geq FFh$) within a same path is null, illustrating an over-specification example (anomaly) of the Calypso standard that should be revised.

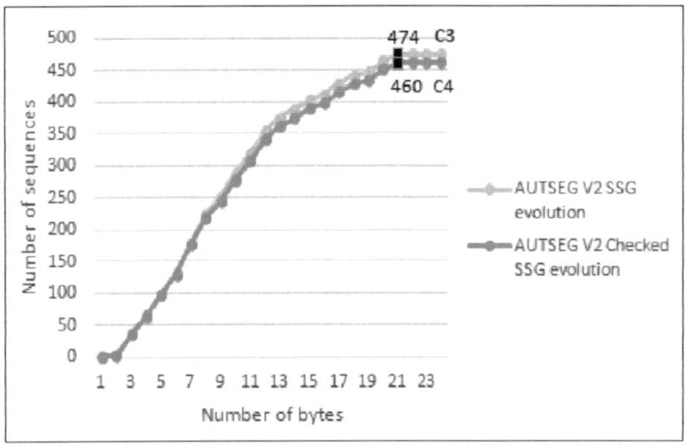

Figure 15. AUTSEG V2 SSG Evolutions.

We show in Fig. 16 an excerpt of generated sequences by AUTSEG V2 detecting another type of anomaly: an under-specification in the card behavior. The *Incomplete Behavior* message reports a missing action on a tested state of the Update-Binary command. Indeed, two actions are defined $(Tag = 54h)$ and $(Tag = 03h)$ at this state. All states where Tag is different from *84* and *3* are missing. We can automatically spot such problems by checking for each parsed state if the union of all outgoing transitions is equal to the whole space. If this property is always true, then the smart card behavior is proved deterministic.

```
Update Binary command Test
------------------------------------------
Sequence:

-AUTSEGINT(CLA==00h OR CLA==94h) -->
-AUTSEGINT(INS==D7h)-->
-Back-Autseg-Open-Session AND not Wrong Key
-AUTSEGINT(P1==00h) -->
-AUTSEGINT(P2>=00h AND P2<=1Eh) -->
-AUTSEGINT(SFI>=00h AND SFI<=FFh)
-AUTSEGINT <other> -->
-AUTSEGINT(EFTYPE==01h) -->
-AUTSEGINT(Lc>=07h AND Lc<=FFH) -->
-AUTSEGINT(Tag==54h) -->
----> Incomplete Behavior!

Post transitions:
Parse expression AUTSEGINT (Tag == 54h)
Parse expression AUTSEGINT (Tag == 03h)
------------------------------------------
```

Figure 16. Smart Card Under-Specification.

As explained before, we get the execution context of each generated sequence at the end of this operation. The next step is then to backtrack all critical states of the Calypso standard (all final states of 33 commands). Fig. 17 shows a detailed example of backtracking from the final state of the SV Undebit command that emits SW6200 code. We identify from the global extracted preconditions Back-Autseg-Open-Session and Back-Autseg-Get-SV the list of commands (Open Secure Session and SV Get) to be executed beforehand. Then, we look recursively for all global preconditions of each identified command to trace the complete path to the initial state of

```
Backtrack from state SV Undebit
Postponed Response Data SW6200
--------------------------------------
Backtrack Sequence:

-Back-Autseg-Open-Session --> SW6200
-not Session memory full -->
-AUTSEGINT(Amount<0) -->
-tick --> Autseg Memorize(Amount)
-AUTSEGINT(Lc==14h) -->
-Present SV -->
-Back-Autseg-Get-SV -->
-AUTSEGINT(INS==BCh) -->
-AUTSEGINT(CLA==FAh) -->

Backtrack var is Back-Autseg-Get-SV
Backtrack var is Back-Autseg-Open-Session
Backtrack var is Back-Autseg-Verify-PIN
Prior commands to execute 3
--------------------------------------
```

Figure 17. SV Undebit Backtrack.

the Start command. We observe from the results that the Verify PIN command should proceed the Open Secure Session command. So, the final backtrack path is to trace (local backtrack) the identified commands respectively SV Undebit, SV Get, Open Secure Session and Verify PIN using local preconditions of each command. At the end of this process, we generate automatically 5456 test sets that cover the entire behavior of the studied smart card.

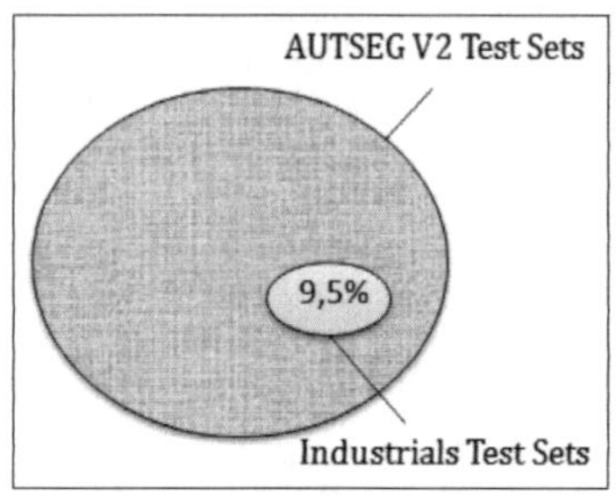

Figure 18. Tests Coverage.

Industry techniques, on the other hand, take much more time to manually generate a mere 520 test sets, covering 9.5% of our tests as shown in Fig. 18.

VI. CONCLUSION

We have proposed a complete automatic testing tool for embedded reactive systems that details all features presented in our previous works AUTSEG V1 and AUTSEG V2. Our testing approach focused on systems executing iterative commands. It is practical and performs well, even with large models where the risk of combinatorial explosion of state space is important. This has been achieved by essentially (1) exploiting the robustness of synchronous languages to design an effective system model easy to analyze, (2) providing an algorithm to quasi-flatten hierarchical FSMs and reduce the state space, (3) focusing on pertinent subspaces and restricting the tests, and (4) carrying out rigorous calculations to generate an exhaustive list of possible test cases. Our experiments confirm that our tool provides expressive and significant tests, covering all possible system evolutions in a short time. More generally, our tool including the SupLDD calculations can be applied to many numerical systems as they could be modelled by FSMs handling integer variables. Since SupLDD is implemented on top of a simple BDD package, we aim in a future work to rebuild SupLDD on top of an efficient implementation of BDDs with complement edges [33] to achieve a better library optimization. More generally, new algorithms can be integrated to enhance the LDD library. We aim as well to integrate SupLDD in data abstraction of CLEM [13]. More details about these future works are presented in [34]. Another interesting contribution would be to generate penetration tests to determine whether a system is vulnerable to an attack.

REFERENCES

[1] M. Abdelmoula, D. Gaffé, and M. Auguin, "Automatic Test Set Generator with Numeric Constraints Abstraction for Embedded Reactive Systems: AUTSEG V2," in VALID 2015: The Seventh International Conference on Advances in System Testing and Validation Lifecycle, Barcelone, Spain, Nov. 2015, pp. 23–30.

[2] M. Abdelmoula, D. Gaffé, and M. Auguin, "Autseg: Automatic test set generator for embedded reactive systems," in Testing Software and Systems, 26th IFIP International Conference,ICTSS, ser. Lecture Notes in Computer Science. Madrid, Spain: springer, September 2014, pp. 97–112.

[3] B. Seljimi and I. Parissis, "Automatic generation of test data generators for synchronous programs: Lutess v2," in Workshop on Domain specific approaches to software test automation: in conjunction with the 6th ESEC/FSE joint meeting, ser. DOSTA '07. New York, NY, USA: ACM, 2007, pp. 8–12.

[4] L. DuBousquet and N. Zuanon, "An overview of lutess: A specification-based tool for testing synchronous software," in ASE, 1999, pp. 208–215.

[5] B. Blanc, C. Junke, B. Marre, P. Le Gall, and O. Andrieu, "Handling state-machines specifications with gatel," Electron. Notes Theor. Comput. Sci., vol. 264, no. 3, 2010, pp. 3–17. [Online]. Available: http://dx.doi.org/10.1016/j.entcs.2010.12.011 [Accessed 15 November 2016]

[6] J. R. Calam, "Specification-Based Test Generation With TGV," CWI, CWI Technical Report SEN-R 0508, 2005. [Online]. Available: http://oai.cwi.nl/oai/asset/10948/10948D.pdf [Accessed 15 November 2016]

[7] D. Clarke, T. Jéron, V. Rusu, and E. Zinovieva, "Stg: A symbolic test generation tool," in TACAS, 2002, pp. 470–475.

[8] L. Bentakouk, P. Poizat, and F. Zaïdi, "A formal framework for service orchestration testing based on symbolic transition systems," Testing of Software and Communication Systems, 2009.

[9] D. Xu, "A tool for automated test code generation from high-level petri nets," in Proceedings of the 32nd international conference on Applications and theory of Petri Nets, ser. PETRI NETS'11. Berlin, Heidelberg: Springer-Verlag, 2011, pp. 308–317.

[10] J. Burnim and K. Sen, "Heuristics for scalable dynamic test generation," in Proceedings of the 2008 23rd IEEE/ACM International Conference on Automated Software Engineering, ser. ASE '08. Washington, DC, USA: IEEE Computer Society, 2008, pp. 443–446.

[11] G. Li, I. Ghosh, and S. P. Rajan, "Klover: a symbolic execution and automatic test generation tool for c++ programs," in Proceedings of the 23rd international conference on Computer aided verification, ser. CAV'11. Berlin, Heidelberg: Springer-Verlag, 2011, pp. 609–615.

[12] C. André, "A synchronous approach to reactive system design," in 12th EAEEIE Annual Conf., Nancy (F), May 2001, pp. 349–353.

[13] A. Ressouche, D. Gaffé, and V. Roy, "Modular compilation of a synchronous language," in Soft. Eng. Research, Management and Applications, best 17 paper selection of the SERA'08 conference, R. Lee, Ed., vol. 150. Prague: Springer-Verlag, August 2008, pp. 157–171.

[14] C. André, "Representation and analysis of reactive behaviors: A synchronous approach," in Computational Engineering in Systems Applications (CESA). Lille (F): IEEE-SMC, July 1996, pp. 19–29.

[15] G. Berry and G. Gonthier, "The esterel synchronous programming language: Design, semantics, implementation," Sci. Comput. Program., vol. 19, no. 2, Nov. 1992, pp. 87–152. [Online]. Available: http://dx.doi.org/10.1016/0167-6423(92)90005-V [Accessed 15 November 2016]

[16] N. Halbwachs, P. Caspi, P. Raymond, and D. Pilaud, "The synchronous dataflow programming language lustre," in Proceedings of the IEEE, 1991, pp. 1305–1320.

[17] A. C. R. Paiva, N. Tillmann, J. C. P. Faria, and R. F. A. M. Vidal, "Modeling and testing hierarchical guis," in Proc.ASM05. Universite de Paris 12, 2005, pp. 8–11.

[18] A. Wasowski, "Flattening statecharts without explosions," SIGPLAN Not., vol. 39, no. 7, Jun 2004, pp. 257–266. [Online]. Available: http://doi.acm.org/10.1145/998300.997200 [Accessed 15 November 2016]

[19] I. Chiuchisan, A. D. Potorac, and A. Garaur, "Finite state machine design and vhdl coding techniques," in 10th International Conference on development and application systems. Suceava, Romania: Faculty of Electrical Engineering and Computer Science, 2010, pp. 273–278.

[20] M. Fujita, P. C. McGeer, and J. C.-Y. Yang, "Multi-terminal binary decision diagrams: An efficient datastructure for matrix representation," Form. Methods Syst. Des., vol. 10, no. 2-3, Apr. 1997, pp. 149–169.

[21] Y.-T. Lai and S. Sastry, "Edge-valued binary decision diagrams for multi-level hierarchical verification," in Proceedings of the 29th ACM/IEEE Design Automation Conference, ser. DAC'92. Los Alamitos, CA, USA: IEEE Computer Society Press, 1992, pp. 608–613.

[22] R. E. Bryant and Y.-A. Chen, "Verification of arithmetic circuits with binary moment diagrams," in Proceedings of the 32Nd Annual ACM/IEEE Design Automation Conference, ser. DAC '95. New York, NY, USA: ACM, 1995, pp. 535–541.

[23] L. Arditi, "A bit-vector algebra for binary moment diagrams," I3S, Sophia-Antipolis, France, Tech. Rep. RR 95–68, 1995.

[24] E. Clarke and X. Zhao, "Word level symbolic model checking: A new approach for verifying arithmetic circuits," Pittsburgh, PA, USA, Tech. Rep., 1995.

[25] M. Ciesielski, P. Kalla, and S. Askar, "Taylor expansion diagrams: A canonical representation for verification of data flow designs," IEEE Transactions on Computers, vol. 55, no. 9, 2006, pp. 1188–1201.

[26] J. Møller and J. Lichtenberg, "Difference decision diagrams," Master's thesis, Department of Information Technology, Technical University of Denmark, Building 344, DK-2800 Lyngby, Denmark, Aug. 1998.

[27] A. J. C. Bik and H. A. G. Wijshoff, Implementation of Fourier-Motzkin Elimination. Rijksuniversiteit Leiden. Valgroep Informatica, 1994.

[28] P. Bouyer, S. Haddad, and P.-A. Reynier, "Timed petri nets and timed automata: On the discriminating power of zeno sequences," Inf. Comput., vol. 206, no. 1, Jan. 2008, pp. 73–107.

[29] S. Chaki, A. Gurfinkel, and O. Strichman, "Decision diagrams for linear arithmetic," in FMCAD. IEEE, 2009, pp. 53–60.

[30] R. S. Boyer, B. Elspas, and K. N. Levitt, "Select a formal system for testing and debugging programs by symbolic execution," SIGPLAN Not., vol. 10, no. 6, Apr. 1975, pp. 234–245. [Online]. Available: http://doi.acm.org/10.1145/390016.808445 [Accessed 15 November 2016]

[31] D. B. Johnson, "A note on dijkstra's shortest path algorithm," J. ACM, vol. 20, no. 3, Jul. 1973, pp. 385–388. [Online]. Available: http://doi.acm.org/10.1145/321765.321768 [Accessed 15 November 2016]

[32] "Ask." [Online]. Available: http://www.ask-rfid.com/ [Accessed 15 November 2016]

[33] K. Brace, R. Rudell, and R. Bryant, "Efficient implementation of a bdd package," in Design Automation Conference, 1990. Proceedings., 27th ACM/IEEE, June 1990, pp. 40–45.

[34] M. Abdelmoula, "Automatic test set generator with numeric constraints abstraction for embedded reactive systems," Ph.D. dissertation, Published in "Génération automatique de jeux de tests avec analyse symbolique des données pour les systèmes embarqués", Sophia Antipolis University, France, 2014.

Engineering a Generic Modular Mapping Framework

Philipp Helle and Wladimir Schamai
Airbus Group Innovations
Hamburg, Germany
Email: {philipp.helle,wladimir.schamai}@airbus.com

Abstract—**This article presents a new framework for solving different kinds of data mapping problems, the Generic Modular Mapping Framework (GEMMA), and the engineering process that lead to its development. GEMMA is geared towards high flexibility for dealing with a large number of different challenges. To this end it has an open architecture that allows the inclusion of application-specific code and provides a generic rule-based mapping engine that allows users without programming knowledge to define their own mapping rules. The paper provides the thought processes that were involved in the engineering of the framework, detailed description of the concepts inherent in the framework and its current architecture. Additionally, the evaluation of the framework in two different application cases, simulation model composition and test bench setup, is described.**

Keywords*–*Mapping; Framework; Simulation Model Composition.

I. Introduction

This article is a revised and extended version of the article [1], which was originally presented at the The Seventh International Conference on Advances in System Simulation (SIMUL 2015).

Recently, several of our research challenges could be reduced to a common core question: How can we match data from one or more data sources to other data from the same and/or different data sources in a flexible and efficient manner? A search for an existing tool that satisfied our application requirements did not yield any results. This sparked the idea of a new common generic framework for data mapping. The goal in designing this framework was to create an extensible and user-configurable tool that would allow a user to define the rules for mapping data without the necessity for programming knowledge and that yet still has the possibility to include application-specific code to adapt to the needs of a concrete application.

Figure 1 shows an example, in which data points from different data sources have mapping relationships. A mapping problem can now be defined as the challenge to identify mappings between data points from (potentially) different data sources. This is what we want to automate.

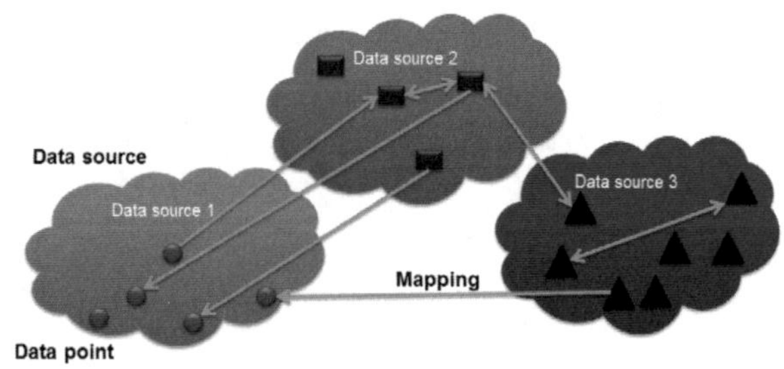

Figure 1. Data mapping

The results of our efforts so far and a first evaluation based on our existing research challenges are presented in this paper.

This paper is structured as follows: Section II provides information regarding related work. Section III provides a detailed description of the framework, its core concepts and its architecture. Next, Section IV describes the application cases that have been used for developing and evaluating the framework so far. Finally, Section V concludes this article.

II. Related Work

The related work can be divided into two major categories: on the one hand, record linkage and data deduplication tools and frameworks, and on the other hand semantic matching frameworks for ontologies.

Record linkage as established by Dunn in his seminal paper [2] and formalised by Felligi and Sunter [3] deals with the challenge to identify data points that correspond with each other in large data sets. Typically, this involves databases of different origin and the question, which of the data on one side essentially are the same on the other side even if their name does not match precisely. The same approach is also called data deduplication [4] where the goal is to identify and remove redundancies in separate data sets. An overview of existing tools and frameworks can be found in [5]. The research work in that area focuses on efficient algorithms for approximate and fuzzy string matching since the size of the data sets involved often leads to an explosion of the run times. These tools [6] often include phonetic similarity metrics or analysis based on common typing errors, i.e., analysis based on the language of the input data. They concentrate on the matching of the string identifiers whereas our framework is more open and flexible in that regard and also includes the possibility to base the matching on available semantic meta-information. The goal in record linkage is always finding data points in different sets representing the same real-world object. Our framework was developed with the goal to match data from different sources that is related but not necessarily referencing the same object.

Semantic matching is a type of ontology matching technique that relies on semantic information encoded in ontologies to identify nodes that are semantically related [7]. They are mostly developed and used in the context of the semantic web [8], where the challenge is to import data from different heterogeneous sources into a common data model. The biggest restriction to their application is that these tools and frameworks rely on the availability of meta-information in the form of ontologies, i.e., formal representations of concepts within a domain and the relationships between those concepts. While our framework can include semantic information, as shown in Section IV-A, it is not a fixed prerequisite.

In conclusion, we can say that our framework tries to fit into a middle ground between record linkage and semantic matching. We use methods applied in both areas but we leave the user the flexibility to choose, which of the features are actually needed in a mapping project.

III. Generic Modular Mapping framework

The Generic Modular Mapping Framework (GEMMA) is designed to be a flexible multi-purpose tool for any problem that requires matching data points to each other. The following subsections will introduce the requirements that were considered during the GEMMA development, the artifacts that make up the core idea behind GEMMA, describe the kind of mapping rules that can be implemented, show the generic process for the usage of GEMMA and describe the software architecture and the current GEMMA implementation.

A. *Mapping*

The basic challenge as defined in the introduction is the mapping of data that do not necessarily match completely in name, type, multiplicity or other details from different data sources to each other as depicted by Figure 1.

Relations between data from different sources and possibly in different formats need to be created. It must be possible to output the generated relations in a user-defined format. This leads to a first draft for a mapping tool, as depicted by Figure 2.

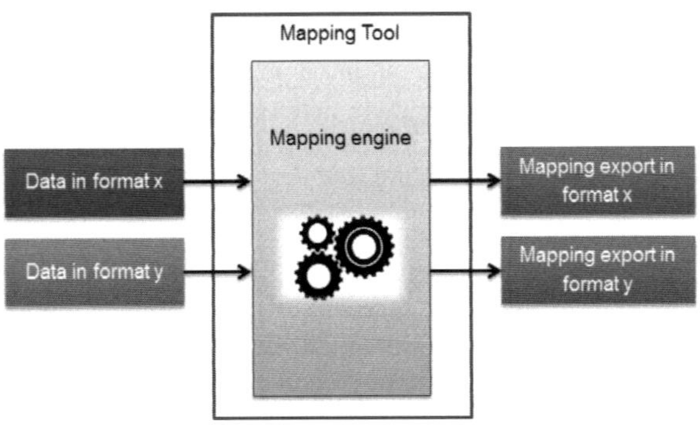

Figure 2. Mapping tool

The mapping tool shall be able to read data from different sources in different formats, then a mapping engine shall be able to create relations between the data and export these relations in different formats.

This is the minimum functionality that such a tool shall provide. In addition to that, there are three major requirements regarding the characteristics of the mapping tool, being **generic** in order to enable applications in different areas with similar challenges; being **modular**, as well as being **interactive**.

B. *Generic*

The requirement for a generic tool stems from the fact that different mapping problems and challenges require different data sources and mapping rules.

This means that the tool shall allow the user to define the rules that govern the creation of mappings. The tool will need to read and interpret such rules in order to be able to create mappings between different input data sets.

Additionally, it shall be possible to setup the current configuration of the mapping tool by means of user-defined configuration. Such a project configuration will contain information, such as where the input data is located, what mapping rules should be used and where the mapping export data should be written to.

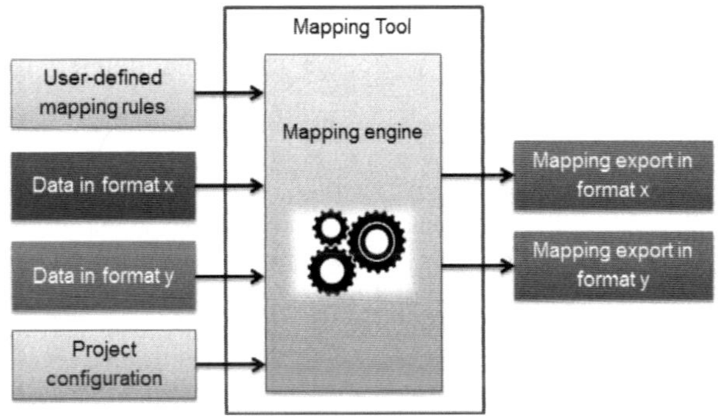

Figure 3. Generic mapping tool

The discussion above leads to an extension of the first draft of the mapping tool which is shown in Figure 3.

C. *Modular*

The requirement for modular software is an extension for the requirement that the software needs to be generic (see Section III-B). Modular programming is a software design technique that emphasizes separating the functionality of a program into independent, interchangeable modules, such that each contains necessary information for executing only one aspect of the desired functionality if required.

We anticipate using the mapping tool in very different contexts and applications with diverse data formats for import and export. To support this, the architecture needs to be modular.

Predefining the interfaces for importer and exporter modules allows creating new modules for specific applications without affecting the rest of the tool. Which modules are used in a specific mapping project can then be defined by the project configuration. A further benefit of the modular architecture is a separation of concerns and responsibilities. Different modules can be created and maintained by different developers or even organizations.

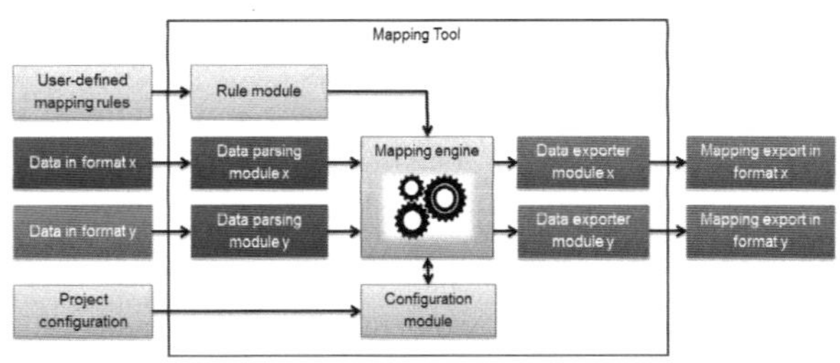

Figure 4. Generic modular mapping tool

The requirement for a modular tool affects the internal architecture of the mapping tool that is shown in Figure 4.

Furthermore, it should be possible to add, change or remove modules from the mapping tool without changes to the core application code. This allows for a packaging of the tool according to user and application needs and enables developing modules that must not be shared, e.g., for confidentiality reasons.

D. Interactive

Based on the assumption that the data in different data sources to be mapped can differ quite substantially in name, type, multiplicity or other details, it is reasonable to assume that a perfect mapping is not always possible. This directly leads to the requirement that the mapping tool needs to be interactive, i.e., allow user-involvement when needed.

An interactive tool displays information to the user and allows user to modify the displayed data. In our setting, this means that the mapping tool shall be able to display the generated mappings between the input data and allow the user to modify these mappings using a Graphical User Interface (GUI).

In order to present the generated mapping data to the user in a meaningful way it is necessary to consider interpretation of the generated mapping data. This requires an additional module: the resolver module. The resolver, as an application-specific module, is aware of application-specific requirements and features. Using this information, the resolver can process the generated mapping data and provide information regarding the application-specific validity of the generated mapping data to users.

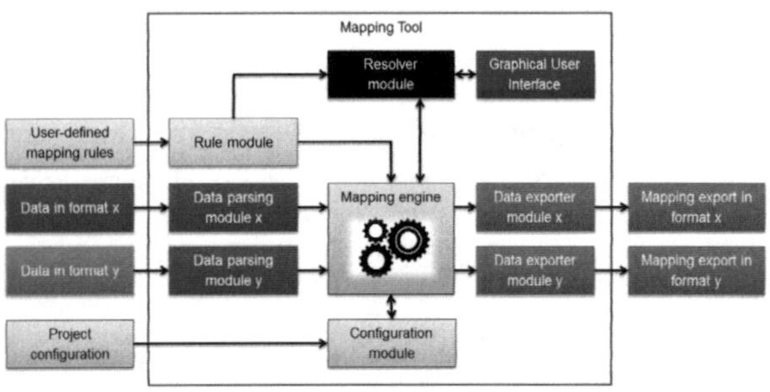

Figure 5. Interactive generic modular mapping tool

The requirement for an interactive tool leads to a change in the tool concept as shown in Figure 5. To further support the idea of a generic and flexible tool for different applications, the GUI module will be optional, i.e., it should be possible to run the mapping tool with or without the GUI.

E. Artefacts

GEMMA is centred around a set of core concepts that are depicted by Figure 6. In an effort to increase the flexibility of GEMMA, the core concepts have been defined in an abstract fashion.

The following artefacts are used:

- **Node** - Something that has properties that can be mapped to some other properties.

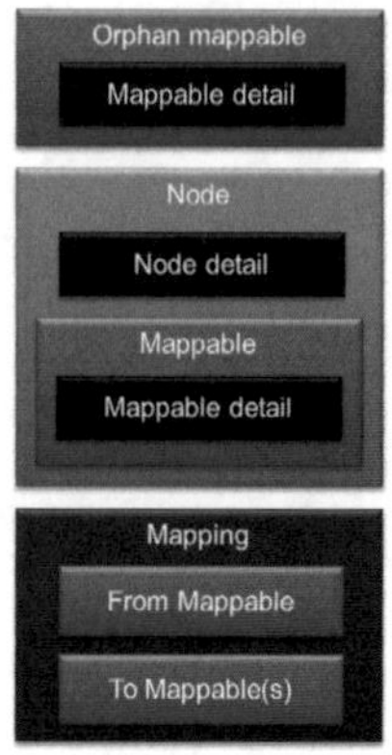

Figure 6. Overview of relevant artefacts

- **Mappable** - Something that can be mapped to some other thing according to specified mapping rules. Orphan mappables are mappables whose owning node is not known or not relevant to the problem.
- **Mapping** - The result of the application of mapping rules, i.e., a relation between one FROM mappable and one or more TO mappables. Note that the semantic interpretation of a mapping highly depends on the application scenario.
- **Mapping rule** - A function that specifies how mappings are created, i.e., how one mappable can be related to other mappables.
- **Mappable or node detail** - Additional attribute of a mappable or a node in the form of a {detail name:detail value} pair. Details are optional and can be defined in the context of a specific application scenario.

To illustrate these abstract definitions, Figure 7 provides a simple example, where real-world objects depicted on the left hand side are represented on the right hand side in the form of our GEMMA concepts.

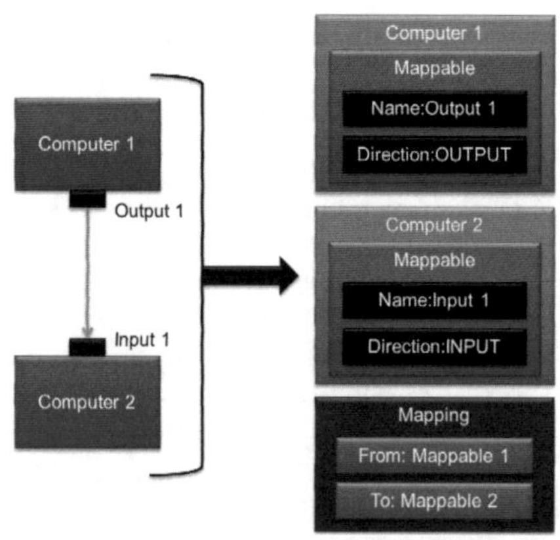

Figure 7. Simple example

In this context, the abstract concept definitions provided above are interpreted as follows:

- **Node** - A computer with input and output ports
- **Mappable** - An input or output port of a computer
- **Mapping** - The connection between ports
- **Mapping rule** - Output ports must be connected to input ports according to some specified criteria such as having the same port name or the same data type.
- **Mappable detail** - Every port has a detail called direction, which defines if the port is an input of output port of the computer

F. Mapping rules

One goal of GEMMA is to allow a large degree of freedom regarding the definition of the mapping rules, so that the framework can be used flexibly for very different kind of application scenarios. So far, the following kinds of mapping rules have been identified and are supported by GEMMA:

- **Exact matching**, e.g., map a mappable to other mappables with the exact same name.
- **Fuzzy matching**, or other forms of **approximate string matching** [9], e.g., map a mappable to other mappables with a similar name (similarity can be based on the Levenshtein distance (LD) [10], i.e., "map" can be matched to "mop" if we allow an LD of 1).
- **Wildcard matching**, e.g., map a mappable to mappables that contain a certain value.
- **RegEx matching**, e.g., map a mappable to mappables based on a regular expression.
- **Tokenized matching**, e.g., split a mappable property into tokens and then map to another mappable with a property that contains each of these tokens in any order.
- **Details**, e.g., map a mappable with value of detail X=x to other mappables with values of details Y=y and Z=z or more concretely, map a mappable with detail direction="output" to mappables with detail direction="input".
- **Structured rewriting** of search term based on name, details and additional data, e.g., construct a new string based on the properties of a mappable and some given string parts and do a name matching with the new string (e.g., new string = "ABCD::" + $mappable.detail(DIRECTION) + "::TBD::" + $mappable.detail(LOCATION) would lead to a search for other mappables with the name "ABCD::Input::TBD::Front").
- **Semantic annotations** such as user-predefined potential mappings (bindings) using mediators as described in [11], e.g., map a mappable whose name is listed as a client of a mediator to all mappables whose name is listed as a provider of the same mediator.

And, of course, any combination of the above mentioned kinds of rules can be used. For example, structured rewriting could also be applied on the target mappables, which would in effect mean defining aliases for every mappable in the mappable database in the context of a rule.

In one GEMMA rule set, several rules can be defined for the same mappable with options for defining their application, e.g., only if the rule with the highest priority does not find any matches then rules with a lower priority are evaluated.

G. Process

The process for the usage of GEMMA is generic for all kinds of applications scenarios and consists of five steps:

1) Import
2) Pre-processing
3) Matching
4) Post-processing
5) Export

The mapping process is configured using an Extensible Markup Language (XML) configuration file that defines which parsers, rules, resolvers and exporters (see Section III-H for a detailed explanation of the terms) will be used in the mapping project. The open character of GEMMA allows implementing different data parsers for importing data, resolvers for post-processing of the mappings and data exporters for exporting data.

Import loads data into the framework. GEMMA provides the interfaces *DataParser*, *MappableSource* and *NodeSource* to anyone who has the need to define a new data parser for an application-specific configuration of GEMMA. All available parsers are registered in an internal parser registry where the Run Configuration can instantiate, configure and run those parsers, which are required by the configuration file. The data will then be stored in the mappable database. As our mappable database uses the full-text search engine Lucene [12], all relevant information from a mappable must be converted into Strings. Each mappable is assigned a unique identifier (ID) from its parser and other required information is stored as detail-value pair in so-called fields as shown in Figure 8.

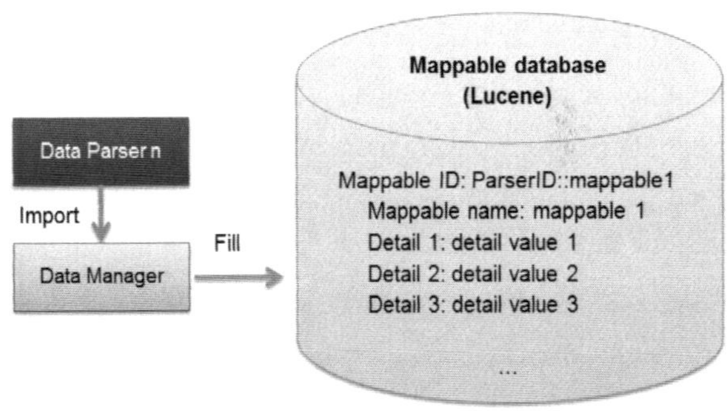

Figure 8. Import process

Pre-processing of data involves selection of mappables that will require matching using whitelists and/or blacklists and structured rewriting of, e.g., mappable names based on mappable details. Pre-processing will be user-defined in a set of rules in a file that can be edited with a standard text editor and does not require programming knowledge. The set of rules that should be applied in one mapping project will be defined by the configuration.

Matching involves running queries on the mappable database to find suitable matches for each mappable that is selected for mapping. The queries are derived from the mapping rules. A mapping is a one to (potentially) many relation between one mappable and all the matches that were found.

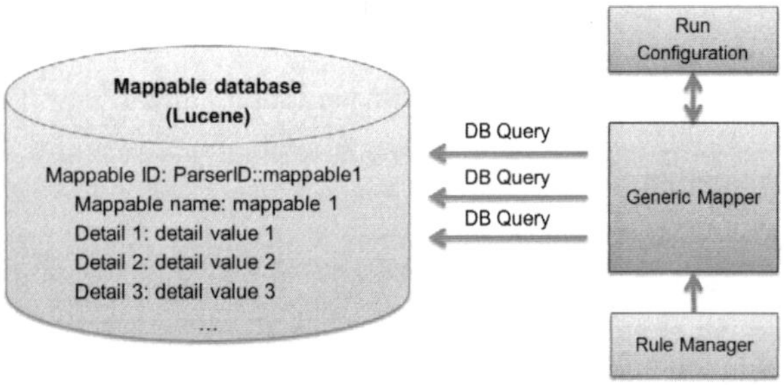

Figure 9. Matching process

As depicted by Figure 9, during the matching process, the generic mapper requests the list of existing mappables from the data manager. For every mappable the mapper retrieves applicable rules from the rule manager and generates queries that are run on the mappable database. The mapper then creates a mapping from the original mappable to the mappables yielded by the query result. The mappings are stored in the data manager.

Post-processing or match resolving is an optional step that is highly driven by the specific application as will be shown in Section IV. It potentially requires the interaction with the user to make a selection, e.g., a mapping rule might say that for a mappable only a one-to-one mapping is acceptable but if more than one match was found then the user must decide which should be selected. Post-processing also allows the user to apply the graphical user interface to review and validate the generated mapping results, to check the completeness and correctness of the defined rules, and to modify mappings manually, e.g., remove a mappable from a mapping if the match was not correct or create a new mapping manually.

Export is also highly application-specific. Exporting involves transformation of the internal data model into an application-specific output file. Similar to the *DataParser* interface, a generic *MappingExporter* interface allows the definition of custom exporters that are registered in an exporter registry where they can be accessed by the run configuration as dictated by the configuration file.

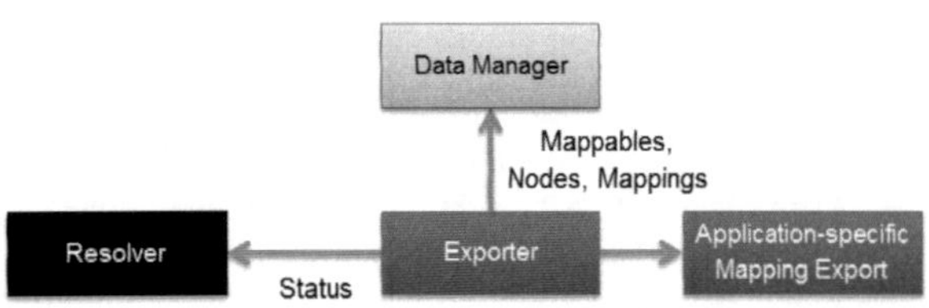

Figure 10. Export process

Each exporter can obtain the available mappables, nodes and mappings from the data manager and the resolver provides an exporter with the status of the elements as depicted by Figure 10. Using this information the exporter creates a mapping export. The mapping export can take many forms, e.g., it can be just an XML file as the standard exporter produces but it can also be an export directly into an application using the application's application programming interface (API). How the data is exported is completely encapsulated in the exporter.

H. *Architecture and implementation*

As already stated before, the Generic Mapping Framework is designed as a flexible answer to all sorts of mapping problems. This is represented in the architecture of the framework, which is depicted in Figure 11 in a simplified fashion. GEMMA modules can be categorized either as core or as application-specific. Core components are common for all GEMMA usage scenarios whereas the application specific components have to be developed to implement features that are very specific to achieve a certain goal. For example, data parsers are application-specific as applications might need data from different sources whereas the mappable database and query engine is a core component that is shared. Table I provides a brief description of the most important modules in GEMMA and their categorization.

TABLE I. GENERIC MAPPING FRAMEWORK MODULES

Module	Description	Core	Specific
Data Parser	Reads data (nodes and/or mappables) into the internal data model and feeds the mappable database		x
Mapper	Generates mappings between mappables based on rules	x	x
GUI	Interface for loading configuration, displaying mappings as well as allowing user-decisions and displaying of data based on resolver as shown in Figure 12	x	
Mappable Database	Stores mappable information and allows searches	x	
Data Manager	Stores mappables, nodes and mappings	x	
Resolver	Resolves mappings based on application specific semantics		x
Rule Manager	Reads mapping rules and provides rules information to other components	x	
Run Configuration	Holds the configuration that defines which parsers, exporters, mapper and rules are used in the current mapping project	x	
Data Exporter	Exports the internal data model into a specific file format		x

GEMMA is implemented in Java. As much as possible, open source libraries and frameworks have been used. The choice for the mappable database, for example, fell on Apache Lucene [12]. Lucene is is a high-performance, full-featured text search engine library. The choice of Lucene might seem odd because we are not using it for its originally intended purpose, indexing and searching of large text files, but it offers a lot of the search capabilities like fuzzy name matching that we need and is already in a very stable state with a strong record of industrial applications.

GEMMA was built on top of the Eclipse Rich Client Platform (RCP) [13], which is a collection of frameworks that enables building modular, pluggable architectures. As shown in Figure 13, the RCP provides some base services on top of which it is possible to build a custom application that may consist of a number of modules that work together in a flexible fashion.

GEMMA is an Eclipse product and uses the Eclipse Open Service Gateway Initiative (OSGi) extension mechanism [14] for registering and instantiating modules. This means that, as

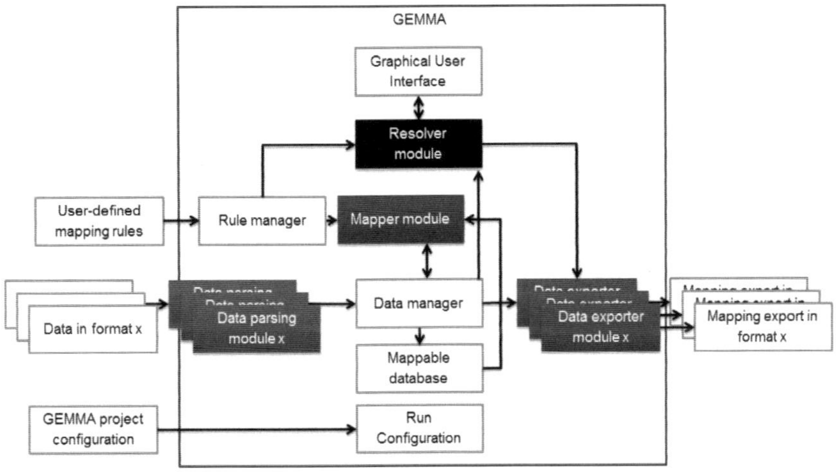

Figure 11. Generic mapping framework architecture

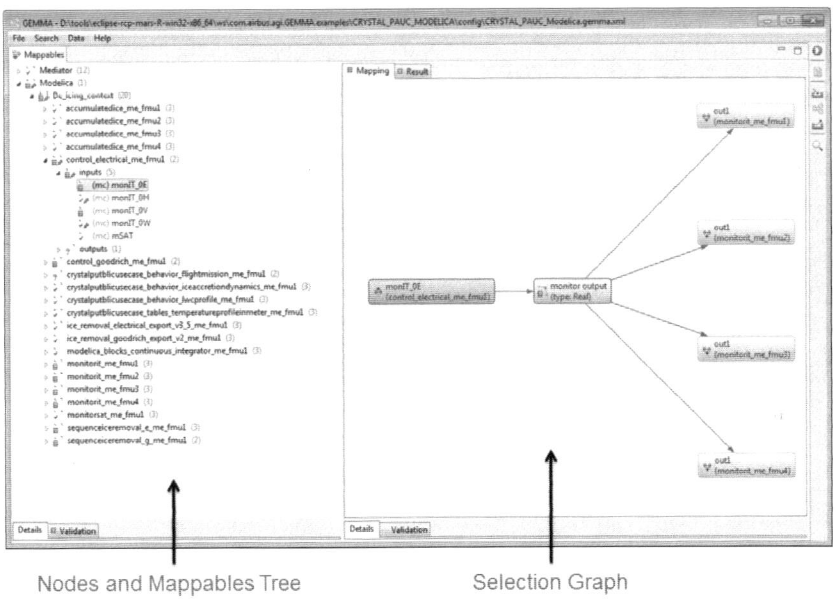

Figure 12. GEMMA graphical user interface

depicted by Figure 14, GEMMA is in essence a collection of Eclipse plugins, some of which can be selected by a user for specific applications, such as the data parsers or the exporters and some of which are fixed, such as the GUI. This architecture allows a tailored deployment of GEMMA.

If some modules are not needed by a user of if a module must not be given to some users, it is possible to remove the plugin from the installation directory of GEMMA without the need for any programming. Only the plugins that are required by a mapping project configuration are needed and instantiated during runtime as shown in Figure 15.

IV. Evaluation

The evaluation so far has been done using two application cases, simulation model composition and test bench setup.

In each of the application cases, four criteria have been evaluated to determine the success of the application of the mapping tool in the use case: mapping rates, adaptability, usability, performance.

- The **mapping rates criterion** includes the number of correct mappings, the number of incorrect mappings (false positives) and the number of missed mappings. As the difficulty of the mapping challenge depends on the characteristics of the input data it is not possible to define thresholds that determine a success of the

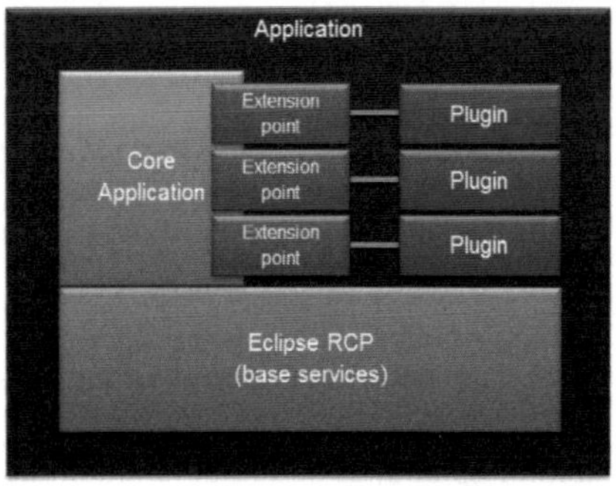

Figure 13. Eclipse RCP

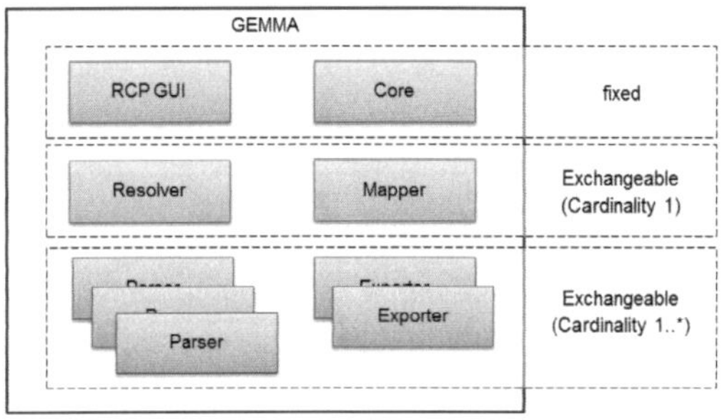

Figure 14. GEMMA as a collection of Eclipse plugins

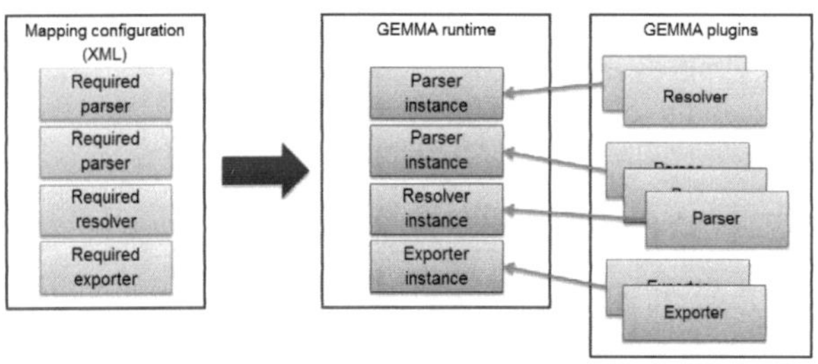

Figure 15. Instantiation of GEMMA modules at runtime

application.

- The **adaptability criterion** is not a measurable criterion. It is a subjective criterion to evaluate how easily and efficiently the mapping tool could be adapted to the needs of a new use case. This mainly focuses on the effort for the definition and validation of the mapping rules as well as the effort for creating or adapting modules that are required by the use case and their integration in the tool.
- Similar to the adaptability criterion, the **usability criterion** is based on feedback from the tool users and their subjective assessment of the effectiveness of using the tool.
- The **performance criterion** mainly refers to speed in terms of tool runtime: runtime for data parsing, mapping, resolving and exporting. As with the mapping rates criterion, a threshold for performance metrics cannot be defined a priori due to the diverse nature of the tool.

A. *Simulation model composition*

The description of the application case simulation model composition requires the introduction of the bindings concept as presented in [11]. The purpose of bindings is to capture the minimum set of information required to support model composition by an automated binding or connecting mechanism. For example, for the outputs of a given component, we wish to identify the appropriate inputs of another component to establish a connection.

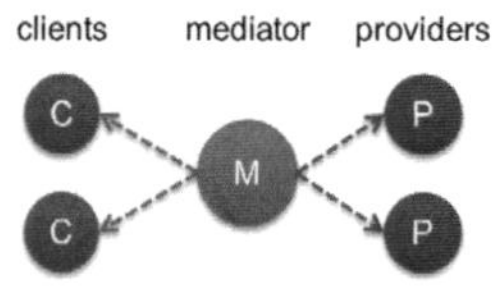

Figure 16. Bindings concept

To this end [11] introduces the notions of clients and providers. Clients require certain data; providers can provide the required data. However, clients and providers do not know each other a priori. Moreover, there may be multiple clients that require the same information. On the other hand, data from several providers may be needed in order to compute data required by one client. This results in a many-to-many relation between clients and providers. In order to associate the clients and the providers to each other the mediator concept is introduced, which is an entity that can relate a number of clients to a number of providers, as illustrated in Figure 16. References to clients and providers are stored in mediators in order to avoid the need for modifying client or provider models.

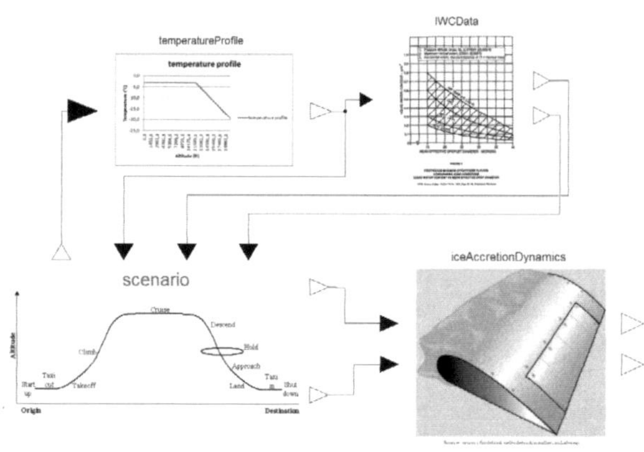

Figure 17. Assembled ice-accretion simulation based on [15]

After the bindings concept was introduced we can now turn to the description of the application case. Generally speaking, the application case is the automatic creation of connections between different model components in a model. Typically in modelling tools, to create a connection between one port of one component to another port of another component requires the user to draw each connection as one line from one port to the other port. If the components' interfaces or the model structure change, then all of the connections have to be checked and some of them have to be redrawn. If we consider a large set of models that have to be changed frequently or if we want to create the models dynamically, then the effort for creating and maintaining the connections between the components in the models becomes a serious issue. The goal of our application case is the formalization of the often implicit rules which the user applies to create the connections to automate this process.

Consider the model depicted by Figure 17, which is a part of the model from the public aerospace use case in the CRYSTAL project [15]. It consists of component models such as flight scenario profile, ice accretion dynamics, and tables for temperature or liquid water content. All of the component models must be interconnected. For example, the temperature profile component requires the current aircraft altitude, which is provided by the flight scenario component; the ice accretions dynamics component requires the current aircraft speed, which is also provided by the scenario component, etc. The individual models were built using the Modelica tool Dymola and exported as Functional Mockup Units [16] (FMUs) in order to be integrated, i.e., instantiated and connected, in a co-simulation environment.

However, assume that the models were created without this specific context in mind. They neither have agreed interfaces, nor do the name and type of the component elements to be connected necessarily match. In order to be able to find the counter parts, i.e., to know that the input of the ice accretion instance should be connected to the appropriate output of the scenario model instance, a dedicated XML file captures some additional information. This way we can capture such interrelations without modifying the models. This data is used as follows: whenever the model "IceAccretionDynamics" is instantiated, bind its input port "aspeed" to the output "port p_v", which belongs to the instance of type "ScenarioMissionProfile1".

Whenever there will be another model that requires the same data, i.e., current aircraft speed, an additional client entry is added to the same mediator. Similarly, whenever there is another model that outputs this data, its corresponding element is referenced in a new provider entry. This approach in particular pays off as soon as there are several models that require or provide the same data. Their connection is then resolved whenever they are instantiated in a specific context model such as the one depicted in Figure 17.

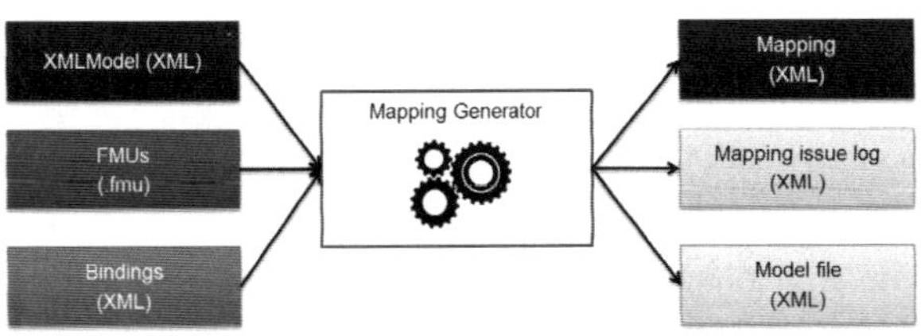

Figure 18. Mapping generator for simulation model composition

In our setting, the bindings specification XML file and the model XML file are application specific sources that are inputs to our generic mapping framework as depicted by Figure 18. The information read from these sources by the application specific parsers is put into the core module mappable database. Two rules are used to query the mappable database to find suitable matches for each mappable. The matching results are then given to the resolver module. This module is aware of the bindings concept and is able to resolve chains of matches and generate a binding for each client and, if necessary, involve the user when an unambiguous mapping is not possible automatically.

In the end, the mapping framework uses a list of FMUs, a description of the simulation model consisting of instances of classes implemented in the FMUs and a description of the bindings in the form of an XML file. The output is then the complete simulation model with all the connections between the simulation instances as sketched by Figure 19.

The evaluation of GEMMA in the simulation model composition application case was considered successful regarding all four evaluation criteria.

B. Test bench setup

The test bench setup application case is driven by the needs of test engineers. They are given a hardware System under Test (SuT), a formal definition of the interfaces of the SuT and other equipment and a description of the specified logic of the SuT, which should be tested. Unfortunately, the formal interface definition has been finalized after the specification of the logic, which means that the signal names in the logic description and the signal names in the formal interface definition, which has been implemented in the SuT, do not match. Today, a significant amount of manual effort is required to discover the correct formal signal name for every logical signal. To ease this, GEMMA has been configured as shown in Figure 20.

The goal of the application case is to find a mapping between the name of a signal used in the description of the SuT logic and the corresponding formal interface signal name as shown in Figure 21.

Since the names of the signals could be quite different, the test bench setup application case required the use of the structured rewriting rule type (see Section III-F). One of the rules for the test bench setup is depicted by Figure 22 in pseudo code. The rule defines a new local variable called *soughtName* whose content depends on some attributes of the mappable (enclosed in $$) and instead of searching for other mappables that have the same or a similar name as the original mappable, GEMMA searches now for mappables whose name is equal to the variable *soughtName*. If a mappable has the attributes *direction*, *type*, *BLOCKID* and *ID* with the respective values OUTPUT, SuT_Type1, 45 and 67 then *soughtName* would take the value *AB_BLOCK45_STATUS_67* and GEMMA will search for and map to another mappable in the database with that name.

The main challenge for this application case was the amount of data. Even for a small SuT, the mappable database contained 350000 mappables and matches had to be found for 2500 mappables. Nevertheless, the application proved to be successful. The total run time is around 30 seconds including the time for data import and export, and the average time per query is 4.5 ms on a standard PC.

The evaluation of GEMMA in the test bench setup application case was considered successful regarding all four evaluation criteria.

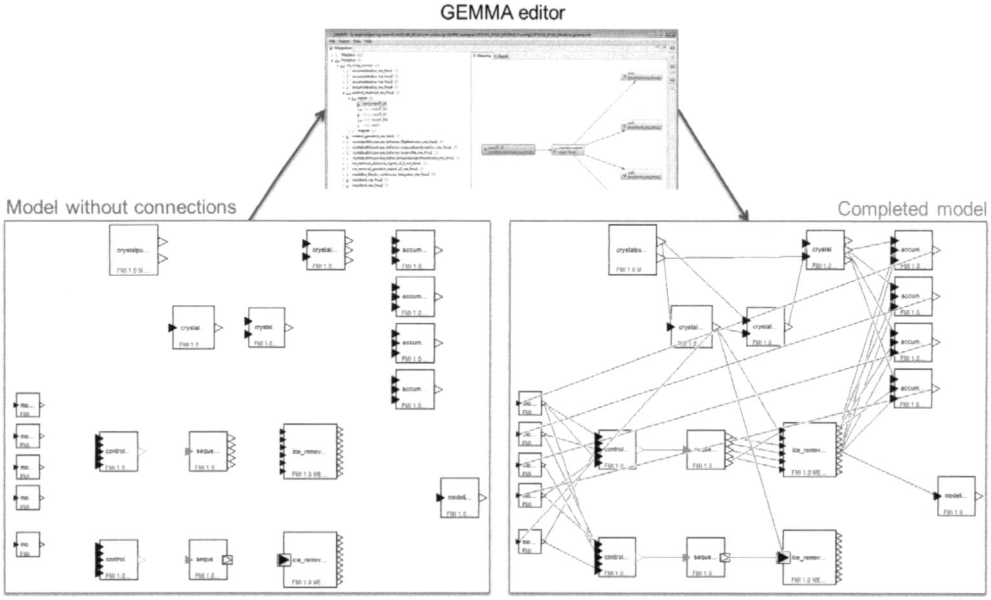

Figure 19. Input and output artefacts of simulation model composition mapper)

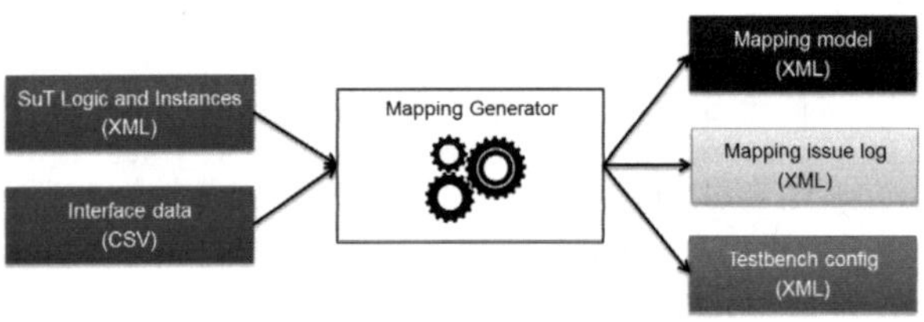

Figure 20. Mapping generator for test bench setup

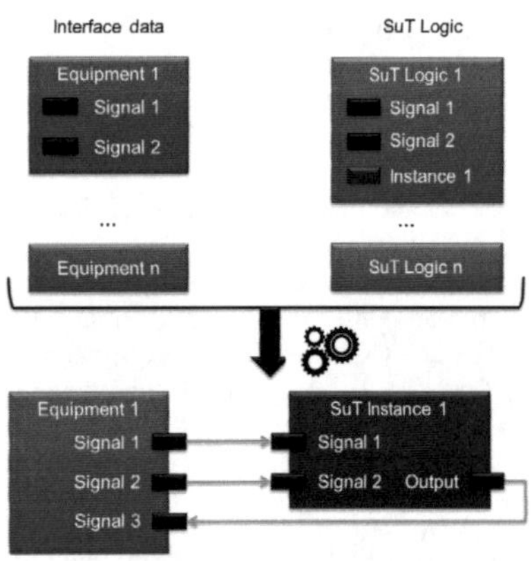

Figure 21. Input and output artifacts of test bench setup mapper

V. Conclusion

In this paper, we introduce a new framework for generic mapping problems, GEMMA. It is geared towards high flexibility for dealing with a number of very different challenges. To this end it has an open architecture that allows the inclusion of application-specific code for reading and exporting data and the resolving of mapping results. Furthermore, it provides a generic rule-based mapping engine that allows users without programming knowledge to define their own mapping rules. So far, the evaluation in the two application cases described in this paper has been highly successful.

The modular architecture based on the Eclipse RCP proved to be especially useful to allow using GEMMA for different purposes. The effort for adapting GEMMA for new applications, i.e., mainly the development of custom parser, resolver and exporter modules is low compared and usually takes a couple of days for an experienced Java developer. This is quite low compared to the effort required for the development of a new application that could satisfy the user needs.

As said in Section II, as far as we know, there is currently no other tool with the same functionality as GEMMA. This prevents a direct comparison in terms of performance of GEMMA with other solutions. For our future work we also plan to compare GEMMA functionally to other solutions that rely on more formalized semantic information in the form of ontologies. Depending on the results of this comparison, this might lead to an extension of GEMMA, so that in addition to the matching based on the Lucene text database there will be the possibility to include the results from a semantic reasoner in the matching process. Another possible extension of GEMMA that we are currently investigating is the inclusion of machine learning technology into GEMMA. Machine Learning could potentially be used to learn from existing mappings and to create or propose to the user new mappings based on that knowledge.

At the same time, we are actively looking for further application cases to mature the framework.

```
foreach SuTLogicInstance:instance
 foreach Mappable:mappable
  if mappable.detail(DIRECTION) == INPUT
   Search Mappable:otherMappables
     with mappable.detail(NAME) == otherMappable.detail(NAME)
   Create mapping from mappable to otherMappables
   elseif mappable.detail(direction) == OUTPUT
    if instance.detail(type) == SuT_Type1
     soughtName = "AB_BLOCK$$mappable.detail(BLOCKID)$$_STATUS_$$mappable.detail(ID)$$"
    elseif instance.detail(type) == SuT_Type2
     soughtName = "BLOCK$$mappable.detail(BLOCKID)$$_STATUS_$$mappable.detail(ID)$$_CD"
    endif
    Search Mappable:otherMappables
     with mappable.detail(NAME) == soughtName
    Create mapping from mappable to otherMappables
  endif
 endfor
endfor
```

Figure 22. One implemented rule for test bench setup (in pseudo code)

REFERENCES

[1] P. Helle and W. Schamai, "Using a generic modular mapping framework for simulation model composition," in SIMUL 2015, The Seventh International Conference on Advances in System Simulation, 2015, pp. 72–78.

[2] H. L. Dunn, "Record linkage*," American Journal of Public Health and the Nations Health, vol. 36, no. 12, 1946, pp. 1412–1416.

[3] I. P. Fellegi and A. B. Sunter, "A theory for record linkage," Journal of the American Statistical Association, vol. 64, no. 328, 1969, pp. 1183–1210.

[4] Q. He, Z. Li, and X. Zhang, "Data deduplication techniques," in Future Information Technology and Management Engineering (FITME), 2010 International Conference on, vol. 1. IEEE, 2010, pp. 430–433.

[5] H. Koepcke and E. Rahm, "Frameworks for entity matching: A comparison," Data & Knowledge Engineering, vol. 69, no. 2, 2010, pp. 197 – 210.

[6] A. K. Elmagarmid, P. G. Ipeirotis, and V. S. Verykios, "Duplicate record detection: A survey," Knowledge and Data Engineering, IEEE Transactions on, vol. 19, no. 1, 2007, pp. 1–16.

[7] F. Giunchiglia, A. Autayeu, and J. Pane, "S-match: An open source framework for matching lightweight ontologies," Semantic Web, vol. 3, no. 3, 2012, pp. 307–317.

[8] Y. Hooi, M. Hassan, and A. Shariff, "A survey on ontology mapping techniques," in Advances in Computer Science and its Applications, ser. Lecture Notes in Electrical Engineering, H. Y. Jeong, M. S. Obaidat, N. Y. Yen, and J. J. J. H. Park, Eds. Springer Berlin Heidelberg, 2014, vol. 279, pp. 829–836.

[9] P. A. Hall and G. R. Dowling, "Approximate string matching," ACM computing surveys (CSUR), vol. 12, no. 4, 1980, pp. 381–402.

[10] V. I. Levenshtein, "Binary codes capable of correcting deletions, insertions, and reversals," in Soviet physics doklady, vol. 10, no. 8, 1966, pp. 707–710.

[11] W. Schamai, P. Fritzson, C. J. Paredis, and P. Helle, "ModelicaML value bindings for automated model composition," in Proceedings of the 2012 Symposium on Theory of Modeling and Simulation-DEVS Integrative M&S Symposium. Society for Computer Simulation International, 2012, p. 31.

[12] M. McCandless, E. Hatcher, and O. Gospodnetic, Lucene in Action. Manning Publications Co., 2010.

[13] J. McAffer, J.-M. Lemieux, and C. Aniszczyk, Eclipse Rich Client Platform. Addison-Wesley Professional, 2010.

[14] R. Hall, K. Pauls, S. McCulloch, and D. Savage, OSGi in action: Creating modular applications in Java. Manning Publications Co., 2011.

[15] A. Mitschke et al., "CRYSTAL public aerospace use case Development Report - V2," ARTEMIS EU CRYSTAL project, Tech. Rep. D208.902, 2015.

[16] T. Blochwitz et al., "The functional mockup interface for tool independent exchange of simulation models," in 8th International Modelica Conference, Dresden, 2011, pp. 20–22.

Falsification of Java Assertions Using Automatic Test-Case Generators

Rafael Caballero Manuel Montenegro
Universidad Complutense, Facultad de Informática
Madrid, Spain
email: {rafacr,mmontene}@ucm.es

Herbert Kuchen Vincent von Hof
University of Münster, ERCIS, Münster, Germany
email: {kuchen,vincent.von.hof}@wi.uni-muenster.de

***Abstract*—We present a technique for the static generation of test-cases falsifying Java assertions. Our framework receives as input a Java program including assertions and instruments the code in order to detect whether the assertion conditions are met by every direct and indirect method call within a certain depth level. Then, any automated test-case generator can be used to look for input examples that falsify the conditions. The transformation ensures that the value obtained for the test-case inputs represents a path of method calls that ends with a violation of some assertion. Our technique deals with Java features such as object encapsulation and inheritance, and can be seen has a compromise between the usual but too late detection of an assertion violation at runtime and an often too expensive complete analysis based on a model checker.**

Keywords–assertion; automatic test-case generation; program transformation; inheritance.

I. INTRODUCTION

The goal of this paper is to present a source-to-source program transformation useful for the static generation of test-cases falsifying Java assertions. In a previous paper [1], we addressed the same goal with a simpler approach which, however, could lead to a combinatorial explosion in the generated program. In this paper, we overcome this problem by introducing a data type containing the aforementioned path of method calls in case of assertion violation.

Using assertions is nowadays a common programming practice and especially in the case of what is known as 'programming by contract' [2], [3], where they can be used, e.g., to formulate pre- and postconditions of methods as well as invariants of loops. Assertions in Java [4] are used for finding errors in an implementation at run-time during the test-phase of the development phase. If the condition in an `assert` statement is evaluated to false during program execution, an *AssertionException* is thrown.

During the same phase, testers often use automated test-case generators to obtain test suites that help to find errors in the program. The goal of our work is to use these same automated test-case generators for detecting assertion violations. However, finding an input for a method $m()$ that falsifies some assertion in the body of $m()$ is not enough. For instance, in the case of preconditions it is important to observe whether the methods calling $m()$ ensure that the call arguments satisfy the precondition, which is the source of the assertion falsification can be an *indirect* call (if in the body of method m_1 there is a call to m_2, then we say that m_1 *calls* m_2 *directly*. When m_2 calls m_3 directly and m_1 calls m_2 directly or indirectly, we say that m_1 *calls* m_3 *indirectly*). Our technique considers indirect calls up to a fixed level of indirection, allowing checking the assertions in the context of the whole program.

In order to fulfill these goals we propose a technique based on a source-to-source transformation that converts the assertions into `if` statements and changes the return type of methods to represent the path of calls leading to an assertion violation as well as the normal results of the original program. Converting the assertions into a program control-flow statement is very useful for white-box, path-oriented test-case generators, which determine the program paths leading to some selected statement and then generate input data to traverse such a path (see [5] for a recent survey on the different types of test-case generators). Thus, our transformation allows this kind of generators to include the assertion conditions into the sets of paths to be covered.

The next section discusses related approaches. Section III presents a running example and introduces some basic concepts. Section IV presents the program transformation, while Section V sketches a possible solution to the problem of inheritance. Section VI shows by means of experiments how two existing white-box, path-oriented test-case generators benefit from this transformation. Finally, Section VII presents our conclusions.

II. RELATED WORK

The most common technique for checking program assertions is model-checking [6]. It is worth observing that, in contrast to model checking, automated test-case generators are not complete and thus our proposal may miss possible assertion violations. However, our experiments show that the technique described in this paper performs quite well in practice and is helpful either in situations where model checking cannot be applied, or as a first approach during program development before using model checking [7]. The overhead of an automated test-case generator is smaller than for full model checking, since data and/or control coverage criteria known from testing are used as a heuristic to reduce the search space.

The origins of our idea can be traced back to the work [8], which has given rise to the so called *assertion-based software testing* technique. In particular, this work can be included in what has been called *testability transformation* [9], which aims to improve the ability of a given test generation method to generate test cases for the original program. An important difference of our proposal with respect to other works such as [10] is that instead of developing a specific test-case generator we propose a simple transformation that allows general purpose test-case generators to look for input data invalidating assertions.

In [1], we took another transformation-based approach to assertion falsification, in which methods containing assertions were transformed to return a boolean value indicating whether an assertion is violated. In the case of a method with several assertions, the transformation generates as many boolean methods as constraints exist in the corresponding method's body, so each method reports the violation of its corresponding assertion. If we want to catch assertion violations obtained through a given sequence of method calls, the transformation shown in [1] generates as many methods as sequences of method calls up to a maximum level of indirection given by the user. However, this could cause an exponential growth in the number of generated methods w.r.t. the indirection level. In this paper, we overcome this problem by defining a type that contains the path leading to an assertion violation, so the test case generator can report assertion violations through different paths by using a single transformed method. An extended abstract of this approach can be found in [11].

III. Conditions, Assertions, and Automated Test-Case Generation

Java assertions allow the programmer to ensure that the program, if executed with the right options, fulfils certain restrictions at runtime. They can be used to formulate, e.g., preconditions and postconditions of methods and invariants of loops. As an example, let us consider the code in Figs. 1 and 2, which introduces two Java classes:

- `Sqrt` includes a method `sqrt` that computes the square root based on Newton's algorithm. The method uses an assertion, which ensures that the computation makes progress. However, the method contains an error: the statement `a1 = a+r/a/2.0;` should be `a1 = (a+r/a)/2.0;`. This error provokes a violation of the assertion for any input value different from 0.0.
- `Circle` represents a circle with its radius as only attribute. The constructor specifies that the radius must be nonnegative. There is also a static method `Circle.ofArea` for building a `Circle` given its area. Besides checking whether the area is nonnegative, this method calls `Sqrt.sqrt` to compute a square root in order to obtain the radius.

Thus, `Circle.ofArea` will raise an assertion exception if the area is negative, but it may also raise an exception even when the area is nonnegative, due to the aforementioned error in `Sqrt.sqrt`.

```
public class Circle {
  private double radius;

  public Circle(double radius) {
    assert radius >= 0;
    this.radius = radius;
  }

  public double getRadius() {
    return radius;
  }

  public static Circle ofArea(double area) {
    assert area >= 0;
    return new Circle(
          Sqrt.sqrt(area / Math.PI)
       );
  }
}
```

Figure 1: Class `Circle`.

Our idea is to use a test-case generator to detect possible violations of these assertions. A test-case generator is typically based on some heuristic, which reduces its search space dramatically. Often it tries to achieve a high coverage of the control and/or data flow. In the `sqrt` example in Fig. 2, the tool would try to find test cases covering all edges in the control-flow graph and all so-called def-use chains, i.e., pairs of program locations, where a value is defined and where this value is used. E.g., in method `sqrt` the def-use chains for variable `a1` are (ignoring the assertion) the following pairs of line numbers: (5,8), (9,11), (9,8), and (9,13).

There are mainly two approaches to test-case generation [5]. One approach is to generate test inputs metaheuristically, i.e., search-based with hill climbing or genetic algorithms, which often involve randomizing components (see [12] for an overview). Another approach is to symbolically execute the code (see, e.g., [13], [14], [15]). Inputs are handled as logic variables and at each branching of the control flow, a constraint is added to some constraint store. A solution of the accumulated constraints corresponds to a test case leading to the considered path through the code. Backtracking is often applied in order to consider alternative paths through the code. Some test-case generators offer hybrid approaches combining search-based techniques and symbolic computation, e.g., EvoSuite [16], CUTE [17], and DART [18].

EvoSuite generates test-cases also for code with `assert` conditions. However, its search-based approach does not always generate test cases exposing assertion violations. In particular, it has difficulties with indirect calls such as the assertion in `Sqrt.sqrt` after a call from `Circle.ofArea`. A reason is that EvoSuite does not model the call stack. Thus, the test-cases generated by EvoSuite for `Circle.ofArea` only expose one of the two possible violations, namely the one related to a negative area.

```
public class Sqrt {
  public static final double eps = 0.00001;

  public double sqrt(double r) {
    double a, a1 = r + eps;

    do {
      a = a1;
      a1 = a+r/a/2.0; //erroneous!
      assert a == 1.0 || (a1 > 1.0 ? a1 < a : a1 > a);
    } while (Math.abs(a - a1) >= eps);

    return a1;
  }
}
```

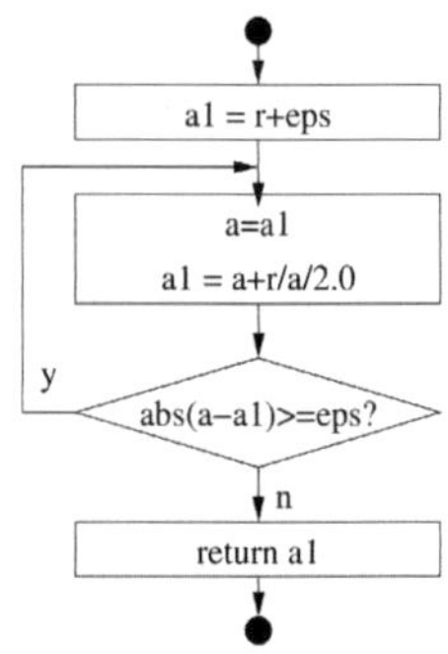

Figure 2: Java method `sqrt` and its corresponding control-flow graph.

There are other test-data generators such as JPet [19] that do not consider `assert` statements and thus cannot generate test-cases for them. In the sequel, we present the program transformation that allows both EvoSuite and JPet to detect both possible assertion violations.

IV. Program Transformation

We start defining the subset of Java considered in this work. Then, we shall define an auxiliary transformation step that *flattens* the input program, so it can be subsequently handled by the main transformation algorithm.

A. Java Syntax

In order to simplify this presentation we limit ourselves to the subset of Java defined in Table I. This subset is inspired by the work of [20]. Symbols e, e_1, ..., indicate arbitrary expressions, b, b_1 ..., indicate blocks, and s, s_1, ..., indicate statements. Observe that we assume that variable declarations are introduced at the beginning of blocks, although for simplicity we often omit the block delimiters '{' and '}'. A Java method is defined by its name, a sequence of arguments with their types, a result type, and a body defined by a block. The table also indicates whether the construction is considered an expression and/or a statement.

The table shows that some expression e can contain subexpression e'. A position p in an expression e is represented by a sequence of natural numbers that identifies a subexpression of e. The notation $e_{|p}$ denotes the subexpression of e found at position p. For instance, given $e \equiv$ `(new C(4,5)).m(6,7)`, we have $e|_{1.2} =$ `(new C(4,5))`$_{|2} = 5$, since e is a method call, the position 1 stands for its first subexpression $e' \equiv$ `new C(4,5)` and the second subexpression of e' is 5. Given two positions p, p' of the same expression, we say the $p < p'$ if p is a prefix of p' or if $p <_{\text{LEX}} p'$ with $<_{\text{LEX}}$ the lexicographic order. For instance, $1 < 1.2 < 2 < 2.1$ (1 prefix of 1.2, $1.2 <_{\text{LEX}} 2$, and 2 prefix of 2.1).

Last statement in `ofArea` method, in which the leftmost innermost call is underlined:

```
return new
    Circle(Sqrt.sqrt(area / Math.PI));
```

After extracting the `Sqrt.sqrt` call:

```
double sqrtResult;
sqrtResult = Sqrt.sqrt(area / Math.PI);
return new Circle(sqrtResult);
```

After extracting the constructor call:

```
double sqrtResult;
sqrtResult = Sqrt.sqrt(area / Math.PI);
Circle circleResult;
circleResult = new Circle(sqrtResult);
return circleResult;
```

Figure 3: Flattening an expression.

For the sake of simplicity we consider the application of a constructor (via the `new` operator) as a method call. A method call that does not include properly another method call as subexpression is called *innermost*. Let e be an expression and $e' = e_{|p}$ an innermost method call. Then, e' is called *leftmost* if every innermost method call $e'' = e_{|p'}$, with $p \neq p'$ verifies $p < p'$.

In the statement example in Fig. 3 the underlined expression is a leftmost innermost method call. The idea behind this concept is that a leftmost innermost expression can be evaluated in advance because it is not part of another method call and it does not depend on other method calls of the same expression due to the Java evaluation order.

TABLE I: Java subset.

Description	Syntax	Expr.	Stat.
creation of new objects	`new C(`e_1`, ...,`e_n`)`	yes	no
casting	`(C) e`	yes	no
literal values	k	yes	no
binary operation	e_1 `op` e_2	yes	no
variable access	`varName`	yes	no
attribute access	`e.x`	yes	no
method call	`e.M(`e_1`, ...,`e_n`)`	yes(*)	yes(**)
variable assignment	`vaName = e`	no	yes
attribute assignment	`e.x = e`	no	yes
conditional statements	`if(e)` b_1 `else` b_2	no	yes
while loop	`while(`e_1`) b`	no	yes
catching blocks	`try` b_1 `catch(C V)` b_2	no	yes
return statements	`return e`	no	yes
assertions	`assert e`	no	yes
block	`{`s_1`; ...; `s_n`;}`	no	yes
block with local variable declaration	`{T V; `s_1`; ...; `s_n`}`	no	yes

(*) Method calls are expressions if their return type is different from `void`
(**) Method calls are statements if they are not contained in another expression

The *minimal statement* of an expression e is a statement s that contains e and there is no statement s' such that s contains s' and s' contains e.

Observe that in Table I neither variable nor field assignments are allowed as part of expressions. This corresponds to the following assumption:

Assumption 1: All the assignments in the program are statements.

Using assignments as part of expressions is usually considered a bad programming practice, as the evaluation of those expressions introduces side effects, namely the modification the variables in scope. Anyway, it is possible to eliminate these expressions by introducing auxiliary variables. For instance, given the following program:

```
int sum = 0;
int x;
while ((x = next()) != -1) {
  sum += x;
}
```

The subexpression `x = next()` can be factored out as follows:

```
int sum = 0;
int x;
x = next();
while (x != -1) {
  sum += x;
  x = next();
}
```

We omit the corresponding transformation for the sake of simplicity.

B. Flattening

Before applying the transformation, the Java program needs to be *flattened*. The idea of this step is to extract each nested method call and assign its result to a new variable without affecting the Java evaluation order.

Algorithm 1 (Flattening expressions): Let B be the body of a method and let $e \equiv o.M(es)$ be an expression in B such that:

1) e is a leftmost-innermost method call, and M is a user defined method
2) e is not the right-hand side of a variable assignment
3) e is not a statement

Let T be the type of e. Finally, let s be the minimal statement associated with e and let V be a new variable name. Then, the following case distinction applies:

1) s is a `while` statement, that is $s \equiv$`while(`e_1`)` $\{e_2\}$. In this case e is a subexpression of e_1, and the flattening of e is obtained replacing s by:

```
{
  T V;
  V = e;
  while (e1[e ↦ V]) {
    e2;
    V = e;
  }
}
```

where the notation $e_1[e \mapsto V]$ stands for the replacement of e by V in e_1.

2) s is not a `while` statement.
Then, the flattening of s is defined as

```
{
  T V;
  V = e;
  s[e ↦ V];
}
```

This process is repeated recursively, until no method call needs to be transformed. Then, the program obtained is called the flattened version of P and is represented by P^F in the rest of the paper. The second part of Fig. 3 shows the flattening of the last statement of the function `Circle.ofArea` in our running example.

C. Program Transformation

The idea of the following program transformation is to instrument the code in order to obtain special output values that represent possible violations of assertion conditions.

In our case, the instrumented methods employ the class `MayBe<T>` of Fig. 5. The overall idea is that a method returning a value of type `T` in the original code returns a value of type `MayBe<T>` in the instrumented code. `MayBe<T>` is in fact an abstract class with two subclasses, `Value<T>` and `CondError<T>` (Fig. 4). `Value<T>` represents a value with the same type as in the original code, and it is used via method `MayBe.createValue` whenever no assertion violation has been found. If an assertion condition is not satisfied, a `CondError<T>` value is returned. There are two possibilities:

- The assertion is in the same method. Suppose it is the i-th assertion in the body of the method following the textual order. In this case, the method returns `MayBe.generateError(name, i);` with `name` the method name. The purpose of method `generateError` is to create a new `CondError<T>` object. Observe that the constructor of `CondError<T>` receives as parameter a `Call` object. This object represents the point where a condition is not verified, and it is defined by the parameters already mentioned: the name of the method, and the position i.
- The method detects that an assertion violation has occurred indirectly through the i-th method call in its body. Then, the method needs to extend the call path and propagate the error. This is done using a call `propagateError(name, i, error)`, where `error` is the value to propagate. In Fig. 4 we can observe that the corresponding constructor of `CondError<T>` adds the new call to the path, represented in our implementation by a list.

The transformation takes as parameters a program P and a parameter not discussed so far: the *level* of the transformation.

```
public static class Value<T>
              extends MayBe<T> {
  private T value;

  public Value(T value) {
    this.value = value;
  }

  @Override
  public boolean isValue() {
    return true;
  }

  @Override
  public T getValue() {
    return value;
  }
}

public static class CondError<T>
              extends MayBe<T> {
  private List<Call> callStack;

  public CondError(Call newElement) {
    this.callStack = new ArrayList<Call>();
    this.callStack.add(newElement);
  }

  public <S> CondError(Call newElement,
                       CondError<S> other) {
    this.callStack =
      new ArrayList<Call>(other.callStack);
    this.callStack.add(newElement);
  }

  public List<Call> getCallStack() {
    return callStack;
  }

  @Override
  public boolean isValue() {
    return false;
  }

  @Override
  public T getValue() {
    return null;
  }
}
```

Figure 4: Classes `Value<T>` and `CondError<T>`.

```
public abstract class MayBe<T> {

  public static class Value<T> extends MayBe<T> {//→ Fig. 4}

  public static class CondError<T> extends MayBe<T> {//→ Fig. 4}

  // did the method return a normal value (no violation)?
  abstract public boolean isValue();

  // value returned by the method.
  abstract public T getValue();

  // called if no condition violation detected. Return same value as before the instrumentation.
  public static <K> MayBe<K> createValue(K value) {
    return new Value<K>(value);
  }

  // called if an assert condition is not verified.
  public static <T> MayBe<T> generateError(String method, int position) {
    return new CondError<T>(new Call(method, position));
  }

  // calls another method whose assertion is not satisfied.
  public static <T,S> MayBe<T> propagateError(String method, int position, MayBe<S> error){
    return new CondError<T>(new Call(method, position), (CondError<S>) error);
  }
}
```

Figure 5: Class MayBe<T>: New result type for instrumented methods.

This parameter is determined by the user and indicates the maximum *depth* of the instrumentation. If $level = 0$ then only the methods including assertions are instrumented. This means that the tests will be obtained independently of the method calls performed in the rest of the program. If $level = 1$, then all the methods that include a call to a method with assertions are also instrumented, checking if there is an indirect condition violation and thus a propagation of the error is required. Greater values for $level$ enable more levels of indirection, and thus allow to find errors occurring in a more specific program context.

The algorithm can be summarized as follows:

Algorithm 2:

Input: P, a Java Program verifying Assumption 1 (all the assignments in the program are statements), and an integer $level \geq 0$.

Output: a transformed program P^T

1) Flatten P delivering P^F as explained in Section IV-B.
2) Make a copy of each of the methods to instrument by replacing the result type by MayBe, as described in Algorithm 3. Call the new program P^C.
3) Replace assertions in P^C by new code that generates an error if the assertion condition is not met, as explained in Algorithm 4. This produces a new program P_0 and a list of methods L_0.
4) For $k = 1$ to $level$: apply Algorithm 5 to P, P_{k-1}, and L_{k-1}. Call the resulting program P_k and list L_k, respectively.
5) Apply your favourite automatic test-data generator to obtain test cases for the methods in L_{level} with respect to P_{level}. Look for the test cases that produce CondError values. Executing the test case with respect to the original program P produces an assertion violation and thus the associated exception displays the trace of method calls that lead to the error, which correponds to the path contained within the CondError object.

Now we need to introduce algorithms 3, 4, and 5.

We assume as convention that it is possible to generate a new method name M' and a new attribute name M^A given a method name M. Moreover, we assume that the mapping between 'old' and 'new' names is one-to-one, which allows to extract name M both from M' and from M^A.

Algorithm 3:

Input: flat Java program P^F verifying Assumption 1.

Output: transformed program P^{Copy} with copies of the methods.

1) Let $P^{Copy} := P^F$.
2) For each method (not constructor) $C.M$ in P^F with result type T:
   a) Include in class C of P^{Copy} a new method $C.M'$ with the same body and arguments as $C.M$, but with return type MayBe<T>

b) Replace each statement

```
return e;
```

in the body of $C.M$ by

```
return MayBe.createValue(e);
```

3) For each constructor $C.M$ in P^F:

a) Include in the definition of class C of program P^{Copy} a new static attribute M^A:

```
static MayBe<C> M^A;
```

b) Create a new method $C.M'$ as a copy of $C.M$ with the same arguments `args` as the definition of $C.M$, but with return type `MayBe<C>` and body:

```
MayBe<C> result=null;
M^A = null;
C constResult = new C(args);

// if no assertion has
// been falsified
if (M^A != null)
  result = M^A;
else
  result =
    MayBe.createValue(constResult);
return result;
```

Algorithm 3 copies the class methods, generating new methods M' for checking the assertions. This is done because we prefer to modify a copy of the method in order to ensure that the change does not affect the rest of the program. Method M' returns the same value as M wrapped by a `MayBe` object.

Observe that in the case of constructors we cannot modify the output type because it is implicit. Instead, we include a new attribute M^A, used by the constructor, to communicate any violation of an assertion. The new method is a wrapper that calls the constructor, which will have been transformed in order to assign a non-null value to M^A in case of an assertion violation (see Algorithm 4). Then, the method checks whether there has been an assertion violation in the constructor (that is whether M^A `!= null` holds) and returns the new value as output result. If, on the contrary, M^A is `null` then no assertion violation has taken place in the constructor and the newly built object is returned wrapped by a `MayBe` object.

In our running example, assume we want to instrument the methods `Sqrt.sqrt`, `Circle.ofArea`, and the constructor of `Circle`. A copy of each of these methods would be generated by Algorithm 3. The new fields and methods are shown in Figure 6. Notice that the condition `circleM != null` in `CircleCopy` will never hold, since the current `Circle` constructor does not alter the `circleM` variable. We will change the code of the `Circle` constructor in the following algorithms.

Inside `Sqrt` class:

```
public MayBe<Double> sqrtCopy(double value) {
   ... // same body as sqrt except the last
   ... // return statement
   return Maybe.createValue(a1);
}
```

Inside `Circle` class:

```
private static MayBe<Circle> circleM;

public MayBe<Circle> CircleCopy(double radius)
{
  MayBe<Circle> result = null;
  circleM = null;
  Circle constResult = new Circle(radius);

  if (circleM != null) {
    result = circleM;
  } else {
    result = Maybe.createValue(constResult);
  }
  return result;
}

public static MayBe<Circle> ofAreaCopy(double
    area) {
  assert area >= 0;
  double sqrtResult;
  sqrtResult = Sqrt.sqrt(area / Math.PI);
  Circle circleResult;
  circleResult = new Circle(sqrtResult);
  return MayBe.createValue(circleResult);
}
```

Figure 6: New methods and fields generated after duplication.

The next step or the transformation handles `assert` violations in the body of methods:

Algorithm 4:

Input: P^{Copy} obtained from the previous algorithm.

Output: – P_0, a transformed program

– L_0, a list of methods in the transformed program

1) Let $P_0 := P^{Copy}$, $L_0 := [\,]$
2) For each method $C.M$ containing an assertion:

a) Let $L_0 := [C.M'|L_0]$, being M' the new method name obtained from M.

b) If $C.M$ is a method with return type T, not a constructor, replace in $C.M'$ each statement `assert exp;` by:

```
if (!exp) return
    MayBe.generateError("C.M", i);
```

with i the ordinal of the assertion counting the assertions in the method body in textual order.

c) If $C.M$ is a constructor, replace in $C.M$ each statement `assert exp;` by:

```
if (!exp) M^A =
    MayBe.generateError("C.M", i);
```

with i as in the case of a non-constructor.

In our running example, we get L_0 = [`Sqrt.sqrtCopy`, `Circle.CircleCopy`, `Circle.ofAreaCopy`], which are the new names introduced by our transformation for the methods with assertions. In `Sqrt.sqrtCopy` the `assert` statement would be replaced by the following,

```
...
if (!(a == 1.0 ||
      (a1 > 1.0 ? a1 < a : a1 > a)))
   return MayBe.generateError("sqrt", 1);
...
```

whereas in `Circle` the transformation would affect the constructor and the `ofAreaCopy` method:

```
public Circle(double radius) {
  if (!(radius >= 0)) {
    circleM = MayBe.generateError("Circle", 1);
    return;
  }
  this.radius = radius;
}

public static MayBe<Circle> ofAreaCopy(double
    area) {
  if (!(area >= 0))
    return MayBe.generateError("ofArea", 1);
  ...
}
```

Finally, the last transformation focuses on indirect calls. The input list L contains the names of all the new methods already included in the program. If L contains a method call $C.M'$, then the algorithm looks for methods $D.L$ that include calls of the form $C.M(args)$. The call is replaced by a call to $C.M'$ and the new value is returned. A technical detail is that in the new iteration we keep the input methods that have no more calls, although they do not reach the level of indirection required. The level must be understood as a maximum.

Algorithm 5:

Input: – P, a Java flat Program verifying Assumption 1

– P_{k-1}, the program obtained in the previous phase

– A list L_{k-1} of method names in P_{k-1}

Output: – P_k, a transformed program

– L_k, a list of methods in the P_k

1) Let $P_k := P_{k-1}$, $L_k := L_{k-1}$
2) For each method $D.L$ in P including a call $x = C.M$ with $C.M$ such that $C.M'$ is in L_{k-1}:
   a) Let i be the ordinal of the method call in the method body and y a new variable name'
   b) If $C.M'$ is in L_k, then remove it from L_k.
   c) Let $L_k := [D.L'|L_k]$
   d) If $D.L$ is a method of type T, not a constructor then replace in $D.M'$ the selected call to $x = C.M$ by:

```
MayBe<T> y = C.M';
if (!y.isValue()) return
  MayBe.propagateError("D.L", i, y);
x = y.getValue();
```

   e) If $D.L$ is a constructor, then let x' be a new variable name. Replace in the constructor $D.L$ the selected call to $x = C.M$ by:

```
MayBe<T> y = C.M';
if (!y.isValue()) M^A =
  MayBe.propagateError("D.L", i, y);
x = y.getValue();
```

   where M^A is the static variable associated to the constructor and introduced in Algorithm 3.

```
public class Sqrt {
  public static final double eps = 0.000001;

  public static double sqrt(double r) { ... }

  public static MayBe<Double> sqrtCopy(double
      r) {
    double a, a1 = 1.0;
    a = a1;
    a1 = a+r/a/2.0;
    double aux = Math.abs(a-a1);
    while (aux >= eps) {
      a = a1;
      a1 = a+r/a/2.0;
      if (!(a == 1.0 ||
            (a1 > 1.0 ? a1 < a : a1 > a)))
         return MayBe.generateError("sqrt", 1);
      aux = Math.abs(a - a1);
    }
    return MayBe.createValue(a1);
  }
}
```

Figure 7: `Sqrt` class after transformation.

In our example, we have $L_1 = L_0$ since the only indirect call to a method in L_0 is by means of `Circle.ofAreaCopy`, but the latter is already in the list. In fact, $L_k = L_0$ for every $k > 0$.

The transformation of our running example can be found in Figs. 7 and 8. It can be observed that in practice the methods not related directly nor indirectly to an assertion do not need to be modified. This is the case of the `getRadius` method.

```
public class Circle {
  private double radius;
  private static MayBe<Circle> circleM;

  public Circle(double radius) {
    if (!(radius >= 0)) {
      circleM =
        MayBe.generateError("Circle", 1);
      return;
    }
    this.radius = radius;
  }

  public MayBe<Circle> CircleCopy(double
      radius)
  {
    MayBe<Circle> result = null;
    circleM = null;
    Circle constResult = new Circle(radius);

    if (circleM != null) {
      result = circleM;
    } else {
      result = Maybe.createValue(constResult);
    }
    return result;
  }

  public double getRadius() {
    return radius;
  }

  public static Circle ofArea(double area) {
    ...
  }

  public static MayBe<Circle>
      ofAreaCopy(double area) {
    if (!(area >= 0))
      return MayBe.generateError("ofArea", 1);

    MayBe<Double> sqrtResultM;
    sqrtResultM = Sqrt.sqrtCopy(area /
        Math.PI);
    if (!sqrtResultM.isValue())
      return MayBe.propagateError("ofArea", 2,
          sqrtResultM);
    double sqrtResult = sqrtResultM.getValue();

    MayBe<Circle> circleResultM;
    circleResultM = CircleCopy(sqrtResult);
    if (!circleResultM.isValue()) {
      return MayBe.propagateError("ofArea", 3,
          circleResultM);
    }
    Circle circleResult =
        circleResultM.getValue();
    return MayBe.createValue(circleResult);
  }
}
```

Figure 8: `Circle` class after transformation.

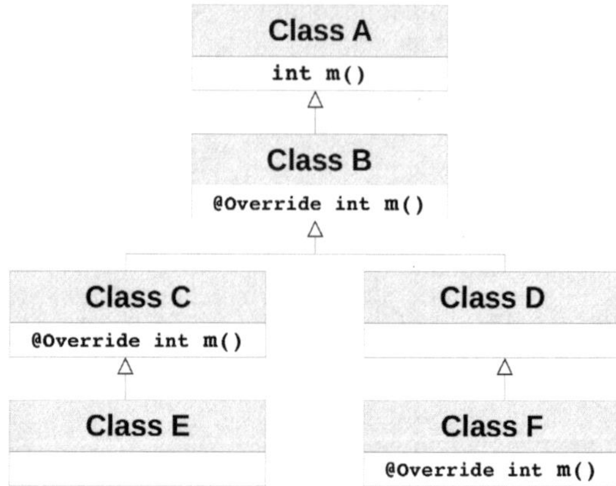

Figure 9: Inheritance example.

V. INHERITANCE

Inheritance poses a new interesting challenge to our proposal. Consider the hierarchy shown in Fig. 9, in which we assume that the implementation of `m()` in `B` contains an assertion, and hence, it is transformed according to Algorithm 4. If there are neither assertions nor calls to `B.m()` in the remaining classes of the hierarchy, it seems that there is no further transformations to apply. However, assume the following method:

```
public int foo(A a) {
  return a.m();
}
```

If we have the call `foo(new B(..))` then it becomes apparent that `foo()` can raise an assertion due to dynamic dispatching, because the call `a.m()` corresponds in this context to a call to `B.m()`. Thus, in order to detect this possible assertion violation, `foo()` needs to be transformed by introducing a `fooCopy()` method containing a call to `a.mCopy()` in its body. In turn, this implies that class `A` must contain a method `mCopy()` as well. Therefore, we create a method `mCopy()` in `A` with the following implementation:

```
public MayBe<Integer> mCopy() {
  return MayBe.createValue(m());
}
```

which wraps the result of `m()` into a `MayBe` value. This wrapper implementation must be replicated in classes `C` and `F` as well, since they also override `m()`.

In general, whenever we create a copy of a method $C.M$, we have to create a copy method with the wrapper implementation in the class where M is defined for the first time in the class hierarchy, and in each descendant C' of C overriding M unless there is another class between C and C' in the hierarchy which

TABLE II: Detecting assertion violations.

Method	Total	EvoSuite P	EvoSuite P^T	JPet P	JPet P^T
Circle.ofArea	2	1	2	0	2
BloodDonor.canGiveBlood	2	0	2	0	2
TestTree.insertAndFind	2	0	2	0	2
Kruskal	1	1	1	0	1
Numeric.foo	2	1	2	0	2
TestLibrary.test*	5	0	5	0	5
MergeSort.TestMergeSort	2	0	1	0	1
java.util.logging.*	5	0	2	-	-

also overrides M, or C' already has a copy M' of the method M (e.g., because $C'.M$ contains another assertion). In the example of Fig. 9, this means that we need to create additional `mCopy()` methods in classes `A`, `C`, and `F`.

An obvious limitation is when we introduce an assertion in methods defined in a library class such as `Object` (for instance, when overriding method `toString`), since we cannot introduce new methods in these classes. Fortunately, introducing assertions when overriding library methods is quite unusual. A possible improvement, still under development, is to look in advance for polymorphic calls. For instance, maybe method `foo()` is never called with arguments of type `C` in the program and there is no need of transforming this class.

VI. Experiments

We observed the effects of the transformation by means of experiments, including the running example shown above, the implementation of the binary tree data structure, Kruskal's algorithm, the computation of the mergesort method, a constructed example with nested if-statements called *Numeric*, an example representing a blood donation scenario *BloodDonor* and two bigger examples, namely a self devised *Library* system, which allows customers to lend and return books and the 6500 lines of code of the package java.util.logging of the Java Development Kit 6 (JDK). In all the cases, the transformation has been applied with level *infinite*, i.e., application of the transformation until a fixed point is reached. In the next step, we have evaluated the examples with different test-case generators with and without our `level=1` program transformation. We have developed a prototype that performs this transformation automatically. It can be found at https://github.com/wwu-ucm/assert-transformer, whereas the aforementioned examples can be found at https://github.com/wwu-ucm/examples.

We have used two test-case generators, JPet and EvoSuite, for exposing possible assertion violations. First of all, we can note that our approach works. In our experiments, all but one possible assertion violation could be detected. Moreover, we can note that our program transformation typically improves the detection rate, as can be seen in Table II. In this table, column *Total* displays for each example the number of possible assertion violations that can be raised for the method. Column P shows the number of detected assertion violations using the test-case generator and the original program, while column P^T displays the number of detected assertion violations after applying the transformation. For instance, in our running example, `Circle.getRadius` can raise the two assertion violations explained in Section III. Without the transformation, only one assertion violation is found by EvoSuite. With the transformation, EvoSuite correctly detects both assertion violations. For JPet no test cases are created for `java.util.logging`, since JPet does not support library method calls. Notice that JPet cannot find any assertion violation without our transformation, since it does not support assertions. Thus, our transformation is essential for tools, that do not support assertions, such as jPet. An improvement in the assertion violation detection rate is observed for all examples.

Additionally, tools that already support assertions to some degree benefit from our program transformation, since it makes the control flow more explicit than the usual assertion-violation exceptions. This helps the test-case generators to reach a higher coverage, as can be seen in Table III. The dashes in the JPet row indicate that JPet does not support assertions and hence cannot be used to detect assertion violations in the untransformed program. Our program transformation often only requires a few seconds and even for larger programs such as the JDK 6 logging package the transformation finishes in 18.2 seconds. The runtime of our analysis depends on the employed test-case generator and the considered example. It can range from a few seconds to several minutes.

VII. Conclusions

We have presented an approach to use test-case generators for exposing possible assertion violations in Java programs. Our approach is a compromise between the usual detection of assertion violations at runtime and the use of a full model checker. Since test-case generators are guided by heuristics such as control- and data-flow coverage, they have to consider a much smaller search space than a model checker and can hence deliver results much more quickly. If the coverage is high, the analysis is nevertheless quite accurate and useful in practice; in particular, in situations where a model checker would require too much time. We tried to use the model checker Java Pathfinder [21] to our examples, but we had to give up, since this tool was too time consuming or stopped because of a lack of memory.

Additionally, we have developed a program transformation that replaces assertions by computations, which explicitly propagate violation information through an ordinary computation involving nested method calls. The result of a computation is encapsulated in an object. The type of this object indicates whether the computation was successful or whether it caused an assertion violation. In case of a violation, our transformation makes the control flow more explicit than the usual assertion-violation exceptions. This helps the test-case generators to reach a higher coverage of the code and enables more assertion violations to be exposed and detected. Additionally, the transformation allows to use test-case generators such as JPet, which do not support assertions.

We have presented some experimental results demonstrating that our approach helps indeed to expose assertion violations

TABLE III: Control and data-flow coverage in percent.

	Binary Tree		Blood Donor		Kruskal		Library		MergeSort		Numeric		StdDev		Circle	
	P	P^T	P	P^T	P	P^T	P	P^T	P	P^T	P	P^T	P	P^T	P	P^T
EvoSuite	90	95	83	91	95	100	63	92	82	82	76	82	71	71	80	100
JPet	–	89	–	99	–	49	–	20	–	87	–	82	–	74	–	100

and that our program transformation improves the detection rate.

Although our approach accounts for the call path that leads to an assertion violation, this path is represented as a chain of object references, so some test case generators might not be able to recreate it in their generated tests. We are studying an alternative transformation that represents the call path in terms of basic Java data types. Another subject of future work is to use the information provided by a dependency graph of method calls in order to determine the maximum call depth level where the transformation can be applied.

ACKNOWLEDGMENT

This work has been supported by the German Academic Exchange Service (DAAD, 2014 Competitive call Ref. 57049954), the Spanish MINECO project CAVI-ART (TIN2013-44742-C4-3-R), Madrid regional project N-GREENS Software-CM (S2013/ICE-2731) and UCM grant GR3/14-910502.

REFERENCES

[1] R. Caballero, M. Montenegro, H. Kuchen, and V. von Hof, "Automatic falsification of Java assertions," in Proceedings of the 7th International Conference in Advances in System Testing and Validation Lifecycle (VALID 2015), T. Kanstren and B. Gersbeck-Schierholz, Eds. IARIA, 2015, pp. 36–41.

[2] B. Meyer, Object-oriented Software Construction (2Nd Ed.), 2nd ed. Upper Saddle River, NJ, USA: Prentice-Hall, Inc., 1997.

[3] R. Mitchell, J. McKim, and B. Meyer, Design by Contract, by Example. Redwood City, CA, USA: Addison Wesley Longman Publishing Co., Inc., 2002.

[4] Oracle, "Programming With Assertions," http://docs.oracle.com/javase/7/docs/technotes/guides/language/assert.html, Retrieved: 8 January 2017.

[5] S. Anand, E. Burke, T. Y. Chen, J. Clark, M. B. Cohen, W. Grieskamp, M. Harman, M. J. Harrold, and P. McMinn, "An orchestrated survey on automated software test case generation," Journal of Systems and Software, vol. 86, no. 8, August 2013, pp. 1978–2001.

[6] W. Visser, K. Havelund, G. Brat, S. Park, and F. Lerda, "Model checking programs," Automated Software Engineering, vol. 10, no. 2, 2003, pp. 203–232.

[7] M. Utting, A. Pretschner, and B. Legeard, "A taxonomy of model-based testing approaches," Softw. Test. Verif. Reliab., vol. 22, no. 5, Aug. 2012, pp. 297–312. [Online]. Available: http://dx.doi.org/10.1002/stvr.456

[8] B. Korel and A. M. Al-Yami, "Assertion-oriented automated test data generation," in Proceedings of the 18th International Conference on Software Engineering, ser. ICSE '96. Washington, DC, USA: IEEE Computer Society, 1996, pp. 71–80.

[9] M. Harman, A. Baresel, D. Binkley, R. Hierons, L. Hu, B. Korel, P. McMinn, and M. Roper, "Testability transformation program transformation to improve testability," in Formal Methods and Testing, ser. Lecture Notes in Computer Science, R. Hierons, J. Bowen, and M. Harman, Eds. Springer Berlin Heidelberg, 2008, vol. 4949, pp. 320–344.

[10] C. Boyapati, S. Khurshid, and D. Marinov, "Korat: Automated testing based on Java predicates," SIGSOFT Softw. Eng. Notes, vol. 27, no. 4, Jul. 2002, pp. 123–133.

[11] R. Caballero, M. Montenegro, H. Kuchen, and V. von Hof, "Checking java assertions using automated test-case generation," in Proceedings of the 25th International Symposium on Logic-Based Program Synthesis and Transformation (LOPSTR), ser. Lecture Notes in Computer Science, M. Falaschi, Ed., vol. 9527. Springer International Publishing, 2015, pp. 221–226.

[12] P. McQuinn, "Search-based software test data generation: A survey," Software Testing, Verification and Reliability, vol. 14, no. 2, 2004, pp. 105–156.

[13] J. C. King, "Symbolic execution and program testing," Commun. ACM, vol. 19, no. 7, 1976, pp. 385–394. [Online]. Available: http://doi.acm.org/10.1145/360248.360252

[14] M. Gómez-Zamalloa, E. Albert, and G. Puebla, "Test case generation for object-oriented imperative languages in CLP," TPLP, vol. 10, no. 4-6, 2010, pp. 659–674. [Online]. Available: http://dx.doi.org/10.1017/S1471068410000347

[15] M. Ernsting, T. A. Majchrzak, and H. Kuchen, "Dynamic solution of linear constraints for test case generation," in Sixth International Symposium on Theoretical Aspects of Software Engineering, TASE 2012, Beijing, China, 2012, pp. 271–274. [Online]. Available: http://dx.doi.org/10.1109/TASE.2012.39

[16] J. P. Galeotti, G. Fraser, and A. Arcuri, "Improving search-based test suite generation with dynamic symbolic execution," in IEEE International Symposium on Software Reliability Engineering (ISSRE). IEEE, 2013, pp. 360–369.

[17] K. Sen, D. Marinov, and G. Agha, "CUTE: A concolic unit testing engine for C," in Proceedings of the 10th European Software Engineering Conference, ser. ESEC/FSE-13. New York, NY, USA: ACM, 2005, pp. 263–272. [Online]. Available: http://doi.acm.org/10.1145/1081706.1081750

[18] P. Godefroid, N. Klarlund, and K. Sen, "DART: directed automated random testing," in Proceedings of the ACM SIGPLAN 2005 Conference on Programming Language Design and Implementation, Chicago, IL, USA, June 12-15, 2005, 2005, pp. 213–223. [Online]. Available: http://doi.acm.org/10.1145/1065010.1065036

[19] E. Albert, I. Cabanas, A. Flores-Montoya, M. Gómez-Zamalloa, and S. Gutierrez, "jPET: An automatic test-case generator for Java," in 18th Working Conference on Reverse Engineering, WCRE 2011, Limerick, Ireland, October 17-20, 2011, 2011, pp. 441–442.

[20] G. Klein and T. Nipkow, "A machine-checked model for a Java-like language, virtual machine and compiler," vol. 28, no. 4, 2006, pp. 619–695.

[21] W. Visser, K. Havelund, G. P. Brat, S. Park, and F. Lerda, "Model checking programs," Autom. Softw. Eng., vol. 10, no. 2, 2003, pp. 203–232. [Online]. Available: http://dx.doi.org/10.1023/A:1022920129859

Evaluation of Some Validation Measures for Gaussian Process Emulation: a Case Study with an Agent-Based Model

Wim De Mulder
and Geert Molenberghs
and Geert Verbeke

Leuven Biostatistics and
Statistical Bioinformatics Centre
KU Leuven and Hasselt University, Belgium
Email: wim.demulder@cs.kuleuven.be,
geert.molenberghs@uhasselt.be,
geert.verbeke@med.kuleuven.be

Bernhard Rengs
and Thomas Fent

Wittgenstein Centre (IIASA, VID/ÖAW, WU)
VID/ÖAW
Vienna, Austria
Email: bernhard.rengs@oeaw.ac.at,
thomas.fent@oeaw.ac.at

***Abstract*—A common way to evaluate surrogate models is by using validation measures. This amounts to applying a chosen validation measure to a test data set that was not used to train the surrogate model. The selection of a validation measure is typically motivated by diverse guidelines, such as simplicity of the measure, ease of implementation, popularity of the measure, etc., which are often not related to characteristics of the measure itself. However, it should be recognized that the validity of a model is not only dependent on the model, as desired, but also on the behavior of the chosen validation measure. Some, although very limited, research has been devoted to the evaluation of validation measures, by applying them to a given model that is trained on a data set with some known properties, and then evaluating whether the considered measures validate the model in an expected way. In this paper, we perform an evaluation of some statistical and non statistical validation measures from another point of view. We consider a test data set generated by an agent-based model and we successively remove those elements from it for which our previously developed Gaussian process emulator, a surrogate model, produces the worst approximation to the true output value, according to a selected validation measure. All considered validation measures are then applied to the sequence of increasingly smaller test data sets. It is desired that a validation measure shows improvement of a model when test data points on which the model poorly performs are removed, irrespective of the validation measure that is used to detect such data points. Our experiments show that only the considered statistical validation measures have this desired behavior.**

***Keywords*–Gaussian process emulation; Agent-based models; Validation.**

I. Introduction and Outline of the Paper

In previous work we applied Gaussian process emulation, a surrogate model, to a training data set generated by an agent-based model that we had developed before [1]. Several alternative implementations of the Gaussian process emulation technique were considered and each of these was evaluated according to two different validation measures. Evaluation of the emulators was performed with respect to a test data set of size 500.

In this paper, we consider a research question that is not given proper attention in the literature, namely the evaluation of validation measures themselves. Although some researchers have examined certain characteristics of validation measures, their research is typically limited to the application of several selected validation measures to a given model that is trained on a data set with some known properties, and then evaluating whether these measures are able to validate these properties, see, e.g., [2], [3], [4]. Although such research is, of course, useful, we take here another perspective on the evaluation of validation measures. We consider the influence on validation measures when elements from the test data set are removed in the order proposed by a fixed validation measure. That is, we select a validation measure and we use that measure to find the element in the test data set for which a given surrogate model produces the worst approximation. We will simply refer to the element of a given test data set in which a given surrogate model produces the worst approximation according to a given validation measure as the worst test data point, and we will use the more vague term bad test data point to denote a test data point in which the surrogate model produces a bad approximation according to the given validation measure. It is then clear that the selected validation measure will show improvement when applied with respect to the reduced test data set, i.e., the elements of the test data set that remain after removing the worst test data point. However, an interesting and important research question is how the *other* validation measures will perform on the same reduced test data set. Will they also consider the selected test data point as the most problematic and thus have improved values when they evaluate the surrogate model on the reduced test data set? Or will they have another view on the test data point that is to be considered as the one where the surrogate model performs worst and, therefore, maybe even show *deterioration* of the surrogate model on the reduced data set?

The operation of removing the worst test data point is then repeatedly performed on the remaining test data set such that a graph of the considered validation measures results. This graph shows the evolution of the validation measures on increasingly smaller test data sets, where each test data set in this sequence does not contain the worst test data point of its predecessor. The whole procedure is then repeated by choosing another validation measure to detect bad test data points and to remove them accordingly. Consequently, another graph of all considered validation measures is produced. These graphs are then analyzed to supply an answer to the following questions. Which validation measures show steady improvement by removing test data points that are designated as bad according to *both* selected validation measures? For which validation measures does the improvement depend on the choice of fixed validation measure that is used to detect bad test data points? Our previously developed Gaussian process emulator that emulates an agent-based model will be used as case study to answer these questions.

The significance of the above research questions is that it is desired to use validation measures whose evaluation of a given model in terms of its performance on a test data set is consistent with respect to other validation measures. That is, if one researcher employs validation measure A and detects a region in input space where the model has low performance, then it is desired that another researcher using validation measure B should see improvement of the model after additional training on points in that region, even though he is using another validation measure. Otherwise, there would be inconsistency between both measures and this would make it impossible to state any justified claim related to the performance of the model. The above described method to evaluate validation measures then simulates the often applied practice of additional training in regions where the given surrogate model performs bad, since such additional training results in improvement in that region. This implies that previously bad test data points will not have that statute anymore and this can be simply simulated by removing them from the test data set.

The outline of the paper is as follows. In Section II, we review Gaussian process emulation and agent-based models to ensure that the paper is self-contained. For the same reason we review our previous work, which is done in Section III. As described above, several validation measures will be considered. Some of them have been developed by statisticians to validate statistical models, such as Gaussian process emulation, while we also consider some validation measures that are popular outside statistical domains and apply to deterministic models. These validation measures are reviewed in Section IV. An in-depth description of and motivation for our experiments is provided in Section V. Results are presented and analyzed in Section VI. Section VII contains a discussion of the experiments, evaluating the implications and meaning of the experimental results.

II. Related work

A short overview of the aspects of our previous work that are relevant for this paper is provided in Section III. In this section, we briefly review Gaussian process emulation and agent-based models.

A. Gaussian process emulation

Gaussian process (GP) emulation provides an approximation to a mapping $\nu : \mathbb{R}^n \to \mathbb{R}$. The approximation to ν, i.e., the emulator, is determined as follows. In the first step, it is assumed that nothing is known about ν. The value $\nu(\mathbf{x})$ for any $\mathbf{x}$ is then modeled as a Gaussian distribution with mean $m(\mathbf{x}) = \sum_{i=1}^{q} \beta_i h_i(\mathbf{x})$, where β_i are unknown coefficients and where h_i represent linear regression functions. The covariance between $\nu(\mathbf{x})$ and $\nu(\mathbf{x}')$, with $\mathbf{x}$ and $\mathbf{x}'$ arbitrary input vectors in $\mathbb{R}^n$, is modeled as

$$\mathrm{Cov}\Big(\nu(\mathbf{x}), \nu(\mathbf{x}') \,|\, \sigma^2\Big) \;=\; \sigma^2 c(\mathbf{x}, \mathbf{x}') \qquad (1)$$

where σ^2 denotes a constant variance parameter and where $c(\mathbf{x}, \mathbf{x}')$ denotes a function that models the correlation between $\nu(\mathbf{x})$ and $\nu(\mathbf{x}')$. In our previous work, we have used the most common choice for c:

$$c(\mathbf{x}, \mathbf{x}') \;=\; \exp\Big[-\sum_i \Big((x_i - x_i')/\delta_i\Big)^2\Big] \qquad (2)$$

with x_i and x_i' the ith component of $\mathbf{x}$ and $\mathbf{x}'$ resp., and where the δ_i represent the so-called correlation lengths. In the second step, training data $(\mathbf{x}_1, \nu(\mathbf{x}_1)), \ldots, (\mathbf{x}_n, \nu(\mathbf{x}_n))$ are used to update the Gaussian distributions to Student's t-distributions via a Bayesian analysis. The mean of the Student's t-distribution in $\mathbf{x}$ is then considered the best approximation to $\nu(\mathbf{x})$. Therefore, we refer to this mean as $\hat{\nu}(\mathbf{x})$. It is given by

$$\hat{\nu}(\mathbf{x}) = m(\mathbf{x}) + U^T(\mathbf{x})A^{-1}([\nu(\mathbf{x}_1), \ldots, \nu(\mathbf{x}_n)]^T - H\boldsymbol{\beta}) \quad (3)$$

with

$$\boldsymbol{\beta} \;=\; (\beta_1, \ldots, \beta_q)^T \qquad (4)$$

$$(5)$$

$$H \;=\; \begin{bmatrix} h_1(\mathbf{x}_1) & \ldots & h_q(\mathbf{x}_1) \\ & \ldots & \\ h_1(\mathbf{x}_n) & \ldots & h_q(\mathbf{x}_n) \end{bmatrix} \qquad (6)$$

and where $U(\mathbf{x})$ contains the correlations, as given by (2), between $\mathbf{x}$ and each of the training data points $\mathbf{x}_i$, and where A is the correlation matrix, containing the correlations between $\mathbf{x}_i$ and $\mathbf{x}_j$ for $i, j = 1, \ldots, n$. The expression (3) shows that the Bayesian analysis adds a correction term to the prior mean $m(\mathbf{x})$ by taking into account the information encapsulated in the training data set. The parameters δ_i can be optimized in terms of maximum likelihood [5], while optimal values for the β_i and for σ^2 can be determined by optimization principles in Hilbert space. For a more detailed account on GP emulation we refer to [6] and [7].

In practical applications, the Student's t-distributions are approximated by Gaussian distributions that are then used for all further operations. The variance of the Gaussian distribution in $\mathbf{x}$, denoted as $v(\mathbf{x})$, gives a measure of the uncertainty in approximating $\nu(\mathbf{x})$ by $\hat{\nu}(\mathbf{x})$. That is, the larger $v(\mathbf{x})$ the more tricky it is to approximate $\nu(\mathbf{x})$ as $\hat{\nu}(\mathbf{x})$. A 95% confidence interval for the true output $\nu(\mathbf{x})$ is given by $[\hat{\nu}(\mathbf{x}) - 2\sqrt{v(\mathbf{x})}, \hat{\nu}(\mathbf{x}) + 2\sqrt{v(\mathbf{x})}]$. An analytical formula for $v(\mathbf{x})$ is given in [7].

The main use of an emulator lies in the critical property that its execution is typically much faster than running the full model ν [8].

An example application of GP emulation is provided in Fig. 1. The model to be approximated is the function $f(x) = x\sin(x)$. The training data points (referred to as observations in the figure) are shown as red dots, while the approximation (called prediction in the figure), given by (3), is denoted by a blue line. A 95% confidence interval can be constructed as outlined above and this is also shown in the figure. It is seen that an emulator is an interpolator, i.e., the approximation is exact in the training data points and the confidence interval

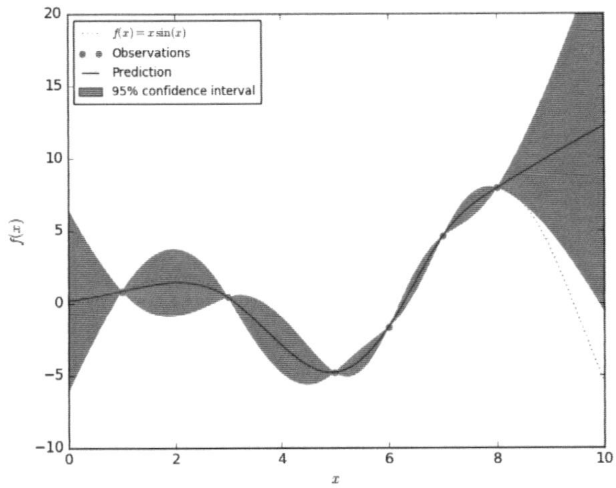

Figure 1. Example application of GP emulation
(From http://scikit-learn.org/stable/modules/gaussian_process.html)

in these points have length zero. Another typical property of a GP emulator is clearly noticed from the figure: the length of the confidence intervals increases with increasing distance to the nearest training data point. This property is intuitively clear, since moving away from a training data point means moving away from a point where there is precise information about an output value of the function to be approximated. One final observation is the large discrepancy between $f(x)$ and the emulator over the interval $(0.8, 1]$, which does not contain any training data point. Such a behavior is often observed for approximation techniques and shows that extrapolation should be avoided if possible [9].

B. Agent-based models

An agent-based model (ABM) is a computational model that simulates the behavior of and interactions between autonomous agents. A key feature is that population level phenomena are studied by explicitly modeling the interactions of the individuals in these populations [10], [11]. The systems that emerge from such interactions are often complex and might show regularities that were not expected by researchers in the field who solely relied on their background knowledge about the characteristics of the lower-level entities to make predictions about the higher-level phenomena. In [12], the authors describe situations for which agent-based modeling can offer distinct advantages to conventional simulation approaches. Some include:

- There is a natural representation as agents.
- It is important that agents learn and engage in dynamic strategic behaviors.
- The past is no predictor of the future.
- It is important that agents have a dynamic relationship with other agents, and agent relationships form and dissolve.

Examples of situations where ABMs have been successfully applied are infectious disease transmission [13], the development of risk behaviors during adolescence [14], the simultaneous study of the epidemiological and evolutionary dynamics of Influenza viruses [15], the sector structure of complex financial systems [16] and pedestrian movement [17]. ABMs are especially popular among sociologists who model social life as interactions among adaptive agents who influence one another in response to the influence they receive [18], [19], [20], [21].

Since nonlinear interactions and successive simulation steps are key ingredients of an agent-based model, such models are often computationally expensive. Consequently, if the model has to be executed on a large set of given input points, e.g., to determine parameter values that minimize an error criterion between model output and observed data, this task can often only be accomplished within a reasonable time by relying on emulation. Surprisingly, it is only recently that one has started to realize the use of Gaussian process emulation in analyses with agent-based models [22], [23], [24], [25], [26], [27], [28].

III. Previous Work

A. Our agent-based model

In previous work, we developed an ABM to analyze the effectiveness of family policies under different assumptions regarding the social structure of a society [29]. In our model the agents represent the female partner in a household and are heterogeneous with respect to age, household budget, parity, and intended fertility. A network of mutual links connects the agents to a small subset of the population to exchange fertility preferences. The agents are endowed with a certain budget of time and money which they allocate to satisfy their own and their children's needs. We assume that the agent's and their children's consumption levels depend on the household budget but increase less than linearly with household budget. This implies that wealthier households have a higher savings rate. If the household's intended fertility exceeds the actual parity and the disposable budget suffices to cover the consumption needs of another child, the household is subject to the corresponding age-specific fertility. If an additional child is born, other agents may update their intended fertility.

We considered two components of family policies: 1. the policy maker provides a fixed amount of money or monetary equivalent per child to each household and 2. a monetary or nonmonetary benefit proportional to the household income is received by the household. The output on the aggregate level that is simulated by the ABM consists of the cohort fertility, the intended fertility and the fertility gap. Here, as in previous work, we restrict attention to the output component cohort fertility. The input variables include the level of fixed and income dependent family allowances, denoted by b^f and b^v, and parameters that determine the social structure of a society, such as a measure for the agents' level of homophily α, and the strength of positive and negative social influence, denoted by pr_3 and pr_4 resp.

Our simulations revealed a positive impact of both fixed and income dependent family allowances on completed cohort fertility and on intended fertility, and a negative impact of fixed and income dependent child supports on the fertility gap. However, several network and social influence parameters are such that they do not only influence fertility itself but also the effectiveness of family policies, often in a detrimental

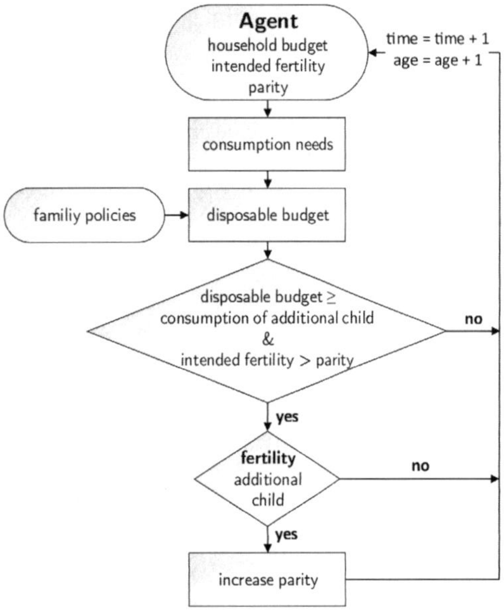

Figure 2. The decision making process in a household

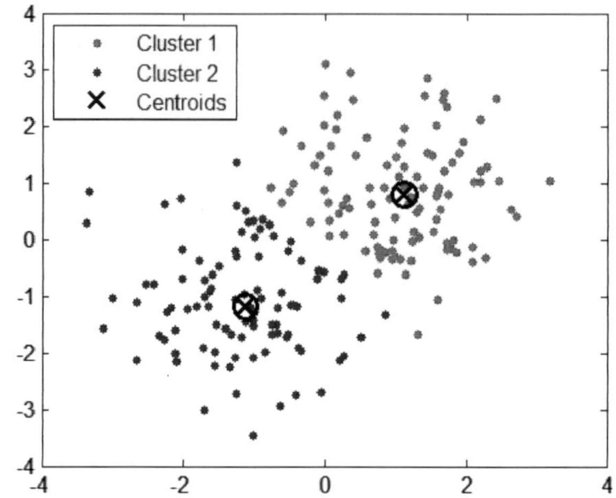

Figure 3. Illustration of k-means for two-dimensional data set with $k = 2$ (*From http://mines.humanoriented.com/classes/2010/fall/csci568/portfolio_exports/mvoget/cluster/cluster.html*)

way. For instance, while a higher degree of homophily among the network partners has a positive effect on fertility, family policies may be less effective in such a society. Therefore, policymakers aiming to transfer a certain policy mix that has proved successful from one country to another one ignoring differences in the social structure may fail. Family policies can only be successful if they explicitly take into account the characteristics of the society they are assigned for.

A flow-chart of the simulations performed by the ABM is provided in Fig. 2. Our model and the sociological hypotheses derived from application of it are extensively described in our previous work [29].

B. Data set generated by agent-based model

The input variables of our ABM are given equidistant values from the input domain and the ABM is applied to generate the corresponding outputs. As input domain we considered the variables b^f, b^v, α, pr_3 and p_4, a selection of the larger amount of variables that were used in the ABM. These five variables were found to have the largest influence on the outcomes. On the output side we restrict attention to one variable, namely cohort fertility. The ABM was applied to 10,732 vectors in the input domain, resulting in a large training data set. A test data set containing 500 input-output pairs was generated, the use of which will be described below.

C. Gaussian process emulation applied to our agent-based model

We applied GP emulation to our ABM. However, the large training data set necessitated us to adapt the originally developed GP emulation technique described in Section II-A. The reason is that the inverse of the correlation matrix is needed in the analytical formulation of the emulator. As this matrix is of quadratic order in the training data set size, it is obvious that the inverse operation cannot be performed (at least not in a numerically stable way). Therefore, we proceeded as follows.

First, we applied k-means [30], a popular cluster analysis algorithm, to subdivide the very large training data set into clusters. Cluster analysis is the unsupervised partitioning of a data set into groups, also called clusters, such that data elements that are member of the same group have a higher similarity than data elements that are member of different groups. Similarity is expressed in terms of a user-defined distance measure, such as the commonly used Euclidean distance which we employed. An illustration of the k-means principle is provided by Fig. 3. The application of k-means to our training data set resulted in 34 clusters with sizes ranging from 15 to 500. Implementation details are described in our previous work [1]. An emulator was then constructed for each of the resulting clusters.

Secondly, values of the parameters of each of the emulators were determined. Determination of the parameters β_i and σ^2 is simple, as analytical expressions exist for their optimal values (see, e.g., [31]). However, such expressions do not exist for the δ_i. These are typically obtained by applying the maximum likelihood principe, as described in [5]. This amounts to optimizing their joint density function which is a nontrivial task here as this function is a $\mathbb{R}^5 \to \mathbb{R}$ mapping (there are five correlation lengths, one for each of the input variables b^f, b^v, α, pr_3 and pr_4), potentially having many local optima. We used genetic algorithms [32] to perform this optimization task. Genetic algorithms are a type of heuristic optimization method that mimics some aspects of the process of natural selection, in that a population of candidate solutions to an optimization problem is evolved toward better solutions. This is done by applying certain operators, called mutation, crossover and reproduction, to the set of candidate solutions. These operators have been inspired by the principles of their biological counterparts and ensure that the population as a whole becomes fitter, i.e., the set of candidate solutions improves gradually according to a chosen error criterion. Fig. 4 illustrates the basic idea of genetic algorithms. Key advantages of genetic algorithms

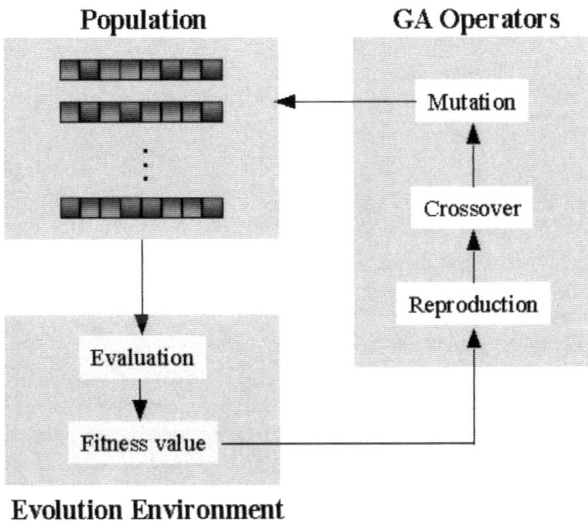

Figure 4. Illustration of genetic algorithms
(From http://www.ewh.ieee.org/soc/es/May2001/14/Begin.htm)

are that they only employ function evaluations (and thus not, e.g., information about the derivative, as is required by many other optimization methods, such as, for example, gradient descent) and that they are well suited to avoid getting stuck in local optima [33], [34], [35]. Both characteristics make them particularly useful to optimize the density function of the correlation lengths. For implementation details we again refer to our previous work.

Finally, given an input point $\mathbf{x}$ we determine an approximation to the output of the ABM in $\mathbf{x}$ as the output generated by the emulator that corresponds to the cluster closest to $\mathbf{x}$. We define the distance from a point to a cluster as the minimum of all distances from that point to any training data point that is member of the considered cluster. Obviously, there are other ways to combine the 34 emulators into one approximator. However, experimental results in our previous work demonstrated that the described approximator performs better than some alternative methods to combine the emulators.

In summary, when we speak of the output of the emulator in $\mathbf{x}$ we refer to the output of the emulator that was trained with the part of the full training data set that constitutes the cluster to which $\mathbf{x}$ is closest in terms of the described minimum distance. The notation $\nu(\mathbf{x})$ is used to denote the output of the ABM in $\mathbf{x}$, while $\hat{\nu}(\mathbf{x})$ refers to the output of the emulator in that input point.

IV. Validation Measures

We consider several validation measures that can evaluate the performance of a given emulator. Two of them are related to popular measures in statistics, namely the average interval score and the average absolute individual standardized error. They take the uncertainty in the approximation generated by the emulator into account. Five other measures (Nash-Sutcliffe efficiency, coefficient of determination, index of agreement, relative Nash-Sutcliffe efficiency and relative index of agreement) are non statistical measures and have been used in a variety of fields. A final, extremely simple measure, is just the average of the absolute relative differences between approximations and true outputs. The values of the measures are determined with respect to a given test data set T.

A. Average interval score

The quality of a confidence interval $[l(\mathbf{x}), u(\mathbf{x})]$ around $\hat{\nu}(\mathbf{x})$ can be evaluated using the interval score described in [36]. Given an $(1-\alpha)\%$ confidence interval $[l(\mathbf{x}), u(\mathbf{x})]$, with $\alpha = 0.05$ chosen in this paper, the interval score is defined as

$$IS(\mathbf{x}) = \Big(u(\mathbf{x}) - l(\mathbf{x})\Big) + \frac{2}{\alpha}\Big(l(\mathbf{x}) - \nu(\mathbf{x})\Big)\mathbf{1}_{\{\nu(\mathbf{x})<l(\mathbf{x})\}} + \frac{2}{\alpha}\Big(\nu(\mathbf{x}) - u(\mathbf{x})\Big)\mathbf{1}_{\{\nu(\mathbf{x})>u(\mathbf{x})\}} \quad (7)$$

where $\mathbf{1}_{\{expr\}}$ refers to the indicator function, being 1 if expression $expr$ holds and 0 otherwise. This scoring rule rewards narrow intervals, while penalizing lack of coverage. The lower its value, the higher the quality of the confidence interval. In terms of the average interval score, the given emulator is perfect when the value of the average interval score equals zero. This can only happen when $l(\mathbf{x}) = u(\mathbf{x}) = \nu(\mathbf{x})$. The first equality implies that the confidence interval is reduced to a single point, and if this is combined with the other equality we find that the value of this single point equals the value of the emulator. Thus, the perfect case occurs when the estimate equals the true value and when, at the same time, there is no uncertainty about how well the predicted value approximates the true one. Or in other words: the estimate equals the true value and we *know* that this is the case. The average interval score is simply the average of $IS(\mathbf{x})$ over all considered test points $\mathbf{x}$. An important advantage of the average interval score is that, unlike many other validation measures, this measure simultaneously evaluates the uncertainty in the approximation as given by the confidence interval, and the quality of the approximation. The first term in (7) evaluates the amount of uncertainty in the approximation: the larger the uncertainty related to the approximation, the larger the first term. The second and third term evaluate the quality of the approximation. If the true value is outside the confidence interval, and thus far from the approximation in a certain sense, one of both terms will be large. For some other work where this measure is used, we refer to [37] and [38].

B. Average absolute individual standardized error

Given $\mathbf{x}$, the corresponding individual standardized error [39] is given by

$$SE(\mathbf{x}) = \frac{\nu(\mathbf{x}) - \hat{\nu}(\mathbf{x})}{\sqrt{v(\mathbf{x})}} \quad (8)$$

This measure takes both the approximation and the constructed confidence interval into account, just as the average interval score discussed in Section IV-A. The measure SE, given by equation (8), is very useful since it allows to evaluate the magnitude of SE in a rather straightforward way. As outlined in Section II-A, the distributions of the approximations are approximately Gaussian. This implies that if the emulator properly represents ν, the distribution of SE is approximately standard normal. Thus, we expect that about 95% of SE values are smaller than 2 in absolute value. That is, if there are a considerable number of test points $\mathbf{x}$ for which the absolute value of $SE(\mathbf{x})$ is larger than 2, then this is a clear warning that the emulator might not perform well. This convenient evaluation of a given emulator is an important advantage over the average interval score, where we do not have such reference values. The average interval score is only useful when at least two different emulators are to be compared to each other, while SE can be used to evaluate a single emulator. On the other hand, the average interval score has the benefit of not making any assumption about the distribution of the approximations. Taking absolute values and averaging over all considered test data points, we obtain our average absolute individual standardized error.

C. Nash-Sutcliffe efficiency

The Nash-Sutcliffe efficiency (NSE), proposed in [40], is determined as

$$NSE = 1 - \frac{\sum_{\mathbf{x}\in T}\Big(\nu(\mathbf{x}) - \hat{\nu}(\mathbf{x})\Big)^2}{\sum_{\mathbf{x}\in T}\Big(\nu(\mathbf{x}) - \overline{\nu}\Big)^2} \quad (9)$$

with $\overline{\nu}$ the average of $\nu(\mathbf{x})$ over all elements of T. The range of NSE lies between 1.0 (perfect fit) and -∞. An NSE of lower than zero indicates that $\overline{\nu}$ would have been a better predictor than the calculated approximations $\hat{\nu}(\mathbf{x})$. The fact that the Nash-Sutcliffe efficiency squares differences between true and estimated values implies that large values have large influence while small values are almost neglected, which might or might not be desired for the application at hand [4]. Furthermore, while the NSE is a convenient and normalized measure of model performance, it does not provide a reliable basis for comparing the results of different case studies [41]. Nevertheless, NSE is a popular measure for the evaluation of models, especially of hydrological models [42].

D. Coefficient of determination

The coefficient of determination r^2 is the square of the Pearson correlation coefficient:

$$r^2 = \left(\frac{\sum_{\mathbf{x}\in T}(\nu(\mathbf{x}) - \overline{\nu})(\hat{\nu}(\mathbf{x}) - \overline{\hat{\nu}})}{\sqrt{\sum_{\mathbf{x}\in T}(\nu(\mathbf{x}) - \overline{\nu})^2}\sqrt{\sum_{\mathbf{x}\in T}(\hat{\nu}(\mathbf{x}) - \overline{\hat{\nu}})^2}}\right)^2 \quad (10)$$

where $\overline{\hat{\nu}}$ refers to the averages of $\hat{\nu}(\mathbf{x})$ over the test data points. The measure is widely applied by statisticians [43].

The values of r^2 are between 0 and 1. The measure describes how much of the observed dispersion is explained by the estimation. A value of zero means no correlation at all, whereas a value of 1 means that the dispersion of the estimations is equal to that of the true values. Although many authors consider the coefficient of determination a useful measure of success of predicting the dependent variable from the independent variables [44], the fact that only the dispersion is quantified is a major drawback of r^2. A surrogate model that systematically over- or underestimates all the time can still result in good r^2 values close to 1.0 even if all estimations are critically wrong [45], [46].

E. Index of agreement

The index of agreement d was proposed in [47] to overcome the insensitivity of NSE and r^2 to differences in the true and estimated means and variances. It is defined as:

$$d = 1 - \frac{\sum_{\mathbf{x}\in T}\Big(\nu(\mathbf{x}) - \hat{\nu}(\mathbf{x})\Big)^2}{\sum_{\mathbf{x}\in T}\Big(|\hat{\nu}(\mathbf{x}) - \overline{\nu}| + |\nu(\mathbf{x}) - \overline{\nu}|\Big)^2} \quad (11)$$

Due to the mean square error in the numerator, d is also very sensitive to large values and rather insensitive to small values, as is the case for NSE. The range of d is $[0, 1]$ with 1 denoting perfect fit.

Practical applications of d show that it has some disadvantages [45]. First, relatively high values, say more than 0.65, may be obtained even for poor surrogate model fits. Secondly, systematic over- or underestimation can, as with the coefficient of determination, be masked by high values of d. There exist several variations on the above definition of the index of agreement, for example, by considering absolute differences instead of squared differences [48] or by removing the approximations $\hat{\nu}(\mathbf{x})$ from the denominator [49].

F. Relative Nash-Sutcliffe efficiency

The NSE described above quantifies the difference between the original model and the surrogate model in terms of absolute values. As a result, an over- or underestimation of higher values has, in general, a greater influence than those of lower values. Therefore, one has introduced the following *relative* NSE [45]:

$$NSE_{rel} = 1 - \frac{\sum_{\mathbf{x}\in T}\left(\frac{\nu(\mathbf{x}) - \hat{\nu}(\mathbf{x})}{\nu(\mathbf{x})}\right)^2}{\sum_{\mathbf{x}\in T}\left(\frac{\nu(\mathbf{x}) - \overline{\nu}}{\overline{\nu}}\right)^2} \quad (12)$$

Some recent research where the relative NSE is used include [50] and [51].

G. Relative index of agreement

The same idea can be applied to the index of agreement, resulting in the *relative* index of agreement [45]:

$$d_{rel} = 1 - \frac{\sum_{\mathbf{x}\in T}\left(\frac{\nu(\mathbf{x}) - \hat{\nu}(\mathbf{x})}{\nu(\mathbf{x})}\right)^2}{\sum_{\mathbf{x}\in T}\left(\frac{|\hat{\nu}(\mathbf{x}) - \overline{\nu}| + |\nu(\mathbf{x}) - \overline{\nu}|}{\overline{\nu}}\right)^2} \quad (13)$$

H. Average absolute relative difference

Given a test data point $\mathbf{x}$, we can evaluate the quality of the approximation as the absolute relative difference between $\nu(\mathbf{x})$ and $\hat{\nu}(\mathbf{x})$ as follows:

$$RD(\mathbf{x}) = \left|\frac{\hat{\nu}(\mathbf{x}) - \nu(\mathbf{x})}{1/2(\hat{\nu}(\mathbf{x}) + \nu(\mathbf{x}))}\right| \quad (14)$$

The average absolute relative difference, denoted ARD, is then the average of $RD(\mathbf{x})$ over all considered test data points.

This measure has the disadvantage of being unbounded, which makes it difficult to evaluate whether the obtained value is, e.g., large or very large. However, the fact that this measure is very simple makes it easy to interpret.

V. Description of the Experiments

We experimentally evaluate how the described validation measures evolve when we successively remove elements from the test data set. Three methods are considered to remove elements. First, removal in terms of the absolute individual standardized error. That is, we calculate all validation measures for the full test data set T consisting of 500 test points. Then we remove the element with the largest absolute individual standardized error and calculate the validation measures again with respect to this reduced test data set. This procedure is repeated until only two elements remain (we do not calculate the measures for a test data set consisting of one element since this makes some measures, such as r^2, undefined due to division by zero). Secondly, removal in terms of the absolute relative difference, where the element with the largest absolute relative difference is removed first, then the element with the second largest absolute relative difference, etc. The third removal method discards elements in a purely random way.

Our experiments are related to the well established practice of evaluating a model with respect to some test data set and enlarging the training data set if the evaluation indicates poor performance. Preferably, the training data set is extended with bad points, i.e., points for which a chosen validation measure indicates large discrepancy between the true output value and the generated approximation, since it is intuitive to consider such points as lying in regions of input space where training was not performed properly. The points with which the training data set is extended should then be removed from the test data set. However, our purpose here is not to consider the influence of the extension of the training data set on the performance of the model, since it is clear that overall performance will, in general, be improved by extending learning to regions that were not given proper attention in a previous learning step. Rather, our goal is to assess the influence of removing bad data points from the test data set on our validation measures. Of course, it is obvious that removing the element with the largest absolute individual standardized error will result in an improvement of the average absolute individual standardized error. What is less obvious, however, is how this will affect the other validation measures. Thus, a first research question is to what extent the values of the described validation measures are sensitive to the choice of criterion that is used to describe a test data point as bad. From another perspective, this research question asks if the validation measures are compatible. That is, if a test point is regarded as bad by a certain measure, do all the other measures agree with this, in the sense that removing such an element improves their value? This research question is of the utmost importance, as it is desired that our evaluation of the goodness-of-fit of a model is only, or at least mainly, dependent on the model and not on the choice of validation measure. Furthermore, even when it would hold that all validation measures improve by removing test points that are bad according to a certain measure, they might not improve to the same extent. Some measures might improve very significantly when one bad point is removed, while other measures might encounter only a marginal benefit. It is also important to detect such differences, if they exist, between validation measures, since an overly optimism in the improvement of a model after having extended training might not be justified if the improvement according to other measures would only show incremental improvement. Indeed, such a case would point to an artifact of the chosen validation measure rather than to inherent characteristics of the improved model.

The random removal of elements serves as a benchmark case: validation measures should improve much more in response to the removal of bad points according to a well chosen validation measure than according to a removal that is completely random.

VI. Results

The results are shown in Figs. 5-12. Each figure displays the evolution of one of the eight considered validation measures, described in Section IV, as elements are progressively discarded from the test data set, and this for each of the three removal methods (i.e., according to the absolute individual standardized error, according to the absolute relative difference and via random removal).

It is seen that, at first sight, the average interval score, the average absolute individual standardized error, the Nash-Sutcliffe efficiency, the coefficient of determination, and the index of agreement behave as desired: they all gradually improve as the worst element of the current test data set is removed. However, a closer look at Figs. 7-9 reveals that the Nash-Sutcliffe efficiency, the coefficient of determination and the index of agreement evaluate the emulator as becoming worse for the removal of, approximately, the first 20 elements when removal is done according to the absolute relative difference.

Although the relative versions of the Nash-Sutcliffe efficiency and of the index of agreement have been developed to compensate certain deficiencies of these measures, we observe that these extensions do not result in unequivocally better behavior in our experiments. Their behavior with respect to the removal of elements according to the absolute individual standardized error is quite erratic, almost indiscernible from their behavior when removal is random. On the other hand, these relative measures show more consistent behavior in terms of removal according to the absolute relative difference. Whereas the non relative Nash-Sutcliffe efficiency and the non relative index of agreement become worse by removing the approx. first 20 elements and only steadily increase after having reduced the test data set by these 20 elements, the relative counterparts increase steadily from the removal of the first element on.

Our simplest validation measure, the average absolute relative difference, decreases steadily if removal is with respect to the absolute relative difference. But this is of course a trivial observation, as it is obvious that a measure improves if elements are discarded that are bad according to that same measure. Much more relevant is that the average absolute relative difference shows undesired behavior when elements are removed according to their absolute individual standardized error. Although its global trend is decreasing until about 350 elements are deleted, it suddenly starts to increase after that turning point.

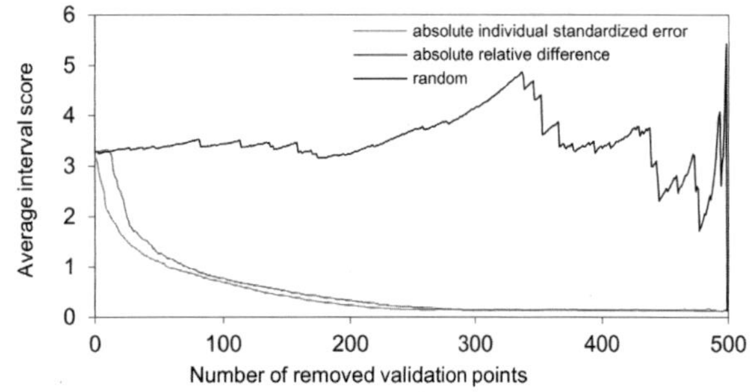

Figure 5. Average interval score

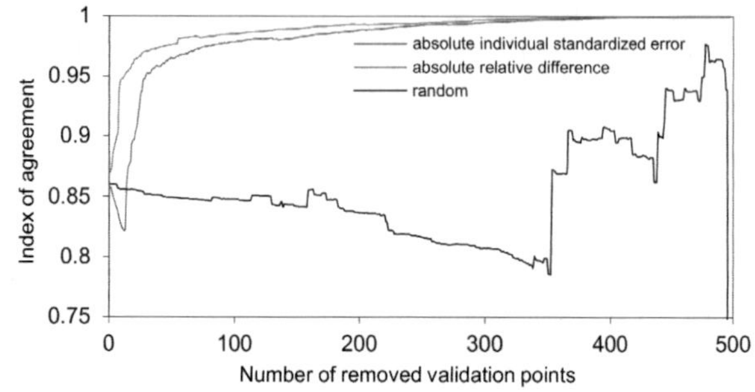

Figure 9. Index of agreement

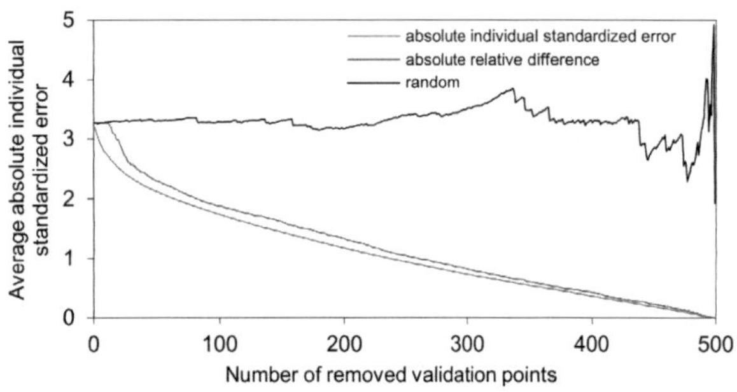

Figure 6. Average absolute individual standardized error

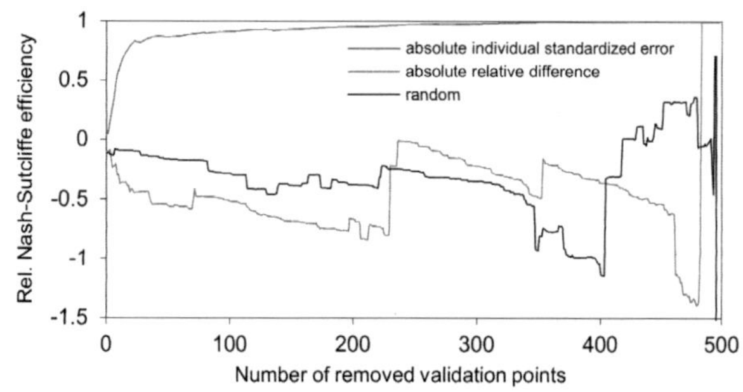

Figure 10. Relative Nash-Sutcliffe efficiency

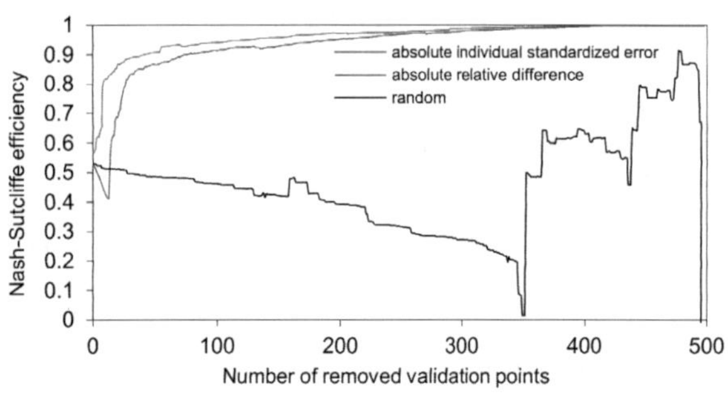

Figure 7. Nash-Sutcliffe efficiency

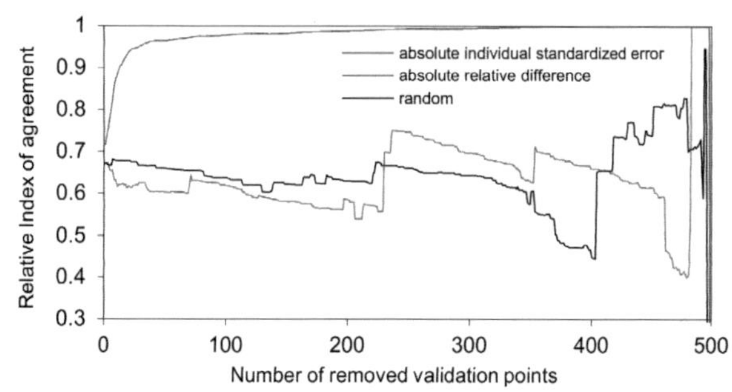

Figure 11. Relative index of agreement

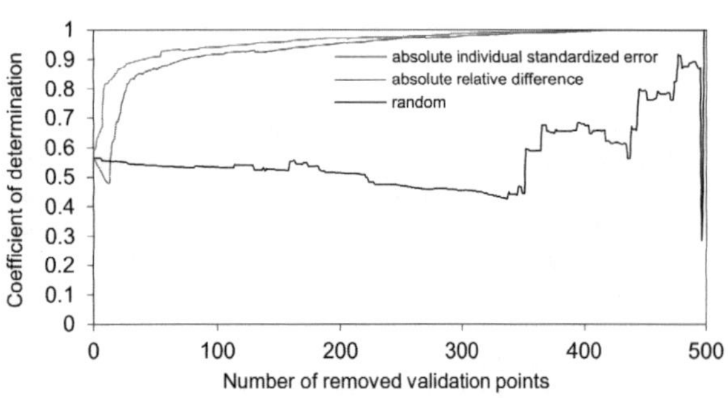

Figure 8. Coefficient of determination

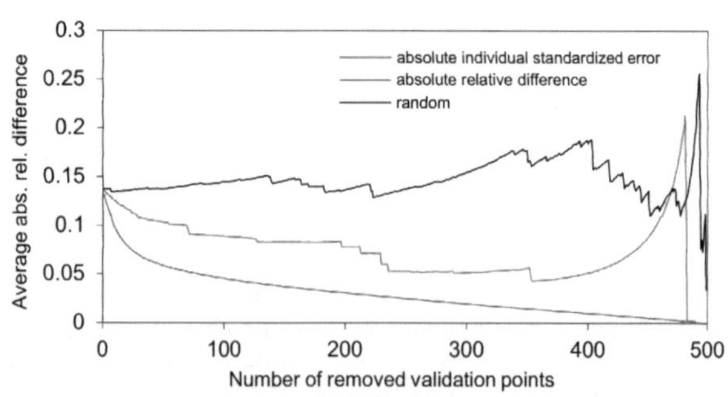

Figure 12. Average absolute relative difference

VII. Discussion

The experiments indicate that the average interval score and the average absolute individual standardized error have the most desired behavior. Whether a point is labeled 'bad' according to its absolute individual standardized error or according to its absolute relative difference, removing the worst element from the test data set results in better values of both measures. We remind that only these two measures take the uncertainty in the approximation into account (see Section IV). Thus, our experiments suggest that statistical surrogate models, such as Gaussian process emulation, have certain benefits over deterministic surrogate models, such as polynomial approximation, in particular that the uncertainty in the approximation is also modeled. This uncertainty measure should then be taken into account in validating the model.

Comparing Fig. 5 and Fig. 6, the main difference between the average interval score and the average absolute individual standardized error is that the first one reacts much more pronounced to the removal of elements, at least concerning the removal of about the first half of all elements. The decrease of the average interval score appears to be of exponential order, while the average absolute individual standardized error seems to improve only linearly except for the first dozen or so elements. This indicates that one should be careful to report an improvement in a model as very significant when the average interval score is used as validation measure, since part of the improvement might be solely due to characteristics inherent in that validation measure. It is advised to validate the model in terms of both the average interval score and the average absolute individual standardized error.

The other measures do not show steady improvement with respect to either the average interval score or the average absolute individual standardized error. Remarkably, each of these other measures *do* improve steadily in terms of *one* of these measures. The Nash-Sutcliffe efficiency, the coefficient of determination and the index of agreement improve consistently when removal of elements is performed according to the absolute individual standardized error, as is seen from Figs. 7, 8, and 9. On the other hand, the relative Nash-Sutcliffe efficiency, the relative index of agreement and, of course, the average absolute relative difference show steady improvement in terms of the absolute relative difference. This implies that these measures are sensitive to the criterion that is used to measure the quality of the approximation in a certain point. A point that is designated as bad, i.e., low quality of approximation in that point, according to the absolute individual standardized error might not be recognized as such by the aforementioned six non statistical validation measures. The same applies to measuring the quality of approximation in a point by the absolute relative difference.

VIII. Conclusion and Future Work

In this paper, we have evaluated eight validation measures for surrogate models: the average interval score, the average absolute individual standardized error, the Nash-Sutcliffe efficiency, the coefficient of determination, the index of agreement, the relative Nash-Sutcliffe efficiency, the relative index of agreement and the average absolute relative difference. The first two measures are statistical in nature, taking into account the uncertainty of the approximation generated by the surrogate model. The other measures are solely based on the generated approximation values. The evaluation was performed using a Gaussian process emulator that was applied to an agent-based model. We developed both Gaussian process emulator and agent-based model in previous work.

Our method of evaluating validation measures has, as far as we are aware of, not been applied yet. We consider a test data set and successively remove those elements from it for which our emulator produces the worst approximation to the true output value, in terms of the absolute individual standardized error. The considered validation measures are then applied to the sequence of increasingly smaller test data sets. The same procedure is applied with removal of test data points in terms of the absolute relative difference. It is desired that a validation measure shows improvement of a model when test data points on which the model poorly performs are removed, irrespective of the measure that is used to detect such data points. Our experiments indicate that only the average interval score and the average absolute individual standardized error have this desired behavior.

Our work has some practical implications:

- Statistical surrogate models, which not only produce an approximation to or estimation of the output in a given input point but also a measure for the uncertainty in the approximation, are preferred over deterministic models. Evaluation of such a model should then be done by a statistical validation measure that takes this uncertainty measure into account, such as the average interval score and the average absolute individual standardized error.
- It is bad practice to evaluate a given model in terms of a single validation measure, as the value of this measure might not only reflect the performance of the model but also certain inherent artifacts of the measure itself. Evaluating a model using several measures ensures different perspectives on the performance of the model, and thus avoids an overly optimistic or pessimistic view on its performance that might not be justified.

As future research, it would be interesting to evaluate other validation measures according to our evaluation procedure. Especially recently developed validation measures that are meant to extend or improve previously developed measures should be evaluated. Examples include:

- A relatively recent alternative to the index of agreement that is dimensionless, bounded by -1.0 and 1.0 and for which the authors claim that it is more rationally related to model accuracy than are other existing indices [52].
- Another alternative to the index of agreement that is also dimensionless and bounded [53]. The authors demonstrate the use and value of their index on synthetic and real data sets, but an evaluation in line with our procedure would increase justification of their claims.
- A bounded version of the Nash-Sutcliffe efficiency [54].

Our experiments show that such an additional evaluation is not superfluous, as modifications to existing measures that in terms of analytical formulation seemingly compensate some clear drawbacks of the existing measure might not show as consistent behavior in practice as one is inclined to anticipate.

ACKNOWLEDGMENT

The authors acknowledge funding from the KU Leuven funded Geconcerteerde Onderzoeksacties (GOA) project New approaches to the social dynamics of long-term fertility change [grant 20142018;GOA/14/001].

REFERENCES

[1] W. De Mulder, B. Rengs, G. Molenberghs, T. Fent, and G. Verbeke, "Statistical emulation applied to a very large data set generated by an agent-based model," in Proceedings of the 7th International Conference on Advances in System Simulation, SIMUL, 2015, pp. 43–48.

[2] Y. Liu, Z. Li, H. Xiong, X. Gao, and J. Wu, "Understanding of internal clustering validation measures," in Proceedings of the IEEE International Conference on Data Mining. IEEE, 2010.

[3] M. Brun, C. Sima, J. Hua, J. Lowey, B. Carroll, E. Suh, and E. Dougherty, "Model-based evaluation of clustering validation measures," Pattern Recognition, vol. 40, 2007, pp. 807–824.

[4] D. R. Legates and G. J. McCabe Jr., "Evaluating the use of goodness-of-fit measures in hydrologic and hydroclimatic model validation," Water Resources Research, vol. 35, 1999, pp. 233–241.

[5] I. Andrianakis and P. G. Challenor, "The effect of the nugget on Gaussian process emulators of computer models," Computational Statistics and Data Analysis, vol. 56, 2012, pp. 4215–4228.

[6] A. O'Hagan, "Bayesian analysis of computer code outputs: A tutorial," Reliability Engineering & System Safety, vol. 91, 2006, pp. 1290–1300.

[7] J. Oakley and A. O'Hagan, "Bayesian inference for the uncertainty distribution of computer model outputs," Biometrika, vol. 89, 2002, pp. 769–784.

[8] J. Gómez-Dans, P. Lewis, and M. Disney, "Efficient emulation of radiative transfer codes using Gaussian processes and application to land surface parameter inferences," Remote Sensing, vol. 8, 2016, doi:10.3390/rs8020119.

[9] D. Larose and C. Larose, Eds., Data mining and predictive analytics. Wiley, 2015.

[10] N. Gilbert, Ed., Agent-based models: quantitative applications in the social sciences. SAGE Publications, Inc, 2007.

[11] F. C. Billari, T. Fent, A. Prskawetz, and J. Scheffran, Eds., Agent–Based Compuational Modelling: Applications in Demography, Social, Economic, and Environmental Sciences, ser. Contributions to Economics. Springer, 2006.

[12] C. Macal and M. North, "Agent-based modeling and simulation: Abms examples," in Proceedings of the 2008 Winter Simulation Conference, 2008, pp. 101–112.

[13] L. Willem, Agent-based models for infectious disease transmission: exploration, estimation & computational efficiency. PhD thesis, 2015.

[14] N. Schuhmacher, L. Ballato, and P. van Geert, "Using an agent-based model to simulate the development of risk behaviors during adolescence," Journal of Artificial Societies and Social Simulation, vol. 17, no. 3, 2014.

[15] B. Roche, J. M. Drake, and P. Rohani, "An agent-based model to study the epidemiological and evolutionary dynamics of influenza viruses," BMC Bioinformatics, vol. 12, no. 87, 2011.

[16] J.-J. Chen, L. Tan, and B. Zheng, "Agent-based model with multi-level herding for complex financial systems," Scientific Reports, vol. 5, 2015.

[17] A. Crooks, A. C. X. Lu, S. Wise, J. Irvine, and A. Stefanidis, "Walk this way: improving pedestrian agent-based models through scene activity analysis," ISPRS International Journal of Geo-Information, vol. 4, no. 3, 2015, pp. 1627–1656.

[18] M. Macy and R. Willer, "From factors to factors: computational sociology and agent-based modeling," Annual Review of Sociology, vol. 28, 2002, pp. 143–166.

[19] F. Bianchi and F. Squazzoni, "Agent-based models in sociology," Wiley Interdisciplinary Reviews: Computational Statistics, vol. 7, 2015, pp. 284–306.

[20] F. Squazzoni, Ed., Agent-based computational sociology. Wiley, 2012.

[21] A. El-Sayed, P. Scarborough, L. Seemann, and S. Galea, "Social network analysis and agent-based modeling in social epidemiology," Epidemiologic Perspectives & Innovations, vol. 9, 2012, doi: 10.1186/1742-5573-9-1.

[22] G. Dancik, D. Jones, and K. Dorman, "Parameter estimation and sensitivity analysis in an agent-based model of Leishmania major infection," Journal of Theoretical Biology, vol. 262, 2010, pp. 398–412.

[23] J.-S. Lee, T. Filatova, A. Ligmann-Zielinska, B. Hassani-Mahmooei, F. Stonedahl, and I. e. a. Lorscheid, "The complexities of agent-based modeling output analysis," Journal of Artificial Societies and Social Simulation, vol. 18, 2015, doi: 10.18564/jasss.2897.

[24] J. Sexton and Y. Everingham, "Global sensitivity analysis of key parameters in a process-based sugarcane growth model: a Bayesian approach ," in Proceedings of the 7th International Congress on Environmental Modelling and Software, 2014.

[25] A. Heppenstall, A. Crooks, L. See, and M. Batty, Eds., Agent-based models of geographical systems. Springer, 2011.

[26] D. Heard, G. Dent, T. Schifeling, and D. Banks, "Agent-Based models and microsimulation," Annual Review of Statistics and Its Application, vol. 2, 2015, pp. 259–272.

[27] J. Bijak, J. Hilton, and E. Silverman, "From agent-based models to statistical emulators," in Joint Eurostat/UNECE Work Session on Demographic Projections, 2013.

[28] J. Castilla-Rho, G. Mariethoz, M. Rojas, R. Andersen, and B. Kelly, "An agent-based platform for simulating complex human-aquifer interactions in managed groundwater systems," Environmental Modelling & Software, vol. 73, 2015, pp. 305–323.

[29] T. Fent, B. Aparicio Diaz, and A. Prskawetz, "Family policies in the context of low fertility and social structure," Demographic Research, vol. 29, 2013, pp. 963–998.

[30] A. Jain and R. Dubes, Eds., Algorithms for clustering data. Prentice Hall College Div, 1988.

[31] J. Oakley and A. O'Hagan, "Bayesian inference for the uncertainty distribution of computer model outputs," Biometrika, vol. 89, 2002, pp. 769–784.

[32] M. Mitchell, Ed., An introduction to genetic algorithms. MIT Press, 1998.

[33] P. Fleming and A. Zalzala, Eds., Genetic algorithms in engineering systems. The Institution of Engineering and Technology, 1997.

[34] E. Sanchez, Ed., Genetic algorithms and fuzzy logic systems: soft computing perspectives. Wspc, 1997.

[35] L. Chambers, Ed., The practical handbook of genetic algorithms: new frontiers. CRC Press, 1995.

[36] T. Gneiting and A. Raftery, "Strictly proper scoring rules, prediction, and estimation," Journal of the American Statistical Association, vol. 102, 2007, pp. 359–378.

[37] N. Cahill, A. Kemp, B. Horton, and A. Parnell, "Modeling sea-level change using errors-in-variables integrated Gaussian processes," The Annals of Applied Statistics, vol. 9, 2015, pp. 547–571.

[38] C. Lian, C. Chen, Z. Zeng, W. Yao, and H. Tang, "Prediction intervals for landslide displacement based on switched neural networks," IEEE Transactions on Reliability, vol. 65, 2016, pp. 1483–1495.

[39] L. Bastos and A. O'Hagan, "Diagnostics for Gaussian process emulators," Technometrics, vol. 51, 2009, pp. 425–438.

[40] J. Nash and J. Sutcliffe, "River flow forecasting through conceptual models, Part I - A discussion of principles," Journal of Hydrology, vol. 10, 1970, pp. 282–290.

[41] B. Schaefli and H. Gupta, "Do Nash values have value?" Hydrological Processes, vol. 21, 2007, pp. 2075–2080.

[42] H. Gupta, H. Kling, K. Yilmaz, and G. Martinez, "Decomposition of the mean squared error and NSE performance criteria: Implications for improving hydrological modelling," Journal of Hydrology, vol. 377, 2009, pp. 80–91.

[43] N. Sören Blomquist, "A note on the use of the coefficient of determination," The Scandinavian Journal of Economics, vol. 82, 980, pp. 409–412.

[44] N. Nagelkerke, "A note on a general definition of the coefficient of determination," Biometrika, vol. 78, 1991, pp. 691–692.

[45] P. Krause, D. Boyle, and F. Bäse, "Comparison of different efficiency criteria for hydrological model assessment," Advances in Geosciences, vol. 5, 2005, pp. 89–97.

[46] J. Liao and D. McGee, "Adjusted coefficients of determination for logistic regression," The American Statistician, vol. 57, 2003, pp. 161–165.

[47] C. Willmot, "On the validation of models," Physical Geography, vol. 2, 1981, pp. 184–194.

[48] C. Willmott, S. Ackleson, R. Davis, Feddema, K. Klink, D. Legates, J. O'Donnell, and C. Rowe, "Statistics for the evaluation and comparison of models," Journal of Geophysical Research, vol. 90, 1985, pp. 8995–9005.

[49] C. Willmott, S. Robeson, and K. Matsuura, "A refined index of model performance," International Journal of Climatology, vol. 32, 2012, pp. 2088–2094.

[50] M. Barbouchi, R. Abdelfattah, K. Chokmani, N. B. Aissa, R. Lhissou, and A. E. Harti, "Soil salinity characterization using polarimetric InSAR coherence: Case studies in Tunisia and Morocco," IEEE Journal of Selected Topics in Applied Earth Observations and Remote Sensing, vol. 8, 2015, pp. 3823–3832.

[51] D. M. M. Ahouansou, S. K. Agodzo, S. Kralisch, L. O. Sintondji, and C. Fürst, "Analysis of the hydrological budget using the J2000 model in the Pendjari River Basin, West Africa," Journal of Environment and Earth Science, vol. 5, 2015, pp. 24–37.

[52] C. Willmott, S. Robeson, and K. Matsuura, "A refined index of model performance," International Journal of Climatology, vol. 32, 2011, pp. 2088–2094.

[53] G. Duveiller, D. Fasbender, and M. Meroni, "Revisiting the concept of a symmetric index of agreement for continuous datasets," Scientific Reports, vol. 6, 2016, doi:10.1038/srep19401.

[54] T. Mathevet, C. Michel, V. Andréassian, and C. Perrin, "A bounded version of the Nash-Sutcliffe criterion for better model assessment on large sets of basins," in IAHS Red Books Series no. 307. IAHS, 2006.

Combining spectral and spatial information for heavy equipment detection in airborne images

Katia Stankov
R&D department
Synodon Inc.
Edmonton AB Canada
e-mail: katia.stankov@usherbrooke.ca

Boyd Tolton
R&D department
Synodon Inc.
Edmonton AB Canada
e-mail: boyd.tolton@ synodon.com

***Abstract* - Unsupervised construction on the pipeline right-of-way may provoke pipe rupture and consequently gas leaks. Heavy equipment is seen as a clue for construction activity. Monitoring the pipeline right-of-way for heavy equipment is therefore important for environmental and human safety. Remotely sensed images are an alternative to expensive and time consuming foot patrol. Existing image processing methods make use of previous images and/or external data. Both are not always available. We propose a new method for image processing to detect heavy equipment without the need of auxiliary data. We first detect potential heavy equipment locations and then use spatial descriptors and spectral information to eliminate false alarms. The method was validated in different environments – urban, vegetation, open excavation – and in different seasons. The experiments demonstrated the capacity of the method to detect heavy equipment without the use of previous images and/or external data.**

Keywords-remote sensing image processing; right-of-way threats detection; differential morphological profile; spectral information; Hausdorff distance.

I. INTRODUCTION

Unsupervised construction activity on oil and gas pipeline's Right-of Way (ROW) may lead to pipeline rupture and leaks. The periodic surveillance of the ROW for the presence of heavy equipment or construction machinery, referred also as ROW threats, is therefore vital to protect the human safety and to prevent ecological damage. Pipeline networks span thousands of kilometers and may be located in remote and difficult to access areas. Airborne and satellite images are considered to complete the surveys. Computer based methods to detect construction machinery in these images represent an alternative of the slow and tedious task of visual image analysis.

In our previous paper [1] we presented a method for heavy equipment detection in airborne images, based on the differential morphological profile and spatial characteristics of the objects. In this paper, we present a notable improvement of the method by analyzing spectral information as well. We have also shown expanded experiments to support the method's achievements.

The paper is organized as follows. In Section II we give the state-of-the-art, Section III presents the methodology, in Section IV we provide results, validation and discussion, and in Section V a conclusion.

II. STATE-OF-THE-ART

The automation of the process of heavy equipment detection in airborne images faces difficulties from different origin: great variety of vehicles; uneven flight altitude; different view and orientation of the images; variable illumination conditions; occlusion by neighboring objects, and others [2]. In addition, construction vehicles are sometimes very similar to transportation vehicles. All these make the development of pattern recognition algorithms for ROW threat detection a challenging remote sensing image processing task.

Existing methods extract characteristic features to decrease the differences between construction vehicles (decrease the intra-class heterogeneity), while increasing the inter-class heterogeneity, i.e., make heavy equipment more distinguishable from other objects. In [3], scale-invariant feature transform was applied on previously defined scale invariant regions to receive object descriptors and detect vehicles. Presuming that local distribution of oriented gradients (edge orientations) is a good indicator for the presence of an object, Dalal [4] proposed the accumulative Histogram of the Oriented Gradients (HOG). In [5], the authors mapped HOG to Fourier domain to achieve rotation invariance and used kernel Support Vector Machine (SVM) to classify the data and identify construction vehicles. Using local textural descriptors and adaptive perception based segmentation, the authors in [2] sequentially eliminate background objects from the image, such as buildings, vegetation, roads, etc. The remaining potential threat locations are divided into several parts to extract and evaluate descriptive features and match them against template data. Extraction of local phase information allowed the separation between structure details and local energy (contrast) [6]. Afterwards, based on previously defined image template, the authors in [6] created a voting matrix to detect construction vehicles. An interesting approach to derive the template images from the processed image itself was proposed in [7]. The authors created an immune network and first trained image areas against vehicles samples; next, they processed the whole images in a similar way to detect vehicles. However, the vehicles samples were defined by human operator. Potential vehicle locations were derived through rule based classifier applied on numerous spatial and gray-level features computed on a segmented image in [8]. Statistical classifier was then used to assign objects to the vehicle class. Though this method avoids the definition of template images, it involved manual image analysis to design training samples.

Exploiting the fact that heavy equipment has a larger number of right corners than natural objects, the authors in [9] defined target and background templates from the images. They used Harris corner detector to perform a first fast processing of UAV images and to reject background. In the second stage of the method the authors compared the performance of four classifiers (k Nearest Neighbors, Support Vector Machine, Decision Trees and Random Tress) and two feature extraction algorithms (HOG and Gabor coefficients). Best results were achieved with Gabor coefficients and Random Trees classifier. However, the results were more consistent while using a set of indoor images of model vehicles, taken in a sand box, than with the set defined from the images.

To decrease the large sets of templates needed to train and test the classifier, the authors in [10] developed a novel system based on the AdaBoost classifier. They applied it on SAR images to detect three types of vehicles and achieved recognition rates above 95% with a very limited training set. Gabor wavelet of SAR images was used to extract descriptive feature parameters in [11] to identify several types of vehicles.

Synthetic aperture radar images provide all weather coverage and are not restricted to the presence of daylight illumination. This property proved very efficient for change detection and potential threat localization [12]. Additional high spatial resolution optical images are to be analyzed to identify positive alarms.

To fully avoid the need of image template, potential threats locations are assessed with the aid of change detection in [13], next auxiliary data is used to decide upon the presence of a threat.

A common trait of existing methods is that the successful recognition of heavy equipment is impossible without complete set of image templates, previous images, and/or auxiliary data. These are not always available in practice. Airborne images of the pipeline ROW are taken only when a customer orders a survey. Previous images are not available when it comes to a new customer. Acquiring auxiliary data or building complete set of templates for the large variety of heavy equipment vehicles will significantly increase the cost of the survey. All of the above made existing methods not applicable in our case, thus we opted for a method that involves the interpretation of individual images.

The new methodology for heavy equipment detection we present in this paper avoids both the need of template images, and the need of auxiliary data or previously acquired images. In addition to increased flexibility, it also makes the performance of the method independent of the quality of the external data. As in our previous method [1], we first localize potential threats by detecting areas of high frequency of the image that correspond to the size of construction machinery and compute spatial descriptors. Unlike the previous method, where we used all the descriptors at once to discriminate between threats and other objects, here we consecutively eliminate non threats locations. The significant improvement of the recognition came from the inclusion of spectral information. We analyze spectral information on the inner parts of the potential locations retained in the previous steps to refine the results. In the following section we give a step by step description of the method.

III. Description of the Method

The method may be roughly divided in three parts. First, we find potential threat locations. In the next step these locations are treated as objects, and spatial indices are derived to eliminate the ones that are certainly no threats. Finally, we introduce spectral information to further tune the results. A detailed description is given in Fig. 4.

A. *Finding potential threat locations*

To build our method we take advantage of the fact that construction vehicles have non-flatten surfaces, which creates inequality in the intensity of surface pixels and together with their outer edges make that they appear as areas of high frequency in the image. Therefore, potential threat locations may be found by identifying areas of high frequencies that are in the range of heavy equipment size. We apply the differential morphological profile on the gradient of the image to find areas of high frequency.

1) Differential Morphological Profile (DMP): DMP is an iterative algorithm that performs opening/closing by reconstruction with a structuring element (SE) to find structures that are brighter/darker than their surroundings. The size of the SE is increased in the consecutive iteration and the result is extracted from the result of the previous iteration. As we are searching for structures that are brighter than their surroundings, we used only the opening by reconstruction to compute the DMP, as follows [14]. Let the vector $\Pi\gamma(x)$ be the opening profile at the point x of image I defined by:

$$\Pi\gamma(x) = \{\Pi\gamma_\lambda : \Pi\gamma_\lambda = \gamma^*_\lambda(x), \forall\lambda \in [0,...,n]\} \quad (1)$$

where $\gamma^*_\lambda(x)$ is the morphological opening by reconstruction operator and the size of the $SE = \lambda$.

The DMP $\Delta\gamma(x)$ is a vector that stores a measure of the slope between consecutive iterations of the opening profile corresponding to the increased size of the SE:

$$\Delta\gamma(x) = \{\Delta\gamma_\lambda : \Delta\gamma_\lambda = |\Pi\gamma_\lambda - \Pi\gamma_{\lambda-1}|, \forall\lambda \in [1,...,n]\} \quad (2)$$

When the SE size exceeds the object size, the background intensity values are assigned to the object. Thus, by extracting two consecutive results, bright objects that correspond or are bigger than the size of the corresponding SE are retained. The object is eliminated in the consecutive iteration if it is smaller than the SE. Thus by knowing when, in what level of the DMP, an object disappeared one may conclude about its size.

The DMP has to be applied on a grayscale image, usually the brightness (the maximum between the red, green and blue channel - RGB) is used. Here we introduce a new technique based on the Color Invariant Model developed by Gevers and Smeulders [15].

2) Invariant Color Model: The invariant color model computes the angles of the reflection vector and is invariant to illumination intensity and viewing direction [15].

$$C1 = \arctan (R/\max\{G,B\}) \quad (3)$$

$$C2 = \arctan (G/\max\{R,B\}) \quad (4)$$

$$C3 = \arctan (B/\max\{R,G\}) \quad (5)$$

The model was designed to compensate for matte and dull surfaces and increases the differences in the inner parts of the construction machinery, which are sometimes attenuated in RGB. To enhance these inequalities, we generate a new image using the maximum between C1, C2, and C3, and compute the gradient of this image.

The gradient of an image measures the directional changes of the intensity levels of an image. Because these changes are greater towards the edges of an object, the gradient highlights the transitions between objects. The uneven surface of heavy equipment may be related to as composed from few small objects, which in the gradient image generated from the invariant color model will appear as a high concentration of edges.

3) Computing the gradient: To obtain the gradient of the image we use the measure of the discontinuity D_{xy} at each pixel with image coordinates x and y [16]:

$$D_{xy} = \sqrt{G_x^2 + G_y^2} \quad (6)$$

where G_x and G_y are the gradients at an image pixel in the x (horizontal) and y (vertical) directions, respectively. To compute the gradient we approximated the partial derivative in the horizontal direction with the central difference between columns; and in the vertical direction – with the central difference between rows, based on Sobel kernel.

As shown in Fig. 1, the gradient of the image derived from the invariant color model produces an aggregation of edges in the inner parts of the threats, which allow for better differentiating construction machinery from other vehicles, compared to the gradient obtained from the brightness image. The higher the gradient value of a pixel, the higher the possibility that it belongs to an edge. To retain edges we threshold the gradient image derived from the invariant color model using the Otsu's method.

4) Localizing areas of high frequency: To find areas of high frequency we applied the DMP on the gradient image. The separation between objects with DMP depends on the size of the SE used for the opening by reconstruction [17]. To fit inner parts of heavy equipment machinery we derived the set of SEs from the size of these parts in accordance with the spatial resolution of the image. In our case, the size of the image pixel is 9 cm, which allowed using a set of SE ranging from 4x4 to 12x12 pixels with an increment of 4. When using DMP, objects situated closer than the size of the SE may be merged together in the corresponding DMP level. The set of SE we used was kind of compromise between retaining the whole construction vehicle and avoiding the merge with nearby objects. To eliminate irrelevant locations we first used spatial information.

Unlike our previous method where we used all relevant spatial properties simultaneously to apply principal component analysis (PCA) and reduce false positives, here we first eliminated irrelevant locations based on the thresholding of few spatial properties. Next, we introduced spectral information and together with additional spatial property, we used the PCA to further refine the detection. As in the feature space the discrimination between classes is not linear [18] this two steps filtering proved to be more efficient.

B. *Spatial information*

For each DMP level, we find out connected components

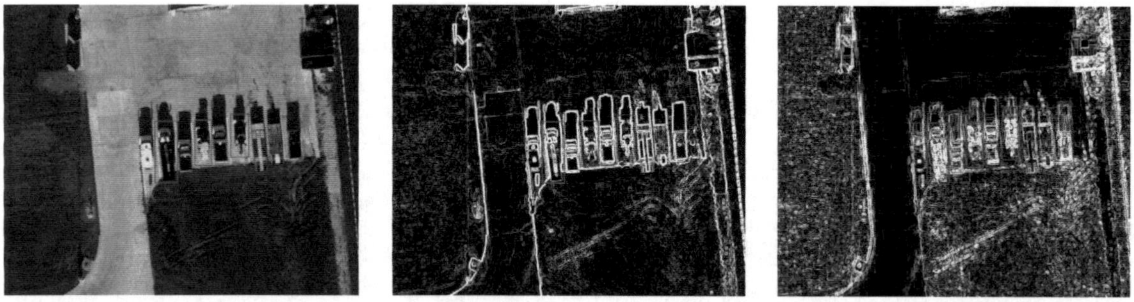

(a) (b) (c)

Figure 1. Gradient image. (a) Original RGB (b) Gradient of the brigthness image (from the original RGB); (c) Gradient of the maximum between C1, C2 and C3 (the invariant color model). Heavy equipment is given in red rectangles. The inavriant color model enhances the edges in the inner parts of the heavy euipment, and in result the threats are more distinguishible from other vehicles in (c), compared to (b).

and obtained image objects for which spatial properties may be computed. To each one of the spatial properties we assigned thresholds with a large margin of error in order to ensure only objects that for certain are not threats will be removed. As we further refine the results we were not concerned in this step of the method about the number of false positives. Following is a description of the spatial properties that better discriminate heavy equipment from other objects together with the way we set an appropriate threshold for them:

1) Area: As stated earlier threats may merge with background depending on the interaction between their size and the size of the SE. For example, construction machinery is often situated in areas with digging activity. Digging is characterized by soil piles, which cast shadow and produce edge like effect in images and may merge with nearby objects. Sometimes, the distance between threats may be smaller than the size of the SE and consequently they will merge in the corresponding level of the DMP. As in these cases larger objects will correspond to heavy equipment, we defined a high threshold value for area (10000 pixels) and removed objects above it.

2) Elongation: Heavy equipment has rectangular shape. The ratio between the major and the minor axis length of the object is a good indicator for the rectangularity of a shape. Higher values for this ratio correspond to objects with linear extension such as roads. Square shapes obtain values closer to 1. We gave a large margin between 1.1 and 5.

3) Curvature: We approximate the curvature with the radius of the circle that fits the best the contours of the object. First we fill the objects, next we find the coordinates of the contour of the filled objects to solve the least mean square problem and calculate the radius of the circle. The curvature is given by 1/radius [19]. The curvature of a straight line will be zero, so the greater the ratio 1/radius, the greater the curvature of the curve. We are searching therefore for objects whose curvature is greater than 0 and lower than some value corresponding to curved shapes. As we eliminate lines based on the elongation property we are not concerned to impose a lower threshold to the curvature. To define an upper threshold we use the Hough transform.

4) Hough transform: Hough transform is useful technique to fit straight lines to object boundaries. For small round objects it finds zero lines. We use the Matlab implemented algorithm with the only constraint of 100 peaks in the parametric space, and find the minimum curvature of the objects that received no lines after the Hough transform. We use this minimum curvature value of the most curved objects in the image to define an upper threshold on the curvature.

To further refine the results and decide whether an object belongs to the class of heavy equipment we analyzed also spectral information.

C. Assigning objects to the class of heavy equipment

To assign objects to the class of heavy equipment we use spectral information, vegetation mask, and a property called edgeness. We designed decision rules to determine whether an object may represent a threat.

1) Spectral properties: We analyze spectral information derived from the inner parts of the objects because the spectra of their contours may be affected by the transition between objects and therefore not a good indicator of the spectral properties of the object. As heavy equipment is painted in saturated colors it appears as bright spot in at least one of the invariant color bands C1, C2, and C3, and as dark spots in the remaining bands, on the contrary of other manmade objects or the background, which have average values in all of the channels. We generate two images; one

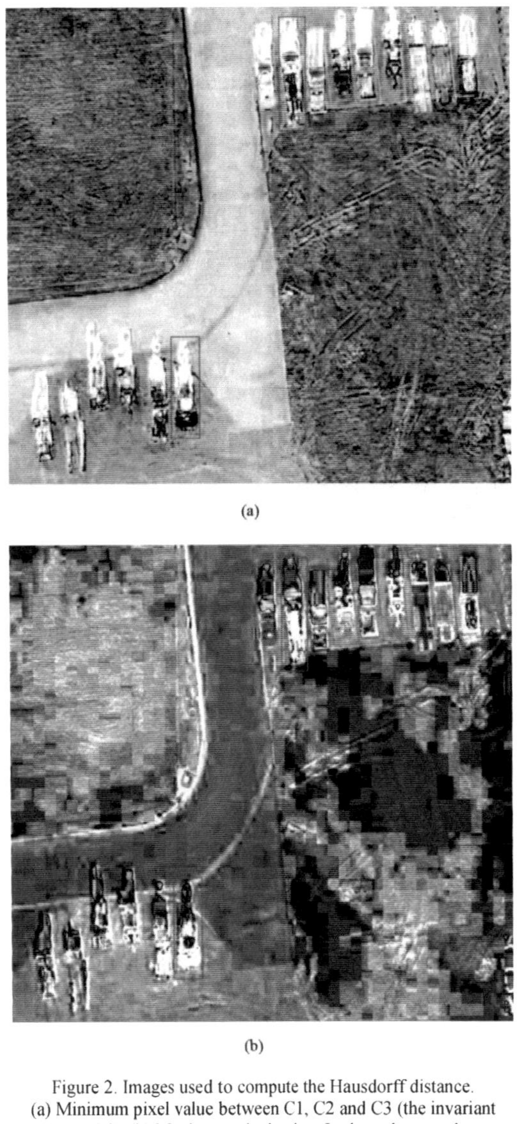

(a)

(b)

Figure 2. Images used to compute the Hausdorff distance. (a) Minimum pixel value between C1, C2 and C3 (the invariant color model); (b) Maximum pixel value. In the red rectangles are given examples of heavy equipement. Lower values in (a) correspond to higher values in (b).

takes the minimum between the three new channels for each pixel (Fig. 2 (a)) and the other one – the minimum (Fig. 2 (b)).

To assess the differences between the maximum and minimum of the set of pixels occupying the inner parts of objects, we use the Hausdorff distance. It is an efficient measure to estimate the mismatch between two sets of points without being influenced by variance or noise [20].

Given two sets of points A = {a_1, …., a_n} and B = {b_1, …., b_n}, the Hausdorff distance is defined as [20]:

$$H(A,B) = \max(h(A,B), h(B,A)) \quad (7)$$

where

$$h(A,B) = \max_{a \in A} \min_{b \in B} \| a - b \| \quad (8)$$

and ||.|| is some norm. We used the Euclidean distance.

The Hausdorff distance first identifies the point of given set A that is farthest from any point in set B and then computes the distance from this point to its nearest neighbor in B and vice versa, from the point of B that is farthest from any other point of A, it finds the distance to the nearest neighbor in A. Then it takes the maximum between the two distances. Thus, every point in one set is within the Hausdorff distance from some other point in the other set and vice versa [20].

We calculate the Hausdorff distance between the two sets of pixels values obtained from the maximum and minimum images received from the C1, C2, and C3 bands. As heavy equipment vehicles have saturated colors they will receive higher values for the Hausdorff distance. Moreover, a larger amount of their pixels will reside within this margin, according to the per pixel difference between the maximum and the minimum of the C1, C2, and C3 channels. We compute the percent of pixels in the whole object whose differences between the maximum and the minimum of the C1, C2, and C3 channels are within the Hausdorff distance for the corresponding object. In the rest of the paper we refer to this property as spectral mismatch occupancy (SMO). Construction machinery receives higher SMO values, as most of the pixels are in the margins defined by the Hausdorff distance. Would we define a threshold on the saturation image to compute the SMO, we would receive higher values for other objects too. We illustrate this in Fig. 3. As shown, the Hausdorff distance allowed to better differentiate the levels of saturation.

To define whether an object may belong to the class of

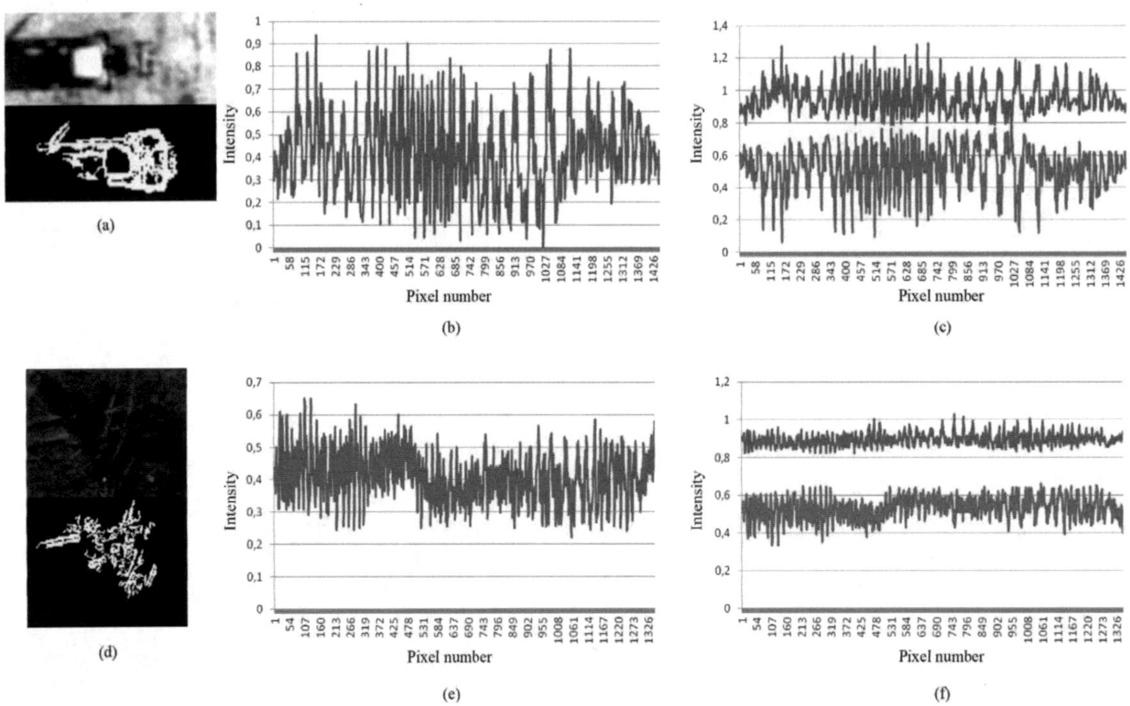

Figure 3. Saturation versus Hausdorff distance: (a) Heavy euqipment, original RGB (above), corresponding object (below); (b) Saturation profile of the object in (a); (c) Maximum and minimum profile of the object in (a); (d) Background object, original RGB (above), corresponding object (below); (e) Saturation profile of the object in (b); (f) Maximum and minimum profile of the object in (b). For the heavy equipment in (a) the Hausdorff distance is equal to 0.59, the SMO is 0.24. For the object in (d) Hausdorff distance equals 0.52, SMO – 0.2.

heavy equipment we compare the SMO to the vegetation occupancy.

2) Compare SMO to vegetation occupancy and apply decision rules: First, we compute the vegetation index from the RGB bands, because the airborne images we work with have only these three bands:

$$Vegetation\ Index = (Green - Red)/(Green + Red) \quad (9)$$

Using the Otsu's threshold method, we generate a vegetation mask. The vegetation occupancy of an object is obtained as the percent of masked pixels in the object area.

The difference between SMO and vegetation occupancy varies according to the scene. To adapt our method we apply the following rules to retain ROW threats.

In scenes occupied mostly by green vegetation, a single threat will have definitely higher SMO than vegetation occupancy, compared to other objects. Thus, if less than 10 percent of the objects have higher SMO than vegetation occupancy, we assume that this is the case and retain these objects (Fig. 6 (a)). However, when the scene is occupied by buildings, excavations, or the image is taken in winter season when no green vegetation is present, but only leafless trees and shrubs, the vegetation mask may also cover part of the heavy equipment and the predominance of SMO over vegetation occupancy is not so evident.

In cases where there is a lack of strict distinction between vegetation and other objects (the SMO is less than the vegetation occupancy for all of the objects or more than 10 percent of the objects have higher SMO than vegetation occupancy), we use the property called edgeness. It is obtained by dividing the area of the object by the number of edge pixels of the object. To receive the area of the object we fill the boundary of the object. As stated earlier, because of the surface inequalities of construction vehicles, they will receive higher edgeness than vegetation areas, or other transport vehicles as shown in Fig. 1 (c).

We concatenate the two properties: 1) the difference between SMO and vegetation occupancy; 2) the edgeness value. Then we computed the principal component analysis and divided the objects according to their first principal score, setting the median of the scores as a threshold. To decide which group to retain we used the ratio between the eigenvalues of the covariance matrix of each group. Threats have higher intra-class heterogeneity compared to other objects. The ratio between the eigenvalues is a good indicator for heterogeneity [21], thus we used the ratio of the eigenvalues of the covariance matrix. Greater values correspond to greater heterogeneity, thus we retained the group that produced higher value for the eigenvalue's ratio.

Step by step results together with a flow chart of the method are given in Fig. 4.

D. Post-processing

As the images may not contain threats at all, we included a step of automate post-processing to refine the results. We used a vector composed from the Hausdorff distance and the SMO. We then sorted the magnitude of the vector and computed the slope of the tangent at each point. A point

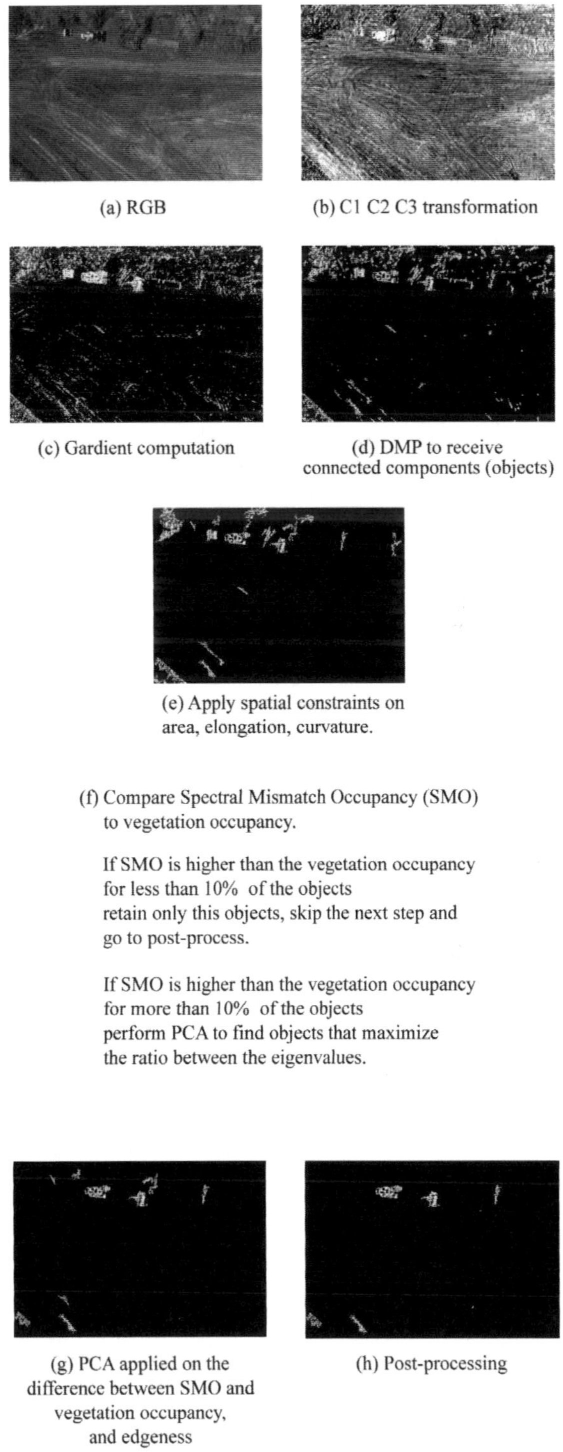

Figure 4. Flow chart of the proposed method. From (a) to (h) - the consecutive steps.

represents the sorted magnitude value for each object. An empirically derived threshold was set to retain objects whose slope was less than the threshold. The rationale here is that if the objects belong to the class of threat their magnitude will be similar and therefore the slope of the tangent will be less than this ratio. If no threat were retained the values for the magnitude will be quite different and the slope will be higher than the threshold. As shown in Fig. 5 this step was efficient to further refine the results.

IV. RESULTS AND VALIDATION

We present some results in Figs. 6, 7 and 8. We indicated true detections – heavy equipment that are present in the image and were identified by the method – with rectangles with yellow contours; false alarms, or false positives – objects that were identified by the method as threats, but are actually not threats – with rectangles with red contours, and missed detection – heavy equipment that is present in the image but was not identified as such by the method – with rectangles with green contours.

As may be seen from Fig. 6 the method performs well in different scenes – forest (a), urban scene (c), abandoned site (e), and ongoing excavations (g). These different backgrounds provide low (abandoned site – (e)) to high contrast (ongoing excavations – (g)). Despite that, the method successfully detected ROW threats. We explain this with the improved spectral contrast obtained with the invariant color model. In Fig. 6 (c) many transportation vehicles were present, which are usually a source of confusion with heavy equipment. The edgeness property allowed for better separation between them. Similar results are shown in Fig. 7 ((a) and (e)).

Fig. 7 (c) shows a typical case of missing a threat. Although both vehicles are very similar, only one was detected. The other one was merged with the nearby fence and treated as a linear object. Fig. 7 (g) demonstrates the capacity of the method to detect threats when there is an accumulation of objects with size similar to this of heavy equipment, that appear as areas of high frequency. However, in this case, many false alarms were also detected as threats.

In Fig. 8 we demonstrate the limitation of the method. When a single threat is present in the image, other objects may be misinterpreted as threats and the real threat omitted. In our opinion, the main reason for this is that while performing the PCA we assume the presence of only two classes. This may be improved by using cluster analysis, applied on the objects principal component scores. In Fig. 8 (c, e and g) we demonstrate typical cases of false alarms. We believe that more rigorous post- processing step would decrease their number.

To validate the accuracy of the method we compared the results to manually detected threats. We refer to the latter as ground truth data. A set of 300 images taken from different surveys was processed. The image size is 1200x800 pixels with average pixel resolution of 9 cm. The detection rate was 83.9% - heavy equipment machines that are present in the ground truth data and were detected by the algorithm. This is a slight improvement compared to our previous method, where the detection rate was 82.6%. However, in the current experiment the images are more heterogeneous, taken from different seasons, as opposite to the previous test where we used images of the same flight day. Also, visual comparison reveals that the number of false positive was significantly reduced.

To place our method among other algorithms for threat detection we compare its achievement to the results reported in [9]. The authors compared several classifiers. Our method, with the detection rate of 83.9% performs slightly better than the kNN classifier (83.3%) and less than the regression trees and SVM classifiers – 85.7% and 93.3%, respectively. However, these classifiers were applied on rural scene only and used template models. As we demonstrated above, our method performs well in different scenes, without using templates or auxiliary data. We may say therefore that it has a potential and we focus our further developments to improve the detection rate and reduce the false detections.

At this stage of the development of the algorithm we are less concerned with the rate of false recognition, as the results are reviewed by an operator. We consider including additional descriptors to reduce the number of false positives events while increasing the detection rate.

The limitation of the method is related to the spatial resolution of the image. In our opinion, the method performance may decrease when applied on images with much lower spatial resolution, more than 1 meter for example, as it relies explicitly on information taken from an increasing neighborhood.

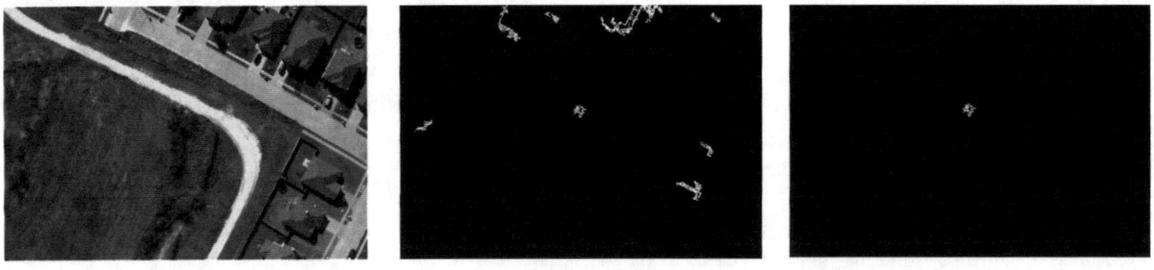

(a) (b) (c)

Figure 5. Post-processsing. (a) Original RGB; (b) Processed image; (c) Results after post-processing.

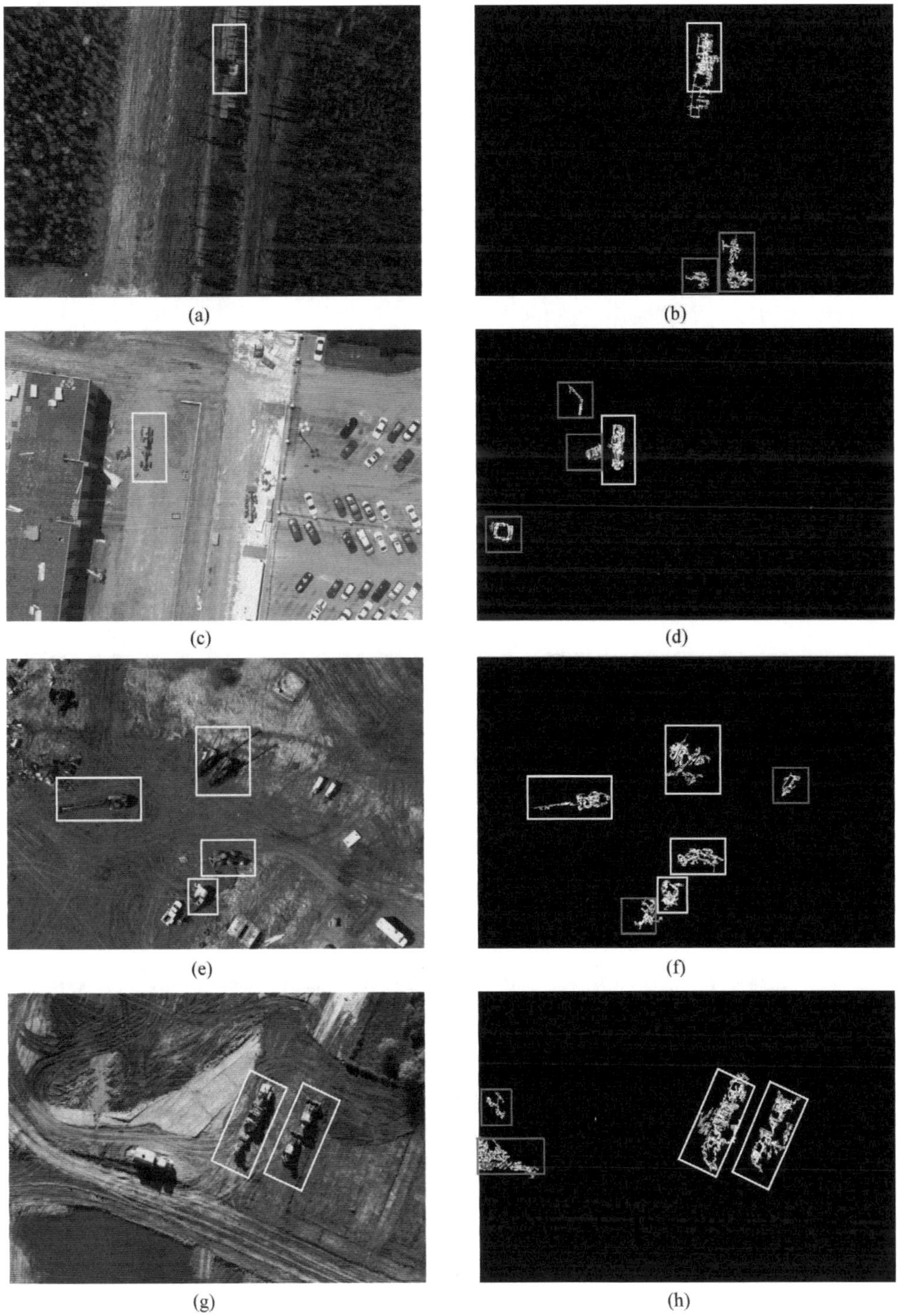

Figure 6. Results. Left column original RGB image. Righ column – detection. Rectangles with yellow contours indicate true detections; rectangles with red contours - false alarms; rectangles with green contours - missed detections.

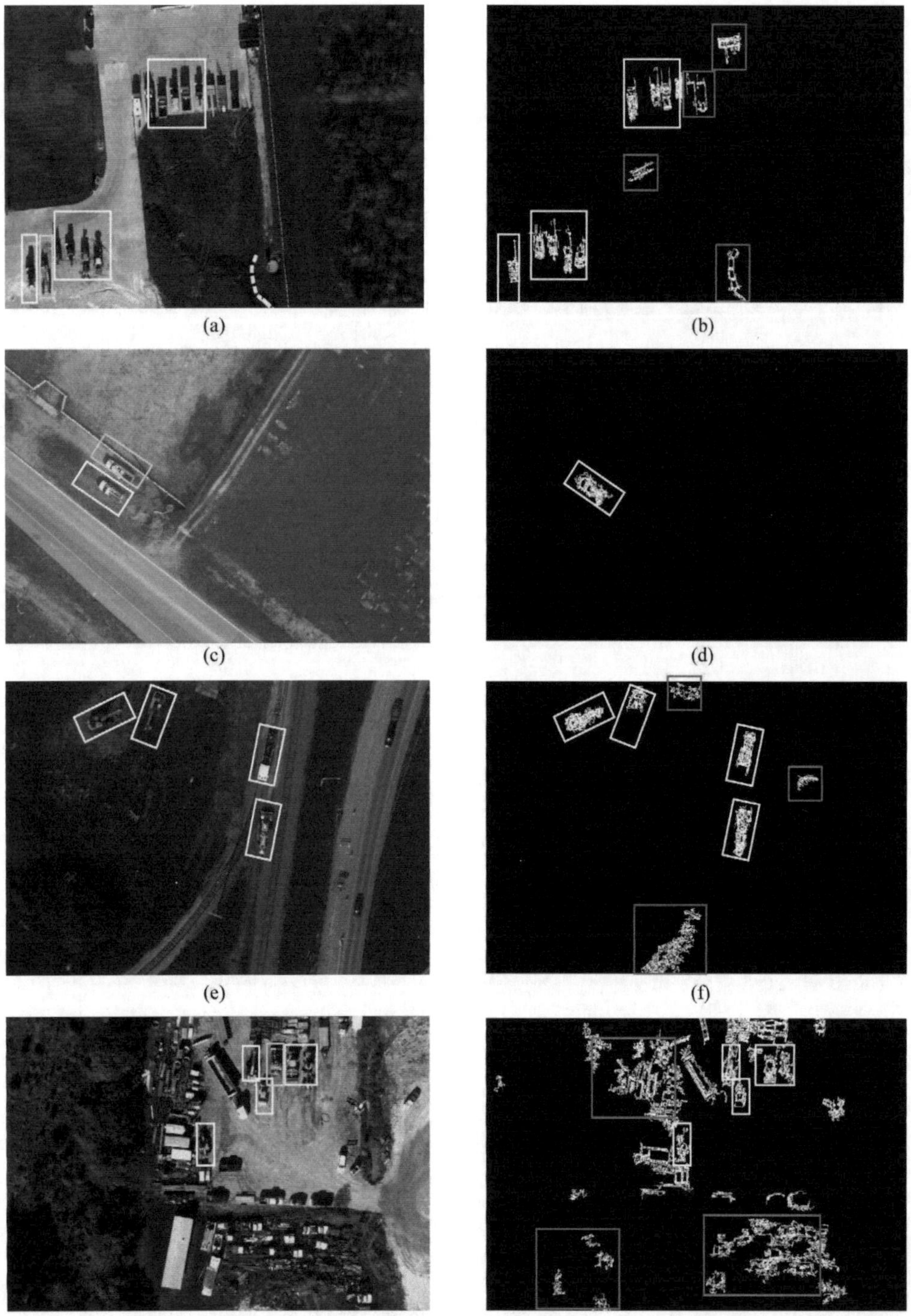

Figure 7. Results. Left column original RGB image. Righ column – detection. Rectangles with yellow contours indicate true detections; rectangles with red contours - false alarms; rectangles with green contours - missed detections.

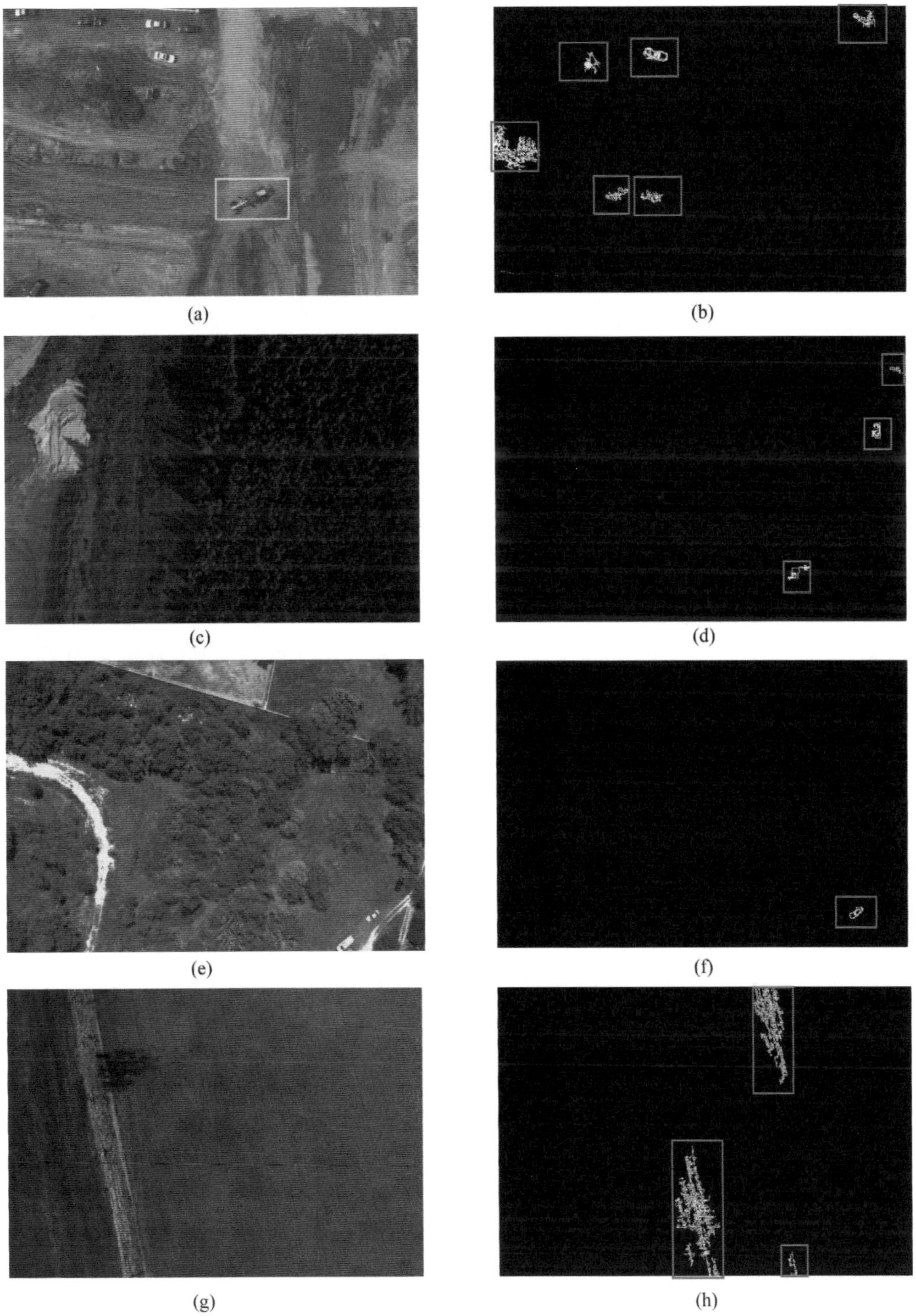

Figure 8. Results. Left column original RGB image. Righ column – detection. Rectangles with yellow contours indicate true detections; rectangles with red contours - false alarms; rectangles with green contours - missed detections.

V. Conclusion

In this paper, we presented a novel methodology for heavy equipment detection. The method first detects high frequency areas in the image that may represent potential heavy equipment locations, and then compute spatial descriptors and explore spectral information to eliminate false detections. It does not involve the use of external data, or previously acquired images, which makes it more flexible, compared to already existing algorithms. An improvement compared to our previous method [1] is due to the exploration of spectral information all along the spatial descriptors. Our method compares favorably to other methods for threat detection. On the contrary of other studies, we tested it in different scenes – urban, forest, excavation areas. The experiments proved its efficiency for surveillance of the pipeline ROW, which is important for human safety and ecological damage prevention. The results are promising and we believe that the method has the potential to replace the manual processing of the images.

Acknowledgment

This research was funded by Alberta Innovates Technology Future. The authors would like to express their gratitude for the support provided by the Industry Associate Program of the institution.

References

[1] K. Stankov and B. Tolton, "Differential morphological profile for threat detection on pipeline right-of-way. Heavy equipment detection," The Eighth International Conference on Advanced Geographic Information Systems, Applications, and Services (Geoprocessing 2016), IARIA, Apr 2016, pp. 76-77, ISSN: 2308-393X , ISBN: 978-1-61208-469-5.

[2] V. Asari, Vijayan, P. Sidike, C. Cui, and V. Santhaseelan. "New wide-area surveillance techniques for protection of pipeline infrastructure." SPIE Newsroom, 30 January 2015, DOI: 10.1117/2.1201501.005760

[3] G. Dorko and C. Schmid, "Selection of scale-invariant parts for object class recognition," IProceedings of the 9th International Conference on Computer Vision, Nice, France, pp. 634–640, 2003.

[4] N. Dalal and B. Triggs, "Histograms of oriented gradients for human detection," IEEE Conference on Computer Vision and Pattern Recognition, pp. 886-893, 2005

[5] A. Mathew and V. K. Asari, "Rotation-invariant Histogram Features for Threat Object Detection on Pipeline Right-of-Way," in Video Surveillance and Transportation Imaging Applications 2014, edited by Robert P. Loce, Eli Saber, Proc. of SPIE-IS&T Electronic Imaging, SPIE vol. 9026, pp. 902604-1-902604-1, 2014 SPIE-IS&T doi: 10.1117/12.2039663

[6] B. Nair, V. Santhaseelan, C. Cui, and V. K. Asari, "Intrusion detection on oil pipeline right of way using monogenic signal representation," Proc. SPIE 8745, 2013, p. 87451U, doi:10.1117/12.2015640

[7] H. Zheng and L. Li, "An artificial immune approach for vehicle detection from high resolution space imagery," IJCSNS International Journal of Computer Science and Network Security, vol.7 no.2, pp. 67-72, February 2007.

[8] L. Eikvil, L. Aurdal, and H. Koren, "Classification-based vehicle detection in high resolution satellite images," ISPRS Journal of Photogrammetry and Remote Sensing, vol. 64, issue 1, pp. 65-72, January 2009. doi.org/10.1016/j.isprsjprs.2008.09.005

[9] J. Gleason, A. Nefian, X. Bouyssounousse, T. Fong, and G. Bebis, "Vehicle detection from aerial imagery," 2011 IEEE International Conference on Robotics and Automation, pp. 2065-2070, May 2011.

[10] Y. Sun, Z. Liu, S. Todorovic, and J. Li, "Synthetic aperture radar automatic target recognition using adaptive boosting," Proceedings of the SPIE, Algorithms for Synthetic Aperture Radar Imagery XII, 5808, pp. 282-293, May 2005.

[11] P. Vasuki and S. M. M. Roomi, "Man-made object classification in SAR images using Gabor wavelet and neural network classifier," Proc. IEEE. Devices, Circuits and Systems Int. Conf., India, pp. 537–539, IEEE 2012.

[12] Roper, W. E. and Dutta, S. "Oil Spill and Pipeline Condition Assessment Using Remote Sensing and Data Visualization Management Systems," George Mason University, 4400 University Drive, 2006.

[13] M. Zarea, G. Pognonec, C. Schmidt, T. Schnur, J. Lana, C. Boehm, M. Buschmann, C. Mazri, and E. Rigaud, "First steps in developing an automated aerial surveillance approach," Journal of Risk Research, vol.13(3–4): pp. 407–420, 2013 doi:10.1080/13669877.2012.729520.

[14] J. A. Benediktsson, M. Pesaresi, and K. Arnason, "Classification and feature extraction from remote sensing images from urban areas based on morphological transformations," IEEE Transactions on Geoscience and Remote Sensing, vol. 41(9), pp. 1940–1949, 2003.

[15] T. Gevers and A. W. M. Smeulders, "Color based object recognition," Pattern Recognit., vol. 32, pp. 453–465, Mar. 1999.

[16] H. Wang and D. Suter, "Color image segmentation using global information and local homogeneity," in: Proc. VIIth Digital Image Computing: Techniques and Applications, Sun C., Talbot H., Ourselin S. and Adriaansen T., Eds., Sydney, pp. 89-98, Dec. 2003.

[17] G.K. Ouzounis, M. Pesaresi, and P. Soille, "Differential area profiles: decomposition properties and efficient computation," IEEE Transactions on Pattern Analysis and Machine Intelligence, vol. 34, no. 8, pp. 1533-1548, Aug. 2012.

[18] X. Chen, T. Fang, H. Huo, and D. Li, "Graph-based feature selection for object-oriented classification in VHR airborne imagery," IEEE Transactions on Geoscience and Remote Sensing, vol. 49 (1), pp. 353–365, 2011.

[19] https://www.mathworks.com/matlabcentral/newsreader/view_thread/152405

[20] D. P. Huttenlocher, G. Klanderman, and W. J. Rucklidge,. "Comparing images using the Hausdorff distance," IEEE Trans. Pattern Anal. Mach. Intell. 15, 9, pp. 850–863, 1993.

[21] F. O'Sullivan, S. Roy, and J. Eary, "A statistical measure of tissue heterogeneity with application to 3D PET sarcoma data," Biostatistics vol. 4, pp. 433–448, 2003.

Management Control System for Business Rules Management

Koen Smit
Digital Smart Services
HU University of Applied Sciences Utrecht
Utrecht, the Netherlands
koen.smit@hu.nl

Martijn Zoet
Optimizing Knowledge-Intensive Business Processes
Zuyd University of Applied Sciences
Sittard, the Netherlands
martijn.zoet@zuyd.nl

Abstract — **With increasing investments in business rules management (BRM), organizations are searching for ways to value and benchmark their processes to elicitate, design, specify, verify, validate, deploy, execute and govern business rules. To realize valuation and benchmarking of previously mentioned processes, organizations must be aware that performance measurement is essential, and of equal importance, which performance indicators to apply as part of performance measurement processes. However, scientific research on BRM, in general, is limited and research that focuses on BRM in combination with performance indicators is nascent. The purpose of this paper is to define performance indicators for previously mentioned BRM processes. We conducted a three round focus group and three round Delphi Study, which led to the identification of 14 performance indicators. In this paper, we re-address and - present our earlier work [33], yet we extended the previous research with more detailed descriptions of the related literature, findings, and results, which provide a grounded basis from which further, empirical, research on performance indicators for BRM can be explored.**

Keywords-Business Rules Management; Business Rules; Performance Measurement; Performance Indicator.

I. INTRODUCTION

Business rules are an important part of an organization's daily activities. Many business services nowadays rely heavily on business rules to express assessments, predictions and decisions [7][27]. A business rule is [23] "*a statement that defines or constrains some aspect of the business intending to assert business structure or to control the behavior of the business.*" Most organizations experience three challenges when dealing with business rules management: 1) consistency challenges, 2) impact analysis challenges, and 3) transparency of business rule execution [4]. A consistent interpretation of business rules ensures that different actors apply the same business rules, and apply them consistently. This is a challenge since business rules are often not centralized, but they are embedded in various elements of an organization's information system instead. For example, business rules are embedded in minds of employees, part of textual procedures, manuals, tables, schemes, business process models, and hard-coded as software applications. Impact assessment determines the impact of changes made to business rules and the effect on an existing implementation. Currently, impact assessments can take significant time, which results in situations where the business rules already have changed again while the impact assessment is still ongoing [2]. Transparency, or business rules transparency, indicates that organizations should establish a system to prove what business rules are applied at a specific moment in time. To tackle the previously mentioned challenges and to improve grip on business rules, organizations search for a systematic and controlled approach to support the discovery, design, validation and deployment of business rules [7][32]. To be able to manage or even address these challenges, insight has to be created concerning business rule management processes at organizations. This can be achieved using performance management, which can provide insight into an organization's current situation, but can also point towards where and how to improve. However, research on performance management concerning BRM is nascent.

The measurement of performance has always been important in the field of enterprise management and, therefore, has been of interest for both practitioners and researchers [9]. Performance measurement systems are applied to provide useful information to manage, control and improve business processes. One of the most important tasks of performance management is to identify (and properly) evaluate suitable Performance Indicators (PI's) [13]. The increase of interest and research towards identifying the right set of indicators has led to 'standard' frameworks and PI's tailored to a specific industry or purpose. Examples of such frameworks are the balanced scorecard, the total quality management framework, and the seven-S model [19][31]. Moreover, research on standard indicators is increasingly performed for sales and manufacturing processes. To the knowledge of the authors, research, which focuses on performance measures for BRM is absent. This article extends the understanding of performance measurement with regard to the BRM processes. To be able to do so, the following research question is addressed: "*Which performance indicators are useful to measure the BRM processes?*"

This paper is organized as follows: In section two we provide insights into performance management and performance measurement. This is followed by the exploration of performance measurement Systems in section three. In section four, we provide an overview of the BRM capabilities and their goals. In section five, we report upon the research method utilized to construct our set of PI's. Next, the data collection and analysis of our study is described in section six. In section seven, our results, which led to our PI's for BRM are presented. This is followed by a critical view of the research method and results of our study and how future research could be conducted in section eight. Lastly, in section nine, we discuss what conclusions can be drawn from our results.

II. Performance Management and Performance Measurement

When examining PI's and what role it plays in the performance measurement and performance management domains, the first essential question is what is meant by these terms. In theory and practice, multiple different acronyms are adhered to when trying to define the concept of performance management [9]. In our research we adhere to the popular definition provided by Amaratunga & Baldry [3]: "*Performance Management is the use of Performance Measurement information to effect positive change in organizational culture, systems and processes, by helping to set agreed-upon performance goals, allocating and prioritizing resources, informing managers to either confirm or change current policy or programme directions to meet these goals, and sharing results of performance in pursuing those goals.*" This definition instantly elaborates upon the relationship between performance measurement (utilizing PI's) and performance management. Additionally, the definition includes multiple domains (culture, systems, and processes) and takes into account the overall goal of performance management. Performance Measurement plays an important role in the Performance Management Processes, and is defined as [25]: "*The process by which the efficiency and effectiveness of an action can be quantified.*" To visualize the relationship between both concepts, Kerklaan [19] created a basis for the performance feedback loop that could be utilized when a performance management and performance measurement solution need to be designed, see Figure 1.

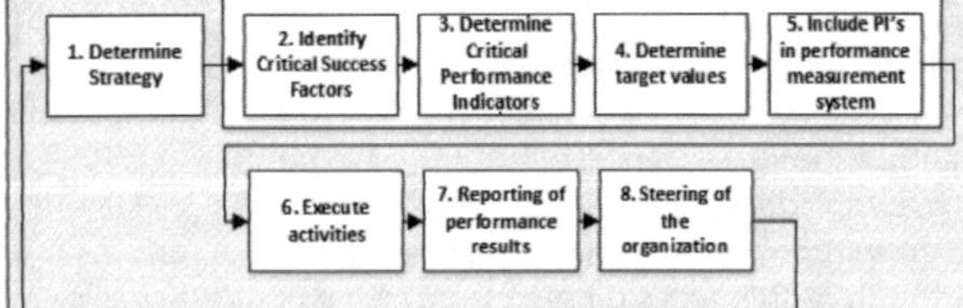

Figure 1. Performance Measurement within Performance Management

III. Performance Measurement Systems

Taking into account possible research avenues in the light of Performance Management and Performance Measurement, Ferreira and Otley [13] identified the demand for a holistic view for researching and designing Performance Management solutions. In their work, a selection of 12 key aspects are highlighted that make up the core of the Performance Management Systems Framework. The framework consists of 8 aspects that are the building blocks of a Performance Management System; 1. Vision and mission 2. Key success factors, 3. Organization structure, 4. Strategies and plans, 5. Key performance measures, 6. Target setting, 7. Performance evaluation, and 8. Reward systems. Furthermore, the remaining four key aspects comprise; 9. Information flows, systems, and networks, 10. Use of the Performance Management System, 11. Performance Management System change, and 12. Strength and coherence, which represent the contextual and cultural factors of an organization. As the first four key aspects are relevant, but already being explored by researchers in the field of BRM, our focus in this study lies on the exploration and development of the fifth key aspect; key performance measures. As performance measures are operationalized in performance measurement systems we first analyze more in depth what a performance measurement system entails and what types of performance measurement systems are utilized for what goals.

The aim of using a performance measurement system is to provide a closed loop control system in line with predefined business objectives. In scientific literature and industry, an abundance of performance management systems exists [14]. Although a lot of performance systems exist, in general, they can be grouped into four base types [19]: 1) consolidate and simulate, 2) consolidate and manage, 3) innovate and stimulate, and 4) innovate and manage. The predefined business objectives, and, therefore, the creation of the closed loop control system, differ per base-type. In the remainder of this section, first, the four performance measurement system base-types will be discussed, after which the registration of a single performance measure will be presented. Subsequently, the processes will be discussed for which the performance management system is created. The last paragraph will focus on bringing all elements together.

Performance measurement systems of the first base-type, *consolidate and stimulate,* are utilized to measure and stimulate the current system performance. The formulation process of PI's is usually performed with employees that work with the system, possibly in combination with direct management, and is, therefore, a bottom-up approach. Examples of this type of performance measurement system are the "control loop system" or "business process management system". Performance measurement systems, that focus purely on measuring and maintaining the current performance level, are classified as the second base-type *consolidate and manage*. Consolidate and manage is a purely top-down approach in which PI's are formulated by top management based on the current strategy. Each PI defined by the top-management is translated into multiple different underlying PI's by each lower management level. Two examples of performance measurement systems of this type are "management by objectives" and "quality policy development". The third base-type, *innovate and stimulate*, focuses on the customer and the product or service delivered to the customer by the organization. To define the PI's, first, the quality attributes of the product or service delivered to the customer need to be defined. Based on these quality attributes, PI's for each business process that contributes to the product or service is defined. An example of a performance measurement system of this type is Quality Function

Deployment (QFD). The fourth base-type, *innovate and manage*, focuses on the future of the organization while managing the present. It is a top-down approach in which PI's are formulated, based on the strategy of the organization. Furthermore, these PI's are then translated to the lower echelons of the organization. Moreover, PI's that are used to manage the current state of the organization are specified. The combination of both measures is used to make sure that the company is performing well while at the same time steering it into the future. An example of this performance measurement system type is the Balanced Score Card.

In addition to choosing the (combination of) performance measurement system(s), the individual performance indicators (PI's) of which the performance measurement system is composed have to be defined. A PI is defined as [19]: *"an authoritative measure, often in quantitative form, of one or multiple aspects of the organizational system."* Scholars as well as practitioners debate on which characteristics must be registered with respect to PI's [18][26]. Comparative research executed by [25] identified a set of five characteristics each scholar applies: 1) the PI must be derived from objectives, 2) the PI must be clearly defined with an explicit purpose, 3) the PI must be relevant and easy to maintain, 4) the PI must be simple to understand, and 5) the PI must provide fast and accurate feedback.

IV. BUSINESS RULES MANAGEMENT

The performance measurement system in this paper is developed for the elicitation, design, specification, verification, validation, deployment, and execution process of BRM. To ground our research a summary of BRM is provided here.

BRM is a process that deals with the elicitation, design, specification, verification, validation, deployment, execution, evaluation and governance of business rules for analytic or syntactic tasks within an organization to support and improve its business performance [8], see Figure 2.

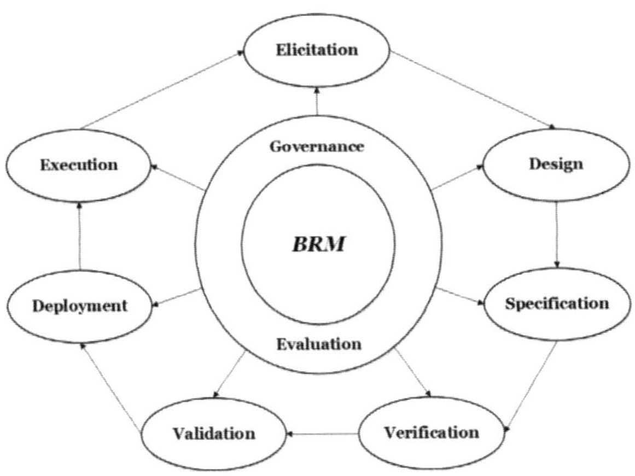

Figure 2. BRM capability overview.

The purpose of the elicitation capability is twofold. First, the purpose is to determine the knowledge that needs to be captured from various legal sources to realize the value proposition of the business rules. Different types of legal sources from which knowledge can be derived are, for example, laws, regulations, policies, internal documentation, guidance documents, parliament documents, official disclosures, implementation instructions, and experts. Depending on the type of knowledge source(s), for example documentation versus experts, different methods, processes, techniques and tools to extract the knowledge are applied [21]. The output of the elicitation capability is the knowledge required to design the business rule architecture. The second purpose is to conduct an impact analysis is if a business rule architecture is already in place. The business rule architecture itself is the output to be realized by the design capability. The business rule architecture consists of a combination of context designs and derivation structures. A context design is a set of business knowledge (in terms of business rules and fact types) with a maximum internal cohesion and a minimal external coherence, which adheres to the single responsibility principle [22]. The relationship between different context designs is depicted in a derivation structure. After the business rule architecture is designed, the contents of each individual context design need to be specified in the specification capability. The purpose of the specification capability is to write the business rules and create the fact types needed to define or constrain some particular aspect of the business. The output of the specification capability is a specified context that contains business rules and fact types. After the business rule architecture is created it is verified (to check for semantic / syntax errors) and validated (to check for errors in its intended behavior). The first happens in the verification capability of which the purpose is to determine if the business rules adhere to predefined criteria and are logically consistent. For example, a business rule could contain multiple verification errors, such as domain violation errors, omission errors, and overlapping condition key errors. If errors are identified, two scenarios can occur. First, the business rules can be specified based on the current elicitated, designed and specified knowledge. Secondly, the design or specification could be altered. Verification errors not properly addressed could result in the improper execution of the value proposition in the execution capability later on in the BRM processes [34]. When no verification errors are identified, the created value proposition is reviewed in the validation capability. The purpose of the validation capability is to determine whether the verified value proposition holds to its intended behavior [35]. To be able to do so, two processes can be applied. First, scenario-based testing can be applied. The scenario-based testing applies pre-defined test sets to check the behavior. Secondly, colleague-based testing can be applied. In this case, a colleague checks if the context is in concurrence with law. When validation errors are identified the created element (i.e. decision, business rule, fact type) is rejected and an additional cycle of the elicitation, design, specification, and verification capabilities must be initiated to resolve the validation error. Validation errors not properly identified or addressed could lead to economic losses or loss of reputation [35]. When no validation errors are identified the context is approved and marked for deployment. The purpose of the deployment capability is to transform the verified and validated value proposition to implementation-dependent executable business rules. However, this does not necessarily imply that the actor that utilizes the value proposition is a system, as the value proposition could also be used by subject-matter experts [34]. An implementation-dependent value proposition can be source code, handbooks or procedures [23]. The output of the deployment capability is then executed in the execution capability, which delivers the actual value proposition. To realize the added value, human or information system actors execute the business rules. Overall, covering the full range of capabilities described earlier, two more capabilities are of importance; governance and monitoring. The governance capability consists of three sub-capabilities; version management, traceability, and validity management [23]. The goal of the versioning capability is to capture and keep track of version data regarding the elements created or modified in the elicitation, design, specification, verification, validation, deployment and execution capabilities. Proper version control as part of the BRM processes allows organizations to keep track what elements are utilized in the execution and deliverance of their added value. For example, the governmental domain needs to support several versions of a regulation as it takes into account different target groups under different conditions. The traceability capability is utilized to create relationships between specific versions of elements used in the value proposition. The goal of the traceability capability is to make it possible to trace created elements, as parts of the value proposition, to the corresponding laws and regulations on which they are based. Another goal of the traceability capability is the foundation it forms for impact analysis when new or existing laws and regulations need to be processed into the value proposition. The third sub-capability comprises validity management. The goal of validity management is to be able to provide, at any given time, a specific version of a value proposition. Validity management is utilized to increase transparency. Transparency is achieved as validity management enables organizations to provide when a specific value proposition was, is or will be valid. Lastly, the monitoring capability observes, checks and keeps record of not only the execution of the value proposition but also the full range of activities in the previously explained BRM capabilities that are conducted to realize the value proposition. The goal of the monitoring capability is to provide insights into how the BRM capabilities perform and, additionally, suggest improvements [5].

To further ground our research a summary of artefacts that are utilized in the BRM processes by the Dutch government are provided here, see also a schematic overview of the concepts in Figure 3.

Overall, a difference is made between implementation-independent design and implementation-dependent design of artefacts (these are: scope, context, business rule, fact type model, and facts). An implementation-independent artefact is always designed in a notation that is not adjusted to accommodate a specific system.

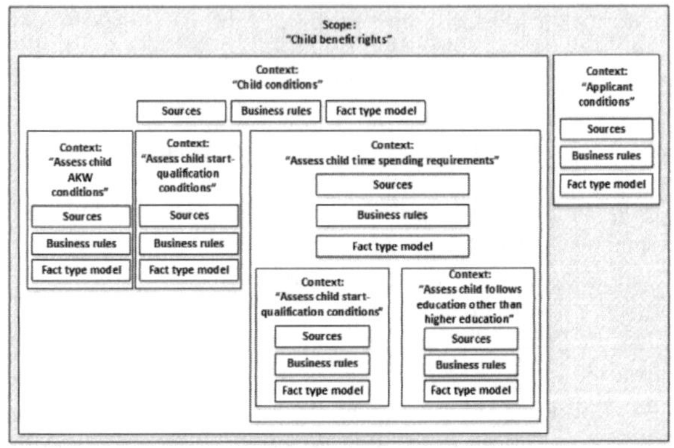

Figure 3. Overview of the relationship between a scope and multiple contexts

On the other hand, an implementation-dependent artefact is adjusted to a specific system, and thus can only be utilized in relation to that specific system. The highest level abstraction artefact is referred to as a scope. The scope is dynamic in size as it represents the established limits of the value proposition that must be realized in the elicitation, design, specification, verification and validation processes. A scope could be further divided into one or multiple collections of knowledge, containing sources, business rules, and fact type models [16]. This is also referred to as a context. A context is characterized by a maximum internal coherence and a minimal external coherence. The goal of a context is the identification of artefacts that can be independently developed within the defined scope. A context contains one or more sources, a fact type model, and business rules. A source can be defined as an authority that imposes requirements to the value proposition that has to be realized, for example, published laws and regulations from the parliament, court decisions, regulations promulgated by executive governmental branches, and international treaties. A fact type model provides an overview of terms and the relationship between these terms, which represent facts. For example, a country (term) has a province (term) or state (state), which contains a city (term). In the elicitation, design and specification processes the collection of a scope containing all underlying artefacts is defined as a scope design. Consequently, the same holds for a context containing source(s), a fact type model, and business rules, which is defined as a context design. Each of the BRM capabilities described can be measured and should be measured to continuously improve the process and stay competitive and innovative. The actual measurements applied depends on the base-type(s) the organization chooses to apply. The four base types are based on two main axes. The first axis described the current focus of the organization: consolidating versus innovating. On the other hand, the management style is described by the second axis: stimulate versus control, which leads to the question for which base type performance measurements are most needed?

The current trend in business rules management is a shift from an information technology perspective towards a broader information systems perspective. Therefore, researchers and scientist are interested in measuring the current state of business rules management implementations and capabilities [20][28][34]. An important question when measuring the current state is that organizations want to compare and benchmark their implementations, processes, and capabilities. For this purpose, multiple initiatives are started, for example, expert group BRM [17], the blue chamber [6]. This trend of comparing different parts of a BRM implementation also concerns the comparison of different rule sets built for the same solutions. An example of this are the challenges released by the decision management community [10]. Every month they release a problem for which different vendors provide their solutions such that they can be compared to each other. To manage and improve the different BRM capabilities/processes insight has to be created regarding the current situation of these processes. Thus, on the current focus of the organization axis we adopt the consolidating perspective over the innovating perspective for this study.

The selection of the participants should be based on the group of individuals, organizations, information technology, or community that best represents the phenomenon studied [33]. In this study, we want to measure the current practice of the work of the employees that perform the capabilities. This implies that we will apply a bottom-up approach and will involve employees working on business rules and their direct management. Therefore, on the second axis we focus on the stimulating over controlling, thereby adopting the perspective of the first base-type, consolidate and stimulate, as described in detail in section three.

Our focus per PI will be on the characteristics as defined by [18]: 1) derived from objectives, 2) clearly defined with an explicit purpose, 3) relevant and easy to maintain, 4) simple to understand, and 5) provide fast and accurate feedback. These PI's form the basis to build a framework that organizations can utilize to design their BRM evaluation process focused on evaluating and improving its business performance.

V. Research Method

The goal of this research is to identify performance measurements that provide relevant insight into the performance of the elicitation, design, specification, verification, validation, deployment, execution, and governance processes of BRM. In addition to the goal of the research, also, the maturity of the research field is a factor in determining the appropriate research method and technique. The maturity of the BRM research field, with regard to non-technological research, is nascent [20][27][34]. Focus of research in nascent research fields should lie on identifying new constructs and establishing relationships between identified constructs [12]. Summarized, to accomplish our research goal, a research approach is needed in which a broad range of possible performance measurements are explored and combined into one view in order to contribute to an incomplete state of knowledge.

Adequate research methods to explore a broad range of possible ideas / solutions to a complex issue and combine them into one view when a lack of empirical evidence exists consist of group-based research techniques [11][24][29][30]. Examples of group based techniques are Focus Groups, Delphi Studies, Brainstorming and the Nominal Group Technique. The main characteristic that differentiates these types of group-based research techniques from each other is the use of face-to-face versus non-face-to-face approaches. Both approaches have advantages and disadvantages, for example, in face-to-face meetings, provision of immediate feedback is possible. However, face-to-face meetings have restrictions with regard to the number of participants and the possible existence of group or peer pressure. To eliminate the disadvantages, we combined the face-to-face and non-face-to-face technique by means of applying the following two group based research approaches: the Focus Group and Delphi Study.

VI. Data Collection and Analysis

Data for this study is collected over a period of six months, through three rounds of focus groups (rounds 1, 2 and 3: experts focus group) and a three-round Delphi study (rounds 4, 5 and 6 Delphi study), see Figure 4. Between each individual round of focus group and Delphi Study, the researchers consolidated the results (rounds 1, 2, 3, 4, 5, 6 and 7: research team). Both methods of data collection and analysis are further discussed in the remainder of this section.

A. *Focus Groups*

Before a focus group is conducted, a number of key issues need to be considered: 1) the goal of the focus group, 2) the selection of participants, 3) the number of participants, 4) the selection of the facilitator, 5) the information recording facilities, and 6) the protocol of the focus group. The goal of the focus group was to identify performance measurements for the performance of the elicitation, design, specification, verification, validation, deployment, execution, and governance capabilities of BRM. The selection of the participants should be based on the group of individuals, organizations, information technology, or community that best represents the phenomenon studied [33]. In this study, organizations and individuals that deal with a large amount of business rules represent the phenomenon studied. Such organizations are often financial and government institutions. During this research, which was conducted from September 2014 to December 2014, five large Dutch government institutions participated. Based on the written description of the goal and consultation with employees of each government institution, participants were selected to take part in the three focus group meetings. In total, ten participants took part, which fulfilled the following positions: two enterprise architects, two business rules architects, three business rules analysts, one project manager, and two policy advisors. Each of the participants had, at least, five years of experience with business rules. Delbecq and van de Ven [11] and Glaser [15] state that the facilitator should be an expert on the topic and familiar with group meeting processes. The selected facilitator has a Ph.D. in BRM, has conducted 7 years of research on the topic, and has facilitated many (similar) focus group meetings before. Besides the facilitator, five additional researchers were present during the focus group meetings. One researcher participated as 'back-up' facilitator, who monitored if each participant provided equal input, and if necessary, involved specific participants by asking for more in-depth elaboration on the subject. The remaining four researchers acted as a minute's secretary taking field notes. They did not intervene in the process; they operated from the sideline. All focus groups were video and audio recorded. A focus group meeting took on average three and a half hour. Each focus group meeting followed the same overall protocol, each starting with an introduction and explanation of the purpose and procedures of the meeting, after which ideas were generated, shared, discussed and/or refined.

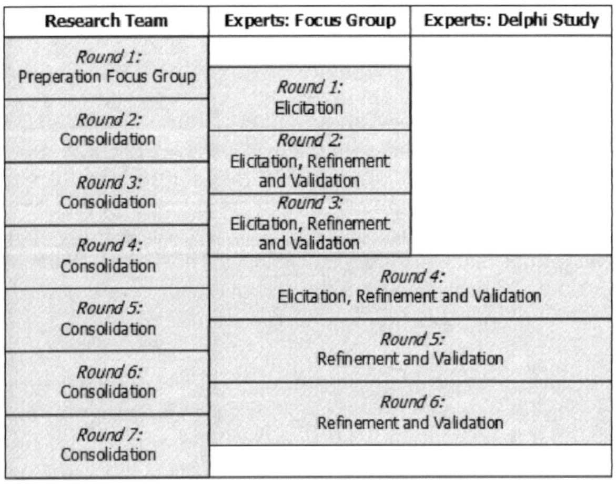

Figure 4. Data collection process design

Prior to the first round, participants were informed about the purpose of the focus group meeting and were invited to submit their current PI's applied in the BRM process. When participants had submitted PI's, they had the opportunity to elaborate upon their PI's during the first focus group meeting. During this meeting, also, additional PI's were proposed. For each proposed PI, the name, goal, specification and measurements were discussed and noted. For some PI's, the participants did not know what specifications or measurements to use. These elements were left blank and agreed to deal with during the second focus group meeting. After the first focus group, the researchers consolidated the results. Consolidation comprised the detection of double PI's, incomplete PI's, conflicting goals and measurements. Double PI's exist in two forms: 1) identical PI's and 2) PI's, which are textually different, but similar on the conceptual level. The results of the consolidation were sent to the participants of the focus group two weeks in advance for the second focus group meeting. During these two weeks, the participants assessed the consolidated results in relationship to four questions: 1) "Are all PI's described correctly?", "2) Do I want to remove a PI?" 3) "Do we need additional PI's?", and 4) "How do the PI's affect the design of a business rule management solution?". This process of conducting focus group meetings, consolidation by the researchers and assessment by the participants of the focus group was repeated two more times (round 2 and round 3). After the third focus group meeting (round 3), saturation within the group occurred leading to a consolidated set of PI's.

B. Delphi Study

Before a Delphi study is conducted, also a number of key issues need to be considered: 1) the goal of the Delphi study, 2) the selection of participants, 3) the number of participants, and 4) the protocol of the Delphi study. The goal of the Delphi study was twofold. The first goal was to validate and refine existing PI's identified in the focus group meetings, and the second goal was to identify new PI's. Based on the written description of the goal and consultation with employees of each organization, participants were selected to take part in the Delphi study. In total, 36 participants took part. Twenty-six experts, in addition to the ten experts that participated in the focus group meetings, of the large Dutch government institutions were involved in the Delphi Study, which was conducted from November 2014 to December 2014. The reason for involving the ten experts from the focus groups was to decrease the likelihood of peer-pressure amongst group members. This is achieved by exploiting the advantage of a Delphi Study, which is characterized by a non-face-to-face approach. The non-face-to-face approach was achieved by the use of online questionnaires that the participants had to return via mail. Combined with the ten participants from the focus groups, the twenty-six additional participants involved in the Delphi Study had the following positions: three project managers, four enterprise architects, ten business rules analyst, five policy advisors, two IT-architects, six business rules architects, two business consultants, one functional designer, one tax advisor, one legal advisor, and one legislative author. Each of the participants had, at least, two years of experience with business rules. Each round (4, 5, and 6) of the Delphi Study followed the same overall protocol, whereby each participant was asked to assess the PI's in relationship to four questions: 1) "Are all PI's described correctly?", "2) Do I want to remove a PI?" 3) "Do we need additional PI's?", and 4) "How do the PI's affect the design of a BRM solution?"

VII. RESULTS

In this section, the overall results of this study are presented. Furthermore, the final PI's are listed. Each PI is specified using a specific format to convey their characteristics in a unified way. Before the first focus group was conducted, participants were invited to submit the PI's they currently use. This resulted in the submission of zero PI's, which is in conformance with the literature described in section four. Since this result can imply a multitude of things (e.g., total absence of the phenomena researched or unmotivated participants), further inquiry was conducted. The reason that no participants submitted PI's was because none of the participants had a formal performance measurement system in place. Some measured BRM processes, but did so in an ad-hoc and unstructured manner.

TABLE I. EXAMPLE OF PI RESULT: TIME MEASUREMENT TO DEFINE, VERIFY, AND VALIDATE A BUSINESS RULE.

PI 09: The amount of time units needed to define, verify, and validate a single business rule. **Goal**: Shortening the time needed to deliver defined, verified, and validated business rules.	
S	The number of time units per selected single business rule: • Measured over the entire collection of context designs; • During the design process; • (Sorted by selected context design); • (Sorted by selected complexity level of a business rule); • (Sorted by selected scope design); • (Sorted by selected time unit).
M	• Context design • Business rule • Complexity level of a business rule • Scope design • Time unit

A. *First Focus Group*

The first focus group meeting resulted in 24 PI's. As stated in the previous section, for each PI the name, goal, specification, and measurements were discussed and noted. This led to two discussions: 1) different levels of abstraction and 2) person-based measurements. The discussion with regards to the abstraction level of sorting indicates that a specific organization chooses for a different level of detail when exploring the KPI. For example, in PI09, '*the number of time units per selected single business rule*' can be sorted by scope design or by context design. The first is a higher abstraction level then the latter. Because the goal of the research is to formulate a set of PI's that can be widely applied, the choice has been made to add sorting possibilities. In Table I, dimensions are displayed between brackets, for example, sorted by selected context design. Therefore, each organization can choose to implement the PI specific to their needs. The second discussion was if PI's are allowed to be configured to monitor a specific individual. For example, '*the number of incorrectly written business rules per business rule analyst.*' The difference in opinion between the participants could not be bridged during this session. Since the discussion became quite heated during the meeting, it was decided that each expert would think about and reflect on this question outside the group and that this discussion would be continued in the next focus group meeting. After the first focus group, the results have been analyzed and sent to the participants.

B. *Second Focus Group*

During the second focus group, the participants started to discuss the usefulness of the PI's. This resulted in the removal of ten conceptual PI's. The ten PI's were discarded because they did not add value to the performance measurement process concerning BRM. This resulted into 14 remaining PI's, which had to be further analyzed by the researchers. Also, the discussion about the PI's formulated to measure specific individuals was continued. At the end, only three participants thought this was reasonable. The other seven disagreed and found it against their organization's ethics. Therefore, the group reached a consensus that this dimension should be added as optional.

C. *Dimensions*

The respondents discussed per PI the dimensions they should be measured by. In total, this resulted into five new dimensions. The first dimension is *the business rule complexity level*. The business rule complexity describes the effort it takes to formulate one business rule. The participants did state that, currently, no widely supported hierarchy to express the dimension level complexity exists. Two examples were provided by different respondents. The first example came from a respondent which indicated that business rule complexity can be determined by the amount of existing versus non-existing facts in the fact model that are utilized in a business rule, the impact a business rule has on other business rules when modified or removed, and the type of business rule. The second example came from a respondent which indicated that they use two languages to write business rules in. The complexity, in this case, is influenced by the language in which the business rule is written.

The second dimension represents the time unit that is used in the PI statement. The participated organizations all indicated different time units as part of their PI's due to differences in release schedules or reporting requirements. For example, one of the participated organizations currently adheres to a standard period of three months, while another adheres to a standard period of six months due to agreements with their parent ministry that publishes new or modified laws and regulations in the same cycle of six months. For example, the PI (09): '*The number of time units required to define, verify, and validate a single business rule*', is sorted by the dimension time unit.

The third dimension represents the roles and individuals. One observation regarding the third dimension, focusing on the utilization of roles in PI's, are the different labels for very similar or equivalent roles the participated organizations utilize in their BRM processes. For example, the PI (02): '*The frequency of corrections per selected context design, emerging from the verification process, per business analyst and per type of verification error*' can be sorted by the measure '*business analyst.*' The business analyst role is a generic role, which each organization can replace by a specific role. Examples of roles other respondents applied are: "*business rules writer*", "*business rules analyst*" or "*business rule expert.*"

The fourth dimension represents the error type, which describes the specific errors that can occur. Error types are applied as measures in two PI's: PI 07 (validation errors) and PI 08 (verification errors). With respect to verification errors three types can be recognized: 1) context error types, 2) business rules errors, and 3) fact type errors. Examples of specific errors are: circularity error, consequent error, unnecessary condition fact type error, interdeterminism error, overlapping condition key coverage error, unused fact type error and domain violation error. Not every organization can measure every error type, as this depends on the language and tool they apply. Therefore, the dimension can vary per organization.

The fifth dimension represents the implementation of the business rules: implementation-independent versus implementation-dependent. In this first case, an organization elicits, designs, specifies, verifies and validates the business rules in an implementation-independent way. Therefore, the PI also focuses on the implementation-independent part. However, one of the participated organizations already designs, specifies, verifies and validates the business rules in an implementation-dependent environment. In this case the PI's focus on the implementation-dependent part.

D. The Third Focus Group

During the third focus group, the participants discussed the remaining 14 final PI's, which led to the further refinement of goals, specifications, and measurements. Additionally, the subject-matter experts expressed a certain need to categorize PI's into well-known phases within the development process of business rules at the case organizations. From the 14 remaining PI's, nine PI's were categorized as business rule design PI's, two PI's were categorized as business rule deployment PI's, and three PI's were categorized as business rules execution PI's.

E. Delphi Study

After the third focus group, the 14 PI's were subjected to the Delphi Study participants. In each of the three rounds, no additional PI's were formulated by the 26 experts. However, during the first two rounds, the specification and measurement elements of multiple PI's were refined. During the third round, which was also the last round, no further refinements were proposed and participants all agreed to the 14 formulated PI's, which are presented in Table II.

TABLE II. PI'S for BRM

PI 01: The frequency of corrections per selected context design emerging from the verification process.

Goal: Improve upon the design process of business rules.

PI 02: The frequency of corrections per selected context design, emerging from the verification process, per business analyst and per type of verification error.

Goal: Improving the context design.

PI 03: The frequency of corrections per selected context design emerging from the validation process per complexity level of a business rule.

Goal: Improve upon the design process of business rules.

PI 04: The frequency of corrections per selected context design emerging from the validation process per type of validation error.

Goal: Improve upon the validation process for the benefit of improving the context design.

PI 05: The frequency of corrections per selected context architecture emerging from the design process per scope design.

Goal: Improve upon the design process for the benefit of improving the context architecture.

PI 06: The frequency of instantiations per selected context design

Goal: Provide insight into the possible instances of a context design.

PI 07: The frequency per selected type of validation error.

Goal: Improve upon the design process for the benefit of improving the context design.

PI 08: The frequency per selected type of verification error

Goal: Improve upon the design process for the benefit of improving the context design.

PI 09: The number of time units required to define, verify, and validate a single business rule.

Goal: Shortening the lead time of a business rule with regard to the design process.

PI 10: The frequency of deviations between an implementation dependent context design and an implementation independent context design.

Goal: Improve upon the deployment process.

PI 11: The frequency of executions of an implementation dependent business rule.

Goal: Gaining insight into what business rules are executed.

PI 12: The frequency of execution variants of a scope design.

Goal: Gaining insight into what decision paths are traversed to establish different decisions.

PI 13: The number of time units required for the execution per execution variant.

Goal: Shortening the lead time of an execution process with regard to enhancing an execution variant.

PI 14: The amount of business rules that cannot be automated.

Goal: Provide insight into what business rules cannot be automated.

Analyzing the defined PI's showed that three out of fourteen (PI 11, 12, and 14) are PI's that can be classified as *'innovate and manage'* PI's. PI number eleven and twelve focus on the number of times a business rule is executed, thereby providing insight on which business rules are most applied. PI twelve goes beyond that and shows which variants of business rules are executed. In other words, it shows the characteristics of the decision based on which citizens or organizations get services. This insight can be used to determine how many and which citizens or organizations are affected by changing specific laws (and, therefore, business rules). In other words, this can be used to further support the development of law. PI fourteen indicated the amount of business rules that cannot be automated, in other words, that need to be executed manually. This can also provide an indication of the amount of workload that organizations encounter due to the manual execution of these specific business rules. This PI can be used to decide if these business rules should be executed manually or that they should be reformulated in such a manner that they can be executed mechanically.

VIII. Discussion and Future work

From a research perspective, our study provides a fundament for PI measurement and benchmarking of the elicitation, design, specification, verification, validation, deployment, execution, and governance capabilities of BRM. In addition to the PI's, one of the biggest discussion has been the question whether a PI should be measured per individual person. Regarding this discussion most respondents in our research agreed that PI's should not measure the performance of an individual person. This could be related to the fact that the sample group didn't contain respondents from a commercial organization where it might be more accepted that the performance of an individual person is measured. From the perspective of performance management systems we focused on the base type 1) consolidate and simulate. When BRM implementations become more mature, innovation should be encouraged and PI's for the base types 3) innovate and stimulate, and 4) innovate and manage should be measured. From an economic perspective, our research results contribute to the design of a proper performance measurement design for the BRM capabilities in order to provide insights about how organizational resources are utilized and how they could be utilized more effectively.

Another discussion focused on the terminology applied to formulate the PI's. The discussion started because the organizations that employ the participants applied different terms and definitions to describe the same elements. This is mainly caused by the different business rule management methods used, business rule management systems applied, business rule language(s) used or business rule engines implemented by the participating organizations. Most of the proprietary systems apply their own language, thereby decreasing interoperability. For example, one organization has implemented Be Informed, which applies the Declarative Process Modeling Notation while another organization implemented The Annotation Environment, which applies Structured Dutch. Therefore, the terminology chosen to formulate the PI's is neutral. However, the terms of the PI's can be adapted to the specific organization.

Several limitations may affect our results. The first limitation is the sampling and sample size. The sample group of participants is solely drawn from government institutions in the Netherlands. While we believe that government institutions are representative for organizations implementing business rules, further generalization towards non-governmental organizations, amongst others, is a recommended direction for future research. Taken the sample size of 36 participants into account, this number needs to be increased in future research as well. Another observation is the lack of PI's regarding some BRM capabilities described in section four. This could have been caused due to participants focusing on a specific BRM capability in practice, limiting the input of PI's regarding other BRM capabilities. Future research should focus on including participants, which are responsible for one capability (taking into account to cover all capabilities) a combination of BRM capabilities, or all BRM capabilities (higher level management).

This research focused on identifying new constructs and establishing relationships given the current maturity of the BRM research field. Although the research approach chosen for this research type is appropriate given the present maturity of the research field, research focusing on further generalization should apply different research methods such as qualitative research methods, which also allow incorporating a larger sample size in future research regarding PI's for BRM.

IX. Conclusion

This research investigated PI's for the elicitation, design, acceptance, deployment and execution of business rules with the purpose of answering the following research question: "*Which performance measurements are useful to measure the BRM processes?*" To accomplish this goal, we conducted a study combining a three round focus group and three round Delphi Study. Both were applied to retrieve PI's from participants, 36 in total, employed by five governmental institutions. This analysis revealed fourteen PI's. We believe that this work represents a further step in research on PI's for BRM and maturing the BRM field as a whole.

References

[1] M. M. Zoet, K. Smit, and E. Y. de Haan, "Performance Indicators for Business Rule Management," Proceedings of the Eighth International Conference on Information, Process, and Knowledge Management - EKNOW, Venice, 2016.

[2] M. Alles, G. Brennan, A. Kogan, and M. Vasarhelyi, "Continuous monitoring of business process controls: A pilot implementation of a continuous auditing system at Siemens," International Journal of Accounting Information Systems, 7, 2006, pp. 137-161. doi: 10.1016/j.accinf.2005.10.004

[3] D. Amaratunga and D. Baldry, "Moving from performance measurement to performance management," Facilities, 20(5/6), 2002, pp. 217-223.

[4] D. Arnot and G. Pervan, "A critical analysis of decision support systems research," Journal of information technology, 20(2), 2005, pp. 67-87.

[5] M. Baject and M. Krisper, "A methodology and tool support for managing business rules in organisations," Information Systems, 30, 2005, pp. 423-443.

[6] Blue Chamber, "Legislation to services: an approach for agile execution of legislation," 2013.

[7] J. Boyer and H. Mili, "Agile Business Rules Development: Process, Architecture and JRules Examples," Heidelberg: Springer, 2011.

[8] J. Breuker and W. Van De Velde, "CommonKADS Library for Expertise Modelling: reusable problem-solving components," Amsterdam: IOS Press/Ohmsha, 1994.

[9] G. Cokins, "Performance Management: Integrating Strategy Execution, Methodologies, Risk, and Analytics," Hoboken: John Wiley & Sons, Inc., ISBN13: 9780470449981, 2009.

[10] Decision Management Community, "DMcommunity" Retrieved November, 2016, from https://www.dmcommunity.org.

[11] A. L. Delbecq and A. H. Van de Ven, "A group process model for problem identification and program planning," The Journal of Applied Behavioral Science, 7(4), 1971, pp. 466-492.

[12] A. Edmondson and S. McManus, "Methodological Fit in Management Field Research," Academy of Management Review, 32(4), 2007, pp. 1155-1179.

[13] A. Ferreira and D. Otley, "The design and use of performance management systems: An extended framework for analysis," Management accounting research, 20(4), 2009, pp. 263-282.

[14] M. Franco-Santos, L. Lucianetti, and M. Bourne, "Contemporary performance measurement systems: A review of their consequences and a framework for research," Management Accounting Research, 23(2), 2012, pp. 79-119.

[15] B. Glaser, "Theoretical Sensitivity: Advances in the Methodology of Grounded Theory," Mill Valley, CA: Sociology Press, 1978.

[16] I. Graham, "Business Rules Management and Service Oriented Architecture," New York: Wiley, 2006.

[17] Handvestgroep Publiek Verantwoorden, "Together means more," HPV, Den Haag, 2013, pp. 22-23.

[18] M. Hudson, A. Smart, and M. Bourne, "Theory and practice in SME performance measurement systems," International Journal of Operations & Production Management, 21(8), 2001, pp. 1096-1115.

[19] L. Kerklaan, "The cockpit of the organization: performance management with scorecards," Deventer: Kluwer, 2007.

[20] A. Kovacic, "Business renovation: business rules (still) the missing link," Business Process Management Journal, 10(2), 2004, pp. 158-170.

[21] S. H. Liao, "Expert System Methodologies and Applications - A Decade Review from 1995 to 2004," Expert Systems with Applications, 28(1), 2004, pp. 93-103

[22] R. Martin, "Agile Software Development: Principles, Patterns and Practices," New York, 2003.

[23] T. Morgan, "Business rules and information systems: aligning IT with business goals," London: Addison-Wesley, 2002.

[24] M. K. Murphy, N. Black, D. L. Lamping, C. M. McKee, C. F. B. Sanderson, and J. Askham, "Consensus development methods and their use in clinical guideline development," Health Technology Assessment, 2(3), 1998, pp. 31-38.

[25] A. Neely, H. Richards, H. Mills, K. Platts, and M. Bourne, "Designing performance measures: a structured approach," International Journal of Operations and Production, 17(11), 1997, pp. 1131-1152.

[26] A. Neely, "The evolution of performance measurement research: developments in the last decade and a research agenda for the next," International Journal of Operations & Production Management, 25(12), 2005, pp. 1264-1277.

[27] M. L. Nelson, J. Peterson, R. L. Rariden, and R. Sen, "Transitioning to a business rule management service model: Case studies from the property and casualty insurance industry," Information & Management, 47(1), 2010, pp. 30-41.

[28] M. L. Nelson, R. L. Rariden, and R. Sen, "A Lifecycle Approach towards Business Rules Management," Proceedings of the 41st Hawaii International Conference on System Sciences, Hawaii, 2008.

[29] C. Okoli and S. D. Pawlowski, "The Delphi method as a research tool: an example, design considerations and applications," Information & Management, 42(1), 2004, pp. 15-29.

[30] R. Ono and D. J. Wedemeyer, "Assessing the validity of the Delphi technique," Futures, 26(3), 1994, pp. 289-304.

[31] V. Owhoso and S. Vasudevan, "A balanced scorecard based framework for assessing the strategic impacts of ERP systems," Computers in Industry, 56, 2005, pp. 558-572.

[32] R. Ross, "Business Rule Concepts," Houston: Business Rule Solutions, LLC, 2009.

[33] A. Strauss and J. Corbin, "Basics of qualitative research: Grounded theory procedures and techniques," Newbury Park: Sage Publication, INC, 1990.

[34] M. M. Zoet, "Methods and Concepts for Business Rules Management," Utrecht: Hogeschool Utrecht, 2014.

[35] M. M. Zoet and J. Versendaal, "Business Rules Management Solutions Problem Space: Situational Factors," Proceedings of the 2013 Pacific Asia Conference on Information Systems, Jeju, 2013.

Big Data for Personalized Healthcare

Liseth Siemons, Floor Sieverink, Annemarie Braakman-Jansen, Lisette van Gemert-Pijnen
Centre for eHealth and Well-being Research
Department of Psychology, Health, and Technology
University of Twente
Enschede, the Netherlands
(l.siemons, f.sieverink, l.m.a.braakman-jansen, j.vangemert-pijnen)@utwente.nl

Wouter Vollenbroek
Department of Media, Communication & Organisation
University of Twente
Enschede, the Netherlands
w.vollenbroek@utwente.nl

Lidwien van de Wijngaert
Department of Communication and Information Studies
Radboud University
Nijmegen, the Netherlands
l.vandewijngaert@let.ru.nl

Abstract - **Big Data, often defined according to the 5V model (volume, velocity, variety, veracity and value), is seen as the key towards personalized healthcare. However, it also confronts us with new technological and ethical challenges that require more sophisticated data management tools and data analysis techniques. This vision paper aims to better understand the technological and ethical challenges we face when using and managing Big Data in healthcare as well as the way in which it impacts our way of working, our health, and our wellbeing. A mixed-methods approach (including a focus group, interviews, and an analysis of social media) was used to gain a broader picture about the pros and cons of using Big Data for personalized healthcare from three different perspectives: Big Data experts, healthcare workers, and the online public. All groups acknowledge the positive aspects of applying Big Data in healthcare, touching upon a wide array of issues, both scientifically and socially. By sharing health data, value can be created that goes beyond the individual patient. The Big Data revolution in healthcare is seen as a promising and innovative development. Yet potential facilitators and barriers need to be faced first to reach its full potential. Concerns were raised about privacy, trust, reliability, safety, purpose limitation, liability, profiling, data ownership, and loss of autonomy. Also, the importance of adding the people-centered view to the rather data-centered 5V model is stressed, in order to get a grip on the opportunities for using Big Data in personalized healthcare. People should be aware that the development of Big Data advancements is not self-evident.**

Keywords - Big Data; personalized healthcare; eHealth.

I. INTRODUCTION

The "Big Data" revolution is a promising development that can significantly advance our healthcare system, promoting personalized healthcare [1]. Imagine a system that analyzes large amounts of real-time data from premature babies to detect minimal changes in the condition of these babies that might point to a starting infection. Science fiction? No, IBM and the Institute of Technology of the University of Ontario developed a system that enables physicians to respond much sooner to a changing condition of the baby, saving lives, and leading to a significantly improved quality of care for premature babies [2].

We are standing at the beginning of the "Big Data" revolution. Many different definitions exist for "Big Data". Where Mayer-Schönberger and Cukier [2] focus on the new insights and economic value that can be obtained from Big Data in contrast to traditional smeller settings, Wang & Krishnan [3] refer to Big Data as complex and large data sets that can no longer be processed using the traditional processing tools and methods. Yet another definition comes from Laney [4], who defines Big Data according to 3 assets (often referred to as the 3V-model) that require new, cost-effective forms of information processing to promote insight and decision making, including: 1) high-volume (i.e., the quantity of data), 2) high-velocity (i.e., the speed of data generation and processing), and 3) high-variety (i.e., the amount of different data types). Marr [5] expanded this 3V model to the 5V model by adding 2 additional Vs: veracity (i.e., the accuracy or trustworthiness of the data) and maybe the most important asset: value (i.e., the ability to turn the data into value).

Though this is just a grasp out of all the definitions available, there is one thing they have in common: The use of Big Data for analysis and decision making requires a change of thought from knowing "why" to knowing "what". Where we focused on small, exact datasets and causal connections in the past (i.e., knowing "why"), we now focus on gathering or linking large amounts of (noisy) data, with which we can demonstrate the presence of (unexpected) correlational connections (i.e., knowing "what") [2]. As a result, we will obtain (and apply) new insights that we did not have before. Insights that can not only be lifesaving, as demonstrated by the example of IBM and the University of Ontario, but that also opens the door towards more personalized medicine [6-8]; i.e., where medical decisions, medications, and/or products are tailored to the individual's personal profile instead of to the whole patient group. For example, when genetic biomarkers in pharmacogenetics are used to determine the best medical treatment for a patient [6] or when data from thousands of patients that have been treated in the past is being analyzed to determine what treatment best fits the individual patient that is under treatment now (e.g., in terms of expected treatment effects and the risk for severe side-effects given the patient's personal characteristics like age, gender, genetic features, etc.).

This shift towards more personalized healthcare is reflected in the change of focus within healthcare from a disease-centered approach towards a patient-centered approach, empowering patients to take an active role in the decisions about their own health [8]. As a result, an increasing number of technologies (e.g., Personal Health Records) are being launched by companies to support chronically ill people in the development of self-management skills [9].

The past decades have also shown a rapid growth in the amount of (personal) data that is digitally collected by individuals via wearable technologies that may or may not be stored on online platforms for remote control [2, 6-8, 10], or shared via other online sources like social media. Social media have become socially accepted and used by a growing group of people [11]. They use it, for example, to share data collected by activity, mood, nutrition and sleep trackers on a variety of online platforms (such as Facebook, Twitter, blogs or forums). These data provide new opportunities for healthcare to personalize and improve care even further [12-14]. Furthermore, the data and messages shared via these tools provide insight in vast amounts of valuable information for scientific purposes. For example, [14] used the data from Twitter to predict flu trends and [15] used social media as a measurement tool for the identification of depression. The information gleaned from social media has the potential to complement traditional survey techniques in its ability to provide a more fine-grained measurement over time while radically expanding population sample sizes [15].

By combining clinical data with personal data on, for instance, eating and sleeping patterns, life style, or physical activity level, treatment and coaching purposes can be tailored to the needs of patients even better than before and are, therefore, seen as the key towards a future with optimal medical help [6]. However, it also confronts us with new technological and ethical challenges that require more sophisticated data management tools and data analysis techniques. This vision paper aims to better understand the technological and ethical challenges we face when using and managing Big Data in healthcare as well as the way in which it impacts our way of working, our health, and our wellbeing.

This paper builds on first insights obtained from Big Data experts as already described in [1] and adds the perspectives of healthcare workers (HCWs) and the online public. Section I describes the background of Big Data in literature. Section II describes the procedure of the meetings with experts (focus group; individual meetings) and HCWs (interviews), and describes how the online public's associations with Big Data in a health context were assessed. Section III presents the results, which are discussed more into depth in Section IV. Finally, Section V concludes this paper, describing a number of implications for research using Big Data in healthcare and addressing some future work.

II. Methods

The impact and challenges of Big Data will be examined from three different perspectives: 1) from the perspective of Big Data experts [1], 2) from the perspective of HCWs, and 3) from the perspective of the online public. Different methods were used to gather information from each group. Where a focus group was planned with the Big Data experts, this turned out to unfeasible with HCWs because of their busy schedule. That is why individual interviews were scheduled with them. Finally, to evaluate the perspective of the online public, social media posts were scraped and analyzed.

A. *Focus group with experts*

Many potential issues regarding the use of Big Data have already been mentioned in the literature, newspapers, social media, or debates, and panel discussion websites. However, many of these media sources do not specifically address the healthcare setting and only focus on a limited set of issues at a time (e.g., the privacy and security issues).

To gain more in depth insights into the pros and cons of using Big Data in personalized healthcare, a focus group was organized [16]. The aim was to gain a variety of opinions regarding the scientific and societal issues that play a role in using and managing Big Data to support the growing needs for personalized (and cost-effective) healthcare.

Purposeful sampling was used in the formation of the focus group, meaning that the selection of participants was based on the purpose of the study [16]; i.e., to map the experts' variety and range of attitudes and beliefs on the use of Big Data for (personalized) healthcare purposes. To gather a broad perspective of viewpoints, multiple disciplines were invited to join the expert meeting, resulting in a panel of 6 experts in Big Data research and quantified self-monitoring from different scientific disciplines: psychology, philosophy, computer science, business administration, law, and data science. Participants were recruited at the University of Twente (the Netherlands), based on their societal impact, expertise, and experiences with conducting Big Data research. Individual face to face meetings were conducted to validate the focus group results.

The focus group took 2 hours in total and was facilitated by LS and FS (authors). All participants signed an informed consent for audiotaping the focus group and for the anonymous usage of the results in publications. LVGP and ABJ took additional notes during the discussion. Group discussion was encouraged and participants were repeatedly asked to share their concerns and thoughts.

In preparation of the focus group discussion, literature and multiple sources of (social) media were searched for information on potential Big Data issues that might play a role. During the discussion itself, experts were asked to write down as many issues as they could think of that might become relevant using Big Data for healthcare. Flip-overs were used to express the issues and experts had to categorize these issues into overall concepts that covered the issues. They named these overall concepts themselves by thinking aloud. These concepts are presented in this vision paper. The focus group was audio taped and transcripts were made by authors of this paper. Loose comments without any further specification were excluded to ensure the results are not a representation of the authors' interpretation. Ethical approval for the scientific expert meeting and the consent procedure was obtained by the ethics committee of the University of Twente.

B. *Interviews with healthcare workers*

Based on the results of the focus group, an interview scheme was constructed to assess how HCWs perceive and experience the issues that were identified. Questions were formulated open-ended to encourage HCWs to elaborate on their perceptions of and experiences with Big Data (or eHealth applications) in healthcare. For each question, HCWs were asked to think aloud and to elaborate on their thoughts. Interviews were transcribed verbatim afterwards and a coding scheme was developed.

A total of 6 physicians with experience in Big Data were interviewed. Participants received a first description of the aim of the interviews by e-mail and, in addition, each interview started with a 1.5 minute long movie presenting the interview's subject: Big Data eHealth applications in healthcare. All participants were interviewed in their work setting. Interviews were semi-structured and continued until the interviewer felt that all questions were answered and no new information could be expected. This took about 60 minutes on average. Participants gave informed consent for audiotaping the interviews and for the anonymous usage of the results in publications. The study was approved by the ethics committee of the University of Twente. No additional ethical approval was necessary from the medical ethical committee.

C. *Online public's associations with Big Data in a health context*

Though Big Data receives a lot of attention nowadays, little is known about the publics' associations with the term Big Data in health contexts. With the digitalization of society, the online public that uses social media channels encloses a large proportion of the potential users of Big Data-driven technological applications in healthcare. Furthermore, the content within the social media provides new opportunities to identify the associations made by the online public in relation to Big Data in a healthcare setting. These associations provide a better understanding of the concerns, opportunities, and considerations that the health sector must take into account.

As such, Coosto, a social media monitoring tool (www.coosto.com), was used as a first explorative analysis to analyze these associations among social media users, using multiple data sources (social networks, microblogs, blogosphere, forums) in both Dutch and English.

The identification of the online public's perceptions regarding the terms they use when discussing about Big Data in relation to healthcare was completed by following three phases. In the first phase, social media posts were scraped, based on 6 search queries in the Dutch social media monitoring tool Coosto (Table I). To avoid issues caused by word variations (for example: healthcare, health-care, health care) and synonyms, an extensive list of different spellings was used in each search query. The terms selected for the search query were derived from a systematic analysis of synonyms in academic literature, popular literature, and websites and Google search results. To treat (longer) blog posts and (shorter) tweets equally, each sentence of all posts was analyzed separately in the second phase. More citations and shares means that more online users are interested in that particular topic.

TABLE I. SEARCH QUERIES

Search query
1. "big data" "e-health" OR "ehealth" OR "e health"
2. "big data" "healthcare" OR "health care" OR "health-care"
3. "big data" "care"
4. "big data" "sensors" OR "health" OR "e-health" OR "e health" OR "ehealth" OR "care" OR "healthcare" OR "health care" OR "health-care" OR "wellness" OR "wellbeing" OR "well-being"
5. "big data" "wearables" OR "health" OR "e-health" OR "e health" OR "ehealth" OR OR "care" OR "healthcare" OR "health care" OR "health-care" OR OR "wellness" OR "wellbeing" OR "well-being"
6. "big data" "domotica"

The second phase was aimed at extracting the most commonly used (combinations of) terms in the collected social media posts and measuring the proximity (the relative distance (similarity)) of these terms. The more frequently two terms are mentioned simultaneously in the whole dataset the higher the proximity between these two (combinations of) terms. Based on a codebook (Appendix 1) consisting of terms that are related to and associated with Big Data and/or healthcare, the most frequently mentioned terms in the social media posts were identified. The codebook terms were selected based on a systematic analysis of scientific and popular literature (including references) and websites (including links to other websites), news articles, social media posts (e.g., Twitter), and Google search results. In our design, the sentences of analysis were considered as the cases, and the terms in these messages – after properly filtering for example the stop words, hyperlinks and @mentions – as the variables. The next step in our analysis was to find the terms (e.g., privacy) or phrases (e.g., Internet of Things) from the codebook in the sentences (cases). The sentences without any of the terms were omitted from further analysis. Thus, a matrix was operated that contained terms as the variables in the columns and sentences as cases in the rows. The cells in the matrix consisted of binary data (whether or not a particular term occurs in the sentences). A proximity measurement [17] indicates what combinations of terms are most prevalent.

In the third phase, the main objective was to determine what terms are mostly associated with Big Data in the context of healthcare within the social media. To do so, the open-source network analysis and visualization software package Gephi (http://gephi.github.io/) was used to visualize the interrelationships between (groups of) terms in a semantic network [18]. The binary matrix formed the basis for the semantic network graph. Due to the reasonably large dataset and the minimum agreement between the terms, the correlations have been relatively low. Therefore, all correlations higher than 0.02 were included in the actual analysis. The terms which served as the basis for the search queries were then removed from the semantic network analysis, since the preservation of these terms in the search results would produce biased results because they will occur significantly more than in reality may be assumed.

III. Results

Results are presented separately for each group: 1) Big Data experts, 2) HCWs, and 3) the online public.

A. *Focus group meeting with experts*

The results can be subdivided in 3 categories: 1) empowerment, 2) trust, and 3) data wisdom.

1) *Empowerment*

What does it mean when you monitor your activities, food intake, or stress 24 hours a day using technologies like smart wearables? What drives people to use these 24 hour monitoring devices and what do they need to understand the data generated by these systems? Do they understand the algorithms that are used to capture our behaviors and moods in pictures and graphs? Who owns the data and how to control the maintenance of that data? How to avoid a filtered scope on our lives ignoring others that are out of our affinity groups? The concept of empowerment captures topics as autonomy, freedom, and having control.

Big data evokes a discussion about freedom and autonomy. Autonomy concerns our critical view on how to use technology, while freedom is more about our way of living and thinking. It might, therefore, be more important to focus on freedom instead of autonomy: understanding how you are being influenced and taking a stance against that instead of trying to keep everything away. The focus group made a distinction between positive freedom and negative freedom; two common concepts within the field of philosophy. Positive freedom is the freedom to do something yourself (e.g., to decide for yourself that you want to share your data), whilst negative freedom is the freedom to keep things away, protecting yourself (e.g., when you do not give permission to companies to link your data with other sources). Not losing control, being able to use, share and understand your data is one of the topics when discussing freedom, self-efficacy using self-monitoring technologies.

Empowerment forces us to think about having control, who has the power through the use of Big Data? There might be just a small elite that understands the algorithms and with the increasing complexity, this elite will become even smaller in the future. This can create a division between people who can access and understand the algorithms and people who do not.

Empowering by personalization is one of the aims of the participatory society. Big data can be a leverage to realize this by creating a personal profile, providing the right information, at right moments to enable just in time coaching. Though it can be useful to put people in a profile, the danger of profiling is that you can never leave the assigned group again; once assigned to a group means always assigned to that group. Profiling might be suffocating to people because it creates uncertainty about what people know about you, what data are being collected, and for what purposes. Also, it is often unclear how to determine the norm to which people are compared when assigning them to a group (i.e., standardization, losing freedom). Furthermore, being assigned to a profile might lead to discrimination and certain prejudices/biases. Questions that arise are: How can profiling be used in a sensible/sound way? And who is responsible when mistakes are being made based on a certain profile?

2) *Trust*

Trust will become a key concept in a data driven society. This concept captures more than privacy and security issues. Trust refers to topics as how to create faith in data management and data maintenance, and how to make sense of these data for humans.

Privacy issues become particularly relevant when the linkage of anonymous datasets leads to re-identification. Encryption of the data might prevent identification of individuals, but transparency is not always possible (e.g., when analyzing query logs with search terms). In the end it is all about creating trust to overcome uncertainty or anxiety for a digital world.

People often give consent to institutions to use their data for certain purposes in return for the (free) use of the product or service. However, data can be (re)used for other purposes as well or can be sold to other interested parties, even though that is not always allowed. This leads to great concerns: e.g., healthcare insurance companies who use treatment data for other purposes on a more personal level (for instance, for determining a personalized health insurance premium based on your personal data about your health and lifestyle). It is not that people do not want to share data, they already do this using Facebook or Google services, but they want to understand what happens with the data, in particularly when it concerns the health domain.

Self-monitoring technologies, with no doctors or nurses involved in the caring process, are provided more and more by institutions. Smart algorithms can be applied to personalize data in such a way so you can manage your health and wellbeing yourself. However, these algorithms decide what information you get to see, based on information about you as a user (e.g., search history, Facebook friends, location). This will influence trust in the healthcare system, using data from your device compared to personal advices given by your doctor or nurse.

3) *Data Wisdom*

There is a rapid growth of self-monitoring technologies, but little is known about the reliability and validity of these systems. The lack of evidence for causality can lead to unreliability as well. Furthermore, how can you tell what you are actually measuring? How can the correlations that are found be validated? Does it really say what we think it says or are it just assumptions?

Data wisdom is the concept that captures scientific and societal topics. Scientific refers to how to create data wisdom, in several ways. Those who generate data are not the ones that have the knowledge to analyze, those who analyze lack domain insight (technologies, behaviors). Different kinds of expertise will be needed in the future to deal with Big Data. For instance, expertise to analyze Big Data, expertise to develop and understand the working of algorithms, or expertise in data interpretation and visualizations. The use of data to personalize healthcare demands for new knowledge to support critical and creative thinking to understand data driven decisions and to watch the impact on science, health and society. We all know the disaster with google flu trends, but we have to learn from these failures to set the agenda for future research in using several sources of data (geospatial data, medical data, technology device data) to develop predictive models about health and wellbeing. We have to search for new models, methods to deal with huge datasets, search for patterns rather than testing hypotheses based on small data. Results are not causal-driven but correlational-driven. This requires a change in thought. The golden rule for Randomized Clinical Trials will no longer be the ultimate format for health sciences. New methods are needed to get a grip on "big", how many data (critical mass) is needed and how rich and mature should data be to make meaningful decisions? How to add qualitative experiences and expertise to Big data? Numbers do not tell the whole story, and a clinical eye is important to interpret data in the context of individual health and wellbeing.

Societal refers to the implications for healthcare, addressing topics as ethics, values for a meaningful life. How to avoid a division between people who can access and understand the data and analytics that rule the decisions about treatments and lifestyle advices, and people that cannot? Knowledge and skills are needed to empower people and people should participate in debates about the values of data for self-regulations on the level of individuals, communities and society. Transparency and trust are the key-topics in that debate. Digging into data starts with a scientific and societal debate on the vales of data for a smart and healthy society.

B. *Interviews with healthcare workers*

Again, the results can be subdivided in the 3 categories: 1) empowerment, 2) trust, and 3) data wisdom.

1) *Empowerment*

Physicians recognize the advantages of data sharing. For instance, it provides them easy insight in treatment outcomes, which is an important instrument for quality of care. Yet though the large majority of people probably do not have any problems with sharing their data, patients cannot be forced to share their data and should give informed consent first. Nevertheless, patients often do not understand where they give permission for. What if they change their minds, is it possible to undo their data sharing? What if the data is already shared with different disciplines, will they all be refused access after withdrawing the data sharing approval? Possibly, an independent supervisor should be appointed the task to safeguard the proper handling of patient data (at least till data encryption).

There was no consensus among the physicians about data ownership. Some argue the data is primarily of the patient, but the hospital or healthcare practitioner should be able to gain access to it as well when they have to give account for their actions. On the other hand, it is the physician who writes most of the medical data down in the patient's personal health record, so it can be argued that he owns (that part of) the data (as well).

Next, the physicians argued that profiling as a concept is nothing new. Current practice is already to gather as much information as possible from a patient and to "go through a checklist" of characteristics, symptoms, or complaints before deciding which treatment might be best. Yet profiling based on Big Data might make this process more accurate, improving treatment outcomes. Especially in complex cases, profiling based on Big Data might be of significant value. It promotes personalized healthcare. Concerns about profiling mainly involve drawing conclusions with far-reaching consequences based on incomplete/imprecise data and the unauthorized misuse of data by third parties, like insurance companies. Also professionals might lose professional skills when they do not have to think for themselves anymore.

When using Big Data for predictive modeling proposes (e.g., to predict the chance you might get lung cancer in the next 5 years), people have the "right not to know". Within a certain boundary that is. If national health is in danger, personal rights do not weigh up to national security. Patients should be informed at an early stage about their rights and about who is liable when something goes wrong. In case of treatment decisions, the physician is most of the time liable if something goes wrong. In the Netherlands, physicians are guilty until proven innocent in case of an accusation. When using Big Data algorithms in treatment decisions, physicians should still think for themselves whether the provided advice by a system appears to be reasonable, because they make the final judgment about the best possible treatment for their patient. That is not different from the current process in which a physician also has to deal with information from, for instance, radiology, long-term research, laboratory results, etc. It does not matter whether choices are based on Big Data or not, the physician needs to keep thinking as a doctor. Yet liability is not always clear. For instance, what if a patient wears a smart watch that registers his blood pressure, but the device has a defect. Who is liable? The manufacturer or supplier of the device? But how to deal with liability when the patient uses the device in an ignorant way? Who is liable then? Who has to prove what and how is it regulated? It will be a long juridical procedure because rules are not clear and straightforward in cases like this.

2) *Trust*

Physicians definitely recognize the importance of secure data management. Data management might be outsourced to a third party, on condition that the liability in case of data leaks is properly arranged. Yet physicians might also play an important role in data management, since they are needed for data interpretation. Furthermore, there should be restricted access to sensitive patient data. For instance, when implementing a patient portal, it can be decided to only grant the patient and his own physician access to the portal. In addition, it is of utmost importance that the portal's communication and data transport mechanisms between the patient and the physician are thoroughly thought through, to minimize the risk on data leaks and cyber-attacks.

Opinions on the need to understand the underlying algorithms of the system were divided. Yet most physicians do want to know the basic reasoning behind the algorithms. They fear to lose their professional clinical skills when blindly following the system, without thinking for themselves anymore. They also argue that the standards and guidelines in the medical field exist because the reasoning behind them are clear. They would never trust a computer without at least some insight into the underlying principles, the reliability of the results, and the parameters that were taken into account. Others, however, express no need to understand the algorithms, but they do argue that the algorithms should be checked by a group of experts.

3) Data Wisdom

When asking about their (future) profession, physicians acknowledge the added value of Big Data systems. The medical field encompasses an enormous amount of data that has been collected over the years. It would be helpful if the data from all the existing different platforms could be combined into one overall system to make it surveyable for both clinical and scientific purposes. When the Big Data revolution offers new opportunities for combining this data using innovative data management tools, many new medical and scientific research questions can be explored. When the right algorithms are being developed, Big Data systems might be more accurate than the patient and physician together could ever be, improving quality of care. For instance, when monitoring a patient's condition at home, the data is send to the physician via an interactive application right away (i.e., real-time, 24/7), changes can be detected at an early stage, and (remote) treatment can be provided timely. Also, certain risk factors can be detected and controlled at an early stage. Such applications can improve treatment outcomes and significantly reduce healthcare costs.

A certain expertise is needed to translate the enormous amount of data into clinically relevant pieces of information. These Big Data specialists might be appointed from outside the hospital, although the hospital might not have the financial means to do this. Nevertheless, when implemented, Big Data applications can serve as medical decision aids that help the physicians to combine and process all the available data real quick or it could be used for e-consults, where the patient can login onto the system to see lab results, to make appointments, or to ask questions. As a result, patients need to visit the physician less often. An important note that was made, is the need for guidance to the patients. For instance, if a patient suddenly notices a drop in his blood pressure from 120 to 90, he might think: "oh, I am dying". However, it is still within the norm and this should be explained to the patient to reassure him.

The physicians also recognize the challenges that come with the application of Big Data systems in healthcare. First of all, not all patients will be able to use such systems. For instance, elderly or cognitively impaired patients might not understand the working mechanisms and do not know how to interpret the results. Furthermore, the physicians already always base their decisions on data and it does not really matter where that data comes from (and, as such, whether it is called "Big Data"). What really matters is that the data is reliable. When you start digging into the data without any clinical expertise, chances are that you will find a significant result. However, it might have no clinical meaning and relevance at all. Data collection and data interpretation cost time (and money) as do the development and testing of the underlying algorithms. People (and insurance companies) should be aware of the imperfections of the system and should not blindly follow it as if it is the golden rule. The system does not replace the physician. The physician still makes the decisions and they will only use a Big Data system if it is proven to be more effective than current practice.

C. Online public's associations with Big Data in a health context

For the social media analysis, a total of 5.852 social media posts (blogs, forums, microblogs, and social networks) were crawled and scraped, with a total of 59.281 sentences from a time period of five years, with a focus on Big Data in the context of healthcare. In Appendix 1, the frequencies of emerging words are given. Fig. 1 shows the semantic graph consisting of 49 nodes (interrelationships) and 174 edges (collections of terms). The larger the node, the higher the frequency with which the term is mentioned in relation to Big Data in the context of healthcare. The weight of the edges is determined by the proximity between the terms.

With the modularity algorithm [19], ten clusters of terms were established that are often used together. The modularity metric is a well-known exploration concept to identify a network that is more densely connected internally than with the rest of the network [20]. Five of the major ten clusters are (Fig. 1): concerns (red), opportunities (violet), personalized healthcare (green), infrastructure (yellow), and applications (blue). These clusters cover 92 percent of the associations. The remaining clusters (8 percent) are solitary nodes or dyads and have a lack of power.

When evaluated per cluster, the cluster concerns shows the most frequent associations with the terms: 1) privacy, 2) regulations, 3) reliability, 4) algorithms, 5) transparency, and 6) legislations. The terms that are mentioned the most in the cluster involving the opportunities of Big Data in the context of healthcare are 1) innovation, 2) future, 3) development, 4) technology, 5) challenges, 6) start-up and 7) revolution; whereas the personalized healthcare cluster shows the most frequent associations with the terms 1) quantified self, 2) medicine, and 3) personalization. In the infrastructure cluster, the most associated terms with Big Data and healthcare are 1) cloud, 2) service, 3) platform, and 4) software. And finally, the majority of social media posts related to applications focus on 1) S-Health app, 2) Healthkit, and 3) Healthtap.

On average, the vast majority of terms are related to more than one other term (average degree: 7.102). The average degree is a numerical measure of the size for the neighborhood of an individual node [21]. The terms most associated with Big Data in the context of healthcare that

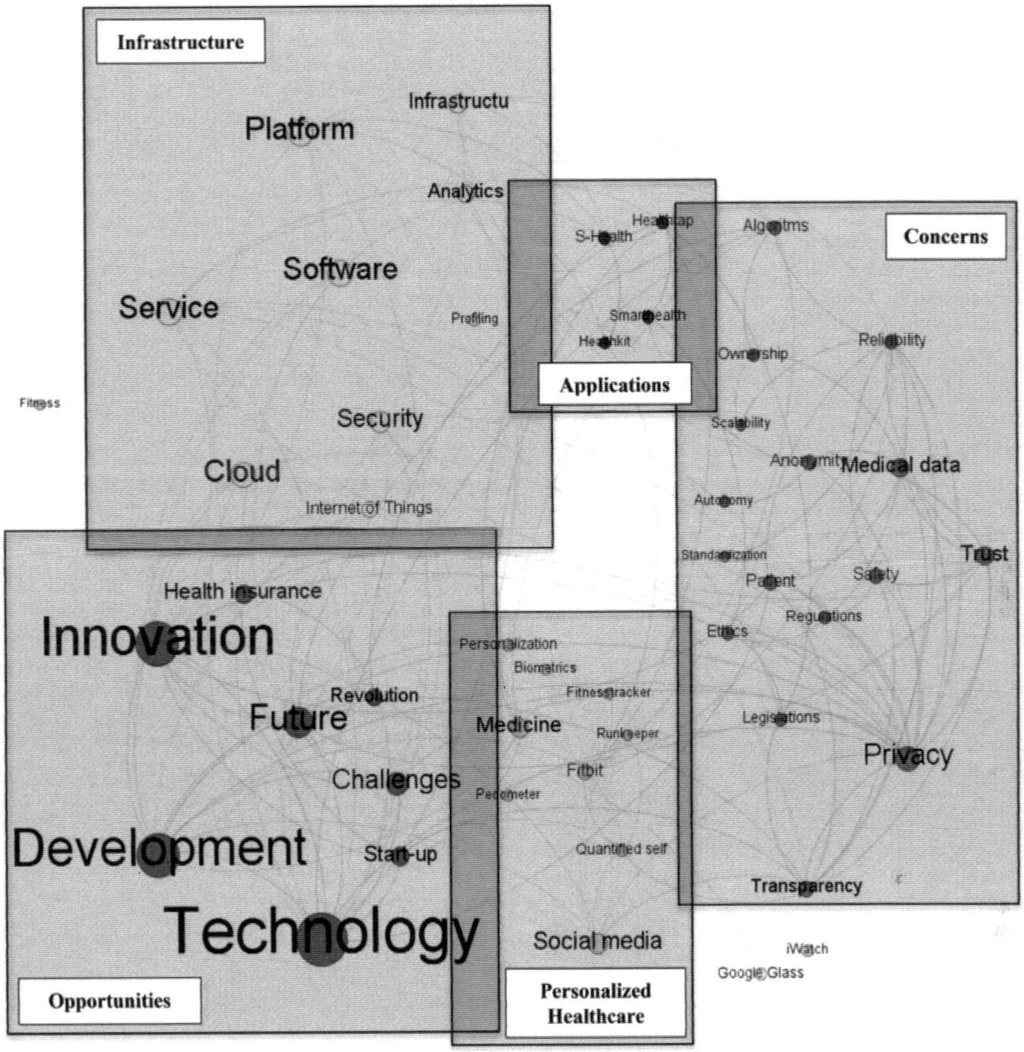

Figure 1. Total semantic network graph (49 nodes – 174 edges).

have a reciprocal degree with other terms in this study are: technology (11), cloud (11), privacy (8), innovation (8), software (8), service (7), development (7), and platform (6). The most frequently mentioned terms in the social media are: technology (1.726), innovation (1.361), development (1.337), future (794), service (638), platform (618), software (610), cloud (581), and privacy (545).

IV. Discussion

With this study we aimed to set a first step in understanding how Big Data impacts healthcare and which critical factors need to be taken into account when using Big Data to personalize healthcare. This was examined from three different perspectives: 1) scientific Big Data experts, 2) HCWs, and 3) the online public.

Results show that Big Data touches upon a wide array of issues, both scientifically and socially. In general, experts and HCWs discussed the future of Big Data on a meta-level, from the perspective of their expertise and their discipline, while the online public considered Big Data more from a consumer-perspective, as end-users of wearables and other technologies. The experts and HCWs make a distinction between promises and concerns depicted as crucial for successfully using and managing Big Data to support the growing needs for personalized healthcare and two rather identical clusters (concerns and opportunities) were found in the social media analyses as well. Concerns are mainly about trust, reliability, safety, purpose limitation, liability, profiling, data ownership (which is unclear), and autonomy, which is consistent with literature [2, 6, 7]. Perhaps the most well-known concern bears upon our privacy [6, 7]. For a great deal, these privacy concerns are associated with potential misuse of data by, for instance, insurance companies [6, 10]. If these privacy concerns are not dealt with appropriately, the public's trust in technological applications might diminish severely [10]. According to the HCWs, patients are often unaware of what is being collected, who is able to view it, and what decisions are being made based on that information. Transparency is needed, people should know what they give informed consent for when they decide to share their data and what happens if they change their mind after some time.

Both experts and HCWs acknowledge the need for a new sort of expertise to be able to understand the algorithms (or at least the basic reasoning behind them) and to interpret the data that is being generated by the technology. At the end, the technology does not replace the physician but they supplement each other. Quality of care can be improved and personalized healthcare becomes the future. Personalized healthcare received a lot of attention in the expert group and among the HCWs. Telemonitoring is seen as a promising development, enabling the physician to react quickly on changes in the clinical status of a patient 24/7, improving the patient's prognosis. In social media personalized healthcare showed clear associations with the Quantified Self movement, medicine, and personalization. Though the semantic network graph (Fig. 1) only visualized the interrelationships between the (groups of) terms without providing it with an interpretation, this result does demonstrate that the emergence of personalized healthcare and the Quantified Self movement receives a lot of attention in science as well as in society. Yet the main themes discussed by the online public did not include personalized healthcare that much, but rather focused on the technological innovation brought by Big Data, the infrastructure that is needed to make this happen, and privacy issues. The need for a good infrastructure was something the experts also stressed, whereas HCWs focused less on this technological aspect of Big Data.

Some other differences between the groups could be identified as well. An aspect specifically addressed by the HCWs is a concern about a potential loss of their autonomy, control, and professional skills if they " blindly" follow an algorithm and do not have to think for themselves anymore. The technology has to respect and keep into account their medical autonomy. Furthermore, experts were rather concerned about the misuse of profiling, whereas HCWs stated that profiling in itself is nothing new. According to the experts, the danger of profiling is that you can never leave the assigned group again. Also, profiling might be suffocating to people because it creates uncertainty about what people know about you, what data is being collected, and for what purpose. Profiling might lead to discrimination and certain prejudices/biases and people might experience the feeling that they lose control. On the other hand, HCWs claim that "profiling is something we have always done, otherwise you cannot start any treatment". HCWs believe that Big Data has the potential to increase its accuracy even further. One concern they do have, in correspondence with the experts, is about the potential misuse of profiling by third parties like insurance companies.

Though these results provide a broad overview of promises as well as barriers that need to be taken into account when using Big Data in healthcare, a few important limitations should be taken into consideration when interpreting the results. At first, we only performed one focus group. This provided us with diverse insights, but we are not able to determine if saturation has been reached [16]. Still, we do expect that we covered a rather broad area, given the multidisciplinary composition of the group and the large variety of expertise they brought into the discussion. To ensure the accuracy of the results and to prevent that the results represent the interpretation of the researchers, clarification and follow-up questions were asked in case of ambiguity to ensure the validity of the results. As such, we believe that the findings provide an accurate exploration of issues that play a role when using Big Data for personalization purposes in healthcare, from a scientific perspective as well as from a societal perspective.

Secondly, only 6 physicians were interviewed, potentially providing a rather limited view on how HCWs in general think about Big Data. However, that was also not the intent of this study. The aim was to gain a better understanding of technological and ethical challenges that need to be faced when using and managing Big Data in healthcare, as well as to gain insight into its impact on our way of working, our health, and our wellbeing. The interviews with the physicians provide some important first insights for this that can be studied further. All physicians had knowledge of and/or experience with Big Data in some way, to ensure they were able to discuss the topics that were addressed. The interview scheme was constructed based on the input from experts to make sure the same themes were addressed, allowing us to compare the results. At the same time the interview scheme was semi-structured and questions were formulated open-ended to allow the physicians to raise other thoughts as well, enriching the data.

Another limitation is that the results from the perspective of the online public might be colored, as the data are restricted to those who use social media. Therefore, a completely reliable reflection of how the general (online) public thinks or speaks about Big Data in the context of healthcare cannot be given at this moment.

Finally, none of the experts or healthcare workers turned out to be a strong adversary of Big Data in healthcare, even though they did provide some critical comments. As such, it would be interesting to extent the results with the opinions of strong adversaries. After all, for sake of implementation, it is important to take their concerns into consideration as well.

V. Conclusion and Future Work

Big Data is seen as the key towards personalized healthcare. However, it also confronts us with new technological and ethical challenges that require more sophisticated data management tools and data analysis techniques. This vision paper aimed to better understand the technological and ethical challenges we face when using and managing Big Data in healthcare as well as the way in which it impacts our way of working, our health, and our wellbeing. A mixed-methods approach (including a focus group, interviews, and an analysis of social media) was used to gain a broader picture about the pros and cons of using Big Data for personalized healthcare from three different perspectives: Big Data experts, HCWs, and the online public. All groups acknowledge the positive aspects of applying Big Data in healthcare, touching upon a wide array of issues, both scientifically and socially. By sharing health data, value can be created that goes beyond the individual patient. The Big Data revolution in healthcare is seen as a promising and innovative development.

Yet the development of these advancements is not self-evident and potential facilitators and barriers need to be addressed first. Concerns were raised, mainly about privacy, trust, reliability, safety, purpose limitation, liability, profiling, data ownership, and loss of autonomy. Also, trust in the technological applications is essential to overcome uncertainty or anxiety for a digital world. To achieve this, a first condition is that privacy and security issues are dealt with appropriately. People should be able to decide for themselves whether or not to share their data and with whom. Also, algorithms should be transparent (at least to a certain degree) to the users (e.g., physicians) to make them meaningful. Reliability should be assured and different kinds of expertise need to evolve. Expertise to analyze Big Data, to develop and understand the working of algorithms, and to interpret and visualize the data in a meaningful way. Moreover, technology should be embedded in our way of working and living. As such, technology should supplement the work of physicians, not replace it, respecting the medical autonomy. The digitalization of society is an ongoing process and the “Big Data” revolution is already changing science, healthcare, and society.

In general, Big Data is described according to the 5V model (Volume, Velocity, Variety, Veracity and Value) [5]. Yet this paper stresses the importance of adding the people-centered view to this rather data-centered 5V model, in order to get a grip on the opportunities for using Big Data in personalized healthcare. Following this view, this vision paper aimed to discuss Big Data topics for personalized healthcare that need to be investigated further to 1) develop new methods and models to better measure, aggregate, and make sense of previously hard-to-obtain or non-existent behavioral, psychosocial, and biometric data, and 2) to develop an agenda for Big Data research to transform and improve healthcare. Topics include:

- Health analytics: Advanced methods (machine learning) and models to analyze Big Data.
- Predictive modelling: To set up smart models to predict behaviors, to prevent diseases, and to personalize healthcare.
- Visualization of data: How to present data meaningful (to the patient as well as the HCW) to support decision making?
- Integration of (mobile) technology with data-platforms to enable automated services and to tailor feedback.
- Disruptive models (new actors, role-players in data driven systems).

ACKNOWLEDGMENT

The authors thank the participants of the focus group as well as the healthcare workers that were interviewed for their valuable input in this study.

REFERENCES

[1] J. E. W. C. van Gemert-Pijnen, F. Sieverink, L. Siemons, and L. M. A. Braakman-Jansen, "Big data for personalized and persuasive coaching via self-monitoring technology," The Eigth International Conference on eHealth, Telemedicine, and Social Medicine (eTELEMED 2016), IARIA, 2016, pp. 127-130, ISBN: 978-1-61208-470-1.

[2] V. Mayer-Schonberger and K. Cukier, Big data: a revolution that will transform how we live, work, and think. New York, NY: Houghton Mifflin Harcourt, 2013.

[3] W. Wang and E. Krishnan, "Big data and clinicians: a review on the state of the science," JMIR Med Inform, vol. 2, pp. e1, 2014, doi:10.2196/medinform.2913.

[4] D. Laney, 3D Data management: Controlling data volume, velocity, and variety. Stamford, CT: META Group Inc., 2001.

[5] B. Marr, Big Data: Using SMART big data, analytics and metrics to make better decisions and improve performance. West Sussex, United Kingdom: John Wiley & Sons, 2015.

[6] S. Klous and N. Wielaard, We are big data. The future of the information society [Wij zijn big data. De toekomst van de informatiesamenleving]. Amsterdam: Business Contact, 2014.

[7] T. B. Murdoch and A. S. Detsky, "The inevitable application of big data to health care," JAMA, vol. 309, pp. 1351-1352, 2013, doi:10.1001/jama.2013.393.

[8] N. V. Chawla and D. A. Davis, "Bringing big data to personalized healthcare: a patient-centered framework," J Gen Intern Med, vol. 28, pp. S660-665, 2013, doi:10.1007/s11606-013-2455-8.

[9] F. Sieverink, L. M. A. Braakman-Jansen, Y. Roelofsen, S. H. Hendriks, R. Sanderman, H. J. G. Bilo, et al., "The diffusion of a personal health record for patients with type 2 diabetes mellitus in primary care," International Journal on Advances in Life Sciences, Vol. 6, pp. 177-183, 2014.

[10] P. Kamakshi, "Survey on big data and related privacy issues," International Journal of Research in Engineering and Technology, vol. 3, pp. 68-70, 2014.

[11] A. M. Kaplan and M. Haenlein, "Users of the world, unite! The challenges and opportunities of Social Media," Business Horizons, vol. 53, pp. 59-68, 2010.

[12] R. Batool, W. A. Khan, M. Hussain, J. Maqbool, M. Afzal, and S. Lee, "Towards personalized health profiling in social network," Information Science and Service Science and Data Mining (ISSDM), 2012 6th International Conference on New Trends in (IEEE, 2013), 2012 pp. 760-765, ISBN: 978-89-94364-20-9.

[13] F. Greaves, D. Ramirez-Cano, C. Millett, A. Darzi, and L. Donaldson, "Harnessing the cloud of patient experience: using social media to detect poor quality healthcare," BMJ quality & safety, vol. 22, pp. 251-255, 2013, doi: 10.1136/bmjqs-2012-001527.

[14] R. Nagar, Q. Yuan, C. C. Freifeld, M. Santillana, A. Nojima, R. Chunara, et al., "A case study of the New York city 2012-2013 influenza season with daily geocoded Twitter data from temporal and spatiotemporal perspectives," J Med Internet Res, vol. 16, pp. e236, 2014, doi: 10.2196/jmir.3416.

[15] M. De Choudhury, S. Counts, and E. Horvitz, "Social media as a measurement tool of depression in populations,"

Proceedings of the 5th Annual ACM Web Science Conference (ACM 2013), 2013, pp. 47-56, ISBN: 978-1-4503-1889-1.

[16] R. A. Krueger and M. A. Casey, Focus groups - a practical guide for applied research. Thousand Oaks, CA: Sage, 2015.

[17] D. Wishart, CLUSTAN user manual, 3rd ed., Edinburgh: Program Library Unit, Edinburgh University, Inter-university research councils series, 1978.

[18] M. Bastian, S. Heymann, and M. Jacomy, "Gephi: an open source software for exploring and manipulating networks," Proceedings Third International ICWSM Conference, 2009, pp. 361-362.

[19] V. D. Blondel, J.-L. Guillaume, R. Lambiotte, and E. Lefebvre, "Fast unfolding of communities in large networks," Journal of Statistical Mechanics: Theory and Experiment, vol. 10, pp. P10008, 2008, doi: 10.1088/1742-5468/2008/10/P10008.

[20] M. E. Newman, "Modularity and community structure in networks," Proceedings of the National Academy of Sciences, 2006, vol. 103, pp. 8577-8582, doi: 10.1073/pnas.0601602103.

[21] J. Scott, Social network analysis. London: Sage, 2012.

SUPPORTING INFORMATION - APPENDIX 1

WORD FREQUENCY TERMS "BIG DATA" – "HEALTHCARE.

Term*	**Word frequency**	**Term**	**Word frequency**
Care	**7469**	Safety	167
Health	**4196**	Anonymity	163
Technology	1726	Patients	153
Innovation	1361	Algorithms	142
Development	1337	Reliability	139
Healthcare	**1320**	Legislations	91
Future	794	Ethics	90
eHealth	**668**	Healthtap	90
Service	638	S Health	89
Platform	618	Ownership	83
Software	610	Smarthealth	81
Cloud	581	Personalization	81
Privacy	545	**Wellbeing**	**80**
Challenges	484	Regulations	74
Security	400	Google Glass	69
Wearable	**374**	**Domotica**	**55**
Social media	374	Quantified self	53
Big Data	**337**	iWatch	44
Start-up	324	Healthkit	42
Medical data	311	Autonomy	37
Health insurance	310	Profiling	36
Trust	310	Pedometer	34
Medicine	309	Wellness	31
Infrastructure	291	Biometrics	19
Analytics	249	Scalability	13
Revolution	242	Runkeeper	12
Sensors	**229**	Fitnesstracker	11
Transparency	196	**Health condition**	**4**
Fitbit	185	Fitness	2
Internet of Things	185	Standardization	1

* **Bold**: Not included in the data-analysis, since they were also present in the search query. Not bold: Included in the data-analysis.

E-business Adoption in Nigerian Small Business Enterprises

Olakunle Olayinka, Martin George Wynn, Kamal Bechkoum
School of Computing and Technology
University of Gloucestershire
Cheltenham, United Kingdom
e-mail: kunle@kunleolayinka.com, MWynn@glos.ac.uk, KBechkoum@glos.ac.uk

Abstract— **Within the last decade, there has been a global increase in the use of e-business by both large and small companies. Today, it is generally acknowledged that e-business provides a range of opportunities for small businesses to operate and compete effectively; however, in developing countries such as Nigeria, there is very limited research on e-business adoption in the small business sector. This paper reviews existing literature on e-business adoption in developing countries, identifies key issues impacting upon e-business adoption and examines the use of e-business in four Nigerian small businesses using existing analytical models. The results indicate that Small Business Enterprises in Nigeria are indeed benefitting from e-business deployment, and key influencing factors affecting e-business adoption are identified. The study also concludes that different processes in different companies are affected by e-business, but that it is the customer facing processes in the main that have gained most from the adoption of e-business.**

Keywords- e-business; Nigeria; Small Business Enterprises; SBEs; process mapping; e-business models; critical influencing factors.

I. INTRODUCTION

Within the last decade, there has been a general increase in the use of e-business by both large and small corporations across the globe, and recent research suggests there has been an increase in the use of e-business technologies in Nigerian businesses [1]. In developing countries such as Nigeria, as a result of the increased use of the internet [2], and mobile networks penetration [3], current and potential customers of both large and small companies are not only equipped with desktop computers and laptops, but also with mobile devices such as iPads, smart phones and tablets. The demand for e-business capabilities in developing countries is on the increase, but very little research has explored the impact on smaller companies.

In developed countries, research has shown that both large enterprises and small businesses have successfully adopted e-business technologies and processes to gain competitive advantage [4], transform business models [5], and improve relationships with customers and suppliers [6] [7]. Various researchers have also pointed out that the motivation for e-business adoption varies from organization to organization, though it often encompasses reducing transaction costs [8], improved access to national or global markets [9], or increasing bottom-line profit performance [10].

Research conducted by the Organization for Economic Cooperation and Development (OECD) found that over 95% of companies in two thirds of OECD countries use the internet for various business activities [11]. The commercialization of the internet has brought about an increased use of information technology in businesses [12] and today, an increasing number of multinationals and large companies have automated all their business processes; even simple activities such as leave booking and room reservation have now been moved to online portals [13]. Empirical evidence has also shown that e-business adoption could be regarded as a strategy for organizations to compete and outperform competition [4] [5]. However, since developing countries often suffer from infrastructure and internet penetration issues [14], understanding the extent of e-business usage in smaller companies in developing countries has not been of research interest up until now. For the purposes of this research, we use the term Small Business Enterprises (SBEs), being defined as enterprises which employ fewer than 50 persons, while Small to Medium Enterprises (SMEs) are defined as enterprises which employ fewer than 250 persons [15] [16]. The significance of SBEs in many economies of the world is considerable. In Nigeria, SMEs contribute about 46.5% to Nigeria's GDP with SBEs making up 99% of these SMEs.

Using case studies of four Nigerian SBEs, this research investigates e-business adoption in a developing country context. The research utilizes process mapping and other existing frameworks to analyze the current situation in these companies. Following this introduction, Section II reviews relevant literature on e-business in developing countries and e-business frameworks, and positions two research questions for the study. Section III then describes the methodology employed in this study and Section IV presents and discusses the findings to date. Section V provides an analysis of these findings, and Section VI summarises results to date and addresses the two research questions. The final concluding section briefly outlines some future research directions.

II. LITERATURE REVIEW

In 1997, IBM first used the term "e-business" to mean "the transformation of key business processes through the use of internet technologies" [17]. E-business can be viewed as the integration of web technologies with business processes and management practices to increase efficiency and lower costs [18]. The adoption of e-business has been of interest to researchers for several years. In developed countries, numerous researchers [5] [7] [19]–[23] have explored various aspects of e-business, including factors affecting e-business adoption, challenges of adopting e-business, the development of e-business models, and critical factors in successful e-business adoption.

SMEs can contribute in various ways to a nation's economy, offering flexible employment opportunities [9], poverty alleviation [24], and supply chain flexibility [25]. Overall, their contribution to a country's overall GDP growth is significant [26], and e-business adoption in SMEs has been the focus of a number of studies in developed countries, including the UK [10] [27], the USA [28], Australia [19] and in Canada [29]. However, there is still considerable debate in the existing literature on the value and productivity gain e-business has to offer to SBEs [11] [13].

The following two sub-sections critically review, first, relevant literature regarding e-business adoption in developing countries, and, second, existing e-business models and frameworks.

A. E-business Adoption in Developing Countries

Research conducted on e-business in developing countries has identified factors responsible for adoption [30] [31], challenges and barriers to e-commerce adoption [32] [33] [34], the benefits of e-business and consumer attitudes to e-business adoption [35]. While several studies have been carried out in developed countries to investigate some of these topics, when results of such studies are compared with studies in developing countries, it becomes evident that the different environmental, infrastructural and cultural issues predominant in developing countries do not allow for all-encompassing generalizations, hence the need for country specific studies.

Kapurubandara and Lawson [34] investigated the barriers to ICT and e-commerce adoption in Sri-Lanka. Their research indicated that SMEs lag behind and are often skeptical about the uptake of e-business technologies. Their study also suggests that SMEs face unique and significant challenges in the uptake of e-commerce and these challenges could be broadly classified as internal and external barriers. Using data from exploratory pilot studies, surveys and existing literature, they identified nine barriers to the adoption of ICT and e-commerce in Sri-Lanka which include lack of skills, security, cultural and political barriers. Their research also proposed relevant support measures needed by SMEs in developing countries to overcome such barriers.

Quite similarly, Janita and Chong [33] also researched the barriers to B2B e-business adoption in SMEs in Indonesia, a country with the largest proportion of SMEs in South East Asia. Their research identified poor infrastructure, lack of owner or manager motivation, lack of power to influence partners and lack of online policies, as some of the key barriers to e-business adoption by SMEs. They proposed a conceptual framework which consists of six key indicators (Individual, Organisational, Technology, Market & Industry, External Support and Government Support) for analyzing the barriers of B2B e-business adoption in Indonesian SMEs.

More recently, Rahayua and Day [31] conducted a study on Indonesian SMEs to determine factors that affect e-commerce adoption. Their research, which was based on the Technological, Organisational and Environmental theoretical framework (TOE), surveyed 292 Indonesian SMEs and identified 11 variables as important factors that influence adoption of e-commerce in SMEs. These variables are further grouped into four, - technological factors, organizational factors, environmental factors and individual factors.

Hitherto, most relevant studies on Nigerian small businesses have focused primarily on e-commerce, i.e., the buying and selling of good and services online, neglecting the potential of e-business in transforming business processes and core operations in the more traditional "bricks and mortar" companies [8] [24]. In 2011, Olatokun and Bankole [36] investigated the factors influencing e-business technology adoption by SMEs in Ibadan, a city in south western Nigeria. Data was collected by structured questionnaires administered to key personnel in 60 SMEs (30 adopters and 30 non-adopters of e-business), and the results revealed that the age of SMEs was a significant influencing factor on whether e-business was used or not, while company size was of very little significance. It was the younger companies that constituted the majority of e-business users.

Agwu [30] also conducted an investigative analysis of factors affecting e-business adoption and website maintenance of commercial organisations in Nigeria. This case study research gathered information from six organisations based in three geopolitical zones of the country – North, West and East. Overall, 9 managers were interviewed and the results of the study indicated that consumer readiness, IT Skills shortage and internet connectivity are vital to e-business adoption and website maintenance in Nigerian businesses.

As a follow on to previous research, in 2015, Agwu and Murray [37] also researched the barriers to e-commerce adoption by SMEs in Nigeria. The research which was conducted in three states in Nigeria – Lagos, Abuja and Enugu - made use of interviews to gather information from SME owners, and their findings indicated that lack of an e-commerce regulatory security framework, technical skills and basic infrastructures are some of the main factors that hamper e-commerce adoption in Nigeria.

Recently, Erumi-Esin and Heeks [38] researched e-business adoption and use among African Women-Owned SMEs. Their study, which made use of both qualitative and quantitate methods of research, surveyed 140 SMEs in Warri - a commercial city in southern Nigeria. Using questions informed by the Unified Theory of Acceptance and Use of Technology Model (UTAUT), they examined factors that influence adoption in women-owned SMEs in sub-Sharan Africa. Their results indicated that perceived usefulness plays an important role in e-business adoption, market forces serve as drivers, while lack of infrastructure and resources serve as impediments to adoption.

These research initiatives indicate both the current use and potential that e-business has in developing countries such as Nigeria, but no study has focused on Nigerian SBEs. This study aims to fill this research gap and provide insights into the key issues impacting upon e-business adoption in Nigerian SBEs. Rather than look at barriers, success factors or indicators, the research at this stage will attempt to identify the key influencing factors that are impacting the take-up and deployment of e-business in the Nigerian SBE sector.

B. *E-business Models and Frameworks*

To understand and extend the deployment of e-business in companies, researchers, governments and e-business consultants have developed several analytical and operational frameworks [39] [40]. Analytical tools such as process mapping and systems profiling have also been used in previous studies [10] [41].

The DTI Adoption Ladder constitutes one of the earliest e-business frameworks. It breaks down e-business adoption into five stages and suggests that organisations move through these stages in a sequential order [9] [42]. Levy and Powell [43] proposed the "transporter model" as an alternative non-linear e-business adoption model for SMEs. This model suggests that different types of SMEs will view e-business adoption in different ways and identifies four dimensions of e-business deployment in an SME - brochureware, business opportunity, business network and business support.

In order to determine e-business adoption at individual process level – rather than at overall company level - the Connect, Publish, Interact, Transform (CPIT) model was developed by the UK Department of Trade and Industry [44]. This model offers a 2-dimensional matrix to evaluate the impact of e-business technologies across an organisation's main business processes. When compared with the Adoption Ladder, the CPIT model offers a more in-depth assessment of the impact of e-business on SME operations [9]. The Stages of Growth for e-business (SOG-e) model [45] is the combination of a six stage IT maturity model with a six stage Internet Commerce maturity model. However, somewhat akin to the CPIT model, the SOG-e model recognises that it is possible for an organisation to have different levels of e-business maturity in different areas of a business. A related model is that of Willcocks and Sauer [46], who identified 4 main stages through which organisations will pass as they develop and apply the skills needed for successful e-business deployment. The organization gains increased business value from e-business as it attains the new capabilities required to advance to the next stage.

Research studies in developed countries have applied some of these methods and frameworks to evaluate e-business technology and process adoption in SMEs. However, in the context of Nigeria, no study has to date applied similar methods in the analysis of e-business adoption in SBEs. This research will attempt to apply some of these models to Nigerian SBEs, using, as a starting point, a simple top level process mapping technique that has been applied in similar studies [10] [47]. More specifically, it will address the following research questions (RQs):

RQ1. Can these mapping techniques and models of e-business adoption be usefully applied to SBEs in a developing world context?

RQ2. What are the critical influencing factors impacting upon e-business adoption in Nigerian SBEs?

III. RESEARCH METHODOLOGY

Research projects usually adopt a particular philosophical stance based on a research paradigm, for example post-positivism, pragmatism, interpretivism or constructivism [48]. This philosophical stance has a major influence on the choice of research methods and approaches to be used in order to obtain relevant findings [49]. For the purposes of this research, an interpretivist paradigm is adopted, and the research approach is qualitative, using multiple case studies.

The case study method of research has been selected because it is well suited for observations where the researcher aims to probe deeply and analyse with a view to making generalisations about the wider population in which the unit being studied belongs [50] [51]. Furthermore, the use of e-business is quite complex and will often vary from one company to another. According to Yin [52], the case study method of research is well suited for exploratory studies that aim to understand a phenomenon which will often result in the use and review of multiple evidences.

The four case studies (Table I) were selected from a cross-section of SBE industry sectors in Lagos – Nigeria's most populous city and its economic capital. The use of multiple case studies adds greater weight to the research and makes research findings more convincing [52]. Qualitative data was gathered through questionnaires and semi-structured interviews with key personnel in the company case studies. The case studies were identified through existing contacts with company owners and IT managers, and all organisations selected for the study had already attempted to apply e-business within their organisations.

The interview data was used to build a process map of each company, employing a simple technique used in similar studies [41]. Interviewees were also questioned

TABLE I. THE FOUR CASE STUDY COMPANIES

Company	**Date Founded**	**No. of Staff**	**Turnover 2014/15**
ABC Laundries	2010	7	£14,000
GPY Properties	2012	23	£76,000
KDE Energy	2012	10	£235,000
LTE Consulting	2007	7	£24,000

about the functioning and capabilities of existing systems and technologies in each process area of the company concerned, providing the basis for a profiling of existing technology as either worthy of retention, in need of replacement or between the two, pending further evaluation (Fig. 1 to Fig. 4). This again builds on similar studies undertaken in small companies in the UK [54].

While this research is qualitative, exploratory and inductive in nature, some quantitative assessment of company turnover, number of staff and period of e-business usage was done. Necessary approval and consent from participatory organisations were sought and aliases have been used for company and individuals' names. Empirical evidence gathered from these organisations was developed and assessment made against selected models.

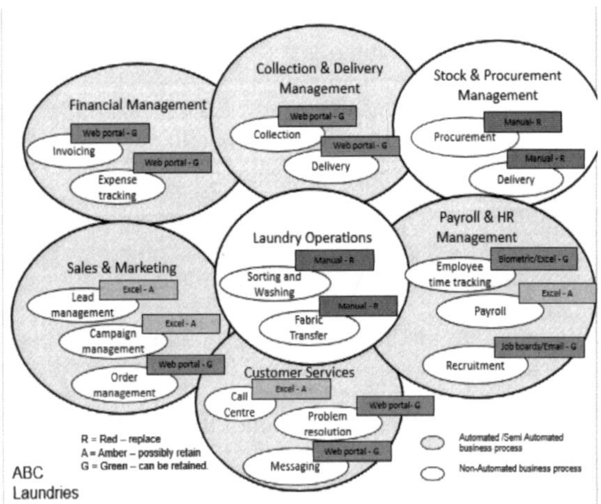

Figure 1. Main business processes and systems profiling at ABC Laundries

IV. FINDINGS

ABC Laundries is a family business founded in 2010. It originated as a home based operation, but has now expanded to become a budget laundry and dry cleaning service for people living in Lagos. The company provides a wide range of laundry and dry cleaning services to people living in the Lagos Metropolis from its locations in Yaba and Surulere (urban areas within Lagos). With its main operations office in Surulere strategically located within the Lagos University Teaching Hospital, ABC Laundries is able to offer its laundry services to students and staff at the hospital, as well as pickup and delivery services to companies, corporate services, and guest houses across Lagos State. Currently, the company turns over circa 6 million Naira (£14,000) per annum, and employs 7 staff. (Staff wages are very low in comparison with developed world norms, averaging less than £1000 a year for these staff). The current business plan is to further increase revenue by expanding the company's customer base and increasing market share.

The management of ABC Laundries view e-business as a key enabler of corporate growth and, to this end, invested in a bespoke web-based system in 2013, to handle its key Sales & Marketing and financial management processes. Prior to this, most business processes were handled by a combination of paper based receipts, Excel spreadsheets and open source accounting tools. However, this became difficult to manage with the opening of a new branch in 2012, and this was the catalyst for investment in a new web portal. The key objectives of this investment were:

1. To provide a system where orders can be captured in real time at both locations.
2. To provide a mechanism to allow staff and customers to track the status of a laundry order from pickup to delivery.
3. To enable top-level financial reporting in real-time.
4. To maintain a database of customers and contact details.

The web portal was implemented in phases, adding new functionality as the old support systems were phased out. The key objectives have been met, with the addition of a few functionality enhancements. The web portal was built using PHP and the MYSQL database. Integration with email servers as well as SMS gateways has enabled emails and SMS notifications to be sent to customers.

GPY Properties is a property development and marketing company founded in 2012. Given Nigeria's housing deficit and the acute absence of quality housing in the country, the company aims to help redress this imbalance through the provision of innovative, high quality and affordable homes.

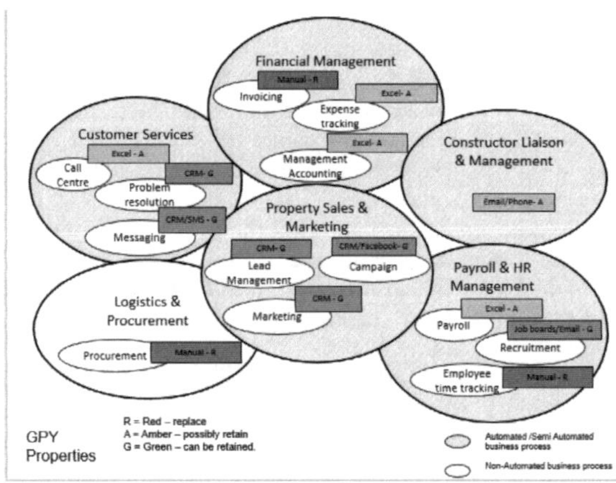

Figure 2. Main business processes and systems profiling at GPY Properties

The company originated as the property sales division of a larger consulting company called PYI Consulting Limited. However, as sales of developed properties increased, the owner decided to hive off the division into a separate corporate entity to focus on property development

Sales & Marketing as its core business. In 2015, the company turned over about 32 million Naira (£76,000) and the forecast for 2016 is even greater, although considering the recent recession in the country, this might be quite ambitious.

GPY Properties maintains a website mainly for marketing properties and showcasing its ongoing projects to customers and potential customers. The company also maintains a cloud based Customer Relationship Management (CRM) system for maintaining and analyzing customer contact details. From time to time, the company also advertises on Facebook and various other property aggregator websites. Invoice generation and other accounting activities are currently managed by Excel spreadsheets, but plans are in place to subscribe to a cloud based accounting solution; the Wave Accounting and Xero Accounting packages are being considered as possible solutions. With three full time staff and twenty contract staff, the company has been able to automate most of its daily business activities concerning customer engagement, internal communication and product marketing.

KDE Energy is an energy solutions company established to meet the energy demands of Nigerians. By offering alternative energy solutions using solar technologies, the company has been able to provide cost effective solutions to both residential and commercial customers. Upon completion of a degree in Electronics in the UK in 2012, the founder returned to Nigeria and subsequently identified an opportunity in the energy sector in Nigeria.

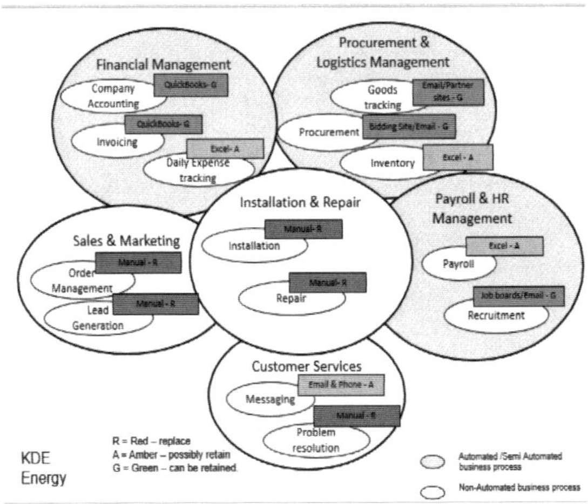

Figure 3. Main business processes and systems profiling at KDE Energy

Today, with only two full-time staff and about eight temporary staff, the company turns over 100 million Naira (£235,000) and has plans to increase this in the coming year. In 2014, KDE Energy invested in a website to provide information about its products and services to potential customers. This investment was part of the company's growth strategy as it intended to take on more commercial projects and having a website made the company look more professional. The company makes use of a cloud based accounting tool for its quarterly accounting and most of the day to day expenses are handled with Microsoft Excel. According the founder, the company is very aware of how e-business positively affects its operations, particularly with the sourcing of goods. However, they do not have a plan in place yet to take orders online or become very active on social media.

LTE Consulting is a training and consulting SBE based in Lagos, Nigeria. The owner founded the company in 2007 after a successful career in the civil service. The company turns over 10 million Naira (£24,000) and principally focuses on training and consulting in West Africa, but with Nigeria as its main focus point. The company offers standard or tailored in-house training, as well as open courses, particularly to the Nigerian financial sector. With staff numbering 4 full-time staff and 3 contractors, the company prides itself on offering quality training courses in customer service, agency marketing, life insurance and management.

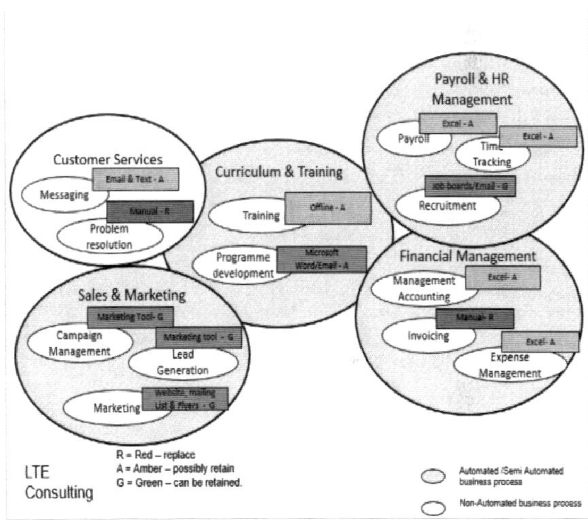

Figure 4. Main business processes and systems profiling at LTE Consulting

The company maintains a website that helps to keep its customers aware of upcoming courses and training. The company also allows bookings to be made on the website but the actual payment/sale is done offline. Furthermore, the company maintains a custom built customer relationship management (CRM) tool that it uses to keep in touch with its customers as well as previous course attendees. After a newsletter is sent out informing previous customers in the database of new course offerings, it is the norm that the company would receive at least 20 related inbound calls within a week. While LTE Consulting still sends out fliers via dispatch riders, the management considers that using the CRM system is cost effective and if their customer base was more IT enabled, they would consider halting their flyer distribution.

V. ANALYSIS

Analysis of e-business deployment in the case study companies was undertaken through the combination of two techniques - process mapping and systems profiling (briefly noted in Section III), and two models - CPIT (a process based e-business model) and the Willcocks and Sauer e-business stage model. Previous research [5] [30] indicates that the use of simple stage based models alone to determine the level of e-business use in an organisation is not sufficient, as different processes may be at different levels. However, even with models that examine technology deployment at process level, such as the CPIT model, there is still the need to adapt these to a small business environment, as the process definitions may not be appropriate to newly-created SBEs. This combination of pre-existing techniques and models, derived and adapted from previous research [10], is used as the framework for analysis of the case studies.

Using data from the questionnaire responses and semi-structured interviews, seven core processes were identified in ABC Laundries (Fig. 1) - Laundry Operations, Financial Management, Sales & Marketing, Collection & Delivery Management, Stock & Procurement Management, Payroll & HR Management and Customer Services. At GPY Properties, there were six core processes (Fig. 2) that the organisation performs – Financial Management, Constructor Liaison & Management, Customer Services, Property Sales & Marketing, Logistics & Procurement and Payroll & HR Management. At KDE Energy, six processes (Fig. 3) were identified - Financial Management, Customer Services, Procurement & Logistics, Installation & Repair, Payroll & HR Management and Sales & Marketing; while at LTE Consulting, five processes were identified (Fig. 4) – Invoicing & Financial Management, Sales & Marketing, Customer Services, Curriculum & Training and Payroll & HR.

Systems profiling was applied to identify e-business systems currently in place in each process area. By employing a simple Red-Amber-Green assessment (Fig. 1 to Fig. 4), systems were assessed to indicate those in need of replacement, those that could possibly be retained and those that were deemed strategically and/or operationally sound. This procedure initiated the analysis of e-business systems at individual process level as well as indicating which processes are automated, semi-automated or non-automated.

A CPIT analysis of ABC Laundries (Fig. 5) provides a more detailed view of the impact of e-business systems at process level. This revealed that e-business systems have made significant impact in the financial management and customer facing processes. Decision-makers within the organisation are easily able to keep track of daily, weekly and monthly revenue from any of the two premises, or remotely, thus helping the organisation to plan effectively and take appropriate action when needed.

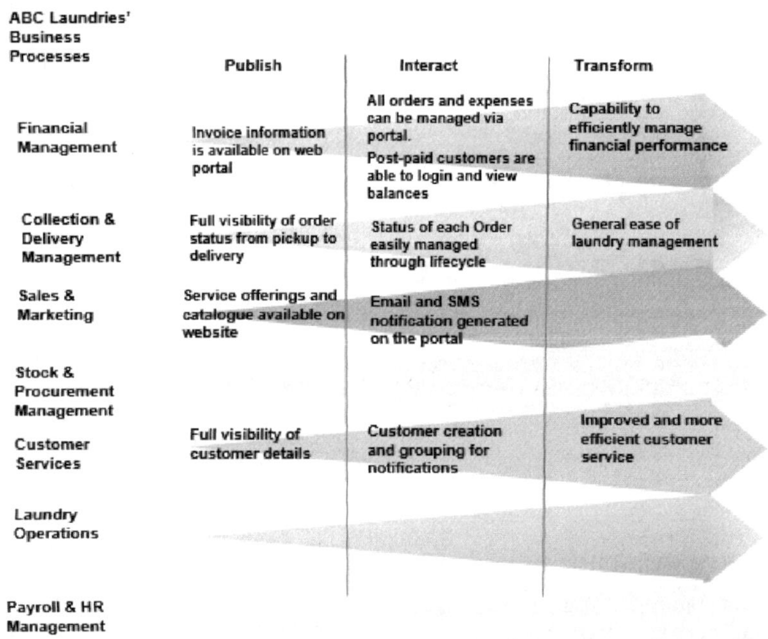

Figure 5. CPIT model applied to ABC Laundries

The Sales & Marketing process has also been made more efficient with the ability to automate and notify selected groups of customer via SMS or emails. There remain further benefits to be gained by automating the communication of marketing information to customers and by making relevant information available across processes. This may allow, for example, special offers to be made to customers in specific geographic locations, with high frequency of delivery, with a mind to keep delivery cost constant and increase orders to be delivered. This type of further development, which is akin to what, in a larger organization, would be termed Business Intelligence, would arguably move the company into the transformation stage on the CPIT model.

GPY Properties has been able to adopt e-business technologies without the need to use in-house IT staff, as it has been able to utilise a cloud based CRM tool. The CPIT model for GPY Properties shows that its Sales & Marketing process is well supported by e-business technology. According to the company's managing director, the strategy to advertise online has helped the company gather new leads - often people with very busy schedules, who would not normally have time to visit the company's office - as well as reach different geographical locations with its advertisements. This year, without doing any advert campaign specifically targeted at the northern part of Nigeria, the company has been able to make two property sales to individuals who live in this location, and a number of further sales in this region are currently in the final stages of completion. One of the current subscribers to its flagship residential estate is a Nigerian who resides in Canada and who saw the advert on the company's Facebook page.

Nevertheless, Fig. 6 shows us that as of now, the deployment of e-business technologies at GPY Properties is restricted to the Sales, Marketing and Customer Service processes. The managing director has affirmed that the volume of data generated by the various departments in the other process areas does not justify further investment in e-business systems at present, although this may change as the organisation expands and takes up more construction projects.

KDE Energy makes use of QuickBooks to maintain its company accounts while day-to-day expenses are tracked using Excel. As can be seen from Fig. 3, the Financial Management, Payroll & HR Management and Procurement & Logistics processes are automated to some degree, while the other three processes are largely manual. The CPIT analysis of KDE Energy (Fig. 7) emphasizes this and clearly indicates that only the Financial Management and Procurement & Logistics processes are adequately supported by e-business technology. However, as indicated by the founder of the company, most of their income is made from transactions with other companies, and this normally emanates from discussions at management level, and therefore there is very little justification for implementing an e-ordering site as there is no demand for it at present. The company's customers do not require it and their competitors are not using it.

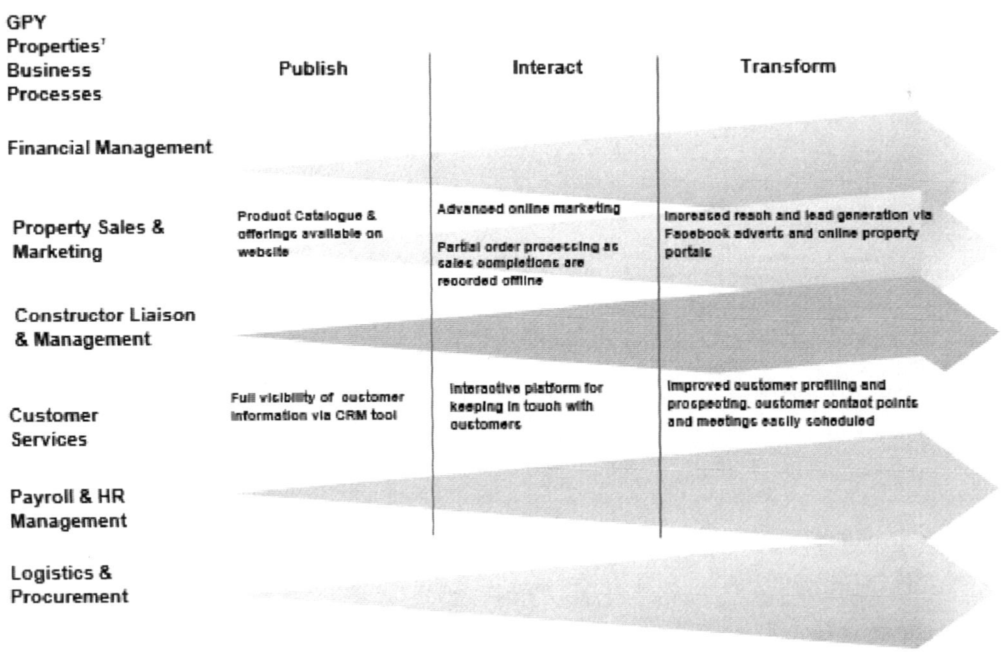

Figure 6. CPIT model applied to GPY Properties

From the system profiling of LTE Consulting (Fig. 4), it can be seen that most processes are automated. The CPIT analysis (Fig. 8) of this company indicates that the business has gained significant value from their e-business deployment, notably in the Sales & Marketing process. The company is very focused on increasing sales, and since the company deals with individuals as well as corporate customers, they are required to constantly keep in touch with customers in order to get new businesses. Email newsletter automation has been cost effective so far.

If we now look at these four companies against Willcocks and Sauer's model [46], the analysis suggests they are all on or between stages 2 and 3 (Fig. 9), whereas other authors [54] have suggested that many small companies do not progress past stage 1 because they often do not see the benefit in investing in capital intensive e-business projects. This apparent contradiction is partly explained by the reduction in cost of e-business infrastructure in recent years, and, partly because of this, it has become a *de facto* norm to use e-business in the Sales & Marketing processes in many organisations, including SBEs. Moreover, in the case study companies investigated here, the management sees e-business as a key enabler to growth.

In ABC Laundries, in particular, their success with e-business to date can be attributed to the phased introduction of new e-business features which has helped the organisation derive value from relatively small scale, staged, expenditure. This has also allowed a phased upgrade in technology, accompanied by appropriate process improvement and staff training, before moving on to focus on another process. Similarly, at GPY Properties, the company has used cloud based systems that offer very low entry costs.

VI. Results

In answer to RQ1 noted earlier in this paper, this research suggests that the e-business adoption models, developed to gauge the impact of e-business in the developed world over a decade ago, are of value today in a developing world context. Although the definition of e-business has evolved, the process mapping technique and the application of models like CPIT can give a clear framework and point of departure for the assessment of e-business in countries like Nigeria; and they clearly show that e-business technologies are bringing value to the studied SBEs, notably in the customer facing processes, which mirrors the early deployment of e-business in the developed world.

As regards RQ2, the analysis of data retrieved from interviews and questionnaires from these four SBEs in the Lagos Metropolis indicates eight *critical influencing factors* (CIFs) impacting e-business adoption in Nigerian SBEs.

A. Owner Perspective

Most SBEs in Nigeria are run by one individual or at most a partnership of two people. Most business decisions are by the owner and his/her perspective is thus critical. In the case of ABC Laundries and LTE Consulting, the company owners were very much in favour of IT and had a general belief that the careful introduction of new systems would make them more productive and profitable. For example, the owner of ABC Laundries made it explicit that he made most of the decisions in the organisation, and that if he had not promoted the use of e-business in his organisation, it would have been difficult for the company to fund the necessary investment, let alone overcome the various challenges the staff encountered as a result of e-business implementation.

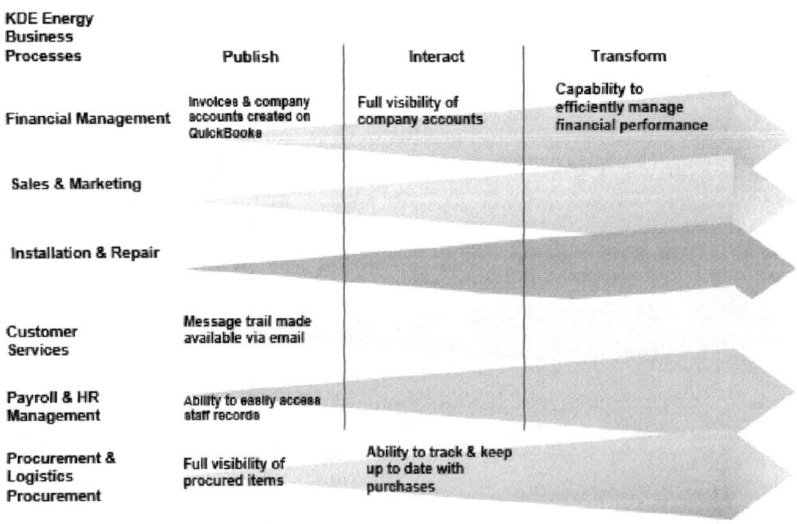

Figure 7. CPIT model applied to KDE Energy

B. Customer/Consumer Perspective

Customer and consumer perspectives are important to most aspects of an SBE operation. Consumers often drive e-business usage in SBEs in Nigeria. In some industry sectors, notably those focused on retail sales, consumers are increasingly expecting a range of web-based services. But in other companies, for example, KDE Energy, the primary customers are other companies that are often not well advanced in the use of e-business themselves, and as such there is no great pressure from the customer side to introduce e-business into customer service processes.

C. Internet Penetration, Cost & Availability

For the purposes of this research, e-business is defined as the use of internet technologies in business processes. Thus, for SBEs in Nigeria to effectively take up e-business, the internet needs to be suitably available at their office and works locations, at acceptable cost. All four companies in this study attested to the importance of internet penetration in their areas. Although this is on the increase in Nigeria generally, it still remains one of the key issues affecting e-business adoption in Nigerian businesses; and with tight cost control often of paramount importance, internet costs are particularly relevant in an SBE environment.

D. Trust

Another key issue affecting e-business adoption in Nigerian SBEs is trust. Trust can be seen as a multifaceted factor as it relates to both staff trust and confidence in the e-business systems and processes, and also customer/consumer trust in online purchases in the Nigerian technology and regulatory environment. Lack of trust has impeded the progression of on-line order capture, as evidenced in these case studies.

E. Government Policies & Regulations

Currently in Nigeria, there are no government policies or incentives regarding the adoption of e-business by SBEs. As already identified in the literature review, this has been a key enabler in the adoption of e-business in the UK and Australia. The move to e-business in Nigeria could be promoted and progressed by Government subsidies for relevant investment, support for skills development and also by acting as an exemplar in using e-business in parastatal authorities and government ministries – for example, for online bidding for government contracts.

F. Investment Costs

As with any infrastructure project in an organisation, there is an initial cost associated with the uptake of e-business -cost of software, cost of hardware devices and general operational and maintenance costs. The average setup cost amongst the four SBEs studied was about 500,000 naira (£1,200). This may seem a relatively small amount, but when compared to the revenue of each of the company, it is a sizeable investment. SBEs also need to be confident regarding payback and benefits. Government incentives to invest in such technology would be of benefit, as would the encouragement of in-country production of appropriate hardware and software systems.

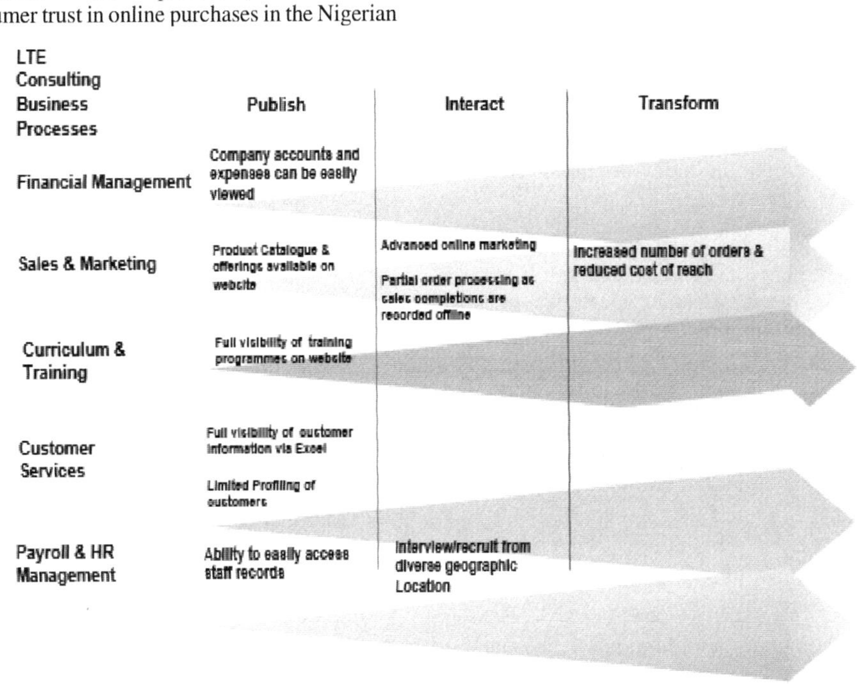

Figure 8. CPIT model applied to LTE Consulting

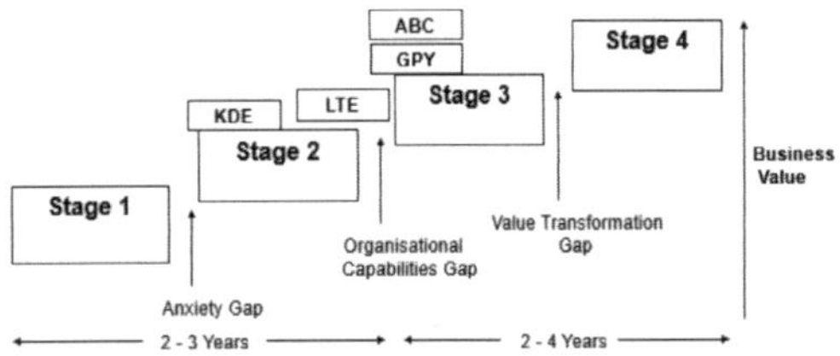

Figure 9. The Four Nigerian SBEs on the E-business Stage Model

Stage 1- Web Presence
- Develop presence
- Develop technology capability

Stage 2- Access Information and Transact Business
- Re-orientate business/technology thinking skills
- Build integrated approach with the web and business systems

Stage 3- Further Integration of Skills, Processes and Technologies
- Reorganise people/structures
- Reengineer processes
- Remodel technology infrastructure

Stage 4- Capability, Leveraging, Experience and Know-How to Maximise Value
- Customer-focused organisation

G. Power availability

Power availability is paramount amongst the key issues influencing e-business adoption in Nigerian SBEs. All the SBEs studied identified power availability as one of the main issues affecting e-business adoption.

On average, Nigerian businesses loose about 10 hours a week to power cuts. This has a major impact on businesses reliant on e-business and other IT systems, making it very difficult to work productively in these periods. Many companies have sought to source alternative sources of power, such as the use of generators, solar panels and inverters. All the companies studied have backup generators, but in two of the companies studied, they have resorted to the use of mobile apps and tablets with long lasting battery power. This can act as a more cost-effective backup than the use of generators in the event of power cuts, as was the case at ABC Laundries.

H. ICT Skills

For any SBE to effectively implement e-business, it will likely need access to third party IT professionals, whilst at the same time, some of its staff need to be proficient in the use of IT. This is problematic in many Nigerian SBEs, where 90% of staff are semi-skilled and have little or no ICT skills or experience. In the case of PYI properties, the company makes good knowledge of IT a pre-requisite for recruitment of most employees. ABC Laundries has a 'buddy' system whereby the more computer literate staff members train other staff for a couple of hours in a week. ICT skills remains a key influencing factor in the uptake of e-business in the SBE sector.

VII. Concluding Remarks

The study clearly shows that e-business technology adoption varies in focus and nature from business to business in Nigerian SBEs. The property and training companies focused on the Customer Services and Sales & Marketing processes, while KDE Energy focused more on

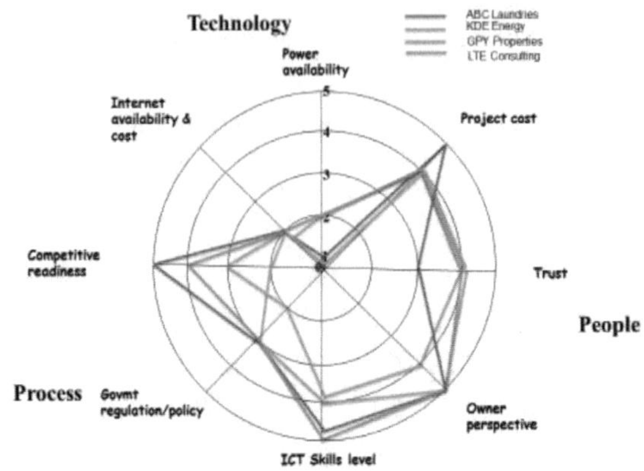

Figure 10. Critical Influencing Factors for the Four Nigerian SBEs

Financial Management and Logistics processes; and ABC Laundries' e-business activity spans the Customer Services, Sales & Marketing and Financial Management processes.

Future research will now build upon existing models to provide an enhanced analytical framework for understanding and progressing e-business deployment in Nigerian SBEs. In particular, the three dimensions of change - technology deployment, process improvement, and people skills enhancement – will be more closely examined to develop a new combined model of e-business implementation. The CIFs in the four case studies (Fig. 10) reinforce the importance of maintaining a balance between these three dimensions of change. These eight CIFs were assessed on a scale of 1-5 (from 1 = low/unacceptable to 5 = high/cost-efficient). Above all, this initial analysis points up the significance of power supply and internet availability problems in a developing country like Nigeria. In the western world, these are often taken for granted, and focus has thus shifted to process change and people skills issues, rather than being on the technology itself. But these case studies suggest that it was the commitment and determination of company owners and the aptitude and skills of the workforce that underpinned successful e-business developments *in spite of* major problems with basic technology support and enabling services. This puts a different perspective on e-business adoption, which has significant implications for the development of the implementation model and associated operational guidelines. The generally negative perception of government regulation and policy is another important finding. These critical influencing factors will be further researched as an integral component of a new implementation framework for e-business projects in a developing world context.

References

[1] O. Olayinka, M. G. Wynn, and K. Bechkoum, "Process Analysis and e-Business Adoption in Nigerian SBEs: A Report on Case Study Research," in eKNOW 2016, The

Eighth International Conference on Information, Process, and Knowledge Management, pp. 57–63, 2016.

[2] Vanguard Nigeria, "Nigeria has 48m active internet users – NITDA," 2014. [Online]. Available: http://www.vanguardngr.com/2014/10/nigeria-48m-active-internet-users-nitda/. [Accessed: 24-Nov-2016].

[3] Paul Budde Communication Pty Ltd, "Nigeria - Mobile Market - Insights, Statistics and Forecasts," Paul Budde Communication Pty Ltd, 2015.

[4] B. A. Wagner, I. Fillis, and U. Johansson, "E-business and e-supply strategy in small and medium sized businesses (SMEs)," Supply Chain Manag. An Int. J., vol. 8, no. 4, pp. 343–354, 2003.

[5] T. Oliveira and M. F. Martins, "Understanding e-business adoption across industries in European countries," Ind. Manag. Data Syst., vol. 110, no. 9, pp. 1337–1354, 2010.

[6] D. Sharma and M. Ranga, "Mobile customer relationship management - A competitive tool," Excel Int. J. Multidiscip. Manag. Stud., vol. 4, no. 7, pp. 37–42, 2014.

[7] T. Oliveira and M. F. Martins, "Firms Patterns of e-Business Adoption: Evidence for the European Union-27," Electron. J. Inf. Syst., vol. 13, no. 1, pp. 47–56, 2010.

[8] W. Olatokun and B. Bankole, "Factors influencing electronic business technologies adoption and use by small and medium scale enterprises (SMEs) in a Nigerian municipality," J. Internet Bank. Commer., vol. 16, no. 3, 2011.

[9] M. Taylor and A. Murphy, "SMEs and e-business," J. Small Bus. Enterp. Dev., vol. 11, no. 3, pp. 280–289, 2004.

[10] M. G. Wynn, P. Turner, and E. Lau, "E-business and process change: two case studies (towards an assessment framework)," Journal of Small Business and Enterprise Development, vol. 20, no. 4, pp. 913–933, 2013.

[11] OECD, "Internet adoption and use: Businesses," OECD Internet Econ. Outlook 2012, 2012.

[12] L. Chen and C. W. Holsapple, "E-Business Adoption Research: State of the Art," J. Electron. Commer. Res., vol. 14, no. 3, pp. 261–286, 2013.

[13] P. Taylor, "The Importance of Information and Communication Technologies (ICTs): An Integration of the Extant Literature on ICT Adoption in Small and Medium Enterprises," Int. J. Econ. Commer. Manag., vol. 3, no. 5, 2015.

[14] M. Kapurubandara, "A model to etransform SMEs in developing countries," Proc. 2008 4th Int. Conf. Inf. Autom. Sustain. ICIAFS 2008, pp. 401–406, 2008.

[15] European Commission, The new SME definition: user guide and model declaration. Office for Official Publications of the European Communities, 2005.

[16] Small and Medium Enterprises Development Agency of Nigeria, "National Policy on Micro, Small and Medium Enterprises," 2014.

[17] D. Chaffey, E-business and E-commerce Management: Strategy, Implementation and Practice. Financial Times Prentice Hall, 2007.

[18] V. Bordonaba-Juste, L. Lucia-Palacios, and Y. Polo-Redondo, "Antecedents and consequences of e-business adoption for European retailers," Internet Res., vol. 22, no. 5, pp. 532–550, 2012.

[19] A. Prananto, J. McKay, and P. Marshall, "Lessons learned from analysing e-business progression using a stage model in Australian Small Medium Enterprises (SMEs)," ACIS 2004 Proc., no. 1969, pp. 75-86, 2004.

[20] D. Chaffey, E-Business and E-Commerce Management - Strategy, Implementation and Practice. 2009.

[21] A. Prananto, J. McKay, and P. Marshall, "A study of the progression of e-business maturity in Australian SMEs: some evidence of the applicability of the stages of growth for e-business model," Proc. PACIS, Adelaide, July, pp. 68–80, 2003.

[22] A. Basu and S. Muylle, "How to plan e-business initiatives in established companies," MIT Sloan Manag. Rev., vol. 49, no. 1, pp. 28-36, 2007.

[23] F. Wu, V. Mahajan, and S. Balasubramanian, "An Analysis of E-Business Adoption and its Impact on Business Performance," J. Acad. Mark. Sci., vol. 31, April, pp. 425–447, 2003.

[24] D. O. Faloye, "The adoption of e-commerce in small businesses: an empirical evidence from retail sector in Nigeria.," J. Bus. Retail Manag. Res., vol. 8, no. 2, 2014.

[25] A. Afolayan, E. Plant, G. R. T. White, P. Jones, and P. Beynon-Davies, "Information Technology Usage in SMEs in a Developing Economy," Strateg. Chang., vol. 24, no. 5, pp. 483–498, 2015.

[26] Bloomberg Business, "Nigerian Economy Overtakes South Africa's on Rebased GDP," Bloomberg Business, 2014. [Online]. Available: http://www.bloomberg.com/news/articles/2014-04-06/nigerian-economy-overtakes-south-africa-s-on-rebased-gdp. [Accessed: 24-Nov-2016].

[27] C. Parker and T. Castleman, "New directions for research on SME-eBusiness: insights from an analysis of journal articles from 2003-2006," J. Inf. Syst. Small Bus., vol. 1, no. 1, pp. 21–40, 2007.

[28] H. D. Kim, I. Lee, and C. K. Lee, "Building Web 2.0 enterprises: A study of small and medium enterprises in the United States," Int. Small Bus. J., vol. 31, no. 2, pp. 156–174, 2013.

[29] P. Ifinedo, "Internet/e-business technologies acceptance in Canada's SMEs: an exploratory investigation," Internet Res., vol. 21, no. 3, pp. 255–281, 2011.

[30] E. M. Agwu, "An investigative analysis of factors influencing E-business adoption and maintenance of commercial websites in Nigeria," Basic Res. J. Bus. Manag. Accounts ISSN 2315-6899 vol. 3, pp. 5–16, 2014.

[31] R. Rahayu and J. Day, "Determinant Factors of E-commerce Adoption by SMEs in Developing Country: Evidence from Indonesia," Procedia - Soc. Behav. Sci., vol. 195, pp. 142–150, 2015.

[32] D. K. Agboh, "Drivers and challenges of ICT adoption by SMES in Accra metropolis , Ghana," J. Technol. Res., vol. 6, pp. 1–16, 2015.

[33] I. Janita and W. K. Chong, "Barriers of b2b e-business adoption in Indonesian SMEs: A Literature Analysis," Procedia Comput. Sci., vol. 17, pp. 571–578, 2013.

[34] M. Kapurubandara and R. Lawson, "Barriers to Adopting ICT and e-commerce with SMEs in Developing Countries : An Exploratory study in Sri Lanka," Univ. West. Sydney, Aust., May, pp. 1–12, 2006.

[35] C. I. Emeti and O. Onyeaghala, "E-Business Adoption and Consumer Attitude in Nigeria," Eur. J. Bus. Manag., vol. 7, no. 21, pp. 76–87, 2015.

[36] W. Olatokun and B. Bankole, "Factors Influencing Electronic Business Technologies Adoption and Use by Small and Medium Scale Enterprises (SMEs) in a Nigerian Municipality," J. Internet Bank. Commer., vol. 16, no. 3, pp. 1–26, 2011.

[37] E. M. Agwu and P. J. Murray, "Empirical Study of Barriers to Electronic Commerce Adoption by Small and Medium Scale Businesses in Nigeria," Int. J. Innov. Digit. Econ., vol. 6, no. 2, pp. 1–19, 2015.

[38] R. Erumi-Esin and R. Heeks, "e-Business Adoption and Use Among African Women-Owned SMEs: An Analytical Study in Nigeria," ICTD 2015 Proc. Seventh Int. Conf. Inf. Commun. Technol. Dev., pp. 11-21, 2015.

[39] P. Jones, E. Muir, and P. B. Davies, "The proposal of a comparative framework to evaluate e-business stages of growth models," Int. J. Inf. Technol. Manag., vol. 5, no. 4, pp. 249-267, 2006.

[40] R. Gatautis and E. Vitkauskaite, "eBusiness Policy Support Framework," no. 5, pp. 35–48, 2009.

[41] M. Wynn, P. Turner, A. Banik, and A. G. Duckworth, "The impact of customer relationship management systems in small businesses," Strategic Change, vol. 25, Issue 6, pp. 655–670, 2016. Published online in Wiley Online Library (wileyonlinelibrary.com) DOI: 10.1002/jsc.2100.

[42] A. Gunasekaran, Modelling and Analysis of Enterprise Information Systems. IGI Pub., 2007.

[43] M. Levy and P. Powell, "Exploring SME internet adoption: towards a contingent model," Electron. Mark., vol. 13, no. 2, pp. 173–181, 2003.

[44] Department of Trade and Industry, Business in the Information Age: International Benchmarking Study 2003. Booz Allen Hamilton, London, 2003.

[45] J. McKay, A. Prananto, and P. Marshall, "E-business maturity: The SOG-e model," in Proceedings of the 11th Australasian Conference on Information Systems (ACIS), pp. 6–8, 2000.

[46] C. Sauer and L. P. Willcocks, Moving to e-business. Random House Business Books, 2000.

[47] M. Wynn and O. Olubanjo, "Demand-supply chain management: systems implications in an SME packaging business in the UK," Int. J. Manuf. Res., vol. 7, no. 2, pp. 198–212, 2012.

[48] J. W. Creswell, Research Design: Qualitative, Quantitative, and Mixed Methods Approaches, Fourth edi. SAGE Publications, 2013.

[49] M. B. Davies, Doing a Successful Research Project: Using Qualitative or Quantitative Methods. Palgrave Macmillan, 2007.

[50] R. B. Burns, Introduction to Research Methods. SAGE Publications, 2000.

[51] D. Silverman, Interpreting Qualitative Data. SAGE Publications, 2015.

[52] R. K. Yin, Case Study Research: Design and Methods. SAGE Publications, 2003.

[53] M. Wynn, P. Turner, H. Abbas, and R. Shen, "Employing Knowledge Transfer to support IS implementation in SMEs," Journal of Industry and Higher Education, vol. 23, no. 2, April, pp. 111-125, 2009.

[54] M. Levy, P. Powell, and P. Yetton, "SMEs: aligning IS and the strategic context," J. Inf. Technol., vol. 16, no. 3, pp. 133–144, 2001.

The State of Peer Assessment: Dimensions and Future Challenges

Usman Wahid, Mohamed Amine Chatti, Ulrik Schroeder
Learning Technologies Research Group (Informatik 9), RWTH Aachen University
Aachen, Germany
{Wahid; Schroeder}@cil.rwth-aachen.de; Chatti@informatik.rwth-aachen.de

Abstract— **Modern day education and learning has moved on from brick and mortar institutions to open learning environments. Massive Online Open Courses (MOOCs) are a perfect example of these learning environments. MOOCs provide a cost and time effective choice for learners across the globe. This has led to new challenges for teachers such as providing valuable and quality assessment and feedback on such a large scale. Recent studies have found peer assessment where learners assess the work of their peers to be a viable and cost effective alternative to teacher/staff evaluation. This study systematically analyzes the current research on peer assessment published in the context of MOOCs and the online tools that are being used in MOOCs for peer assessment. 48 peer reviewed papers and 17 peer assessment tools were selected for the comparison in this study and were assessed on three main dimensions, namely, system design, efficiency and effectiveness. Apart from these dimensions, the study highlights the main challenges of peer assessment. In the light of the comparison and discussion of current research in terms of the identified dimensions, we present future visions and research perspectives to improve the peer assessment process in MOOCs.**

Keywords-Open Assessment; Peer Assessment; Open Learning Environments; MOOC; Blended Learning; Peer Reviews; Peer Feedback; Online Assessment.

I. INTRODUCTION

This paper presents an extended and more detailed version of our paper presented at the eighth international conference on mobile, hybrid, and online learning (eLmL 2016), where we reviewed the existing tools and research directions for peer assessment [1]. The field of education has transformed in recent year, with a growing interest in learner-centered, open, and networked learning models. These include Personalized Learning Environments (PLEs), Open Educational Resources (OER) and Massive Open Online Courses (MOOCs).

Massive Online Open Courses (MOOCs) have revolutionized the field of technology-enhanced learning (TEL). MOOCs enable a massive number of learners from all over the world to attend online courses irrespective of their social and academic backgrounds [2]. MOOCs have been classified in different forms by researchers, e.g., Siemens [3] classifies MOOCs into cMOOCs and xMOOCs. In his opinion cMOOCs allow the learners to build their own learning networks by using blogs, wikis, Twitter, Facebook and other social networking tools outside the confines of the learning platform and without any restriction and interference from the teachers [4]. Whereas, xMOOCs follow a more institutional model, having pre-defined learning objectives, e.g., Coursera, edX and Udacity. Apart from these sMOOCs and bMOOCs have also been introduced as variations of the MOOC platform with sMOOCs catering to a relatively smaller number of participants and bMOOCs combining the in-class and online learning activities to form a hybrid learning environment [3].

Irrespective of the classification, MOOCs require their stakeholders to address a number of challenges including and not limited to the role of university/teacher, plagiarism, certification, completion rates, innovating the learning model beyond traditional approaches and last but not the least assessment [5].

Assessment and Feedback are an integral part of the learning process and MOOCs are no different in this regard. Researchers acknowledge that the Teach-Learn-Access cycle in education cannot function in the absence of quality assessment [6]. However, in the case of MOOCs assessment presents a bottleneck issue due to the massiveness of the course participants and requires increased resources (time, money, manpower etc.) on part of the teachers to provide useful feedback to all the learners for a satisfying academic experience. This limitation causes many MOOCs to use automated assessments, e.g., quizzes with closed questions like multiple choice and fill in the blanks. These questions largely focus on the cognitive aspects of learning, and they are unable to capture the semantic meaning of learners' answers; in particular, in open ended questions [7]. Some other methods used in this scenario make use of crowd sourcing techniques to provide assessment and feedback to students. These methods include portfolios and self-assessment, group feedback and last but not the least peer assessment [8].

Peer assessment offers a scalable and cost effective way of providing assessment and feedback to a massive amount of learners where learners can be actively involved in the assessment processes [9]. A significant amount of research is directed towards exploring peer assessment in MOOCs. While this research discusses many issues such as the effective integration of peer assessment in various MOOC platforms and the improvement of the peer assessment process, it does not cover what has been done in this field for the past years from an analysis point of view.

Since, it is evident that peer assessment is a very viable assessment method in MOOCs, hence, the need for scouting all the available systems and studies becomes paramount in importance as it could be beneficial for future developments as well as provide a good comparison of available tools. In this study, we look at the peer assessment in general and the state of art of peer assessment in the MOOC era along with perceived benefits and challenges of peer assessment. We also look at different tools for peer assessment and the way they try to address the challenges and drawbacks of peer assessment.

The remainder of this paper is structured as follows: Section II introduces peer assessment and its pros and cons. Section III is a review of the related work. Section IV describes the research methodology and how we collected the research data. In Section V, we review and discuss the current research based on several dimensions. Section VI summarises the results of our findings. Section VII presents challenges and future perspectives in peer assessment. Finally, Section VIII gives a conclusion of the main findings of this paper.

II. PEER ASSESSMENT

In recent years, student assessments have shifted from the traditional testing of knowledge to a culture of learning assessments [10]. This culture of assessment encourages students to take an active part in the learning and assessment processes [11]. Peer assessment is one of the flag bearers in this new assessment culture. Peer assessment also known as Peer grading, is defined by Topping as "an arrangement in which individuals consider the amount, level, value, worth, quality or success of the products or outcomes of learning of peers of similar status" [12].

Peer assessment has been leveraged in a wide range of subject domains over the years including natural sciences, social sciences, business, medicine and engineering [13]. According to Somervell [14], at one end of the spectrum peer assessment may involve feedback of a qualitative nature or, at the other, may involve students in the actual marking process. This exercise may or may not entail previous discussion or agreements over criterion. It may involve the use of rating instruments or checklists, which may have been designed by others before the exercise, or designed by the user group to meet its particular needs [15]. The use of peer assessment not only reduces the teacher workload; it also brings many potential benefits to student learning. These benefits include a sense of ownership and autonomy, increased motivation, better learning and high level cognitive and discursive processing [13], [16].

Despite these potential benefits, peer assessment still has not been able to have strong backing from either teachers or students [17]. Both parties have pre-conceived notions of low reliability and validity on their minds when discussing peer assessment [18], [19]. A number of possible factors have been identified for the lack of effectiveness of peer assessment in MOOCs. These factors include the scalability issue, diversity of reviewers, perceived lack of expertise, lack of transparency and fixed grading rubrics [8].

There have been many studies on the effectiveness and usefulness of peer assessment but these studies focus on a certain context and tool, which covers the aspects related to the context of the study. The aim of this paper is to examine the available literature and tools for peer assessment, provide a systematic analysis by reviewing them according to different aspects critical to their usage in the MOOC platform, and provide a bigger picture of the research domain. We will try to highlight the challenges of peer assessment and then provide some viable solutions to overcome these challenges.

III. RELATED WORK

Peer assessment in MOOCs is still an emerging field, hence, we did not find any research directly related to our work. Luxton-Reily [20] made a systematic comparison of a number of online peer assessment tools in 2009, but the study was conducted with limited dimensions for comparing the tools. The study examined tools including legacy systems, and divided the tools in different categories; namely generic, domain specific and context specific. The study identifies the problem that majority of online tools have been used in computer science courses, and most of the tools could not be used outside the context in which they were developed. The context limitations of the tools are the biggest hindrance preventing them from being widely adopted, which gives rise to the need for more general-purpose tools. Luxton-Reily also stressed the need to investigate the quality of the feedback provided by students [20].

Apart from this, another study identifies a number of approaches taken by different peer assessment tools to address the concerns of the involved stakeholders [21]. These approaches include connectivist MOOCs where the onus is on getting superior results through collaboration and not focusing on correctness. Rather, the course is designed in a way to encourage and welcome diverse perspectives from participants. Another approach is the use of calibration like in Calibrated Peer Reviews (CPR), where raters have to evaluate a number of training submissions before they get to evaluate submissions from their peers [22]–[24]. Other approaches highlighted in the study involve making use of a Bayesian post hoc statistical correction method [25]–[27] and to create a credibility index by modifying and refining the CPR method [21].

In comparison to the above-mentioned studies, our study adds a wide range of latest tools and analyzes them over several dimensions based on cognitive mapping approach. The study further provides critical discussion according to each dimension and suggests new areas for future work.

IV. METHODOLOGY

The research methodology used for this study is divided in two parts; namely, identification of eligible studies followed by a cognitive mapping approach to find certain criterion for categorizing and analyzing peer assessment tools.

A. Identification of Eligible Studies

We applied the significant research method of identifying papers from internet resources in our study [28]. This method was carried out in two rounds.

Firstly, we conducted a search in 7 major refereed academic databases. These include Education Resources Information Center (ERIC), JSTOR, ALT Open Access Repository, Google Scholar, PsychInfo, ACM publication,

IEEEXplorer, and Wiley Online Library. We used the keywords (and their plurals) "Peer Assessment", "Peer Review", "Open Assessment", "Assessment in MOOC", and "Peer Assessment in MOOC". As a result, 87 peer-reviewed papers were found.

In the second round, we identified a set of selection criteria as follows:

1- Studies must focus on using peer assessment preferably in a MOOC setting.

2- Studies that focus on design of peer assessment systems or that detail the setting in which peer assessment should be carried out were included.

3- Studies focusing on peer assessment in a manual setting were excluded.

4- Tools older than 10 years have not been included in the study, however the tools having current support are included.

This resulted in a final set of 48 research papers/studies on peer assessment in MOOCs and we extracted a list of 17 peer assessment tools that were used in these studies. These tools include Peer Studio [29], Cloud Teaching Assistant System (CTAS) [30], IT Based Peer Assessment (ITPA) [31], Organic Peer Assessment [32], EduPCR4 [33], GRAASP Extension [34], Web-PA [35], SWoRD (Peerceptiv now) [36], Calibrated Peer Reviews (CPR) [23], [22], [24], Aropä [37], Web-SPA [38], Peer Scholar [39], [40], Study Sync [41], [42], Peer Grader [43] and L²P (Lehr und Lern Portal, RWTH Aachen) Peer Reviews [8]. We also took a look into some open systems providing peer assessment capabilities that could be used in MOOCs as well, namely: TeamMates [44] and TurnItIn [45].

B. Cognitive Mapping Approach

Cognitive mapping is a method that enables researchers to classify and categorize things into several dimensions based on the research questions [46]. The study provides an example of using cognitive mapping to elicit mental models of emotions in the work place by conducting a series of interviews at an office and then code these interviews into maps. These maps were then analyzed to uncover the relationship between the job conditions and the outcomes associated with different kind of emotional experiences at work [46].

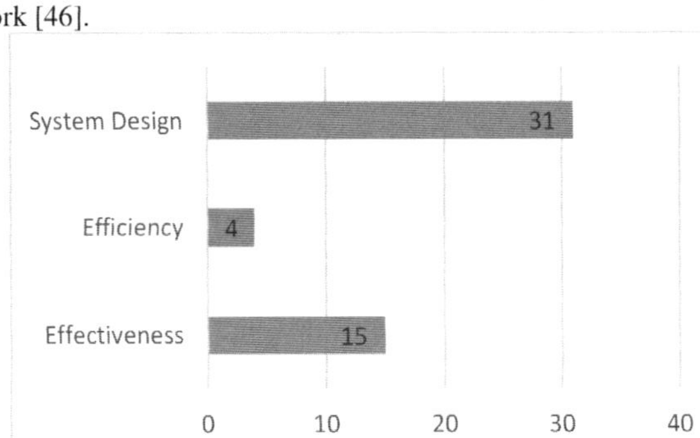

Figure 1. Peer Assessment classification map.

For the sake of our study, we scouted the literature available on peer assessment to form a directed cognitive map for each study identifying main ideas related to peer assessment. These maps were then analyzed for distinct clusters of concepts, grouping similar terms and ideas. After analyzing the clusters, we were able to identify certain dimensions namely: system design, efficiency and effectiveness (see Figure 1), which were all part of the discussed peer assessment systems. These dimensions provide an easy and efficient way to assess different peer assessment tools/studies.

In order to capture the information gained from the literature analysis, we created a detailed field diagram (see Figure 2), which has been partitioned into three categories and ten sub-categories. It is worth mentioning here that some of the sub categories could be mapped to multiple main categories and in such scenarios, we used the best match for better classification.

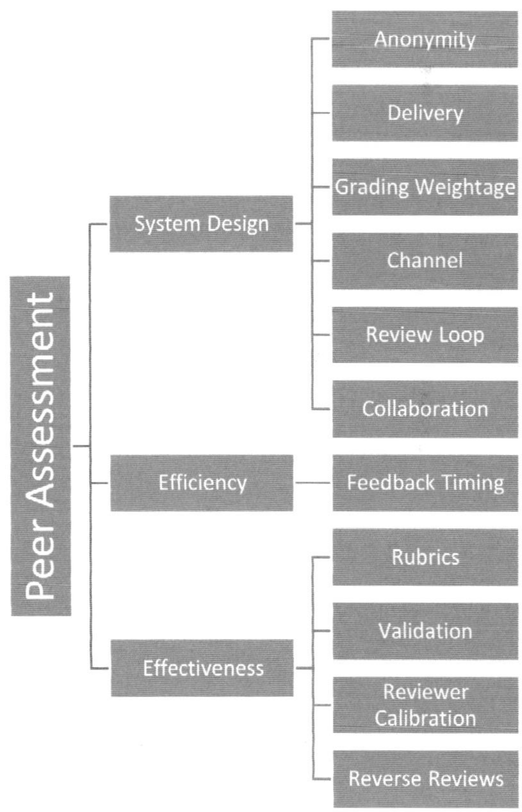

Figure 2. Peer Assessment cognitive map.

Apart from these dimensions, we identified a number of challenges as well for peer assessment from the literature review. The list of challenges of peer assessment includes transparency, credibility, accuracy, reliability, validity, diversity, scalability, and efficiency. *Transparency* refers to the fact that the assessee is aware of how the review process works and has confidence in it. The *credibility* refers to the issue, whether the reviewing person has sufficient knowledge in the subject area and is capable enough of providing credible feedback. *Accuracy* is closely linked to credibility in the sense that if the reviewer has a good mastery of the subject then his/her reviews would tend to be more accurate. *Reliability* is the consistency of grades that different peers would assign to the same assessment, or in other words as inter-rater reliability. Whereas, *validity* is calculated as a correlation coefficient between peer and instructor grades, assuming that the instructor grade is considered a trustworthy benchmark [30]. *Diversity* refers to the different educational backgrounds of the assessors. *Scalability* is inherent to open learning environments with a large number of participants. And last but not the least, *efficiency* related to feedback timing. Studies have shown that the earlier the learners get feedback to their work, the more time they have to improve the final product. Reducing the time, it takes to get feedback to a draft submission automatically allows for a better final product.

The peer assessment dimensions identified earlier try to address some of the challenges presented here in a number of ways, which will be discussed later with the discussion of each peer assessment dimension in the following sections.

V. Discussion

This section deals with the critical analysis of the peer assessment literature based on the cognitive mapping dimensions derived in the previous section. For the critical discussion part, we look at the identified dimensions and then discuss the way in which certain tools cater to that dimension (if at all).

A. System Design

A lot of effort has been put into the design of peer assessment systems, design of certain features provided by the system and the manner in which they are implemented. Nearly 70% of the studies deal in one way or the other with system or a feature design in peer assessment.

In the following sections, we discuss some key features of peer assessment systems and the way they are realized by different tools.

1) Anonymity: Anonymity is a key feature that is to be kept in mind while designing any peer assessment system, as it safeguards the system against any type of bias (gender, nationlity, friendship etc.) to play a factor in the assessment from peers. There are three levels of anonymity namely, single blind: assessor knows the assessee but the assessee has no idea of the assessor, double blind: both assessor and assessee are unaware of each other and finally no anonymity in which the identity of both the assessor and assessee is known to each other. Most of the systems reviewed in this study follow the principle of double blind reviews for the sake of bias free reviews, however, TurnItIn [45] and Study Sync [41] only implement the single blind reviews.Whereas, organic peer assessment [32] has no mention of the feature at all.

Anonymity in peer assessment is also important as it helps increase the reliability of reviews to some extent by removing bias from the system.

2) Delivery: This feature entails the delivery mode of the review, whether it is delivered indirectly (as is the case in most of the MOOC courses), or directly face to face (could be a situation in a bMOOC). All the reviewed systems only support indirect feedback at the moment. Moreover, a study [8] conducted in a bMOOC platform found that students feel more free to voice their evaluations in an indirect way rather than delivering it directly to the assessee. This helps them to give their honest feedback and enables them to be more fair in their assessment.

The in-direct delivery of reviews also serves the purpose of addressing the challenge of accuracy of reviews, as students do not have to worry about giving their feedback face to face to their peers and they can provide honest assessment of peer's work.

3) Grading Weightage: Almost two third of the reviewed systems assign a pre-defined weightage to the review from the peers in the overall grade. This means that the final grade is calculated by combining the grade from the peers and the instructor and assigning certain weightages to each of them. L^2P Peer Reviews [8] implements a novel way of assigning weightage to the reviews from peers, by allowing the teacher to define the weightage per peer review task. This also enables the system to bypass reviews from peers, as the teacher could assign a zero weightage to student reviews.

Moreover, the systems that do not give any weightage to student reviews still use these reviews in order to help the teacher in giving their assessment of the task. The teacher could use the student review as an input to write their own review for the submission.

4) Channel: It is a general principle, the more the merrier/better. Researchers believe that the same holds true for the assessment reviews, as more reviews help the assessee to have multiple inisghts about their work and learn from them instead of a single point of view being forced upon them [8]. However, this also means that every reviewer/reviewing group has to review a greater number of submissions from their peers, which puts extra burdern on the students.

The peer assessment system could handle the channel requirement in two ways, namely single channel: where every submission is reviewed by exacly one peer or peer group, or multi-channel: where the number of reviewers varies and is grater than one. All the reviewed systems provide multi-channel feedback support for the reviews, except the L²P Peer Reviews module, which only offers single channel reviews at the moment [8].

A study conducted at Stanford and University of California, proposed a process of selecting an appropriate number of reviewers needed for each submission by making use of an automated system. Initially the student grade is predicted by a machine learning algorithm, which then estimates the confidence value. This value is used to determine the required number of peer graders. These graders then identify the attributes of the answer with the help of a rubric. Finally, other peer graders then verify whether these attributes actually exist or not. If the results of these peer graders are similar then final score will be generated and if it is not the case then re-identification of attributes takes place by one more peer grader [47]. This automated process aims at putting manageable load on peers by trying to reduce the number of peers required for each submission.

The multi-channel review also paves the way for the peer assessment system to calculate inter-rater reliability from the difference between peer reviews for any submission.

5) Review Loop: The purpose of this feature is to allow the students to work on their assignments in multiple iterations in order to improve the final product and have a better learning outcome. Although, researchers claim it to be a very important feature for any peer assessment tool, only a handful of the reviewed tools actually implement more than one review loops. These systems include PeerStudio [29], EduPCR4 [33], Peerceptiv [36], Aropä [37], Web-SPA [38] and Peer Grader [43].

Peer grader is unique in this respect as it allows for a communication channel between the author and the reviewer to help the authors improve their submissions. The assessor can provide their review that is directly available to the assessee, and then assessee can then in turn improve their original submission untill the deadline. Essentially, it makes use of the single review loop in an efficient way to accommodate multiple loops [43].

6) Collaboration: Collaboration means the ability of the tool to allow students to form and work in small groups. This leads to sharing of ideas inside the group and promotes a healthy learning enviroment. Although many MOOC platforms make use of discussion forums and wikis for enabling collaboration and idea sharing between the students, but we found that only a few systems actually allow the students to form groups and submit their work in groups.

Team mates [44] is an open source tool that allows the students to form smaller groups/teams and submit their work. Also L²P Peer reviews [8], makes use of a separate module Group Workspace in their learning management system to manage student groups. This separate module allows students to work collaboratively in their own workspace online with document sharing and chat functionalities. The peer reviews tool communicates with this module to get the group information for the students and allows group submissions and reviews of the assignments. The L²P Peer reviews tool, also offers the option of individual submissions and feedback, which are available in the individual assignment settings, so the teacher could decide whether to have individual or group work possibilities per assignment.

B. Efficiency

In this section, we list the features that contribute to the overall efficiency of the system. These features allow the system to be more efficient for its users and help them get the most value out of the system. The dimensions discussed here directly relate to the challenge of efficiency of peer assessment systems.

1) Feedback Timing: Research has shown that the optimal timing of a feedback is early in the assessment process, as it gives the learners more time to react and improve their work. Peer Studio, a tool used in Coursera MOOC platfrom proposes an effective way to reduce the review response time. The learners are required to review work from two peers to get an early feedback to their submission. Also, the learners can submit their work any number of times for a peer review and get the review by reviewing others. The system assigns the reviews to reviewers based on certain criteria that includes the users who have submitted their work for review, currently online users etc. A study conducted on the usefulnes of the system concludes that the students in the Fast Feedback condition did better than the No Early Feedback condition group. It also states that on average students scored higher by 4.4% of the assignment's total grade, hence proving the usefulnes of early feedback. The study also claims to have average feedback times of 20 minutes and 1 hour in MOOC and in person classes respectively [29].

C. Effectiveness

Several researchers in TEL have explored how to design effective peer assessment modules with a higher level of user satisfaction. We identified certain features that contribute to the effectiveness of the reviews being provided by the peers, which are discussed in the following sections.

1) Rubrics: Rubrics provide a way to define flexible task specific questions that could include descriptions of each assessment item to achieve fair and consistent feedback for all course participants.

Their have been certain studies that focus on establishing methods to enhance the effectiveness of peer assessment by asking direct questions for the peer to answer, in order to assess the quality of someone's work [8]. This eables the reviewer to easily reflect on the quality of submitted work in a goal oriented manner. Hence, a flexible rubric system becomes a must have feature for any good peer assessment system.

In our study, we found that majority of the reviewed systems offer this feature in one way or the other with a notable exception of Peer Grader. While many tools allow the teachers to define rubrics for tasks, Peerceptiv offers a shared rubric library that allows for templating the rubrics for re-use and editing [36].

Another variation of the use of rubrics in the systems is the way they are handled in peer studio tool. The tool allows the teachers to define rubrics and then enforces the students to answer these questions in a better way by using a technique they call scaffolding comments [29]. The system does this scaffolding by making use of short tips for writing comment below the comments box. The tool provides helpful tips to the reviewers like "Is your feedback actionable?" or it may ask reviewers to "Say more…" when they write "great job!" etc. to enforce the reviewers to write more meaningful comments.

Rubrics are an efficient and effective way of introducing transparency to the peer assessment process, as all the course participants could see the criteria/questions for the evaluation of their submissions. The rubrics also address the challenge of diversity in course participants to some extent. The participants are provided with the same rubrics, which lays a benchmark for them to evaluate the peer submissions in a similar manner.

2) Validation: A number of studies have been carried out on the validation aspect of the reviews provided by peers, i.e., on methods to make sure that the feedback provided the peers is valid and of a certain value. Luo et al. [13] conducted a study, specifically on Coursera platform to evaluate the validity of the reviews from peers. In their study they propose that increasing the number of reviewers and giving prior training to the reviewers on how to review the work of others are some techniques used to bolster the validity of the reviews.

Similar studies focus on other ways to achieve validiy of the reviews, like Peerceptiv measures the validation of reviews to a submission by simply calculating the agreement rate between different reviewers. It takes score difference, consitency and the spread of scores into consideration for evaluating the validity of reviews. Although, this is a minimalistic approach but it still provides a good starting point for other measures to be carried out, to judge the validity of reviews in detail [36].

The validation dimension identified here is linked to several challenges of peer assessment including reliability, accuracy, validity and credibility. By validating the assessment provided by the peers, the peer assessment tool could address these challenges and ensure quality feedback for all course participants.

3) Reviewer Calibration: Calibrated peer reviews [24] along with some other studies carried out in MOOCs [48] propose a different method to achieve system effectivness, namely, reviewer calibration. In this method, the reviewers are required to grade some sample solutions that have been pre-graded by the instructor to train them in the process of providing reviews. The reviewers are not allowed to review the work of their peers, unles they achieve a certain threshold in the review of the sample submission and only then can they review the work of their peers. In the end, the system takes into account the calibration accuracy of the reviewer by assigning weightage to each submitted review.

The calibration of reviewers before the actual review phase increases the level of accuracy of their reviews and also makes it easier to identify credible reviewers from all course participants.

4) Reverse Reviews: Another interesting method to verify the effectiveness of the reviews is to use the reverse review method. Peer Grader [43] and EduPCR4 [33] tools make use of this method to allow the original authors of the reviewed submissions to rate the reviews they received from their peers. The students can specify, whether the review helped them in improving their submission, or was of a certain quality, or helped them understand the topic clearly. This review is then taken into consideration at the time of calculation of the final grade, so the peers who provided better reviews have a chance to better their assignment score.

Aropä varies from other tools in this aspect, as it manages the reverse reviews by giving this option to teachers instead of students [37]. This way teachers could judge the credibility of the review and take it into consideration before providing their own review.

The reverse reviews, also provide an easy and efficient way of creating a credibility index for the course participants, which could be used in later assignments to help the teachers in the grading process.

VI. SUMMARY

Table 1 shows a summary of evaluation of different tools against the dimensions identified in Section IV. The table shows that nearly all the tools reviewed in our study follow a similar system design varying slightly based on the context in which they are used. The only major discrepancy in most tools is their inability to allow students to work in groups (for assignment submission and reviews). Another pattern emerging from studying the table is that more and more tools are giving weightage to the student reviews in the overall grade of the students. This means that the teachers must be sure about the validity and quality of the student reviews, and the system must provide features for its insurance.

Another useful observation is the usage of assessment rubrics by the tools to help students in the process of reviewing their peers. As identified by Yousef et al. [8], rubrics are an easy way to provide learners with task specific questions, allowing the achievement of fair and consistent feedback for all course participants.

In the comparison for the validation, we mention all the tools for whom a study has been conducted for the validation of peer reviews. It does not specify that the tool has some in-built validation mechanism for the reviews provided by peers.

Table 1. A systematic comparison of peer assessment tools

	System Design						Efficiency	Effectiveness			
Tools	**Anonymity**	**Delivery**	**Grading Weightage**	**Channel**	**Review Loop**	**Collaboration**	**Time/Rapid Feedback**	**Rubrics**	**Validation**	**Reviewer Calibration**	**Reverse Reviews**
Peer Studio [29]	Double	InDirect	Yes	Multiple	Multiple	No	Yes	Yes	Yes	No	No
CTAS [30]	Double	InDirect	Yes	Multiple	Single	-	No	Yes	Yes	No	No
ITPA [31]	Yes	InDirect	No	Multiple	Single	-	No	Yes	Not measured	No	No
Organic PA [32]	No	InDirect	No	Multiple	Single	-	No	No	Yes	No	No
EduPCR4 [33]	Double	InDirect	Yes	Multiple	Double	-	No	Yes	Not measured	No	Yes
GRAASP extension [34]	No	InDirect	Yes	Multiple	Single	-	No	Yes	Yes	No	No
Web-PA [35]	Yes	InDirect	Yes	Multiple	Single	Yes	No	Yes	Not measured	No	No
SWoRD/Peerceptiv [36]	Double	InDirect	Yes	Multiple	Double	Yes	No	Yes	Yes	No	No
CPR [22]-[24]	Double	InDirect	Yes	Multiple	Single	No	No	Yes	Yes	Yes	No
Aropä [37]	Yes	InDirect	Yes	Multiple	Double	-	No	Yes	Yes	No	Yes
Web-SPA [38]	Yes	InDirect	No	Multiple	Double	Yes	No	Yes	Yes	No	No
Peer Scholar [39][40]	Double	InDirect	Yes	Multiple	Single	No	No	Yes	Yes	No	No
Study Sync [41][42]	Single	InDirect	No	Multiple	Single	No	No	Yes	Yes	No	No
Peer Grader [43]	Double	InDirect	Yes	Multiple	Double	No	No	No	Yes	No	Yes
L^2P Peer Reviews [8]	Double	InDirect	Yes	Multiple	Single	Yes	No	Yes	Yes	No	No
Team Mates [44]	Double	InDirect	No	Multiple	Single	Yes	No	Yes	Not measured	No	No
TurnItIn [45]	Single	InDirect	No	Multiple	Single	No	No	Yes	Yes	No	No

Table I also highlights an important trend in the field of peer assessment for MOOCs. It shows that most systems are moving on from the basic system design and looking for ways to improve the efficiency and effectiveness of the system. This leads to the use of more innovative ways to ensure the quality of reviews provided by peers, and a focus to find ways on improving the overall user experience and learning. The main reason behind this trend is to decrease the workload on the teachers while addressing the challenges of peer assessment making sure that students get the most out of the course.

VII. CHALLENGES AND FUTURE VISION

MOOCs with their large number of participants pose a challenge when it comes to assessment and feedback, and peer assessment offers a viable solution to the problem. However, peer assessment itself faces many challenges including scalability, reliability, quality and validation. Several studies have focused on overcoming these limitations, as outlined in the previous sections but there is still a lot of room for improvement.

The challenges faced by peer assessment are inherent from the challenges of open assessment in general [49], and the field of learning analytics offers a number of techniques to overcome these challenges. In this section, we try to offer some solutions from the field of learning analytics, which could be used to overcome certain peer assessment challenges.

1) Scalability: The massive number of participants in the MOOC courses requires the feedback provided to students to be scalable as well. This requires the use of certain measures to decrease the time required by the teacher to provide useful feedback to the student submissions. Although, peer assessment tries to lessen the teacher's burden but still the teacher has to be in the loop to ensure quality feedback. To overcome this issue of scalability, we could make use of clustering techniques in a number of ways. We could cluster similar submissions together and in case of peer assessment, the similar reviews (including rubric answers) could also be clustered together to form a single unit. The teacher could easily grade the clusters, in turn, saving valuable time. A similar approach has been used in scaling short answer questions grading with satisfactory results . The study in [50], found out that using clustering to scale feedback not only saves time but it also helps teachers to develop a high-level view of students' understanding and misconceptions.

Another solution to the problem of scalability could be the use of word clouds by extracting important parameters from the submitted work of students. This could help the teacher by providing an overview of the submission and giving a fair idea about the contents. Hence, a teacher could decide if the submission requires in depth review or they could grade based on the provided information.

Further, it can be helpful to leverage statistical methods and visualization techniques (e.g., dashboards) to support teachers in getting a good overview on the provided feedback in a visual manner.

2) Reviewer Credibility/Reliability: There have been cases identified in peer assessment studies, where students do not take the process of reviewing others work seriously. This leads to invalid reviews and casts a doubt over the credibility of the reviews being provided to students. In this scenario, the teacher must be in the loop to ensure valid reviews. One solution to this could be to rate the reviewers using the reverse reviews method and maintain a ranking of reviewers based on these reverse reviews. This way, we could identify possible bad reviewers and they could be screened out for further reviews or they could be urged to provide better reviews. This could lead to the use of predictive analytics methods to predict the accuracy of reviewers based on knowledge in the subject area, received ratings and feedback history etc.

Another approach, could be to use the peer rank method, similar to the page rank method for ranking online search results [51]. The peers are rated based on the ratings they received for their own submissions. The idea behind this approach is that in a usual scenario, the student getting a better grade should have a better grasp of the concept and hence, it is safer to predict that he/she is able to provide better feedback on the topic.

3) Validity: We have already seen the usage of calibration to improve the validity of the reviews. Raman and Joachims make use of a statistical method in their study to ensure the validity of the reviews. They use Bayesian ordinal peer grading to form an aggregated ordering for all the submissions in a course room. The difference in ranking from different peers is also taken into account to ensure the effectiveness and validity of reviews [25].

Another approach could be the usage of semi-automated assessment, as is the case in automatic essay grading systems. The system considers the grade from one human reviewer and the automated assessment grade. If the difference in grades from both sources is greater than a certain threshold, then the system asks for an additional review from a human grader [52]. This technique can be applied to the peer assessment, and if the disagreement between the review from peer and the automated assessment is significant, the system could mark the submission for grading by the teacher or ask for a review from some other peer as well.

4) Quality: Rubrics provide an easy way of improving the quality of the reviews by providing certain questions that a student has to answer in the review process [8]. The peer assessment system could further enhance this by providing a way for the teacher to specify common mistakes that students make, so that the reviewer could look for them in the submission and in turn, improve the quality of the review.

5) System Configuration: Another improvement to the peer assessment tools could be to allow the user to configure different settings from a central location rather than making it a part of system design that could not be altered. Majority of peer assessment systems in use today have pre-defined configuration in features like anonymity, review loops, grading weightage, collaboration etc. These pre-configured settings make it difficult for the tool to be used in a more generic way and in different contexts. Also, a large number of these tools are only used in computer science courses as the teachers could tailor make a tool for their specific needs and use it in their course. These domain specific tools make it impossible for the peer assessment to be used in different disciplines of study uniformly. Hence, a tool that allows its users to configure all these settings could be a lot more useful across different domains and have a higher acceptance rate from users all over the world.

VIII. Conclusion

Peer assessment is a rich and powerful assessment method used in technology-enhanced learning (TEL) to improve learning outcomes as well as learner satisfaction. In this paper, we analysed the research on peer assessment published in the MOOC era, and the tools that could be used to provide peer assessment capabilities in a MOOC. A cognitive mapping approach was used to map the selected studies on peer assessment into three main dimensions namely: system design, efficiency and effectiveness. Furthermore, we identified the challenges of peer assessment and linked them to the system dimensions, which try to overcome these challenges.

The following is a summary of the main findings in our study as well as aspects of peer assessment that need further research, according to each dimension.

A. *System Design*

The analysis of the peer assessment research showed that majority of the systems are designed on similar lines to each other, differing in only a small number of features or the way these features are implemented. Despite these possible differences in implementation, the general idea for different system features remains the same across different tools. However, several features concerning system design need a better acceptance across these tools: (1) Collaboration: The tools should allow the students to work in a collaborative environment and submit their assignments and even review in groups. This could help ease the burden on individual students and the sharing of knowledge would in turn help them achieve better learning objectives. (2) Review Loops: In our opinion, all peer assessment tools should provide at least double review loops, to give students more chances of improvement and in doing so we leverage the peer assessment model in an effective way to achieve better overall results.

B. *Efficiency*

Studies have established the positive effect of timely feedback on student performance but the assessment tools are lagging far behind in this regard. In our opinion, more tools should focus on efficient ways to decrease the feedback time, and focus on more innovations to make the process more efficient.

C. *Effectiveness*

Several methods are being used in peer assessment to increase effectiveness of the reviews and in turn the learners' satisfaction with peer assessment. Although, rubrics, reviewer calibration and reverse reviews are good ideas to improve the effectiveness of the reviews; more and more research must be put into measuring the validity of the reviews provided by peers. Future research needs to find out new ways to record validity of reviews and improvements to this validity.

The systematic comparison of peer assessment tools also reveals certain patterns and trends across the analysed tools. It points out the fact that most tools are quite similar in system design, and the way they carry out the peer assessment process. The difference arises in the way they apply validation and effectiveness techniques to the peer reviews. The study also highlights the shift in focus from basic system design to innovative ways of improving the quality and effectiveness of the reviews provided by peers. It also lists a few techniques that are being used in different peer assessment tools to ensure quality and effectiveness.

The study concludes with providing a list of open challenges in the peer assessment process/systems and proposes certain techniques that could be applied to address these challenges. The proposed solutions include a number of techniques from the field of learning analytics including statistics, prediction, visualizations, and data mining techniques that could prove useful in improving the peer assessment process/tools.

References

[1] U. Wahid, M. A. Chatti, and U. Schroeder, "A Systematic Analysis of Peer Assessment in the MOOC Era and Future Perspectives," in *Proceedings of the Eighth International Conference on Mobile, Hybrid, and On-line Learning, elml 2016*, pp 64-69.

[2] T. Liyanagunawardena, S. Williams, and A. Adams, "The Impact and reach of MOOCs: A developing countries' perspective," *eLearning Pap.*, no. 33, 2013.

[3] G. Siemens, "MOOCs are really a Platform. Elearnspace (2012).".

[4] G. Siemens, "Connectivism: A learning theory for the digital age," 2014.

[5] A. M. F. Yousef, M. A. Chatti, U. Schroeder, M. Wosnitza, and H. Jakobs, "MOOCs-A Review of the State-of-the-Art," in *Proc. CSEDU 2014 conference*, vol. 3, pp. 9–20.

[6] J. R. Frederiksen and A. Collins, "A systems approach to educational testing," *Educ. Res.*, vol. 18, no. 9, pp. 27–32, 1989.

[7] C. Kulkarni, K. P. Wei, H. Le, D. Chia, K. Papadopoulos, J. Cheng, D. Koller, and S. R. Klemmer, "Peer and self assessment in massive online classes," in *Design Thinking Research*, Springer, 2015, pp. 131–168.

[8] A. M. F. Yousef, U. Wahid, M. A. Chatti, U. Schroeder,

and M. Wosnitza, "The Effect of Peer Assessment Rubrics on Learners' Satisfaction and Performance within a Blended MOOC Environment," in *Proc. CSEDU 2015 conference*, vol. 2, pp. 148–159.

[9] R. O'Toole, "Pedagogical strategies and technologies for peer assessment in Massively Open Online Courses (MOOCs)," 2013.

[10] A. Planas Lladó, L. F. Soley, R. M. Fraguell Sansbelló, G. A. Pujolras, J. P. Planella, N. Roura-Pascual, J. J. Suñol Martínez, and L. M. Moreno, "Student perceptions of peer assessment: an interdisciplinary study," *Assess. Eval. High. Educ.*, vol. 39, no. 5, pp. 592–610, 2014.

[11] S. Lindblom-ylänne, H. Pihlajamäki, and T. Kotkas, "Self-, peer-and teacher-assessment of student essays," *Act. Learn. High. Educ.*, vol. 7, no. 1, pp. 51–62, 2006.

[12] K. Topping, "Peer assessment between students in colleges and universities," *Rev. Educ. Res.*, vol. 68, no. 3, pp. 249–276, 1998.

[13] H. Luo, A. C. Robinson, and J.-Y. Park, "Peer grading in a mooc: Reliability, validity, and perceived effects," *Online Learn. Off. J. Online Learn. Consort.*, vol. 18, no. 2, 2014.

[14] H. Somervell, "Issues in assessment, enterprise and higher education: The case for self-peer and collaborative assessment," *Assess. Eval. High. Educ.*, vol. 18, no. 3, pp. 221–233, 1993.

[15] N. Falchikov, "Peer feedback marking: developing peer assessment," *Program. Learn.*, vol. 32, no. 2, pp. 175–187, 1995.

[16] T. Papinczak, L. Young, and M. Groves, "Peer assessment in problem-based learning: A qualitative study," *Adv. Heal. Sci. Educ.*, vol. 12, no. 2, pp. 169–186, 2007.

[17] W. Cheng and M. Warren, "Peer and teacher assessment of the oral and written tasks of a group project," *Assess. Eval. High. Educ.*, vol. 24, no. 3, pp. 301–314, 1999.

[18] N. Falchikov and J. Goldfinch, "Student peer assessment in higher education: A meta-analysis comparing peer and teacher marks," *Rev. Educ. Res.*, vol. 70, no. 3, pp. 287–322, 2000.

[19] O. McGarr and A. M. Clifford, "'Just enough to make you take it seriously': exploring students' attitudes towards peer assessment," *High. Educ.*, vol. 65, no. 6, pp. 677–693, 2013.

[20] A. Luxton-Reilly, "A systematic review of tools that support peer assessment," *Comput. Sci. Educ.*, vol. 19, no. 4, pp. 209–232, 2009.

[21] H. Suen, "Peer assessment for massive open online courses (MOOCs)," *Int. Rev. Res. Open Distrib. Learn.*, vol. 15, no. 3, 2014.

[22] M. E. Walvoord, M. H. Hoefnagels, D. D. Gaffin, M. M. Chumchal, and D. A. Long, "An analysis of calibrated peer review (CPR) in a science lecture classroom," *J. Coll. Sci. Teach.*, vol. 37, no. 4, p. 66, 2008.

[23] A. Russell, O. Chapman, and P. Wegner, "Molecular science: Network-deliverable curricula," *J. Chem. Educ.*, vol. 75, no. 5, p. 578, 1998.

[24] P. A. Carlson and F. C. Berry, "Calibrated peer review/sup TM/and assessing learning outcomes," in *fie*, 2003, pp. F3E1–6.

[25] K. Raman and T. Joachims, "Bayesian Ordinal Peer Grading," in *Proceedings of the Second (2015) ACM Conference on Learning @ Scale*, pp. 149–156.

[26] C. Piech, J. Huang, Z. Chen, C. Do, A. Ng, and D. Koller, "Tuned models of peer assessment in MOOCs," *arXiv Prepr. arXiv1307.2579*, 2013.

[27] I. M. Goldin, "Accounting for peer reviewer bias with bayesian models," in *Proceedings of the Workshop on Intelligent Support for Learning Groups at the 11th International Conference on Intelligent Tutoring Systems*, 2012.

[28] A. Fink, *Conducting research literature reviews: from the Internet to paper*. Sage Publications, 2013.

[29] C. Kulkarni, M. S. Bernstein, and S. Klemmer, "PeerStudio: Rapid Peer Feedback Emphasizes Revision and Improves Performance," in *Proceedings from The Second (2015) ACM Conference on Learning@ Scale*, pp. 75–84.

[30] T. Vogelsang and L. Ruppertz, "On the validity of peer grading and a cloud teaching assistant system," in *Proceedings of the Fifth International Conference on Learning Analytics And Knowledge*, 2015, pp. 41–50.

[31] K. Lehmann and J.-M. Leimeister, "Assessment to Assess High Cognitive Levels of Educational Objectives in Large-scale Learning Services," 2015.

[32] S. Komarov and K. Z. Gajos, "Organic Peer Assessment," in *Proceedings of the CHI 2014 Learning Innovation at Scale workshop*.

[33] Y. Wang, Y. Liang, L. Liu, and Y. Liu, "A Motivation Model of Peer Assessment in Programming Language Learning," *arXiv Prepr. arXiv1401.6113*, 2014.

[34] A. Vozniuk, A. Holzer, and D. Gillet, "Peer assessment based on ratings in a social media course," in *Proceedings of the Fourth International Conference on Learning Analytics And Knowledge*, 2014, pp. 133–137.

[35] P. Willmot and K. Pond, "Multi-disciplinary Peer-mark Moderation of Group Work," *Int. J. High. Educ.*, vol. 1, no. 1, p. p2, 2012.

[36] J. H. Kaufman and C. D. Schunn, "Students' perceptions about peer assessment for writing: their origin and impact on revision work," *Instr. Sci.*, vol. 39, no. 3, pp. 387–406, 2011.

[37] J. Hamer, C. Kell, and F. Spence, "Peer assessment using arop{ä}," in *Proceedings of the ninth Australasian conference on Computing education-Volume 66*, 2007, pp. 43–54.

[38] Y.-T. Sung, K.-E. Chang, S.-K. Chiou, and H.-T. Hou, "The design and application of a web-based self-and peer-assessment system," *Comput. Educ.*, vol. 45, no. 2, pp. 187–202, 2005.

[39] D. E. Paré and S. Joordens, "Peering into large lectures: examining peer and expert mark agreement using peerScholar, an online peer assessment tool," *J. Comput. Assist. Learn.*, vol. 24, no. 6, pp. 526–540, 2008.

[40] S. Joordens, S. Desa, and D. Paré, "The pedagogical anatomy of peer-assessment: Dissecting a peerScholar assignment," *J. Syst. Cybern. Informatics*, vol. 7, no. 5, 2009.

[41] B. McCrea and M. Weil, "On Cloud Nine: Cloud-Based Tools Are Giving K-12 Collaboration Efforts a Boost," *J. (Technological Horizons Educ.*, vol. 38, no. 6, p. 46, 2011.

[42] D. L. White, "Gatekeepers to Millennial Careers: Adoption of Technology in Education by Teachers," *Handb. Mob. Teach. Learn.*, p. 351, 2015.

[43] E. F. Gehringer, "Electronic peer review and peer grading in computer-science courses," *ACM SIGCSE Bull.*, vol. 33,

no. 1, pp. 139–143, 2001.

[44] G. Goh, X. Lai, and D. C. Rajapakse, "Teammates: A cloud-based peer evaluation tool for student team projects," 2011.

[45] S. Draaijer and P. van Boxel, "Summative peer assessment using 'Turnitin' and a large cohort of students: A case study," 2006.

[46] S. McDonald, K. Daniels, and C. Harris, "Cognitive mapping in organizational research In C. Casssell & G. Symon (Eds.), Essential guide to qualitative methods in organizational research (pp. 73-85)." London: Sage, 2004.

[47] C. E. Kulkarni, R. Socher, M. S. Bernstein, and S. R. Klemmer, "Scaling short-answer grading by combining peer assessment with algorithmic scoring," in *Proceedings of the first ACM conference on Learning@ scale conference*, 2014, pp. 99–108.

[48] J. Wilkowski, D. M. Russell, and A. Deutsch, "Self-evaluation in advanced power searching and mapping with google moocs," in *Proceedings of the first ACM conference on Learning@ scale conference*, 2014, pp. 109–116.

[49] A. M. Chatti, V. Lukarov, H. Thüs, A. Muslim, F. A. M. Yousef, U. Wahid, C. Greven, A. Chakrabarti, and U. Schroeder, "Learning Analytics: Challenges and Future Research Directions," *eleed*, vol. 10, no. 1, 2014.

[50] M. Brooks, S. Basu, C. Jacobs, and L. Vanderwende, "Divide and Correct: Using Clusters to Grade Short Answers at Scale," in *Proceedings of the First ACM Conference on Learning @ Scale Conference*, 2014, pp. 89–98.

[51] T. Walsh, "The peerrank method for peer assessment," *arXiv Prepr. arXiv1405.7192*, 2014.

[52] H. Chen and B. He, "Automated Essay Scoring by Maximizing Human-Machine Agreement.," in *EMNLP*, 2013, pp. 1741–1752.

Knowledge Processing and Advanced Application Scenarios With the Content Factor Method

Claus-Peter Rückemann
Westfälische Wilhelms-Universität Münster (WWU),
Leibniz Universität Hannover,
North-German Supercomputing Alliance (HLRN), Germany
Email: ruckema@uni-muenster.de

Abstract—**This paper presents the developments and results on knowledge processing for advanced application scenarios. The processing and discovery is based on the new Content Factor (CONTFACT) methodology used for data description and analysis. The Content Factor method can be applied to arbitrary data and content and it can be adopted for many purposes. Normed factors and variants can also support data analysis and knowledge discovery. This paper presents the algorithm, introduces into the norming of Content Factors, and discusses advanced examples, practical case studies, and implementations based on long-term knowledge resources, which are continuously in development. The Content Factor can be used with huge structured and even unstructured data resources, allows an automation, and can therefore also be used for long-term multi-disciplinary knowledge. The methodology is used for advanced processing and also enables methods like data rhythm analysis and characterisation. It can be integrated with complementary methodology, e.g., classification and allows the application of advanced computing methods. The goal of this research is to create new practical processing algorithms based on the general and flexible Content Factor methodology and develop advanced processing components.**

Keywords–Data-centric Knowledge Processing; Content Factor (CONTFACT) method; Data Rhythm Analysis; Universal Decimal Classification; Advanced Computing.

I. Introduction

The application of the Content Factor method has created new flexible means for the enhancement of knowledge resources and for knowledge discovery processes. This extended research is based on the results from multi-disciplinary projects enhancement of knowledge resources and discovery by computation of Content Factors. The fundaments of the new Content Factor method were presented at the INFOCOMP 2016 conference in Valencia, Spain [1].

This research presents complex use cases for knowledge processing and advanced application scenarios in context with the computation of Content Factors and discusses the results. Information systems handling unstructured as well as structured information are lacking means for data description and analysis, which is data-centric and can be applied in flexible ways. In the late nineteen nineties, the concept of in-text documentation balancing has been introduced with the knowledge resources in the LX Project. Creating knowledge resources means creating, collecting, documenting, and analysing data and information. This can include digital objects, e.g., factual data, process information, and executable programs, as well as realia objects. Long-term means decades because knowledge is not isolated, neither in space nor time. All the more, knowledge does have a multi-disciplinary context. Data [2] and data specialists [3] are becoming increasingly important. Data repositories are core means [4] for long-term knowledge and are discussed to be a core field of activities [5].

Therefore, after integration knowledge should not disintegrate, instead it should be documented, preserved, and analysed in context. The extent increases with growing collections, which requires advanced processing and computing. Especially the complexity is a driving force, e.g., in depth, in width, and considering that parts of the content and context may be continuously in development. Therefore, the applied methods cannot be limited to certain algorithms and tools. Instead there are complementary sets of methods.

The methodology of computing factors [6] and patterns [7] being representative for a certain part of content was considered significant for knowledge resources and referred material. Fundamentally, a knowledge representation is surrogate. It enables an entity to determine consequences without forcing an action. For the development of these resources a definition-supported, sortable documentation-code balancing was created and implemented.

The Content Factor (CONTFACT) method advances this concept and integrates a definition-supported sortable documentation-code balancing and a universal applicability. The Content Factor method is focussing on documentation and analysis. The Content Factor can contain a digital 'construction plan' or a significant part of digital objects, like sequenced DeoxyriboNucleic Acid (DNA) does for biological objects [8]. Here, a construction plan is what is decided to be a significant sequence of elements, which may, e.g., be sorted or unsorted. Furthermore, high level methods, e.g., "rhythm matching", can be based on methods like the Content Factor.

This paper is organised as follows. Section II summarises the state-of-the-art and motivation, Sections III and IV introduce the Content Factor method and an example for the application principle. Section V shows basic Content Factor examples, explains flags, definition sets, and norming. Sections VI and VII introduce the background and provide the results from 8 application scenarios and implementations. Section VIII discusses aspects of processing and computation. Sections XI and X present and evaluation and main results, summarise the lessons learned, conclusions and future work.

II. STATE-OF-THE-ART AND MOTIVATION

Most content and context documentation and knowledge discovery efforts are based on data and knowledge entities. Knowledge is created from a subjective combination of different attainments, which are selected, compared and balanced against each other, which are transformed, interpreted, and used in reasoning, also to infer further knowledge. Therefore, not all the knowledge can be explicitly formalised.

Classification has proven to be a valuable tool for long-term and complex information management, e.g., for environmental information systems [9]. Conceptual knowledge is also a complement for data and content missing conceptual documentation, e.g., for data based on ontologies used with dynamical and autonomous systems [10].

Growing content resources means huge amounts of data, requirements for creating and further developing advanced services, and increasing the quality of data and services. With growing content resources content balancing and valuation is getting more and more important.

Knowledge and content are multi- and inter-disciplinary long-term targets and values [11]. In practice, powerful and secure information technology can support knowledge-based works and values. Computing goes along with methodologies, technological means, and devices applicable for universal automatic manipulation and processing of data and information. Computing is a practical tool and has well defined purposes and goals.

Most measures, e.g., similarity, distance and vector measures, are only secondary means [12], which cannot cope with complex knowledge. Evaluation metrics are very limited, and so are the connections resulting from co-occurences in given texts, e.g., even with Natural Language Processing (NLP), or clustering results in granular text segments [13].

Evaluation can be based on word semantic relatedness, datasets and evaluation measures, e.g., the WordSimilarity 353 dataset (EN-WS353) for English texts [14]. The development of Big Data amounts and complexity up to this point show that processing power is not the sole solution [15]. Advanced long-term knowledge management and analytics are on the rise.

Value of data is an increasingly important issue, especially when long-term knowledge creation is required, e.g., knowledge loss due to departing personnel [16]. Current information models are not able to really quantify the value of information. Due to this fact one of the most important assets [17], the information, is often left out [18]. Today a full understanding of the value of information is lacking. For example, free Open Access contributions can bear much higher information values than contributions from commercial publishers or providers.

For countless application scenarios the entities have to be documented, described, selected, analysed, and interpreted. Standard means like statistics and regular expression search methods are basic tools used for these purposes.

Anyhow, these means are not data-centric, they are volatile methods, delivering non-persistent attributes with minimal descriptive features. The basic methods only count, the result is a number. Numbers can be easily handled but in their solelity such means are quite limited in their descriptiveness and expressiveness.

Therefore, many data and information handling systems create numbers of individual tools, e.g., for creating abstracts, generating keywords, and computing statistics based on the data. Such means and their implementations are either very basic or they are very individual. Open Access data represents value, which must not be underestimated for the development of knowledge resources and Open Access can provide new facilities [19] but it also provides challenges [20].

The pool of tools requires new and additional methods of more universal and data-centric character – for structured and unstructured data.

New methods should not be restricted to certain types of data objects or content and they should be flexibly usable in combination and integration with existing methods and generally applicable to existing knowledge resources and referenced data. New methods should allow an abstraction, e.g., for the choice of definitions as well as for defined items.

III. THE CONTENT FACTOR

The fundamental method of the Basic Content Factor (BCF), κ_{B} – "Kappa-B" –, and the Normed Basic Content Factor (NBCF), $\overline{\kappa}_{\mathrm{B}}$, can be described by simple mathematical notations. For any elements o_i in an object o, holds

$$o_i \in o\,. \tag{1}$$

The organisation of an object is not limited, e.g., a reference can be defined an element. For κ_{B} of an object o, with elements o_i and the count function c, holds

$$\kappa_{\mathrm{B}}(o_i) = c(o_i)\,. \tag{2}$$

For $\overline{\kappa}_{\mathrm{B}}$ of an object o, for all elements n, with the count function c, holds

$$\overline{\kappa}_{\mathrm{B}}(o_i) = \frac{c(o_i)}{\displaystyle\sum_{i=1}^{n} c(o_i)}\,. \tag{3}$$

All normed κ for the elements o_i of an object o sum up to 1 for each object:

$$\sum_{i=1}^{n} \overline{\kappa}_{\mathrm{B}}(o_i) = 1\,. \tag{4}$$

For a mathematical representation counting can be described by a set o and finding a result n, establishing a one to one correspondence of the set with the set of 'numbers' $1, 2, 3, \ldots, n$. It can be shown by mathematical induction that no bijection can exist between $1, 2, 3, \ldots, n$ and $1, 2, 3, \ldots, m$ unless $n = m$. A set can consist of subsets. The method can, e.g., be applied to disjoint subsets, too. It should be noted that counting can also be done using fuzzy sets [21].

IV. ABSTRACT APPLICATION EXAMPLE

The methodology can be used with any object, independent if realia objects or digital objects. Nevertheless, for ease of understanding the examples presented here are mostly considering text and data processing. Elements can be any part of the content, e.g., equations, images, text strings, and words.

In the following example, "letters" are used for demonstrating the application. Given is an object with the sample content of 10 elements:

$$\mathtt{A\ T\ A\ H\ C\ T\ O\ A\ R\ Z} \tag{5}$$

For this example it is suggested that A and Z are relevant for documentation and analysis. The relevant elements, AAAZ, in an object of these 10 elements for element A means $3/10$ normed so the full notation is

$$\mathtt{AAAZ}/10 \text{ with } \overline{\kappa}_{\mathrm{B}}(\mathtt{A}) = 3/10 \text{ and } \overline{\kappa}_{\mathrm{B}}(\mathtt{Z}) = 1/10\,. \tag{6}$$

In consequence, the summed value for AAAZ/10 is

$$\overline{\kappa}_{\mathrm{B}}(\mathtt{A},\mathtt{Z}) = 4/10\,. \tag{7}$$

AAAZ in an object of 20 elements, for element A means 3/20 normed, which shows that it is relatively less often in this object. 3/22 for element A for this object would mean this object or an instance in a different development stage, e.g., at a different time or in a different element context. The notation

$$\{i_1\}, \{i_2\}, \{i_3\}, \ldots, \{i_n\}/n \tag{8}$$

of available elements holds the respective selection where $\{i_1\}, \{i_2\}, \{i_3\}, \ldots, \{i_n\}$ refers to the definitions of element groups. Elements can have the same labels respectively values. From this example it is easy to see that the method can be applied independent from a content structure.

V. Practical Content Factor Examples

The following examples (Figures 1, 2, 4, 3, 5) show valid notations of the Normed Basic Content Factor $\overline{\kappa}_{\mathrm{B}}$, which were taken from the LX Foundation Scientific Resources [22]. The LX Project is a long-term multi-disciplinary project to create universal knowledge resources. Application components can be efficiently created to use the resources, e.g., from the Geo Exploration and Information (GEXI) project. Any kind of data can be integrated. Data is collected in original, authentic form, structure, and content but data can also be integrated in modified form. Creation and development are driven by multifold activities, e.g., by workgroups and campaigns. A major goal is to create data that can be used by workgroups for their required purposes without limiting long-term data to applications cases for a specific scenario. The usage includes a targeted documentation and analysis. For the workgroups, the Content Factor has shown to be beneficial with documentation and analysis. There are countless fields to use the method, which certainly depend on the requirements of the workgroups. For the majority of use cases, especially, selecting objects and comparing content have been focus applications. With these knowledge resources multi-disciplinary knowledge is documented over long time intervals. The resources are currently already developed for more than 25 years. A general and portable structure was used for the representation.

```
CONTFACT:20150101:MS:{A}{A}{G}{G}{G}/2900
CONTFACT:20150101:M:{A}:=Archaeology|Archeology
CONTFACT:20150101:M:{G}:=Geophysics
```

Figure 1. NBCF $\overline{\kappa}_{\mathrm{B}}$ for an object, core notation including the normed CONTFACT and definitions, braced style.

The Content Factor can hold the core, the definitions, and additional information. The core is the specification of κ_{B} or $\overline{\kappa}_{\mathrm{B}}$. Definitions are assignments used for the elements of objects, specified for use in the core.

Here, the core entry shows an International Standards Organisation (ISO) date or optional date-time code field, a flag, and the CONTFACT core. The definitions hold a date-time code field, flag, and CONTFACT definitions or definitions sets as shown here. Definition sets are groups of definitions for a certain Content Factor. The following examples show how the definition sets work.

```
CONTFACT:20150101:MS:AAG/89
CONTFACT:20150101:M:A:=Archaeology|Archeology
CONTFACT:20150101:M:G:=Geophysics
```

Figure 2. NBCF $\overline{\kappa}_{\mathrm{B}}$ for an object, core notation including the normed CONTFACT and definitions, non-braced style.

```
CONTFACT:20150101:MU:A{Geophysics}{Geology}/89
CONTFACT:20150101:M:A:=Archaeology|Archeology
CONTFACT:20150101:M:{Geophysics}:=Geophysics|
  Seismology|Volcanology
CONTFACT:20150101:M:{Geology}:=Geology|
  Palaeontology
```

Figure 3. NBCF $\overline{\kappa}_{\mathrm{B}}$ for an object, core notation including the normed CONTFACT and definitions, mixed style.

```
CONTFACT:20150101:MU:{Archaeology}{Geophysics}/120
CONTFACT:20150101:M:Archaeology:=Archaeology|
  Archeology
CONTFACT:20150101:M:Geophysics:=Geophysics
```

Figure 4. NBCF $\overline{\kappa}_{\mathrm{B}}$ for an object, core notation including the normed CONTFACT and definitions, multi-character non-braced style.

```
CONTFACT:20150101:MU:vvvvaSsC/70
CONTFACT:20150101:M:v:=volcano
CONTFACT:20150101:M:a:=archaeology
CONTFACT:20150101:M:S:=Solfatara
CONTFACT:20150101:M:s:=supervolcano
CONTFACT:20150101:M:C:=Flegrei
```

Figure 5. NBCF $\overline{\kappa}_{\mathrm{B}}$ for an object from a natural sciences collection, multi-case non-braced style.

Definitions can, e.g., be valid in braced, non-braced, and mixed style. Left values can have different labels, e.g., uppercase, lowercase, and mixed style can be valid. Figure 6 shows an example using Universal Decimal Classification (UDC) notation definitions.

```
CONTFACT:20150101:MS:{UDC:55}{UDC:55}/210
CONTFACT:20150101:M:{UDC:55}:=Earth Sciences. Geological
  sciences
```

Figure 6. NBCF $\overline{\kappa}_{\mathrm{B}}$ for an object from a natural sciences collection, UDC notation definitions, braced style.

Conceptual knowledge like UDC can be considered in many ways, e.g., via classification and via description.

A. Flags

Content Factors can be associated with certain qualities. Sample flags, which are used with core, definition, and additional entries are given in Table I.

TABLE I. SAMPLE FLAGS USED WITH CONTFACT ENTRIES.

Purpose	*Flag*	*Meaning*
Content Factor quality	U	Unsorted
	S	Sorted
Content Factor source	M	Manual
	A	Automated
	H	Hybrid

The CONTFACT core entries can have various qualities, e.g., unsorted (U) or sorted (S). Unsorted means in the order in which they appear in the respective object. Sorted means in a different sort order, which may also be specified. CONTFACT entries can result from various workflows and procedures, e.g., they can be created on manual base (M) or on automated base (A). If nothing else is specified the flag refers to the way object entries were created. Content Factor quality refers to core entries, source also refers to the definitions and information.

The Content Factor method provides the specified instructions. The required features with an implementation can, e.g., implicitly require large numbers of comparisons, resulting in highly computationally intensive workflows on certain architectures. It is the choice of the user to weighten between the benefits and the computational efforts, and potentially to provide suitable environments.

B. Definition sets

Definition sets for object elements can be created and used very flexibly, e.g., word or string definitions. Therefore, a reasonable set of elements can be defined for the respective purpose, especially:

- Definition sets can contain appropriate material, e.g., text or classification.
- Groups of elements can be created.
- Contributing elements can be subsummarised.
- Definition sets can be kept persistent and volatile.
- Definition set elements can be weighted, e.g., by parameterisation of context-sensitive code growth.
- Context sensitive definition sets can be referenced with data objects.
- Content can be described with multiple, complementary definition sets.
- Any part of the content can be defined as elements.

The Content Factors can be computed for any object, e.g., for text and other parts of content. Nevertheless, the above definition sets for normed factors are intended to be used with one type of elements.

C. Normed application

$\overline{\kappa}_{\mathrm{B}}$ is a normed quantity. Norming is a mathematical procedure, by which the interesting quantity (e.g., vector, operator, function) is modified by multiplication in a way that after the norming the application of respective functionals delivers 1. The respective $\overline{\kappa}_{\mathrm{B}}$ Content Factor can be used to create a weighting on objects, e.g., multiplying the number of elements with the respective factor value.

VI. VALUE AND APPRECIATION

The value of objects and collections, e.g., regarding libraries [23], is matter of discussion [24]. Nevertheless, bibliometrics is a very disputable practice with highly questionable results from content point of view and relevance.

Whereas some data is of high scientific value it may currently have less or no economic value [25]. Studies on data genomics has delivered a lot of information [26] on the related aspects.

It is interesting to see that on the other hand the form of the content is associated with resulting citations, e.g., more figures may lead to more citations [27]. However, visual information in scientific literature [28] is only one small aspect, it may also have some value.

The demand for better information and reference services is obvious for scientific knowledge, however in rare cases the question if separate services [29] may be required is still asked [30]. A large implementation, which cannot recognise the value of data and knowledge in huge heterogeneous data sources is surely neither a viable solution nor a desirable state. Basic definitions for "data-centric" and "Big Data" in this context are emphasizing the value:

"The term data-centric refers to a focus, in which data is most relevant in context with a purpose. Data structuring, data shaping, and long-term aspects are important concerns. Data-centricity concentrates on data-based content and is beneficial for information and knowledge and for emphasizing their value. Technical implementations need to consider distributed data, non-distributed data, and data locality and enable advanced data handling and analysis. Implementations should support separating data from technical implementations as far as possible." [31].

"The term Big Data refers to data of size and/or complexity at the upper limit of what is currently feasible to be handled with storage and computing installations. Big Data can be structured and unstructured. Data use with associated application scenarios can be categorised by volume, velocity, variability, vitality, veracity, value, etc. Driving forces in context with Big Data are advanced data analysis and insight. Disciplines have to define their 'currency' when advancing from Big Data to Value Data." [31].

The long-term creation and development of knowledge values as well as next generation services require additional and improved features and new algorithms for taking advantage of high quality knowledge resources and increasing the quality of results.

VII. APPLICATION SCENARIOS AND IMPLEMENTATIONS

The implementation has been created for the primary use with knowledge resources' objects (`lxcontfact`). This means handling of any related content, e.g., documentation, keywords, classification, transliterations, and references. The respective objects were addressed as Content Factor Object (CFO) (standard file extension `.cfo`) and the definition sets as Content Factor Definition (CFD) (standard file extension `.cfd`).

A. Case study: Computing complementation and properties

The following case, consisting of a sequence of short examples shows a knowledge resources object (Figure 7), and three pairs of complementary CONTFACT definition sets and the according $\overline{\kappa}_{\mathrm{B}}$ computed for the knowledge resources object and respective definition sets (Figures 8 and 9; 10 and 11; 12 and 13).

```
object A        %-GP%-XX%---: object A                [A, B, C, D, O]:
                %-GP%-EN%---:                         A B C D O
                %-GP%-EN%---:                         A B C D O
                %-GP%-EN%---:                         A B C D O
                %-GP%-EN%---:                         A B C D O
                %-GP%-EN%---:                         A B C D O
```

Figure 7. Artificial knowledge resources object (LX Resources, excerpt).

Here, the algorithm can count in object entry name (right "object A") and label, keywords (in brackets), and object documentation (lower right block).

```
% (c) LX-Project, 2015, 2016
{A}:=\bA\b
{O}:=\bO\b
```

Figure 8. CONTFACT definition set 1 of 3 (LX Resources, excerpt).

The definition set defines {A} and {O}. The definitions are case sensitive for this discovery. We can compute $\overline{\kappa}_{\mathrm{B}}$ (Figure 9) according to the knowledge resources object and definition set.

```
CONTFACT:BEGIN
CONTFACT:20160117-175904:AU:{A}{A}{O}{A}{O}{A}{O}{A}{O}{A}{O}{A}{O}/32
CONTFACT:20160117-175904:AS:{A}{A}{A}{A}{A}{A}{A}{O}{O}{O}{O}{O}{O}/32
CONTFACT:20160117-175904:M:{A}:=\bA\b
CONTFACT:20160117-175904:M:{O}:=\bO\b
CONTFACT:20160117-175904:M:STAT:OBJECTELEMENTSDEF=2
CONTFACT:20160117-175904:M:STAT:OBJECTELEMENTSALL=32
CONTFACT:20160117-175904:M:STAT:OBJECTELEMENTSMAT=13
CONTFACT:20160117-175904:M:STAT:OBJECTELEMENTSCFO=.40625000
CONTFACT:20160117-175904:M:STAT:OBJECTELEMENTSKWO=2
CONTFACT:20160117-175904:M:STAT:OBJECTELEMENTSLAN=1
CONTFACT:20160117-175904:M:INFO:OBJECTELEMENTSOBJ=object A
CONTFACT:20160117-175904:M:INFO:OBJECTELEMENTSDCM=(c) LX-Project, 2015, 2016
CONTFACT:20160117-175904:M:INFO:OBJECTELEMENTSMTX=LX Foundation Scientific
 Resources; Object Collection
CONTFACT:20160117-175904:M:INFO:OBJECTELEMENTSAUT=Claus-Peter R\"uckemann
CONTFACT:END
```

Figure 9. NBCF $\overline{\kappa}_{\mathrm{B}}$ computed for knowledge resources object and definition set 1 (LX Resources, excerpt).

The result is shown in a line-oriented representation, each line carrying the respective date-time code for all the core, statistics, and additional information. The second complementary set (Figure 10) defines {B} and {D} with its $\overline{\kappa}_{\mathrm{B}}$ (Figure 11).

```
% (c) LX-Project, 2015, 2016
{B}:=\bB\b
{D}:=\bD\b
```

Figure 10. CONTFACT definition set 2 of 3 (LX Resources, excerpt).

```
CONTFACT:BEGIN
CONTFACT:20160117-175904:AU:{B}{D}{B}{D}{B}{D}{B}{D}{B}{D}{B}{D}/32
CONTFACT:20160117-175904:AS:{B}{B}{B}{B}{B}{B}{D}{D}{D}{D}{D}{D}/32
CONTFACT:20160117-175904:M:{B}:=\bB\b
CONTFACT:20160117-175904:M:{D}:=\bD\b
CONTFACT:20160117-175904:M:STAT:OBJECTELEMENTSDEF=2
CONTFACT:20160117-175904:M:STAT:OBJECTELEMENTSALL=32
CONTFACT:20160117-175904:M:STAT:OBJECTELEMENTSMAT=12
CONTFACT:20160117-175904:M:STAT:OBJECTELEMENTSCFO=.37500000
...
```

Figure 11. NBCF $\overline{\kappa}_{\mathrm{B}}$ computed for knowledge resources object and definition set 2 (LX Resources, excerpt).

The third complementary set (Figure 12) defines {C}.

```
% (c) LX-Project, 2015, 2016
{C}:=\bC\b
```

Figure 12. CONTFACT definition set 3 of 3 (LX Resources, excerpt).

The resulting $\overline{\kappa}_{\mathrm{B}}$ is shown in the excerpt (Figure 13).

```
CONTFACT:BEGIN
CONTFACT:20160117-175905:AU:{C}{C}{C}{C}{C}{C}/32
CONTFACT:20160117-175905:AS:{C}{C}{C}{C}{C}{C}/32
CONTFACT:20160117-175905:M:{C}:=\bC\b
CONTFACT:20160117-175905:M:STAT:OBJECTELEMENTSDEF=1
CONTFACT:20160117-175905:M:STAT:OBJECTELEMENTSALL=32
CONTFACT:20160117-175905:M:STAT:OBJECTELEMENTSMAT=6
CONTFACT:20160117-175905:M:STAT:OBJECTELEMENTSCFO=.18750000
...
```

Figure 13. NBCF $\overline{\kappa}_{\mathrm{B}}$ computed for knowledge resources object and definition set 3 (LX Resources, excerpt).

The sum of all elements considered for $\overline{\kappa}_{\mathrm{B}}$ by the respective CONTFACT algorithm in an object is 100 percent. Here, the overall number of

- definitions is $2 + 2 + 1 = 5$,
- elements is 32 (25, 5 keywords, 2 name and label),
- matches is $13 + 12 + 6 = 31$.

The sum of the aggregated $\overline{\kappa}_{\mathrm{B}}$ values for complementary definitions and all relevant elements results in

$$0.40625000 + 0.37500000 + 0.18750000 + 1/32 = 1$$

This also means the used definitions completely cover the elements in an object with their description.

B. Case study: Complex resources and discovery scenario

The data used here is based on the content and context from the knowledge resources, provided by the LX Foundation Scientific Resources [22]. The LX knowledge resources' structure and the classification references [32] based on UDC [33] are essential means for the processing workflows and evaluation of the knowledge objects and containers.

Both provide strong multi-disciplinary and multi-lingual support. For this part of the research all small unsorted excerpts of the knowledge resources objects only refer to main UDC-based classes, which for this part of the publication are taken from the Multilingual Universal Decimal Classification Summary (UDCC Publication No. 088) [34] released by the UDC Consortium under the Creative Commons Attribution Share Alike 3.0 license [35] (first release 2009, subsequent update 2012).

The excerpts (Figures 14, 15, 16), show a CFO from the knowledge resources a CFD and the computed CONTFACT.

```
Vesuvius [Volcanology, Geology, Archaeology]:
         (lat.) Mons Vesuvius.
         (ital.) Vesuvio.
         Volcano, Gulf of Naples, Italy.
         Complex volcano (compound volcano). Stratovolcano, large cone (Gran
          Cono).
         ...
         The most well known antique settlements at the Vesuvius are \lxidx{
          Pompeji}, \lxidx{Herculaneum}, and \lxidx{Stabiae}.
         s. also seismology, phlegra, Solfatara
         %%IML: keyword: volcano, Vesuvius, Campi Flegrei, phlegra, scene of
          fire, Pompeji, Herculaneum, volcanic ash, lapilli, catastrophe,
          climatology, eruption, lava, gas ejection, Carbon Dioxide
         %%IML: UDC:[911.2+55]:[57+930.85]:[902]"63"(4+37+23+24)=12=14
         ...
         Object:              Volcanic material.
         Object-Type:         Realia object.
         Object-Location:     Vesuvius, Italy.
         Object-FindDate:     2013-10-00
         Object-Discoverer:   Birgit Gersbeck-Schierholz, Hannover, Germany.
         Object-Photo:        Claus-Peter Rückemann, Minden, Germany.
         %%IML: media: YES 20131000 {LXC:DETAIL--M-} {UDC:(0.034)(044)770}
          LXDATASTORAGE://...img_3824.jpg
         %%IML: UDC-Object:[551.21+55]:[911.2](37+4+23)=12
         %%IML: UDC: 551.21       :: Vulcanicity. Vulcanism. Volcanoes. Eruptive
          phenomena. Eruptions
         %%IML: UDC: 55           :: Earth Sciences. Geological sciences
         %%IML: UDC: 911.2        :: Physical geography
```

Figure 14. Knowledge resources object (geosciences collection, LX, excerpt).

Labels, language fields, and spaces were stripped. A knowledge object can contain any items required, e.g., including storing data, documentation, classification, keywords, algorithms, references, implementations, in any languages and representations, allowing support tables and algorithms. An object can also include subobjects and references [36] as shown here. Examples of application scenarios for the Content Factor method range from libraries, natural sciences and archaeology, statics, architecture, risk coverage, technology to material sciences [37].

```
% (c) LX-Project, 2009, 2015
{Ve}:=Vesuvius
{Vo}:=\b[Vv]olcano
{Po}:=Pompe[ji]i
{UDC:55}:=Geology
{UDC:volcano}:=UDC.*\b911\b.*\b55\b
```

Figure 15. CONTFACT definition set (geosciences collection, LX, excerpt).

The definition sets can contain anything required for the definitions and additional information for the respective Content Factor implementation, e.g., definitions of elements and groups as well as comments. The left side defines the element used in the Content Factor and the right side states the matching element components. Left value and right value are separated by ":=" for an active definition.

```
CONTFACT:BEGIN
CONTFACT:20160130-235804:AU:{Ve}{Vo}{UDC:55:geology}{Ve}{Ve}{Vo}{Vo}{Vo}{Vo}{Vo
 }{Vo}{Vo}{Ve}{Ve}{Po}{Ve}{Po}{Ve}{Ve}{Ve}{Vo}{Vo}{Vo}{Vo}{Vo}{UDC:volcano}{Vo}{
 Vo}/319
CONTFACT:20160130-235804:AS:{Po}{Po}{UDC:55:geology}{UDC:volcano}{Ve}{Ve}{Ve}{Ve
 }{Ve}{Ve}{Ve}{Ve}{Ve}{Vo}{Vo}{Vo}{Vo}{Vo}{Vo}{Vo}{Vo}{Vo}{Vo}{Vo}{Vo}{Vo}{Vo}{
 Vo}/319
CONTFACT:20160130-235804:M:{Ve}:=Vesuvius
CONTFACT:20160130-235804:M:{Vo}:=\b[Vv]olcano
CONTFACT:20160130-235804:M:{Po}:=Pompe[ji]i
CONTFACT:20160130-235804:M:{UDC:55:geology}:=Geology
CONTFACT:20160130-235804:M:{UDC:volcano}:=UDC.*\b911\b.*\b55\b
CONTFACT:20160130-235804:M:STAT:OBJECTELEMENTSDEF=5
CONTFACT:20160130-235804:M:STAT:OBJECTELEMENTSALL=319
CONTFACT:20160130-235804:M:STAT:OBJECTELEMENTSMAT=28
CONTFACT:20160130-235804:M:STAT:OBJECTELEMENTSCFO=.09180304
CONTFACT:20160130-235804:M:INFO:OBJECTELEMENTSDCM=(c) LX-Project, 2009, 2015
...
CONTFACT:END
```

Figure 16. NBCF $\overline{\kappa}_{\mathrm{B}}$ computed for knowledge resources object and definition set (geosciences collection, LX Resources, excerpt).

The left value can include braces (e.g., curly brackets) in order to support the specification and identification of the left value. The right value can include common representations of pattern specification. The result of which can be seen from the computed CONTFACT.

The example patterns follow the widely used Perl (Practical Extraction and Report Language) regular expressions [38], e.g., `\b` for word boundaries and `[...]` and multiple choices of characters at a certain position.

C. Definitions

Definitions link the elements used in an Content Factor with a certain content. The following figures show examples for a collection object (Figure 17), a related definition set (Figure 18), and a computed CONTFACT (Figure 19).

```
object A       %-GP%-XX%---: object A            [A, B, C, D, O]:
               %-GP%-EN%---:                     A B C D O
               %-GP%-EN%---:                     A B C D O
               %-GP%-EN%---:                     A B C D O
               %-GP%-EN%---:                     A B C D O
               %-GP%-EN%---:                     A B C D O
```

Figure 17. Example of single LX collection object, used with CONTFACT (LX Resources, excerpt).

```
% (c) LX-Project, 2015, 2016
{A}:=\bA\b
{Letter_B}:=\bB\b
{charC}:=\bC\b
{004}:=\bD\b
{Omega}:=\bO\b
```

Figure 18. Example of CONTFACT definitions (LX Resources, excerpt).

The definitions (braced) define single letters in this case. In this representation, the CONTFACT computation sees the right side of the object entry (right of the language flags 'EN' and 'XX').

The computed CONTFACT (Figure 19) uses the braced definitions for building the CONTFACT core.

```
CONTFACT:BEGIN
CONTFACT:20160829-094358:AU:{A}{A}{Letter_B}{charC}{004}{Omega}{A}{Letter_B}{
 charC}{004}{Omega}{A}{Letter_B}{charC}{004}{Omega}{A}{Letter_B}{charC}{004}{
 Omega}{A}{Letter_B}{charC}{004}{Omega}{A}{Letter_B}{charC}{004}{Omega}/32
CONTFACT:20160829-094358:AS:{004}{004}{004}{004}{004}{004}{A}{A}{A}{A}{A}{A}{A}{
 charC}{charC}{charC}{charC}{charC}{charC}{Letter_B}{Letter_B}{Letter_B}{
 Letter_B}{Letter_B}{Letter_B}{Omega}{Omega}{Omega}{Omega}{Omega}{Omega}/32
CONTFACT:20160829-094358:M:{A}:=\bA\b
CONTFACT:20160829-094358:M:{Letter_B}:=\bB\b
CONTFACT:20160829-094358:M:{charC}:=\bC\b
CONTFACT:20160829-094358:M:{004}:=\bD\b
CONTFACT:20160829-094358:M:{Omega}:=\bO\b
CONTFACT:20160829-094358:M:STAT:OBJECTELEMENTSDEF=5
CONTFACT:20160829-094358:M:STAT:OBJECTELEMENTSALL=32
CONTFACT:20160829-094358:M:STAT:OBJECTELEMENTSMAT=31
CONTFACT:20160829-094358:M:STAT:OBJECTELEMENTSCFO=.96875000
CONTFACT:20160829-094358:M:STAT:OBJECTELEMENTSKWO=2
CONTFACT:20160829-094358:M:STAT:OBJECTELEMENTSLAN=1
CONTFACT:20160829-094358:M:INFO:OBJECTELEMENTSOBJ=object A
CONTFACT:20160829-094358:M:INFO:OBJECTELEMENTSDCM=(c) LX-Project, 2015, 2016
CONTFACT:20160829-094358:M:INFO:OBJECTELEMENTSMTX=LX Foundation Scientific
 Resources; Object Collection
CONTFACT:20160829-094358:M:INFO:OBJECTELEMENTSAUT=Claus-Peter R\"uckemann
CONTFACT:END
```

Figure 19. Example of CONTFACT output (LX Resources, excerpt).

The left side values can be used in the core. For application purposes these values can internally be mapped or referenced to other unique values or representations like meta-levels and numbering schemes, e.g., if this practice may provide benefits for a certain implementation.

D. Case study: Rhythm matching and core sequences

As soon as Content Factors have been computed for an object the patterns can be compared with pattern of other objects. The Content Factor method allows to compare occurrences of relevant elements in objects in many ways. The following example shows the "rhythm matching" method on the basis of an object and a definition set (Figure 20), for two computed unsorted CONTFACT core sequences (Figures 21, 22).

```
% (c) LX-Project, 2009, 2015, 2016
{Am}:=\b[Aa]mphora
{Ce}:=[Cc]eramic
{Gr}:=\b[Gg]reek\b
{Pi}:=[Pp]itho[is]
{Ro}:=\b[Rr]oman\b
{Tr}:=[Tt]ransport
{Va}:=[Vv]ases
```

Figure 20. Example of CONTFACT definition set, geoscientific and archaeological resources (LX Resources, excerpt).

```
CONTFACT:20160828-215751:AU:{Am}{Gr}{Ce}{Gr}{Gr}{Ro}{Am}{
 Gr}{Am}{Am}{Va}{Am}{Ce}{Am}{Am}{Pi}{Pi}{Tr}{Tr}{Gr}{Ro}{
 Am}{Am}{Tr}{Am}{Gr}{Ro}{Am}{Tr}{Am}{Tr}{Am}{Am}{Am}{Am}{
 Tr}{Am}{Am}{Am}{Am}{Gr}{Ce}{Ce}{Tr}/474
```

Figure 21. CONTFACT rhythm matching: Computed core for same object (before modification) and definition set (LX Resources, excerpt).

```
CONTFACT:20160828-231806:AU:{Am}{Gr}{Ce}{Gr}{Gr}{Ro}{Am}{
 Gr}{Am}{Am}{Va}{Am}{Ce}{Am}{Am}{Pi}{Pi}{Tr}{Tr}{Gr}{Ro}{
 Am}{Am}{Tr}{Am}{Gr}{Ro}{Am}{Tr}{Am}{Tr}{Am}{Am}{Am}{Am}{
 Tr}{Am}{Am}{Am}{Am}{Gr}{Ce}{Ce}{Tr}{Ce}{Ce}{Tr}{Ce}{Ce}{
 Tr}{Ce}{Ce}{Ce}{Ce}{Pi}{Pi}{Am}/589
```

Figure 22. CONTFACT rhythm matching: Computed core for same object (after modification) and definition set (LX Resources, excerpt).

The comparison shows that relevant passages were appended to the object (italics font). Relevant regarding the rhythm matching means relevant from the object and definition set. Even short sequences like `{Am}{Gr}{Ce}` and even when sorted like `{Am}{Ce}{Gr}` can be relevant and significant in order to compute factors and identify and compare objects. The Content Factor method does not have built-in or intrinsic limitations specifying certain ways of further use, e.g., with comparisons and analysis.

Unsorted CONTFACT are more likely to describe objects and quality, including their internal organisation. Sorted CONTFACT tend to describe objects by their quantities, with reduced focus on their internal organisation.

Objects with larger amount of documentation maybe candidates for unsorted CONTFACT. Objects, e.g., with factual, formalised content maybe candidates for sorted CONTFACT. Combining several methods in a workflow is possible.

Anyhow, the further use of the CONTFACT core, e.g., sorting the core data for a certain comparison, is a matter of application and purpose with respective data.

E. Object Comparison

The Content Factor can be used with arbitrary data, e.g., with knowledge resources, for all objects, referenced data and information, collections, and containers. The example (Figure 23) shows an excerpt of a collection object in an arbitrary stage of creation. The excerpt contains some elements, which can be relevant regarding Content Factor and respective definitions sets.

```
Amphora [Archaeology, Etymology]:
        (greek) amphoreus = ceramic container with two handles.
        (greek) amphí = on both sides.
        (greek) phérein = carry.
        The Greco-Roman term amphora is of ancient Greek origin and has been
         developed during the Bronze Age.
        Container of a characteristic shape and size and two handles.
        Amphoras are a subgroup of antique \lxidx{vases}.
        Most amphoras are made from ceramic material, often clay.
        There are rare amphoras made from stone and metal, like bronze, silver
         or gold.
        Amphoras typically have a volume of 5--50\UD{l}, in some cases 100 or
         more litres.
        Larger containers mostly had the purpose of storage only,
        named pithos and pithoi (pl.).
        ...
        Object:             Amphora, transport.
        Object-Type:        Realia object.
        Object-Relocation: Museu d'Arqueologia de Catalunya, Barcelona, Spain.
        %%IML: media: YES 20111027 {LXC:DETAIL----} {UDC:(0.034)(460)770}
         LXDATASTORAGE://.../img_5831.jpg
        %%IML: media: YES 20111027 {LXC:DOC-------} {UDC:(0.034)(460)770}
         LXDATASTORAGE://.../img_5831.jpg
        %%IML: UDC-Object:[902+903.2+904]+738+738.8+656+(37)+(4)
        %%IML: UDC-Relocation:069.51+(4)+(460)+(23)
        %%IML: label: {MUSEUM-Material:    Ceràmica}
```

Figure 23. Example of LX collection object, matter of change, used with CONTFACT (LX Resources, excerpt).

Figure 24 shows a definition set as used with objects as with the example (Figure 23), instances of which are to be compared.

```
% (c) LX-Project, 2009, 2015, 2016
{Am}:=\b[Aa]mphora
{Ce}:=[Cc]eramic
{Gr}:=\b[Gg]reek\b
{Pi}:=[Pp]itho[is]
{Ro}:=\b[Rr]oman\b
{Tr}:=[Tt]ransport
{Va}:=[Vv]ases
```

Figure 24. Example of CONTFACT definitions, geoscientific and archaeological resources (LX Resources, excerpt).

Definition sets are used when the Content Factor is applied to objects. This definition set is used for comparing an instance of an object with an instance of the same object, which has been modified later.

Figure 25 presents the resulting Content Factor of this implementation, including $\overline{\kappa}_{\mathrm{B}}$ for this context, the core lines (lines 2–3), unsorted (U) and sorted (S), definition set lines (lines 4–10) resolving the used elements, and integrated additional information and statistics (lines 11-20).

```
1  CONTFACT:BEGIN
2  CONTFACT:20160829-123531:AU:{Am}{Gr}{Ce}{Gr}{Gr}{Ro}{Am}{Gr}{Am}{Am}{Va}{Am}{Ce
    }{Am}{Am}{Pi}{Pi}{Tr}{Tr}{Gr}{Ro}{Am}{Am}{Tr}{Am}{Gr}{Ro}{Am}{Tr}{Am}{Tr}{Am}{
    Am}{Am}{Am}{Tr}{Am}{Am}{Am}{Am}{Gr}{Ce}{Ce}{Tr}/496
3  CONTFACT:20160829-123531:AS:{Am}{Am}{Am}{Am}{Am}{Am}{Am}{Am}{Am}{Am}{Am}{Am}{Am
    }{Am}{Am}{Am}{Am}{Am}{Am}{Am}{Ce}{Ce}{Ce}{Ce}{Gr}{Gr}{Gr}{Gr}{Gr}{Gr}{Gr}{Pi}{
    Pi}{Ro}{Ro}{Ro}{Tr}{Tr}{Tr}{Tr}{Tr}{Tr}{Tr}{Va}/496
4  CONTFACT:20160829-123531:M:{Am}:=\b[Aa]mphora
5  CONTFACT:20160829-123531:M:{Ce}:=[Cc]eramic
6  CONTFACT:20160829-123531:M:{Gr}:=\b[Gg]reek\b
7  CONTFACT:20160829-123531:M:{Pi}:=[Pp]itho[is]
8  CONTFACT:20160829-123531:M:{Ro}:=\b[Rr]oman\b
9  CONTFACT:20160829-123531:M:{Tr}:=[Tt]ransport
10 CONTFACT:20160829-123531:M:{Va}:=[Vv]ases
11 CONTFACT:20160829-123531:M:STAT:OBJECTELEMENTSDEF=7
12 CONTFACT:20160829-123531:M:STAT:OBJECTELEMENTSALL=496
13 CONTFACT:20160829-123531:M:STAT:OBJECTELEMENTSMAT=44
14 CONTFACT:20160829-123531:M:STAT:OBJECTELEMENTSCFO=.09282680
15 CONTFACT:20160829-123531:M:STAT:OBJECTELEMENTSKWO=2
16 CONTFACT:20160829-123531:M:STAT:OBJECTELEMENTSLAN=2
17 CONTFACT:20160829-123531:M:INFO:OBJECTELEMENTSOBJ=Amphora
18 CONTFACT:20160829-123531:M:INFO:OBJECTELEMENTSDCM=(c) LX-Project, 2009, 2015,
    2016
19 CONTFACT:20160829-123531:M:INFO:OBJECTELEMENTSMTX=LX Foundation Scientific
    Resources; Object Collection
20 CONTFACT:20160829-123531:M:INFO:OBJECTELEMENTSAUT=Claus-Peter R\"uckemann
21 CONTFACT:END
```

Figure 25. Computed CONTFACT, geoscientific and archaeological resources (LX Resources, excerpt).

Additional information maybe required for supporting an integration with an application scenario and practical implementation can be added very flexibly.

Figure 26 presents the resulting core lines after changes to the object.

```
CONTFACT:20160829-123532:AU:{Am}{Gr}{Ce}{Gr}{Gr}{Ro}{Am}{Gr}{Am}{Am}{Va}{Am}{Ce
 }{Am}{Am}{Pi}{Pi}{Tr}{Tr}{Gr}{Ro}{Am}{Am}{Tr}{Am}{Gr}{Ro}{Am}{Tr}{Am}{Tr}{Am}{
 Am}{Am}{Am}{Tr}{Am}{Am}{Am}{Am}{Gr}{Ce}{Ce}{Tr}{Ce}{Ce}{Tr}{Ce}{Ce}{Tr}{Ce}{Ce
 }{Ce}{Ce}{Pi}{Pi}{Am}/510
CONTFACT:20160829-123532:AS:{Am}{Am}{Am}{Am}{Am}{Am}{Am}{Am}{Am}{Am}{Am}{Am}{Am
 }{Am}{Am}{Am}{Am}{Am}{Am}{Am}{Am}{Ce}{Ce}{Ce}{Ce}{Ce}{Ce}{Ce}{Ce}{Ce}{Ce}{Ce}{
 Ce}{Gr}{Gr}{Gr}{Gr}{Gr}{Gr}{Gr}{Pi}{Pi}{Pi}{Pi}{Ro}{Ro}{Ro}{Tr}{Tr}{Tr}{Tr}{Tr
 }{Tr}{Tr}{Tr}{Tr}{Va}/510
```

Figure 26. Computed CONTFACT core after changes, geoscientific and archaeological resources (LX Resources, excerpt).

This method can be used to document and analyse the development of objects over time. It is possible to compare different objects or instances as well as comparing sequences and movements of sequences inside an object. In principle there is no limitation for changes, which can be considered when comparing results. Comparing results with arbitary changes can be reasonable for an application scenario.

Anyway, if one parameter changes at a time then the interpretation from a comparison is most unambiguousness.

F. Multi-lingual Discovery and Concordances

The Content Factor method can also be used for discovery procedures based on multi-lingual definitions (Figures 27, 28, 29). Figure 27 excerpts complementary relevant parts of the collection object (Figure 23).

The parts are relevant for this application regarding Content Factor and respective definitions sets.

```
Amphora         %-GP%-XX%---: Amphora                    [Archaeology, Etymology]:
                %-GP%-EN%---:                            (greek) amphoreus = ceramic
                 container with two handles.
                %-GP%-EN%---:                            (greek) amphí = on both sides.
                %-GP%-EN%---:                            (greek) phérein = carry.
                %-GP%-DE%---:                            (altgriech.) amphoreus =
                 zweihenkliges Tongefäß.
                %-GP%-DE%---:                            (griech.) amphí = auf beiden
                 Seiten.
                %-GP%-DE%---:                            (griech.) phérein = tragen.
...
                %-GP%-XX%---:                            catalan:   \lxidxlangeins{
                 àmphora}
                %-GP%-XX%---:                            english:   \lxidxlangeins{
                 amphore, amphorae / amphoras (pl.)}
                %-GP%-XX%---:                            french:    \lxidxlangeins{
                 amphora}
                %-GP%-XX%---:                            german:    \lxidxlangeins{
                 Amphore}
                %-GP%-XX%---:                            greek:     \lxidxlangzwei{
                 amphora, amphoreas}{$\alpha\mu\varphi o\rho\epsilon\alpha\
                 varsigma$}
                %-GP%-XX%---:                            italian:   \lxidxlangeins{
                 anfora, anfore}
                %-GP%-XX%---:                            latin:     \lxidxlangeins{
                 amphora}
                %-GP%-XX%---:                            spanish:   \lxidxlangeins{
                 àmfora}
```

Figure 27. Example LX collection object, multi-lingual elements, used with CONTFACT (LX Resources, excerpt).

Regarding this case study, the excerpt contains multi-lingual entries (EN, DE) in an object as well as multi-lingual elements in the multi-lingual entries, including translations and transcriptions. Figure 28 excerpts a CONTFACT definition set, which has been generated from concordance references.

```
% (c) LX-Project, 2009, 2015, 2016
{Am}:=[Aa]mphora
{AA}:=[Àà]mphora
{Ae}:=[Aa]mphore
{An}:=[Aa]nfor[ae]
{Af}:=[Àà]mfora
```

Figure 28. Example of CONTFACT definitions, generated from concordance references (LX Resources, excerpt).

In this case different representations of the same term are defined. The resulting core will contain the different distinctable occurences and supports a complex analysis. Figure 29 excerpts the resulting Content Factor core lines.

```
CONTFACT:20160101-220551:AU:{Am}{Ae}{Ae}{Am}{Am}{Ae}{Am}{Am}{Am}{Ae}{Am}{Ae}{Ae
 }{Am}{Am}{Ae}{Am}{Ae}{Am}{Ae}{Ae}{Am}{Am}{Am}{Am}{Am}{Am}{Am}{AA}{Ae}{Am}{Am}{
 Am}{Ae}{Am}{Ae}{An}{An}{Am}{Af}{Ae}{Am}/488
```

Figure 29. Computed CONTFACT core only containing multi-lingual/concordances information (LX Resources, excerpt).

The resulting Content Factor allows to document and analyse multi-lingual entries as well as concordances in many ways, e.g., all the data, dedicated entries or translations. The method also allows to create relations from the context and deduct relevances.

G. Concordances Discovery

Knowledge processing can benefit from creating concordances with the conceptual knowledge [39] as well as concordances can be used with advanced association processing [40].

The Content Factor works with classification references the same way as with patterns and definitions. The application of concordances for the use with Content Factors is therefore comparable but introduces additional complexity at the level of evaluating concordances.

The differences in classification and concordances are resulting from the different level of detail in the collections and containers as well as in different potential of the various classification schemes to describe certain knowledge as can be seen from the different depth of classification. In integration, together the concordances can create valuable references in depth and width to complementary classification schemes and knowledge classified with different classification.

The term concordance is not only used in the simple traditional meaning. Instead, the organisation is that of a meta-concordances concept. That results from the use of universal meta-classification, which in turn is used to classify and integrate classifications. The samples include simple classifications from UDC, Mathematics Subject Classification (MSC) [41], Library of Congress Classification (LCC) [42], and Physics and Astronomy Classification Scheme (PACS) [43].

The Universal Classified Classification (UCC) entries contain several classifications. The UCC blocks provide concordances across the classification schemes. The object classification is associated with the items associated with the object whereas the container classification is associated with the container, which means it refers to all objects in the containers.

Figure 30 excerpts a definition set based on UCC entries.

```
% (c) LX-Project, 2009, 2015, 2016
{UCC:}:=
{UCC:UDC2012:}:=UDC2012:551.21
{UCC:UDC2012:}:=UDC2012:551
{UCC:UDC2012:}:=UDC2012:902/908
{UCC:MSC2010:}:=MSC2010:86,86A17,86A60
{UCC:LCC:}:=LCC:QE521-545
{UCC:LCC:}:=LCC:QE1-996.5
{UCC:LCC:}:=LCC:QC801-809
{UCC:LCC:}:=LCC:CC1-960,CB3-482
{UCC:PACS2010:}:=PACS2010:91.40.-k
{UCC:PACS2010:}:=PACS2010:91.65.-n,91.
```

Figure 30. Concordances information: UCC (LX Resources, excerpt).

In general, the typification for taking advantage of concordances can consider all the according levels spanned by the classification trees. In practice, organising concordances discovery means to care for the individual typecasting, mapping, and referencing with the implementation.

H. Element Groups

The algorithm can be used with discovery procedures using definitions based on element groups (Figures 31, 32, 33).

```
object or       %-GP%-EN%---: object or           [Alternatives]:
                %-GP%-EN%---:                     Archaeology, Archeology.
                %-GP%-DE%---:                     Archäologie.
                %-GP%-EN%---:                     Underwaterarchaeology,
                 Underwaterarcheology.
                %-GP%-DE%---:                     Unterwasserarchäologie.
                %-GP%-EN%---:                     archaeology, archeology.
                %-GP%-DE%---:                     ...archäologie.
```

Figure 31. Example LX collection object for computing Content Factors including element groups (LX Resources, excerpt).

This example (Figure 31) defines a collection object with several main lines. The lines contain terms composed in two languages, with and without umlauts, and using upper case and lower case. A definition set containing an element group delivering several hits is given in Figure 32.

```
% (c) LX-Project, 2009, 2015, 2016
{Boundary_A}:=\b[Aa]rchaeology\b|\b[Aa]rcheology\b|\b[Aa]rchäologie\b
```

Figure 32. Example definition set for computing Content Factors including element groups (LX Resources, excerpt).

The definition set defines an element group of terms with and without umlauts, all choosing lower case and upper case terms with word boundaries.

```
CONTFACT:BEGIN
CONTFACT:20160829-220828:AU:{Boundary_A}{Boundary_A}{Boundary_A}{Boundary_A}{
 Boundary_A}{Boundary_A}/12
CONTFACT:20160829-220828:AS:{Boundary_A}{Boundary_A}{Boundary_A}{Boundary_A}{
 Boundary_A}{Boundary_A}/12
CONTFACT:20160829-220828:M:{Boundary_A}:=\b[Aa]rchaeology\b|\b[Aa]rcheology\b|\b
 [Aa]rchäologie\b
CONTFACT:20160829-220828:M:STAT:OBJECTELEMENTSDEF=1
CONTFACT:20160829-220828:M:STAT:OBJECTELEMENTSALL=12
CONTFACT:20160829-220828:M:STAT:OBJECTELEMENTSMAT=6
CONTFACT:20160829-220828:M:STAT:OBJECTELEMENTSCFO=.50000000
CONTFACT:20160829-220828:M:STAT:OBJECTELEMENTSKWO=1
CONTFACT:20160829-220828:M:STAT:OBJECTELEMENTSLAN=2
CONTFACT:20160829-220828:M:INFO:OBJECTELEMENTSOBJ=object or
CONTFACT:20160829-220828:M:INFO:OBJECTELEMENTSDCM=(c) LX-Project, 2009, 2015,
 2016
CONTFACT:20160829-220828:M:INFO:OBJECTELEMENTSMTX=LX Foundation Scientific
 Resources; Object Collection
CONTFACT:20160829-220828:M:INFO:OBJECTELEMENTSAUT=Claus-Peter R\"uckemann
CONTFACT:END
```

Figure 33. Example CONTFACT output including element groups (LX Resources, excerpt).

This results in one definition and six matches from twelve elements for the CONTFACT: The definitions define groups of alternative element representation subsummarised in the same element group. The subsummarisation may be created for specific purposes, e.g., for different writing for a certain term.

In a Perl notation alternatives are separated with pipe symbols (|). The right side value is used accordingly for counting. The two commented examples in the definition set show using lower and upper case specification for letter and defining word boundaries.

In principle, the definitions are subject of the respective application scenario and creator. Anyhow, it is a good practice to think about the sort order, e.g., to consider more special/-conditions first. In a Content Factor implementation this can mean to use a sort key, a priority or simply place the respective groups on top.

Here, the definitions can include substring alternatives, boundary delimited first-letter case insensitive alternatives, and first-letter case insensitive substring alternatives.

With element groups the alternatives are counted for the respective element group. The implementation of the Content Factor has to make sure to handle the alternatives and the counting appropriately.

VIII. Processing and Computation

It is advantageous if algorithms used with arbitrary content can be adopted for different infrastructure and data-locality, e.g., with different computing, network, and storage resources. This is especially helpful when data quantities are large. Therefore, scalability, modularisation, and dynamical use as well as parallelisation and persistence of individual stages of computation should be handled in flexible ways.

A. Scalability, modularisation, and dynamical use

The algorithms can be used for single objects as well as for large collections and containers, containing millions of entries each. Not only simulations but more and more Big Data analysis is conducted using High Performance Computing. Therefore, data-centric models are implemented expanding the traditional compute-centric model for an integrated approach [44]. In addition to the data-centric knowledge resources, the Content Factor computation routines allow a modularised and dynamical use.

The parts required for an implementation computing a Content Factor can be modularised, which means that not only a Content Factor computation can be implemented as a module but even core, definitions, and additional parts can be computed by separate modules.

Sequences of routine calls can be used in order to modularise complex workflows. The sequence of routine calls used for examples in this case study shows the principle and modular application of respective functions (Figure 34). The modules create an entity for the implemented Content Factor (`contfactbegin` to `contfactend`). They include labels, date, unsorted elements and so on as well as statistics and additional information.

The possibility to modularise the routine calls even within the Content Factor provides the features increased flexibility and scalability, which can be used for individual implementations optimised for distributed and non-distributed Big Data.

```
contfactbegin

contfact
contfactdate
contfacttype
contfactelementsu
contfactref
contfactsum

contfact
contfactdate
contfacttypes
contfactelementss
contfactref
contfactsum

contfactdef

contfact
contfactdate
contfacttypestat
contfact_stat_def_lab
contfact_stat_def

contfact
contfactdate
contfacttypestat
contfact_stat_all_lab
contfact_stat_all

contfact
contfactdate
contfacttypestat
contfact_stat_mat_u_lab
contfact_stat_mat_u

contfact
contfactdate
contfacttypestat
contfact_stat_cfo_lab
contfact_stat_cfo

contfact
contfactdate
contfacttypestat
contfact_stat_kwo_lab
contfact_stat_kwo

contfact
contfactdate
contfacttypestat
contfact_stat_lan_lab
contfact_stat_lan

contfact
contfactdate
contfacttypeinfo
contfact_info_obj_lab
contfact_info_obj

contfact
contfactdate
contfacttypeinfo
contfact_info_dcm_lab
contfact_info_dcm

contfact
contfactdate
contfacttypeinfo
contfact_info_mtx_lab
contfact_info_mtx

contfact
contfactdate
contfacttypeinfo
contfact_info_aut_lab
contfact_info_aut

contfactend



...
```

Figure 34. Sequence of modular high-level CONTFACT routines for `lxcontfact` implementation (LX Resources, excerpt).

In this case atomised modules are used to create entries. The module calls are grouped by their purpose for creating certain entries. In the example one single Content Factor with additional information is created. For example, after the `contfactbegin`, the `contfact`, `contfactdate` up to `contfactsum` create an entry with date / timestamp, type specification, specification of unsorted elements, reference specification (/), and sum. The next block adds a sorted entry to the Content Factor. The contfactdef calculates and adds the definitions used with the above entries. The following blocks add additional information and statistics, e.g., statistics on the number of elements or information on the referred object in the knowledge resources. This means any core entries, statistics and so on can be computed with individual implementations if required.

Application scenarios may allow to compute Content Factors for many objects in parallel. Content Factors can be computed dynamically as well as in batch mode or "pre-computed". Content Factors can be kept volatile as well as persistent. Everything can be considered a set, e.g., an object, a collection, and a container. Content Factors can be computed for arbitrary data, e.g., objects, collections, and containers. A consistent implementation delivers a Content Factor for a collection, which is the sum of the Content Factors computed for the objects contained in the collection. Therefore, an implementation can scale from single on the fly objects to millions of objects, which may also associated with pre-computed Content Factors.

B. *Parallelisation and persistence*

There is a number of modules supporting computation based on persistent data, e.g., in collections and containers. The architecture allows task parallel implementations for multiple instances as well as highly parallel implementations for core routines.

Applications are decollators, which extract objects from collection and containers and compute object based Content Factors. Other applications are slicers and atomisers, which cut data, e.g., objects, into slices or atoms, e.g., lines or strings, for which Content Factors can be computed. Examples in context with the above application scenarios are collection decollators, container decollators, collection slicers, container slicers, collection atomisers, container atomisers, formatting modules, computing modules for (intermediate) result matrix requests.

Content Factor data can easily be kept and handled on persistent as well as on dynamical base. The algorithms and workflows allow the flexible organisation of data locality, e.g., central locations and with compute units, e.g., in groups or containers.

IX EVALUATION

The presented application scenarios and according implementations have shown that many different cases targeting on knowledge processing can benefit from data description and analysis with the Content Factor method.

The case studies showed that the formal description can be implemented very flexibly and successful (`lxcontfact`). Content Factors can be computed for any type of data. The Content Factor is not limited to text processing or even NLP, term-frequencies, and statistics. It has been successfully used with long term knowledge resources and with unstructured and dynamical data. The Content Factor method can describe arbitrary data in a unique form and supports data analysis and knowledge discovery in many ways, e.g., complex data comparison and tracking of relevant changes.

Definition sets can support various use cases. Examples were given from handling single characters to string elements. Definitions can be kept with the Content Factor, together with additional Content Factor data, e.g., statistics and documentation. Any of this Content Factor information has been successfully used to analyse data objects from different sources. The computation of Content Factors is non invasive, the results can be created dynamically and persistent. Content Factors can be automatically computed for elements and groups of large data resources. The integration with data and knowledge resources can be kept non invasive to least invasive, depending on the desired purposes. Knowledge objects, e.g., in collections and containers, can carry and refer to complementary information and knowledge, especially Content Factor information, which can be integrated with workflows, e.g., for discovery processes.

The implementation is as far data-centric as possible. Data and technical implementations can be separated and the created knowledge resources and technical components comply to the above criteria.

The benefits and usability may depend on the field of application and the individual goals. The evaluation refers to the case context presented, which allows a wide range of freedom and flexibility. The benefits for the knowledge resources are additional means for documentation of objects. In detail, the benefits for the example workflows were improved data-mining pipelines, due to additional features for comparisons of objects, integrating developing knowledge resources, and creating and developing knowledge resources.

In practice, the computation of Content Factors has revealed significant benefits for the creation and analysis of large numbers of objects and for the flexibility and available features for building workflows, e.g., when based on long-term knowledge objects. In addition, creators, authors, and users of knowledge and content have additional means to express their views and valuation of objects and groups of objects. From the computational point of view, the computation of Content Factors can help minimise the recurrent computing demands for data.

X. Conclusion

This paper introduced a methodology for data description and analysis, the Content Factor (CONTFACT) method and presented the developments and results on knowledge processing algorithms and discovery for advanced application scenarios.

The paper presents the formal description and examples, a successful implementation, and a practical case study. It has been shown that the Content Factor is data-centric and can describe and analyse arbitrary data and content, structured and unstructured. Data-centricity is even emphasized due to the fact that the Content Factor can be seamlessly integrated with the data. The data locality is most flexible and allows an efficient use of different computing, storage, and communication architectures.

The method can be adopted for many purposes. The Content Factor method has been successfully applied for knowledge processing and analysis with long-term knowledge resources, for knowledge discovery, and with variable data for system operation analysis. It enables to specify a wide range of precision and fuzziness for data description and analysis and also enables methods like data rhythm analysis and characterisation, can be integrated with complementary methodologies, e.g., classifications, concordances, and references.

Therefore, the method allows weighting data regarding significance, promoting the value of data. The method supports the use of advanced computing methods for computation and analysis with the implementation. The computation and processing can be automated and used with huge and even unstructured data resources. The methodology allows an integrated use with complementary methodologies, e.g., with conceptual knowledge like UDC.

It will be interesting to see further various Content Factor implementations for individual applications, e.g., dynamical classification and concordances. Future work concentrates on high level applications and implementations for advanced analysis and automation.

Acknowledgements

We are grateful to the "Knowledge in Motion" (KiM) long-term project, Unabhängiges Deutsches Institut für Multidisziplinäre Forschung (DIMF), for partially funding this implementation, case study, and publication under grants D2014F1P04518 and D2014F2P04518 and to its senior scientific members, especially to Dr. Friedrich Hülsmann, Gottfried Wilhelm Leibniz Bibliothek (GWLB) Hannover, to Dipl.-Biol. Birgit Gersbeck-Schierholz, Leibniz Universität Hannover, and to Dipl.-Ing. Martin Hofmeister, Hannover, for fruitful discussion, inspiration, practical multi-disciplinary case studies, and the analysis of advanced concepts. We are grateful to Dipl.-Ing. Hans-Günther Müller, Cray, for his work on flexible practical solutions to architectural challenges and excellent technical support. We are grateful to all national and international partners in the Geo Exploration and Information cooperations for their constructive and trans-disciplinary support. We thank the Science and High Performance Supercomputing Centre (SHPSC) for long-term support of collaborative research since 1997, including the GEXI developments and case studies.

References

[1] C.-P. Rückemann, "Enhancement of Knowledge Resources and Discovery by Computation of Content Factors," in Proceedings of The Sixth International Conference on Advanced Communications and Computation (INFOCOMP 2016), May 22–26, 2016, Valencia, Spain. XPS Press, 2016, Rückemann, C.-P., Pankowska, M. (eds.), pages 24–31, ISSN: 2308-3484, ISBN-13: 978-1-61208-478-7, ISBN-13: 978-1-61208-061-1 (CDROM), TMDL: infocomp_2016_2_30_60047, URL: http://www.thinkmind.org/download.php?articleid=infocomp_2016_2_30_60047 [accessed: 2016-06-18], URL: http://www.thinkmind.org/index.php?view=article&articleid=infocomp_2016_2_30_60047 [accessed: 2016-06-18].

[2] T. Koltay, "Data literacy for researchers and data librarians," Journal of Librarianship and Information Science, 2015, pp. 1–12, Preprint, DOI: 10.1177/0961000615616450.

[3] E. König, "From Information Specialist to Data Specialist, (German: Vom Informationsspezialisten zum Datenspezialisten)," library essentials, LE_Informationsdienst, March 2016, 2016, pp. 8–11, ISSN: 2194-0126, URL: http://www.libess.de [accessed: 2016-03-20].

[4] R. Uzwyshyn, "Research Data Repositories: The What, When, Why, and How," Computers in Libraries, vol. 36, no. 3, Apr. 2016, pp. 11–14, ISSN: 2194-0126, URL: http://www.libess.de [accessed: 2016-03-20].

[5] E. König, "Research Data Repositories - A new Field of Activities, (in German: Forschungsdaten-Repositorien als ein neues Betätigungsfeld)," library essentials, LE_Informationsdienst, Jun. 2016, 2016, pp. 11–14, ISSN: 2194-0126, URL: http://www.libess.de [accessed: 2016-03-20].

[6] C.-P. Rückemann, "Advanced Content Balancing and Valuation: The Content Factor (CONTFACT)," Knowledge in Motion Long-term Project, Unabhängiges Deutsches Institut für Multidisziplinäre Forschung (DIMF), Germany; Westfälische Wilhelms-Universität Münster, Münster, 2009, Project Technical Report.

[7] C.-P. Rückemann, "CONTCODE – A Code for Balancing Content," Knowledge in Motion Long-term Project, Unabhängiges Deutsches Institut für Multidisziplinäre Forschung (DIMF), Germany; Westfälische Wilhelms-Universität Münster, Münster, 2009, Project Technical Report.

[8] F. Hülsmann and C.-P. Rückemann, "Content and Factor in Practice: Revealing the Content-DNA," KiM Summit, October 26, 2015, Knowledge in Motion, Hannover, Germany, 2015, Project Meeting Report.

[9] C.-P. Rückemann, "Integrated Computational and Conceptual Solutions for Complex Environmental Information Management," in The Fifth Symposium on Advanced Computation and Information in Natural and Applied Sciences, Proceedings of The 13th International Conference of Numerical Analysis and Applied Mathematics (ICNAAM), September 23–29, 2015, Rhodes, Greece, Proceedings of the American Institute of Physics (AIP), vol. 1738. AIP Press, 2016, Simos, T. E., Tsitouras, C. (eds.), ISBN-13: 978-0-7354-1392-4, ISSN: 0094-243X (American Institute of Physics Conference Proceedings, print), ISSN: 1551-7616 (online) (eISSN), DOI: 10.1063/1.4951833.

[10] D. T. Meridou, U. Inden, C.-P. Rückemann, C. Z. Patrikakis, D.-T. I. Kaklamani, and I. S. Venieris, "Ontology-based, Multi-agent Support of Production Management," in The Fifth Symposium on Advanced Computation and Information in Natural and Applied Sciences, Proceedings of The 13th International Conference of Numerical Analysis and Applied Mathematics (ICNAAM), September 23–29, 2015, Rhodes, Greece, Proceedings of the American Institute of Physics (AIP), vol. 1738. AIP Press, 2016, Simos, T. E., Tsitouras, C. (eds.), ISBN-13: 978-0-7354-1392-4, ISSN: 0094-243X (American Institute of Physics Conference Proceedings, print), ISSN: 1551-7616 (online) (eISSN), DOI: 10.1063/1.4951834.

[11] C.-P. Rückemann, F. Hülsmann, B. Gersbeck-Schierholz, P. Skurowski, and M. Staniszewski, Knowledge and Computing. Post-Summit Results, Delegates' Summit: Best Practice and Definitions of Knowledge and Computing, September 23, 2015, The Fifth Symposium on Advanced Computation and Information in Natural and Applied Sciences, The 13th International Conference of Numerical Analysis and Applied Mathematics (ICNAAM), September 23–29, 2015, Rhodes, Greece, 2015.

[12] O. Lipsky and E. Porat, "Approximated Pattern Matching with the L_1, L_2 and L_∞ Metrics," in 15th International Symposium on String Processing and Information Retrieval (SPIRE 2008), November 10–12, 2008, Melbourne, Australia, ser. Lecture Notes in Computer Science (LNCS), vol. 5280. Springer, Berlin, Heidelberg, 2008, pp. 212–223, Amir, A. and Turpin, A. and Moffat, A. (eds.), ISSN: 0302-9743, ISBN: 978-3-540-89096-6, LCCN: 2008938187.

[13] G. Ercan and I. Cicekli, "Lexical Cohesion Based Topic Modeling for Summarization," in Proceedings of The 9th International Conference on Computational Linguistics and Intelligent Text Processing (CICLing 2008), February 17–23, 2008, Haifa, Israel, ser. Lecture Notes in Computer Science (LNCS), vol. 4919. Springer, Berlin, Heidelberg, 2008, pp. 582–592, Gelbukh, A. (ed.), ISSN: 0302-9743, ISBN: 978-3-540-78134-9, LCCN: 2008920439, URL: http://link.springer.com/chapter/10.1007/978-3-540-78135-6_50 [accessed: 2016-01-10].

[14] G. Szarvas, T. Zesch, and I. Gurevych, "Combining Heterogeneous Knowledge Resources," in Proceedings of The 12th International Conference on Computational Linguistics and Intelligent Text Processing (CICLing 2011), February 20–26, 2011, Tokyo, Japan, ser. Lecture Notes in Computer Science (LNCS), vol. 6608 and 6609. Springer, Berlin, Heidelberg, 2011, pp. 289–303, Gelbukh, A. (ed.), ISSN: 0302-9743, ISBN: 978-3-642-19399-6, DOI: 10.1007/978-3-642-19400-9, LCCN: 2011921814, URL: http://link.springer.com/chapter/10.1007/978-3-642-19400-9_23 [accessed: 2016-01-10].

[15] A. Woodie, "Is 2016 the Beginning of the End for Big Data?" Datanami, 2016, January 5, 2016, URL: http://www.datanami.com/2016/01/05/is-2016-the-beginning-of-the-end-for-big-data/ [accessed: 2016-01-10].

[16] M. E. Jennex, "A Proposed Method for Assessing Knowledge Loss Risk with Departing Personnel," VINE: The Journal of Information and Knowledge Management Systems, vol. 44, no. 2, 2014, pp. 185–209, ISSN: 0305-5728.

[17] R. Leming, "Why is information the elephant asset? An answer to this question and a strategy for information asset management," Business Information Review, vol. 32, no. 4, 2015, pp. 212–219, ISSN: 0266-3821 (print), ISSN: 1741-6450 (online), DOI: 10.1177/0266382115616301.

[18] E. König, "The (Unknown) Value of Information (in German: Der (unbekannte) Wert von Information)," library essentials, LE_Informationsdienst, Dez. 2015 / Jan. 2016, 2015, pp. 10–14, ISSN: 2194-0126, URL: http://www.libess.de [accessed: 2016-08-27].

[19] E. König, "Effects of Open Access on Remote Loan and Other Information Resources, (in German: Die Auswirkungen von Open Access auf die Fernleihe und andere Informationsressourcen)," library essentials, LE_Informationsdienst, Jun. 2015, 2015, pp. 11–14, ISSN: 2194-0126, URL: http://www.libess.de [accessed: 2016-03-20].

[20] T. Baich, "Open access: help or hindrance to resource sharing?" Interlending & Document Supply, vol. 43, no. 2, 2015, pp. 68–75, DOI: 10.1108/ILDS-01-2015-0003.

[21] B. Kosko, "Counting with Fuzzy Sets," IEEE Transactions on Pattern Analysis and Machine Intelligence, vol. PAMI-8, no. 4, Jul. 1986, pp. 556–557, ISSN: 0162-8828, DOI: 10.1109/TPAMI.1986.4767822.

[22] "LX-Project," 2016, URL: http://www.user.uni-hannover.de/cpr/x/rprojs/en/#LX [accessed: 2016-06-18].

[23] C. W. Belter and N. K. Kaske, "Using Bibliometrics to Demonstrate the Value of Library Journal Collections," College & Research Libraries, vol. 77, no. 4, Jul. 2016, pp. 410–422, DOI: 10.5860/crl.77.4.410, URL: http://crl.acrl.org/content/77/4/410.full.pdf+html [accessed: 2016-08-20].

[24] E. König, "Demonstrate the Value of Libraries Using Bibliometric Analyses (German: Den Wert von Bibliotheken mittels bibliometrischer Analysen nachweisen)," library essentials, LE_Informationsdienst, Aug. 2016, 2016, pp. 11–16, ISSN: 2194-0126, URL: http://www.libess.de [accessed: 2016-08-20].

[25] E. König, "Most Stored Data is of no Economic Value (German: Die meisten gespeicherten Daten sind ohne wirtschaftlichen Wert)," library essentials, LE_Informationsdienst, Aug. 2016, 2016, pp. 30–32, ISSN: 2194-0126, URL: http://www.libess.de [accessed: 2016-08-20].

[26] "Data Genomics Index 2016," 2016, URL: http://datagenomicsproject.org/Data_Genomics_Index_2016.pdf [accessed: 2016-08-20].

[27] E. König, "More Figures = More Citations (German: Mehr Bilder = mehr Zitierungen)," library essentials, LE_Informationsdienst, Aug. 2016, 2016, pp. 34–35, ISSN: 2194-0126, URL: http://www.libess.de [accessed: 2016-08-20].

[28] P. Lee, J. D. West, and B. Howe, "Viziometrics: Analyzing Visual Information in the Scientific Literature," 2016, URL: http://arxiv.org/abs/1605.04951 [accessed: 2016-08-20].

[29] E. König, "Are Reference Services Still Needed in the Age of Google and Co.? (German: Werden Auskunftsdienste im Zeitalter von Google und Co. noch benötigt?)," library essentials, LE_Informationsdienst, Aug. 2016, 2016, pp. 11–14, ISSN: 2194-0126, URL: http://www.libess.de [accessed: 2016-08-20].

[30] S. P. Buss, "Do We Still Need Reference Services in the Age of Google and Wikipedia?" The Reference Librarian, vol. 57, no. 4, 2016, pp. 265–271, DOI: 10.1080/02763877.2015.1134377, URL: http://dx.doi.org/10.1080/02763877.2015.1134377 [accessed: 2016-08-20].

[31] C.-P. Rückemann, Z. Kovacheva, L. Schubert, I. Lishchuk, B. Gersbeck-Schierholz, and F. Hülsmann, Best Practice and Definitions of Data-centric and Big Data – Science, Society, Law, Industry, and Engineering. Post-Summit Results, Delegates' Summit: Best Practice and Definitions of Data-centric and Big Data – Science, Society, Law, Industry, and Engineering, September 19, 2016, The Sixth Symposium on Advanced Computation and Information in Natural and Applied Sciences (SACINAS), The 14th International Conference of Numerical Analysis and Applied Mathematics (ICNAAM), September 19–25, 2016, Rhodes, Greece, 2016, URL: http://www.user.uni-hannover.de/cpr/x/publ/2016/delegatessummit2016/rueckemann_icnaam2016_summit_summary.pdf [accessed: 2016-11-06].

[32] C.-P. Rückemann, "Enabling Dynamical Use of Integrated Systems and Scientific Supercomputing Resources for Archaeological Information Systems," in Proceedings INFOCOMP 2012, Oct. 21–26, 2012, Venice, Italy, 2012, pp. 36–41, ISBN: 978-1-61208-226-4, URL: http://www.thinkmind.org/download.php?articleid=infocomp_2012_3_10_10012 [accessed: 2016-08-28].

[33] "UDC Online," 2015, URL: http://www.udc-hub.com/ [accessed: 2016-01-01].

[34] "Multilingual Universal Decimal Classification Summary," 2012, UDC Consortium, 2012, Web resource, v. 1.1. The Hague: UDC Consortium (UDCC Publication No. 088), URL: http://www.udcc.org/udcsummary/php/index.php [accessed: 2016-01-01].

[35] "Creative Commons Attribution Share Alike 3.0 license," 2012, URL: http://creativecommons.org/licenses/by-sa/3.0/ [accessed: 2016-01-01].

[36] B. F. S. Gersbeck-Schierholz, "Testimonies of Nature and History in the Napoli and Vesuvius Region, Italy," Media Presentation, January 2014, Hannover, Germany, 2014, URL: http://www.user.uni-hannover.de/zzzzgers/bgs_volcano.html [accessed: 2016-08-27].

[37] F. Hülsmann, C.-P. Rückemann, M. Hofmeister, M. Lorenzen, O. Lau, and M. Tasche, "Application Scenarios for the Content Factor Method in Libraries, Natural Sciences and Archaeology, Statics, Architecture, Risk Coverage, Technology, and Material Sciences," KiM Strategy Summit, March 17, 2016, Knowledge in Motion, Hannover, Germany, 2016.

[38] "The Perl Programming Language," 2016, URL: https://www.perl.org/ [accessed: 2016-01-10].

[39] C.-P. Rückemann, "Creation of Objects and Concordances for Knowledge Processing and Advanced Computing," in Proceedings of The Fifth International Conference on Advanced Communications and Computation (INFOCOMP 2015), June 21–26, 2015, Brussels, Belgium. XPS Press, 2015, pp. 91–98, ISSN: 2308-3484, ISBN-13: 978-1-61208-416-9, URL: http://www.thinkmind.org/download.php?articleid=infocomp_2015_4_30_60038 [accessed: 2016-08-28].

[40] C.-P. Rückemann, "Advanced Association Processing and Computation Facilities for Geoscientific and Archaeological Knowledge Resources Components," in Proceedings of The Eighth International Conference on Advanced Geographic Information Systems, Applications, and Services (GEOProcessing 2016), April 24–28, 2016, Venice, Italy. XPS Press, 2016, Rückemann, C.-P. and Doytsher, Y. (eds.), pages 69–75, ISSN: 2308-393X, ISBN-13: 978-1-61208-469-5, ISBN-13: 978-1-61208-060-4 (CDROM), TMDL: geoprocessing_2016_4_20_30144, URL: http://www.thinkmind.org/download.php?articleid=geoprocessing_2016_4_20_30144 [accessed: 2016-06-05], URL: http://www.thinkmind.org/index.php?view=article&articleid=geoprocessing_2016_4_10_30144 [accessed: 2016-06-05].

[41] "Mathematics Subject Classification (MSC2010)," 2010, URL: http://msc2010.org [accessed: 2015-02-01].

[42] Fundamentals of Library of Congress Classification, Developed by the ALCTS/CCS-PCC Task Force on Library of Congress Classification Training, 2007, Robare, L., Arakawa, S., Frank, P., and Trumble, B. (eds.), ISBN: 0-8444-1186-8 (Instructor Manual), ISBN: 0-8444-1191-4 (Trainee Manual), URL: http://www.loc.gov/catworkshop/courses/fundamentalslcc/pdf/classify-trnee-manual.pdf [accessed: 2015-02-01].

[43] "Physics and Astronomy Classification Scheme, PACS 2010 Regular Edition," 2010, American Institute of Physics (AIP), URL: http://www.aip.org/pacs [accessed: 2015-02-01].

[44] IBM, ""Data-Centric" approach feeds cognitive computing; How to deploy a data-centric methodology for your organization," 2016, ISSN: 2194-0126, URL: http://www-01.ibm.com/common/ssi/cgi-bin/ssialias?htmlfid=DCG12426USEN [accessed: 2016-06-25].

Open Source Software and Some Licensing Implications to Consider

Iryna Lishchuk
Institut für Rechtsinformatik
Leibniz Universität Hannover
Hannover, Germany
e-mail: lishchuk@iri.uni-hannover.de

Abstract — **As more and more areas of science make use of open source software, legal research seeks to reconcile various open source licenses (OSS) (which may be used in a single research project) and explores solutions to allow exploitation of software outcomes in a license-compliant way. In this paper, we consider some licensing implications of open source licenses along with solutions on how to distribute software developments in a license compatible way. The steps undertaken in course of defining a license and checking license compatibility are demonstrated by a case study.**

Keywords - open source software; free software; open source licensing; copyleft.

I. Introduction

As previously discussed in the paper "Licensing Implications of the Use of Open Source Software in Research Projects", presented at INFOCOMP 2016 [1], the use of open source software in IT-projects may produce licensing implications. Such implications may in turn interfere with the plans of the developer on the potential exploitation of newly developed software. However, as we found out and describe below, some potentially risky legal issues can be avoided a priori by applying the basic knowledge of license terms and managing the use of dependencies in a legally and technically skillful way. We describe in simple terms the basic ideas and principles of free and open source software (FOSS) and suggest some guidelines, which should help a developer to make such uses of OSS, which would go in line with the exploitation plans of the developer and the license terms.

Some key areas of computing, such as Apple/Linux/GNU, Google/Android/Linux, rely on open source software. There are numerous platforms and players in the market of OSS, which offer their tools "open source", but dictate their own rules for using their developments. Well-known examples are the Apache Software Foundation (ASF) and the Apache http server; the Mozilla Foundation, whose browser Firefox makes strong competition to Google Chrome and Microsoft Internet Explorer; the Free Software Foundation with its benchmarking GNU project. The bringing of such innovative products to the market enriches the software development community and helps solving various technical problems. On the other hand, binding the use of such products within the rules of the platforms may also cause legal challenges for the developers, who try to combine products of several platforms in one project.

Many research projects use the potential of OSS and contribute to the open source movement as well. One example is the EU FP7 CHIC project in the area of health informatics (full title "Computational Horizons In Cancer (CHIC): Developing Meta- and Hyper-Multiscale Models and Repositories for In Silico Oncology" [2]). CHIC is engaged in *"the development of clinical trial driven tools, services and infrastructures that will support the creation of multiscale cancer hypermodels (integrative models)"* [2]. In the course of this, it makes use of OSS. For example, the hypermodelling framework VPH-HF relies on an open source domain-independent workflow management system Taverna [3], while an open source finite element solver, FEBio, is used in biomechanical and diffusion modeling [4].

CHIC also explores the possibility of releasing the project outcomes "open source" as well. This is part of a wider trend in all areas of scientific research, in which OSS is becoming increasingly popular. However, while the use of OSS may benefit the conduct of the project and promote its outcomes, it may at times limit the exploitation options.

In this paper, we look into the licensing implications associated with the use of OSS and open sourcing the project outcomes. Also, we seek to suggest solutions on how licensing implications (and incompatibility risks) may best be managed. The rest of this paper is organized as follows. Section II describes the notion of FOSS and elaborates on the license requirements for software distribution. Section III addresses peculiarities of the set of GNU General Public Licenses (GPL) and points up some specific aspects stemming from the use of GPL software. In Section IV, we consider some instruments for solving license incompatibility issues. The article concludes by way of a case study in Section V, showing how the use of OSS may impact on future licensing of software outcomes.

II. Free and Open source software

Open source software is not simply a popular term, but it has its own definition and criteria, which we describe below.

A. Open Source Software

According to the Open Source Initiative (OSI), *"Open source doesn't just mean access to the source code. The distribution terms of open-source software must comply with the following criteria..."* [5]. These requirements normally dictate distribution of a program: either in source form (a script written in one or another programming language, such as C^{++}, Java, Python, etc.) or as a compiled executable, i.e., object code (*"a binary code, simply a concatenation of "0"'s and "1"'s."* [6]).

The basic requirements of OSS are as follows:

1. Free Redistribution. The license may not restrict distributing a program as part of an aggregate software distribution and/or may not require license fees.

2. Source Code. The license must allow distribution of the program both in source code and in compiled form. By distribution in object code, the source code should also be accessible at a charge not exceeding the cost of copying (download from Internet at no charge).

3. Derived Works. The license must allow modifications and creation of derivative works and distribution of such works under the same license terms.

4. Integrity of The Author's Source Code. The license may require derivative works and modification to be distinguishable from original, such as by a version number or by name.

5. No Discrimination Against Persons or Groups.

6. No Discrimination Against Fields of Endeavor.

7. Distribution of License. The license terms apply to all subsequent users without the need to conclude individual license agreements.

8. License Must Not Be Specific to a Product. The license may not be dependent on any software distribution.

9. License Must Not Restrict Other Software. The license must not place restrictions on other programs distributed with the open source program (e.g., on the same medium).

10. License Must Be Technology-Neutral. The license may not be pre-defined for a specific technology [5].

There are currently more than 70 open source licenses, which can be categorized according to the license terms.

B. Free Software

One category is free software, which also has its own criteria. As defined by the Free Software Foundation (FSF), a program is free software, if the user (referred to as "you") has the four essential freedoms:

1. *"The freedom to run the program as you wish, for any purpose (freedom 0).*

2. *The freedom to study how the program works, and change it so it does your computing as you wish (freedom 1). Access to the source code is a precondition for this.*

3. *The freedom to redistribute copies so you can help your neighbor (freedom 2).*

4. *The freedom to distribute copies of your modified versions to others (freedom 3). By doing this you can give the whole community a chance to benefit from your changes. Access to the source code is a precondition for this."* [7].

The GPL, in its different versions, is a true carrier of these freedoms and GPL software (when distributed in a GPL compliant way) is normally free. The licenses, which qualify as free software licenses are defined by the FSF [8].

C. Free Software and Copyleft

The mission of free software is to provide users with these essential freedoms. This mission is achieved in a way that not only the original author, who licenses his program under a free license first, but also the subsequent developers, who make modifications to such free program, are bound to release their modified versions in the same "free" way.

Maintaining and passing on these freedoms for subsequent software distributions are usually achieved by the so called copyleft. *"Copyleft is a general method for making a program (or other work) free, and requiring all modified and extended versions of the program to be free as well."* [9]. A copyleft license usually requires that modified versions be distributed under the same terms. This distinguishes copyleft from non-copyleft licenses: copyleft licenses pass identical license terms on to derivative works, while non-copyleft licenses govern the distribution of the original code only.

D. Licensing Implications on Software Distribution

From the whole spectrum of FOSS licenses, mostly the free licenses with copyleft may produce licensing implications on software exploitation. The other free licenses without copyleft are, in contrast, rather flexible, providing for a wider variety of exploitation options, subject to rather simple terms: acknowledgement of the original developer and replication of a license notice and disclaimer of warranties.

Such more relaxed non-copyleft licenses usually allow the code to be run, modified, distributed as standalone and/or as part of another software distribution, either in source form and/or as a binary executable, under condition that the license terms for distribution of the original code are met. Among the popular non-copyleft licenses are: the Apache License [10], the MIT License [11], the BSD 3-Clause License [12], to name but a few. "*Code, created under these licenses, or derived from such code, may "go "closed" and developments can be made under that proprietary license, which are lost to the open source community.*" [13].

The conditions for distributing the original code under these non-copyleft licenses are rather simple. The basic rationale is to keep the originally licensed code under the original license (irrespective whether it is distributed as standalone or as part of software package) and to inform subsequent users that the code is used and the use of that code is governed by its license. The basic principle, which, generally, not only these, but all open source licenses follow, is that the use of the original code and its authors should be acknowledged. For instance, the MIT license requires that "*copyright notice and this permission notice shall be included in all copies or substantial portions of the Software*" [11]. The easiest way to fulfill this license requirement is to keep all copyright and license notices found in the original code intact. By this, the copyright notice, the program license with disclaimer stay replicated (maintained) throughout the whole re-distribution chain.

Failure to do so may, on the one hand, compromise the ability of the developer to enforce his own copyright in parts of the code, which he wrote himself, and, on the other hand, put him at risk of becoming an object of cease and desist action or a lawsuit [13].

E. Copyleft Licenses

At the same time though, the free licenses with copyleft, in promoting the four essential freedoms to the users, may take away the developer's freedom to decide on licensing of his own software, by pre-determining a license choice for him. While supporters of free software speak about copyleft as protecting the rights, some developers, affected by the copyleft against their will, tend to refer "*to the risk of "viral" license terms that reach out to infect their own, separately developed software and of improper market leverage and misuse of copyright to control the works of other people.*" [14].

The GPL Version 2 (GPL v2) [15] and Version 3 (GPL v3) [16] are examples of free licenses with strong copyleft. GPL copyleft looks as follows. GPL v2, in Section 1, allows the user "*to copy and distribute verbatim copies of the Program's source code... in any medium*" under the terms of GPL, requiring replication of the copyright and license notice with disclaimer and supply of the license text. In Section 2, the GPL license allows modifying the program, "*thus forming a work based on the Program, and copy and distribute such modifications or work under the terms of Section 1 above*", i.e., under GPL itself. In doing so, it implies that a developer may distribute his own developments, only if he licenses under GPL. In some cases, this binding rule may place the developer in a dilemma: either to license under GPL or not to license at all.

A more positive aspect of GPL is that at times it may be rather flexible. In particular, not all modes of using a GPL program create a modified version and not all models of software distribution are necessarily affected by GPL.

III. GPL AND GPL COPYLEFT

Among the decisive factors whether software is affected by GPL copyleft are: the mode, in which software uses a GPL program, the version and wording of the applicable GPL license, and the method of how software will be distributed.

A. Mode of Use

The mode of use essentially determines whether a development qualifies as "*a work based on a GPL program*" or not. If because of using a GPL program, software qualifies as a derivative work, i.e., a "*work based on the Program*", then according to the terms of GPL it shall go under GPL [15]. Otherwise, if a program is not a modified version of GPL, then there is no binding reason for it to go under GPL.

In this regard, not all uses of a GPL program will automatically produce a derivative work. For example, developing a software using the Linux operating system, or creating a piece of software designed to run on Java or Linux (licensed under GPL v2 [17]) does not affect licensing of this software (unless it is intended to be included into the Linux distribution as a Linux kernel module). Also, calculating algorithms by means of a GPL licensed R (a free software environment for statistical computing and graphics [18]) in the course of developing a software model does not affect licensing of a model, since the model is not running against the GPL code.

Even so, a distinctive feature of GPL is that, in contrast to the majority of other open source licenses, which do not regard linking as creating a modified version (e.g., Mozilla Public License [19], Apache License [10]), the GPL license considers linking, both static and dynamic, as making a derivative work. Following the FSF interpretation criteria, "*Linking a GPL covered work statically or dynamically with other modules is making a combined work based on the GPL covered work. Thus, the terms and conditions of the GNU General Public License cover the whole combination*" [20]. This is interpretation of GPL license by the FSF and this position is arguable. When testing whether linking programs produces a GPL-derivative, the technical aspects of modification, dependency, interaction, distribution medium and location (allocation) must be taken into account [21].

The controversy Android v Linux [22] illustrates how Google avoided licensing of Android under GPL because the mode, in which it used Linux stayed beyond the scope of Linux GPL license. This case concerned the Android operating system, which relies on the GPL licensed Linux kernel and which was ultimately licensed under the Apache License. Android is an operating system, primarily used by mobile phones. It was developed by Google and consists of the Linux kernel, some non-free libraries, a Java platform and some applications. Despite the fact that Android uses the Linux kernel, licensed under GPL v2, Android itself was licensed under Apache License 2.0. "*To combine Linux with code under the Apache 2.0 license would be a copyright infringement, since GPL version 2 and Apache 2.0 are incompatible*" [22]. However, the fact that the Linux kernel remains a separate program within Android, with its source code under GPL v2, and the Android programs communicate with the kernel via system calls clarified the licensing issue. Software communicating with Linux via system calls is expressly removed from the scope of derivative works, affected by GPL copyleft. A note, added to the GPL license terms of Linux by Linus Torvalds, makes this explicit:

"*NOTE! This copyright does *not* cover user programs that use kernel services by normal system calls - this is merely considered normal use of the kernel, and does *not* fall under the heading of "derived work". Also note that the GPL below is copyrighted by the Free Software Foundation, but the instance of code that it refers to (the linux kernel) is copyrighted by me and others who actually wrote it.*" [17].

Examples of normal system calls are: *fork()*, *exec()*, *wait()*, *open()*, *socket()*, etc. [22]. Such system calls operate within the kernel space and interact with the user programs in the user space [23]. Taking into consideration these technical details, "*Google has complied with the requirements of the GNU General Public License for Linux, but the Apache license on the rest of Android does not require source release."* [22]. In fact, the source code for Android was ultimately released. However, in the view of the FSF, even the use of Linux kernel and release of the Android source code do not make Android free software. As commented by Richard Stallman [22], Android comes up with some non-free libraries, proprietary Google applications, proprietary firmware and drivers. Android deprives the users of the freedom to modify apps, install and run their own modified software and leaves the users with no choice except to accept versions approved by Google. What is most interesting, that the Android code, which has been made available, is insufficient to run the device. All in all, in opinion of Richard Stallman, these "faults" undermine the philosophy of free software [22].

B. GPL Weak Copyleft and Linking Exceptions

Another factor that determines whether a development is subject to GPL copyleft is the form of GPL license used.

Some GPL licenses have so-called weak copyleft. Examples are the GNU Library or "Lesser" General Public License, Version 2.1 (LGPL-2.1) [24] and Version 3.0 (LGPL-3.0) [25].

By the use of these licenses, a program or an application, which merely links to a LGPL program or library (without modifying it), does not necessarily have to be licensed under LGPL. As LGPL-2.1 explains, "*A program that contains no derivative of any portion of the Library, but is designed to work with the Library by being compiled or linked with it, is called a "work that uses the Library". Such a work, in isolation, is not a derivative work of the Library, and therefore falls outside the scope of this License*." [24]. LGPL allows combining external programs with a LGPL licensed library and distributing combined works under the terms at the choice of the developer. What LGPL requires is that the LGPL licensed library stay under LGPL and license of the combined work allow "*modification of the work for the customer's own use and reverse engineering for debugging such modifications*" [24].

Some practical consequences of how a switch from LGPL to GPL in one software product may affect exploitation and usability of another software product are demonstrated by the dispute that arose between MySQL and PHP [21].

PHP is a popular general-purpose scripting language that is especially suited to web development [26]. PHP was developed by the Zend company and licensed under the PHP license, which is not compatible with GPL [27]. PHP is widely used and distributed with MySQL in web applications, such as in the LAMP system (standing for: Linux, Apache, MySQL and PHP), which is used for building dynamic web sites and web applications [28]. MySQL is the world's most popular open source database, originally developed by MySQL AB, then acquired by Sun Microsystems in 2008, and finally by Oracle in 2010 [29].

In 2004, MySQL AB decided to switch the MySQL libraries from LGPL to GPL v2. That is when the controversy arose. The PHP developers responded by disabling an extension in PHP 5 to MySQL. If PHP was thus unable to operate with MySQL, the consequences for the open source community, which widely relied on PHP for building web applications with MySQL, would be serious [21]. To resolve the conflict, MySQL AB came up with a FOSS license exception (initially called the FLOSS License Exception). The FOSS license exception allowed developers of FOSS applications to include MySQL Client Libraries (also referred to as "MySQL Drivers" or "MySQL Connectors") within their FOSS applications and distribute such applications together with GPL licensed MySQL Drivers under the terms of a FOSS license, even if such other FOSS license were incompatible with the GPL [30].

A similar exception may be found in GPL license text of the programming language Java. Java is licensed under GPL v2 with ClassPath Exception [31]. ClassPath is a classic GPL linking exception based on permission of the copyright holder. The goal was to allow free software implementations of the standard class library for the programming language Java [21]. It consists of the following statement attached to the Java GPL license text: "*As a special exception, the copyright holders of this library give you permission to link this library with independent modules to produce an executable, regardless of the license terms of these independent modules, and to copy and distribute the resulting executable under terms of your choice, provided that you also meet, for each linked independent module, the terms and conditions of the license of that module. An independent module is a module which is not derived from or based on this library."* [31].

As we explore further in Section IV, a developer may be motivated to add such linking exceptions to solve GPL-incompatibility issues, which can arise if a GPL program is supposed to run against GPL incompatible programs or libraries. Such linking exception may also allow certain uses of GPL software in software developments, which are not necessarily licensed in a GPL compatible way.

C. Mode of Distribution

Thirdly, the mode of distribution, namely: whether a component is distributed packaged with a GPL dependency or without it, may matter for the application of GPL.

According to the first criterion of OSS, which says that a license must permit distribution of a program either as standalone or as part of "*an aggregate software distribution containing programs from several different sources*" [5], the GPL license allows distributing GPL software "*as a component of an aggregate software*". As interpreted by the FSF, "*mere aggregation of another work not based on the Program with the Program (or with a work based on the Program) on a volume of a storage or distribution medium does not bring the other work under the scope of this License*" [33]. Such an "aggregate" may be composed of a number of separate programs, placed and distributed together on the same medium, e.g., USB. [33].

The core legal issue here is of differentiating an "aggregate" from other "modified versions" based on GPL software. "*Where's the line between two separate programs, and one program with two parts? This is a legal question, which ultimately judges will decide.*" [33]. In the view of the FSF, the deciding factor is the mechanism of communication (exec, pipes, rpc, function calls within a shared address space, etc.) and the semantics of the communication (what kinds of information are exchanged). So, including the modules into one executable file or running modules "*linked together in a shared address space*" would most likely mean "*combining them into one program*". By contrast, when "*pipes, sockets and command-line arguments*" are used for communication, "*the modules normally are separate programs*" [33].

These observations bring us to the following conclusions. Distributing an independent program together with a GPL program on one medium, so that the programs do not communicate with each other, does not spread the GPL of one program to the other programs. Equally, distributing a program, which has a GPL dependency, separately and instructing the user to download that GPL dependency for himself would release a program from the requirement to go under GPL. However, distributing a program packaged with a GPL dependency would require licensing the whole software package under GPL, unless exceptions apply.

D. Commercial Distribution

In contrast to the open source licenses, which allow the code to go "closed" (as proprietary software "*lost to the open source community*" [13]), GPL is aimed to preserve software developments open for the development community. For this reason, GPL does not allow "burying" GPL code in proprietary software products. Against this principle, licensing GPL software in a proprietary way and charging royalties is not admissible.

Alternative exploitation options for GPL components, though, remain. One of these may be to charge fees for distribution of copies, running from the network server as "Software as a Service" or providing a warranty for a fee. For instance, when a GPL program is distributed from the site, fees for distributing copies can be charged. However, "*the fee to download source may not be greater than the fee to download the binary*" [34].

Offering warranty protection and additional liabilities would be another exploitation option. In this regard, GPL allows providing warranties, but requires that such provision must be evidenced in writing, i.e., by signing an agreement. A negative aspect here is that by providing warranties a developer accepts additional liability for the bugs, caused by his predecessors, and assumes "*the cost of all necessary servicing, repair and correction*" [16] for the whole program, including modules provided by other developers. Nonetheless, the business model of servicing GPL software has proven to be quite successful, as the Ubuntu [35] and other similar projects, which distribute and provide services for Linux/GNU software, demonstrate.

At the same time, the open source requirement and royalty free licensing of GPL software are not very convenient for some business models. In this regard, businesses, which are not comfortable with GPL (or, to be more exact, with licensing their software developments under GPL), may on occasion be tempted to test the boundaries of what uses of GPL software are still controlled under the GPL license [36]. This has given rise to a number of lawsuits, involving allegations of improper circumvention of GPL license requirements, one of which we consider in more detail below.

E. GPL and Copyright Relevant Actions

The case in question is Oracle America, Inc. v. Google Inc., C 10-03561 WHA [37]. The case dealt with a question in how far Google´s use of Java´s API violated Oracle´ copyright in Java.

Java is a powerful object oriented programming language, developed by Sun Microsystems, first released in 1996, and acquired by Oracle in 2010. Java is a popular programming language and makes an integral part of many contemporary software. Between 2006 and 2007 Java migrated to GPL v2 and continued under GPL v2, when it was acquired by Oracle in 2010. Java was designed to run on different operating systems and makes use of Java virtual machine for that. "*Programs written in Java are compiled into machine language, but it is a machine language for a computer that doesn't really exist. This so-called "virtual" computer is known as the Java virtual machine*" [38].

Java created a number of pre-written programs, called "methods", which invoke different functions, such as retrieving the cosine of an angle. These methods are grouped into "classes" and organised into "packages". Software developers can access and make use of those classes through the Java APIs [37]. In 2008 Java APIs had 166 "packages", split into more than six hundred "classes", all divided into six thousand "methods".

A very popular Java project is the Open JDK project [39]. Open JDK was released under GPL v2 license with the ClassPath exception. However, the package, which was involved in the dispute, was Java ME phone platform development (known as PhoneMe [40]). The package PhoneMe) did not contain the ClassPath exception. Google built its Android platform for the smartphones using the Java language. The GPL v2 license was inconvenient for Android's business model. So, apparently, Google used the syntax of the relevant Java APIs and the Java virtual machine techniques, but with its own virtual machine called the Dalvik [41] and with its own implementations of class libraries [21]. According to Oracle, Google "*utilized the same 37 sets of functionalities in the new Android system callable by the same names as used in Java*" [37].

By doing that, Google wrote its own implementations of the methods and classes, which it needed. The only one substantial element, which Google copied from Java into Android was the names and headers of 37 API packages in question. Such copying of the headers amounted to replication of the structure, sequence and organization of Java APIs. Oracle claimed copyright infringement, and Google defended with fair use, arguing that Java is an open solution (which Oracle did not dispute) and there was no literal copying of the Java code.

In fact, 9 lines of Java code were copied verbatim into Android, but those 9 lines related to a Java function of 3179 lines called Range Check [37]. The judge assessed such copying as accidental and not substantial enough to qualify for copyright violation.

As regards the structure of Java APIs, the district court qualified the headers and method names in Java APIs as non-copyrightable, referring to the interpretation criteria of the US Copyright Office: "*Even if a name, title, or short phrase is novel or distinctive or lends itself to a play on words, it cannot be protected by copyright*." [42].

In terms of the copying of the declarations and duplicating the command structure of Java APIs, the court found that the command structure of Java APIs amounts to a method of operation – a material not subject to copyright in the US [42]. In Java programming, the specific declarations in the Java APIs designate a method. A method can be implemented in different ways, but is invoked by that specific declaration only. The command format, used to call the methods in Java, reads:

"java.package.Class.method()."

Here, a formula "*a = java.package.Class.method()*" sets the field "a", which is equal to the return of the method called. For example, the following call would call the method from Java:

"int a = java.lang.Math.max (2, 3)"

This command line would instruct the computer to fetch "*the max method under the Math class in the java.lang package, input "2" and "3" as arguments, and then return a "3," which would then be set as the value of "a."* [37].

As interpreted by the district court judge, in Java, each symbol in a command structure is more than a simple name - each symbol carries a task to invoke a pre-assigned function.

Considering that for using Java class methods software developers need to replicate the Java declarations, the judge qualified the command structure of Java APIs as a method of operation – a functional element essential for interoperability, not subject to the US Copyright Act. This position was based on the merger doctrine and non-copyrightability of structures dictated by efficiency: "*... When there is only one way to express an idea or function, then everyone is free to do so and no one can monopolize that expression.*" [37].

However, on appeal, the Federal Circuit Court reversed that ruling [43]. The appellate court found the declaring code and the structure, sequence and organization of packages in Java APIs were entitled to be protected by copyright.

The appellate court supported its decision by the argument that Java programmers were not limited in the way they could arrange the 37 Java API packages at issue and had a choice to organize these API packages in other ways. For instance, instead of using the command format "*java.package.Class.method()*": language – package – class – method, the same method could be called by the format: method – class – package – language. By making a decision to arrange the declarations in Java in this way and by having also other choices, the programmers were not prevented by the factor of efficiency, which would preclude copyright. Rather, the programmers had a scope to exercise their creation, which they, in view of the court, exercised, indeed. This creation, realized in sequencing the Java APIs, amounted to a copyrightable expression. Against these considerations, the court concluded that, "*the structure, sequence, and organization of the 37 Java API packages at issue are entitled to copyright protection.*" [43].

Google argued fair use and petitioned the US Supreme Court to hear the case. The US Supreme Court, referring to the opinion of the US Solicitor General, denied the petition. In the result, a new district court trial began. On 26 of May 2016 the district court jury found that Google´s Android did not infringe Oracle copyrights, because Google´s re-implementation of 37 Java APIs in question amounted to and was protected by fair use. According to a Google spokesperson, *"Today's verdict that Android makes fair use of Java APIs represents a win for the Android ecosystem, for the Java programming community, and for software developers who rely on open and free programming languages to build innovative consumer products."* [44].

This lawsuit, although not concerning the GPL license directly, sheds some light on very important questions of software copyright: free use of Java APIs, copyrightability of interfaces and an attempt "*to control APIs with copyright law*" and counter-balance between copyrights and "fair use" [44]. As established in this case, the APIs, although elements responsible for interoperability, can be protected by copyrights (at least in the opinion of one court of appeals); the APIs, although protected by copyright, may be reused in other software systems, if such re-use is covered by fair use of open and free programming languages, like Java.

Another conclusion, which may be drawn from this litigation, is that copying structure, sequence and organization of someone else's GPL program or APIs, and in the process making a GPL program and a newly developed program compatible with each other, may be not the best solution to avoid GPL copyleft. Such copying may, under some circumstances and unless exempted by "fair use" doctrine, infringe third party copyright and lead to litigation and associated financial costs, which might be spared if compliance with GPL had been observed.

Also, as may be observed, although the programming languages, which comprise ideas and principles, may not be subject of copyright, at least not in the EU [45], Java is an object oriented programming language, which tested this assumption under the US law and has passed the copyrightability test [21].

IV. Managing License Incompatibility

In this section, we consider some examples and practices of managing license incompatibility issues.

A. Exceptions and Permissions

There are about 70 open source licenses and some of them are incompatible with each other in some respect [46]. The FSF made an attempt to analyze open source licenses on compatibility with GPL and published the list of GPL-compatible and GPL-incompatible licenses on the FSF website [8]. Also, compatibility checks and the lists of compatible and non-compatible licenses have been identified by the Apache Software Foundation [47], the Mozilla Foundation [48], etc.

The FSF developments are powerful software and are very popular with the software development community. By that, the specifics of GPL license often causes license incompatibility issues. The reason for this is the position of FSF to consider linking as creating a derivative work: "*Linking a GPL covered work statically or dynamically with other modules is making a combined work based on the GPL covered work. Thus, the terms and conditions of the GNU General Public License cover the whole combination*" [20]. In contrast, in terms of Apache License, Version 2.0, "*Derivative Works shall not include works that remain separable from, or merely link (or bind by name) to the interfaces of, the Work and Derivative Works thereof*" [10]. Also, Mozilla Public License, Version 2.0 (MPL 2.0), which has a weak copyleft, allows "*programs using MPL-licensed code to be statically linked to and distributed as part of a larger proprietary piece of software, which would not generally be possible under the terms of stronger copyleft licenses.*" [48].

However, what approach should a developer adopt, who intends to release his program under GPL, but uses GPL-incompatible dependencies, modules or libraries linking to his code? In this situation, the FSF recommends the developers to provide a permission to do so. The appropriate examples are: systems call exception added by Linus Torvalds to the GPL license terms for Linux [17] or GNU ClassPath exception, aimed at allowing free software implementations of the standard class libraries for Java [31].

For GPL v3, the FSF advises adding the linking permission by making use of Section 7 GPL v3 "Additional permissions". Section 7 GPL v3 allows adding terms that supplement the terms of GPL license by making exceptions from one or more of its conditions [16]. For adding a linking permission to the GPL v3 license text, the FSF advises developers to insert the following text after the GPL license notice:

"*Additional permission under GNU GPL version 3 section 7. If you modify this Program, or any covered work, by linking or combining it with [name of library] (or a modified version of that library), containing parts covered by the terms of [name of library's license], the licensors of this Program grant you additional permission to convey the resulting work. {Corresponding Source for a non-source form of such a combination shall include the source code for the parts of [name of library] used as well as that of the covered work.}*" [32]. If a developer does not want everybody to distribute source for the GPL-incompatible libraries, he should remove the text in brackets or otherwise remove the brackets.

In GPL v2, a developer may add his own exception to the license terms. The FSF recommends the following notice for that:

"*In addition, as a special exception, the copyright holders of [name of your program] give you permission to combine [name of your program] with free software programs or libraries that are released under the GNU LGPL and with code included in the standard release of [name of library] under the [name of library's license] (or modified versions of such code, with unchanged license). You may copy and distribute such a system following the terms of the GNU GPL for [name of your program] and the licenses of the other code concerned{, provided that you include the source code of that other code when and as the GNU GPL requires distribution of source code}.*" [32].

By this, the FSF notes that people who make modified versions of a program, licensed with a linking exception, are not obliged to grant this special exception for their modified versions. GPL v2 allows licensing a modified version without this exception. However, when such exception is added to the GPL license text, it allows the release of a modified version, which carries forward this exception [32].

However, only an original developer, who creates a program from scratch and owns copyrights in it, may add such permission. This would be the case when a developer does programming as a hobby or in his spare time. At the same time, when a developer writes a program in the employment relation, then, according to the work-for-hire doctrine, a developer is the author and owns moral rights in the program (such as a right to be named as the author), however, economic or exploitation rights in the program (such as to distribute or license) pass to the employer [45]. This principle may, however, be derogated from by the contract. On the other hand, when a developer writes a program as a freelance, then, unless the contract foresees otherwise, software copyright would pass to the developer. In case of doubt, it is advisable to check the contractual basis or consult a lawyer.

It may also be said that although such a linking exception may be added and would be valid for a program, which a programmer creates by himself, it would not apply to the parts of other GPL-covered programs. If a developer intends to use parts of other GPL licensed programs in his code, a developer cannot authorize this exception for them and needs to get the approval of the copyright holders of those programs [32].

B. License Upgrade

License upgrade may be considered and suggested as

another option for dealing with license incompatibility. It may be considered, if such upgrade is provided for by the license. This may be explained by the fact that in the process of open source movement, some licenses, issued in initial versions, underwent changes, were adapted and became more flexible and compatible with the other open source licenses.

Examples of license upgrades, which provided for a better license compatibility, include: upgrade of MPL 1.1 to MPL 2.0, Apache 1.1 to Apache 2.0, GPL v2 to GPL v3, BSD original to BSD 3-Clause, etc.

Thus, for instance, whereas the original Mozilla Public License was incompatible with GPL, MPL 2.0 provides an indirect compatibility with GNU GPL version 2.0, the GNU LGPL version 2.1, the GNU AGPL version 3, and all later versions of those licenses. Section 3.3 MPL 2.0 gives a permission to combine software, covered by these GPL licenses, with MPL software and distribute a combined work under a GPL license, but requires to leave the MPL code under MPL [8]. In any case, it is advisable to check the MPL license notices, before making a GPL-MPL-combined work. This is also important, given that developers, who release their software under MPL, may opt out of the GPL-compatibility by listing GPL licenses in Exhibit B "Incompatible With Secondary Licenses", declaring in this way that MPL code is not compatible with the GPL or AGPL. Although software originally released under earlier versions of MPL may be brought to compatibility with GPL by upgrade or dual licensing under MPL 2.0, the software, which is only available under the previous MPL versions, will remain GPL-incompatible. Also, whereas the original BSD license because of its advertising clause was recognized as GPL-incompatible, a modified BSD 3-Clause License complies with GPL [8].

Although GNU GPL accepts BSD 3-Clause License as a lax permissive license, the FSF rather supports Apache v2. Apache v2 has been recognized by the FSF as free software license and compatible with GPL v3. Therefore, Apache v2 programs may be included into GPL v3 projects. However, this compatibility works in one direction only: Apache v2→GPL v3 and does not work vice versa [50]. Thus, software under GNU GPL licenses, including: GPL, LGPL, GPL with exceptions may not be used in Apache products. In opinion of the Apache software foundation, "*the licenses are incompatible in one direction only, and it is a result of ASF's licensing philosophy and the GPL v3 authors' interpretation of copyright law*" [50].

V. CASE STUDY

In this paper, we have considered some licensing implications, which may arise by the use of open source software. We conclude by way of a case study, showing how the use of OSS may affect licensing of a project component.

In this example, let us consider licensing of a repository for computational models. The repository links, by calling the object code, to the database architecture MySQL, licensed under GPL v2 [51], and a web application Django, licensed under BSD 3-Clause License [52].

We may identify the future (downstream) licensing options for the repository in the following way. GPL v2 considers, "*linking a GPL covered work statically or dynamically with other modules making a combined work based on the GPL covered work. Thus, GNU GPL will cover the whole combination*" [20]. In terms of GPL, a repository, which links to GPL MySQL, qualifies as a work based on a GPL program.

Assuming the repository is distributed packaged with MySQL, then, in order to be compliant with GPL license, the repository must go under GPL as well. BSD 3-Clause License is a lax software license, compatible with GPL [8]. GPL permits BSD programs in GPL software. Hence, no incompatibility issues with the BSD licensed Django arise. Section 9 GPL v2, applicable to MySQL, allows a work to be licensed under GPL v2 or any later version. This means, a repository, as a work based on GPL v2 MySQL, may go under GPL v3. Hence, GPL v3 has been identified as a license for this repository. The license requirements for distribution are considered next.

A repository may be distributed in source code and/or in object code. Distribution in object code must be supported by either: (a) source code; (b) an offer to provide source code (valid for 3 years); (c) an offer to access source code free of charge; or (d) by peer-to-peer transmission – information where to obtain the source code. If the repository is provided as "Software as a service", so that the users can interact with it via a network without having a possibility to download the code, release of the source code is not required.

In distributing this repository under GPL v3, the developer must include into each source file, or (in case of distribution in an object code) attach to each copy: a copyright notice, a GPL v3 license notice with the disclaimer of warranty and include the GPL v3 license text. If the repository has interactive user interfaces, each must display a copyright and license notice, disclaimer of warranty and instructions on how to view the license.

Django and MySQL, as incorporated into software distribution, remain under BSD and GPL v2, respectively. Here the BSD and GPL v2 license terms for distribution must be observed. This means, all copyright and license notices in the Django and MySQL code files must be reserved. For Django, a copyright notice, the license notice and disclaimer shall be retained in the source files or reproduced, if Django is re-distributed in object code [12]. Distribution of MySQL should be accompanied by a copyright notice, license notices and disclaimer of warranty; recipients should receive a copy of the GPL v2 license. For MySQL, distributed in object code, the source code should be accessible, either directly, or through instructions on how to get it.

At the same time, as we described above, MySQL GPL

v2 will spread its copyleft effect upon the repository only, if the repository is distributed packaged with GPL-covered MySQL. On the other hand, if the repository is distributed separately from MySQL with clear instructions to the user to download and install MySQL on the user´s machine separately, licensing of the repository will not be affected and the repository may go under its own license. A user, who runs GPL covered MySQL when using the repository, will not be affected by GPL either, because GPL v2 does not consider running a GPL program as producing a license relevant action. According to GPL v2, "*Activities other than copying, distribution and modification are not covered by this License; they are outside its scope. The act of running the Program is not restricted, and the output from the Program is covered only if its contents constitute a work based on the Program (independent of having been made by running the Program). Whether that is true depends on what the Program does.*" [15].

As this case study suggests, licensing software under copyleft licenses, such as GPL, may be a preferred option for keeping the project components open for the software development community. By contrast, the use of dependencies under copyleft licenses will not be suitable for business models, pursuing commercial purposes. If commercial distribution is intended, use of dependencies under lax permissive licenses, such as BSD 3-Clause License, Apache v2 or MIT License would suit these interests better.

VI. CONCLUSIONS

In this paper, we considered the spectrum of FOSS licenses, identified essential criteria of different categories of open source licenses, such as free software and copyleft, and tested different uses of software against license terms.

The three categories of licenses were distinguished:

a) Non-copyleft licenses, examples: Apache and BSD. The use of non-copyleft licenses, in principle, does not cause serious licensing implications, except that the license terms for the distribution of the original code must be observed. The best mode to come to terms with this is to keep all license notices in the original code files intact. The modification and distribution of such software as part of other software and under different license terms is generally allowed, as long as the original code stays under its license.

b) Licenses with weak copyleft, examples: LGPL and MPL. These licenses require that modifications should go under the same license, but programs, which merely link to the code with weak copyleft are released from this obligation. Therefore, linking an application to a program with weak copyleft does not bring an application under the same license terms and, in general, should not limit the licensing options for an application. Distribution of the original code is governed by the original license.

c) Copyleft licenses, example: GPL. GPL requires that modified versions should go under the same license terms and also spreads this requirement to the programs, which merely link to a GPL-program. When testing whether linking programs produces a modified version of GPL-software, the technical aspects of modification, dependency, interaction, distribution medium and location (allocation) must be taken into account. The distribution of programs, developed with the use of or from GPL-software should normally follow the GPL license terms and pass on the same rights and obligations to subsequent licensees. Commercial uses of GPL software are restricted.

ACKNOWLEDGMENT

The research leading to these results has received funding from the European Union Seventh Framework Programme FP7/2007-2013 under grant agreement No 600841. Particular credit is given to Luis Enriquez A. for his insightful Master Thesis "Dynamic Linked Libraries: Paradigms of the GPL license in contemporary software", which was of great help in doing the research.

REFERENCES

[1] I. Lishchuk, "Licensing Implications of the Use of Open Source Software in Research Projects," in Proc. INFOCOMP 2016, The Sixth International Conference on Advanced Communications and Computation, Valencia, Spain, 22-26 May, 2016, ISBN: 978-1-61208-478-7, pp. 18-23.

[2] CHIC, Project, <http://chic-vph.eu/project/> [retrieved: 23 November 2016].

[3] D. Tartarini et al., "The VPH Hypermodelling Framework for Cancer Multiscale Models in the Clinical Practice", In G. Stamatakos and D. Dionysiou (Eds): Proc. 2014 6th Int. Adv. Res. Workshop on In Silico Oncology and Cancer Investigation – The CHIC Project Workshop (IARWISOCI), Athens, Greece, Nov.3-4, 2014 (www.6thiarwisoci.iccs.ntua.gr), pp.61-64. (open-access version), ISBN: 978-618-80348-1-5.

[4] F. Rikhtegar, E. Kolokotroni, G. Stamatakos, and P. Büchler, "A Model of Tumor Growth Coupling a Cellular Biomodel with Biomechanical Simulations", In G. Stamatakos and D. Dionysiou (Eds): Proc. 2014 6th Int. Adv. Res. Workshop on In Silico Oncology and Cancer Investigation – The CHIC Project Workshop (IARWISOCI), Athens, Greece, Nov.3-4, 2014 (www.6thiarwisoci.iccs.ntua.gr), pp.43-46. (open-access version), ISBN: 978-618-80348-1-5.

[5] Open Source Initiative, Open Source Definition, <http://opensource.org/osd> [retrieved: 23 November 2016].

[6] Whelan Associates Inc. v. Jaslow Dental Laboratory, Inc., et al, U.S. Court of Appeals, Third Circuit, November 4, 1986, 797 F.2d 1222, 230 USPQ 481.

[7] GNU Operating System, The Free Software Definition, <http://www.gnu.org/philosophy/free-sw.en.html> [retrieved: 23 November 2016].

[8] GNU Operating System, Various Licenses and Comments about Them, <http://www.gnu.org/licenses/license-list.en.html> [retrieved: 23 November 2016].

[9] GNU Operating System, What is Copyleft?, <http://www.gnu.org/licenses/copyleft.en.html> [retrieved: 23 November 2016].

[10] OSI, Licenses by Name, Apache License, Version 2.0, <http://opensource.org/licenses/Apache-2.0> [retrieved: 6 April, 2016].

[11] OSI, Licenses by Name, The MIT License (MIT), <http://opensource.org/licenses/MIT> [retrieved: 23 November 2016].

[12] OSI, Licenses by Name, The BSD 3-Clause License, <http://opensource.org/licenses/BSD-3-Clause> [retrieved: 23 November 2016].

[13] A. St. Laurent, "Understanding Open Source and Free Software Licensing," O´Reilly, 1 Edition, 2004.

[14] R. Nimmer, "Legal Issues in Open Source and Free Software Distribution," adapted from Chapter 11 in Raymond T. Nimmer, The Law of Computer Technology, 1997, 2005 Supp.

[15] GNU General Public License, Version 2 (GPL-2.0), <http://opensource.org/licenses/GPL-2.0> [retrieved: 23 November 2016].

[16] GNU General Public License, Version 3 (GPL-3.0), <http://opensource.org/licenses/GPL-3.0> [retrieved: 23 November 2016].

[17] The Linux Kernel Archives, <https://www.kernel.org/pub/linux/kernel/COPYING> [retrieved: 23 November 2016].

[18] The R Project for Statistical Computing, R Licenses, <https://www.r-project.org/Licenses/> [retrieved: 23 November 2016].

[19] Mozilla, MPL 2.0 FAQ, <https://www.mozilla.org/en-US/MPL/2.0/FAQ/> [retrieved: 26 November 2016].

[20] GNU Operating System, Frequently Asked Questions about the GNU Licenses, <http://www.gnu.org/licenses/gpl-faq#GPLStaticVsDynamic> [retrieved: 26 November 2016].

[21] L. Enriquez, "Dynamic Linked Libraries: Paradigms of the GPL license in contemporary software," EULISP Master Thesis, 2013.

[22] R. Stallman, "Android and Users' Freedom," first published in The Guardian, <http://www.gnu.org/philosophy/android-and-users-freedom.en.html> [retrieved: 26 November 2016].

[23] H. Kroat, "Linux kernel in a nutshell," O'Reilly, United States, 2007.

[24] Open Source Initiative, Licenses by Name, The GNU Lesser General Public License, version 2.1 (LGPL-2.1), <http://opensource.org/licenses/LGPL-2.1> [retrieved: 26 November 2016].

[25] Open Source Initiative, Licenses by Name, The GNU Lesser General Public License, version 3.0 (LGPL-3.0), <http://opensource.org/licenses/LGPL-3.0> [retrieved: 26 November 2016].

[26] The PHP Group, <http://php.net/> [retrieved: 26 November 2016].

[27] OSI, Licenses by Name, The PHP License 3.0 (PHP-3.0), <https://opensource.org/licenses/PHP-3.0> [retrieved: 26 November 2016].

[28] Building a LAMP Server, <http://www.lamphowto.com/> [retrieved: 26 November 2016].

[29] Oracle, Products and Services, MySQL, Overview, <http://www.oracle.com/us/products/mysql/overview/index.html> [retrieved: 26 November 2016].

[30] MySQL, FOSS License Exception, <https://www.mysql.de/about/legal/licensing/foss-exception//> [retrieved: 26 November 2016].

[31] GNU Operating System, GNU Classpath, <http://www.gnu.org/software/classpath/license.html> [retrieved: 26 November 2016].

[32] GNU Operating System, Frequently Asked Questions about the GNU Licenses, <http://www.gnu.org/licenses/gpl-faq#GPLIncompatibleLibs> [retrieved: 26 November 2016].

[33] GNU Operating System, Frequently Asked Questions about the GNU Licenses, <http://www.gnu.org/licenses/gpl-faq#MereAggregation> [retrieved: 26 November 2016].

[34] GNU Operating System, Frequently Asked Questions about the GNU Licenses, <https://www.gnu.org/licenses/gpl-faq.html#DoesTheGPLAllowDownloadFee> [retrieved: 26 November 2016].

[35] Ubuntu, <http://www.ubuntu.com/> [retrieved: 26 November 2016].

[36] Software Freedom Conservancy, Conservancy Announces Funding for GPL Compliance Lawsuit, VMware sued in Hamburg, Germany court for failure to comply with the GPL on Linux <https://sfconservancy.org/news/2015/mar/05/vmware-lawsuit/> [retrieved: 26 November 2016].

[37] U.S. District Court for the Northern District of California, Ruling of 31 May 2012, Case C 10-03561 WHA, Oracle America, Inc., v. Google Inc.

[38] E. David, "Introduction to Programming using Java," Hobart and William Smith Colleges, 1996.

[39] Java.net, JDK Project, <https://jdk7.java.net/> [retrieved: 26 November 2016].

[40] Java ME phone platform development, <http://java.net/projects/phoneme> [retrieved: 26 November 2016].

[41] B. Cheng and B. Buzbee, "A JIT Compiler for Android's Dalvik VM," May 2010, pp.5-14, <www.android-app-developer.co.uk> [retrieved: 26 November 2016]

[42] U.S. Copyright Office, Circular 34; "Copyright Protection 'Not Available for Names, Titles or Short Phrases", rev. January 2012.

[43] U.S. Court of Appeals for the Federal Circuit, Ruling of 09 May 2014, Oracle America, Inc., v. Google Inc., Appeals from the United States District Court for the Northern District of California in No. 10-CV-3561.

[44] J. Mullin, "Google beats Oracle—Android makes "fair use" of Java APIs," Ars Technica, 26 May 2016, <http://arstechnica.com/tech-policy/2016/05/google-wins-trial-against-oracle-as-jury-finds-android-is-fair-use/> [retrieved: 26 November 2016].

[45] Directive 2009/24/EC of the European Parliament and of the Council of 23 April 2009 on the legal protection of computer programs, Official Journal of the European Union (OJEU), L 111/16 – 111/22, 5 May 2009.

[46] D.Rowland, U.Kohl, A.Charlesworth, "Information Technology Law", 4th edition, Routledge, Taylor&Francis Group, 2012, p. 412 et seq.

[47] The Apache Software Foundation, ASF Legal Previously Asked Questions, <http://www.apache.org/legal/resolved.html> [retrieved: 26 November 2016].

[48] Mozilla, MPL 2.0 FAQ, <https://www.mozilla.org/en-US/MPL/2.0/FAQ/> [retrieved: 26 November 2016].

[49] GNU Operating System, Various Licenses and Comments about Them, BSD original license

[50] The Apache Software Foundation, GPL-Compatibility, <http://www.apache.org/licenses/GPL-compatibility.html> [retrieved: 26 November 2016].

[51] MySQL, MySQL Workbench, <http://www.mysql.com/products/workbench/> [retrieved: 26 November 2016].

[52] Django, Documentation, <https://docs.djangoproject.com/en/1.9/> [retrieved: 26 November 2016].

iaria journals

www.iariajournals.org

International Journal On Advances in Intelligent Systems
issn: 1942-2679

International Journal On Advances in Internet Technology
issn: 1942-2652

International Journal On Advances in Life Sciences
issn: 1942-2660

International Journal On Advances in Networks and Services
issn: 1942-2644

International Journal On Advances in Security
issn: 1942-2636

International Journal On Advances in Software
issn: 1942-2628

International Journal On Advances in Systems and Measurements
issn: 1942-261x

International Journal On Advances in Telecommunications
issn: 1942-2601

International Academy, Research, and Industry Association (IARIA)
412 Derby Way
Wilmington, DE 19810

ISBN 978-1-5108-5635-6

9 781510 856356

CURRAN ASSOCIATES INC.
proceedings.com